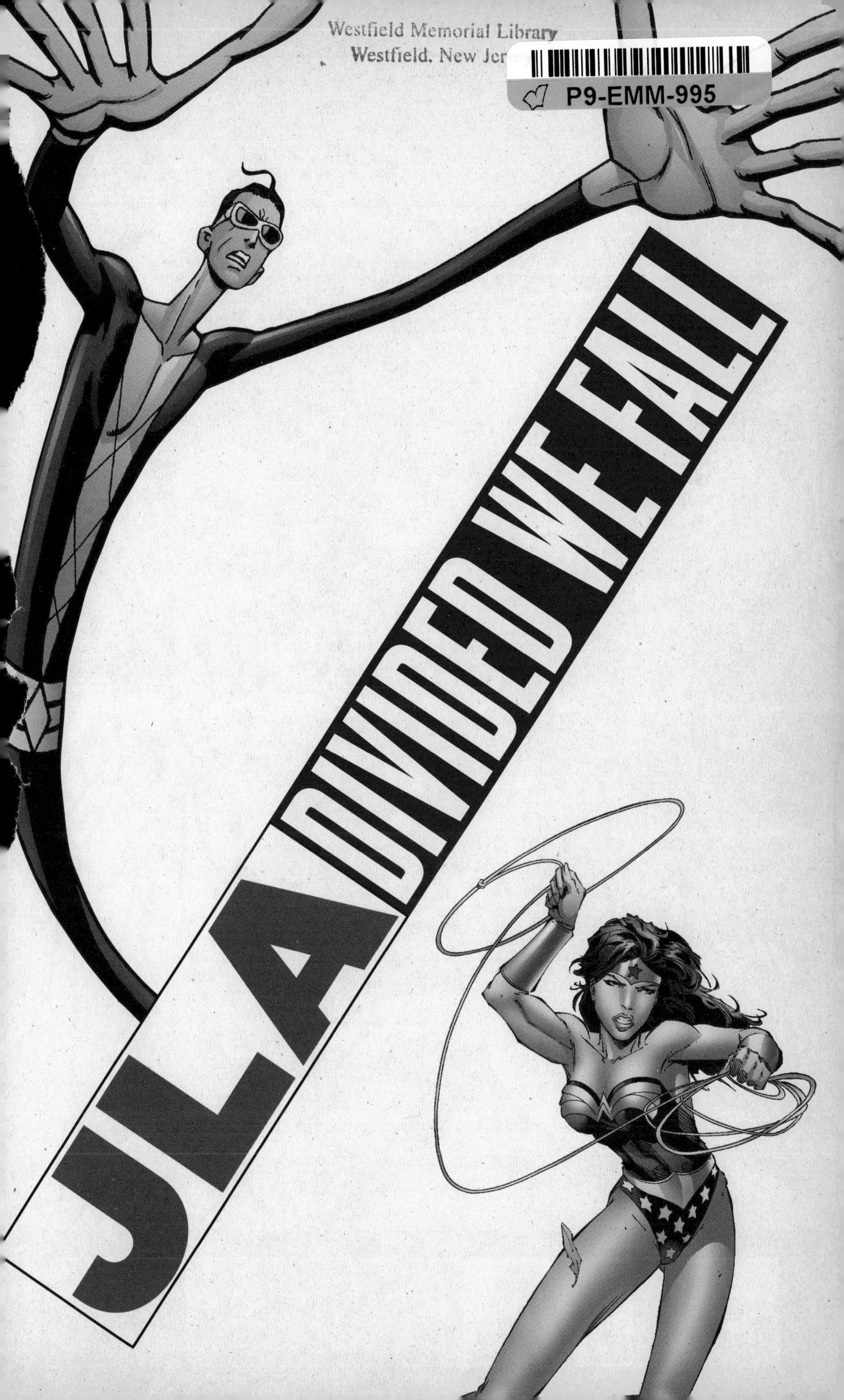
JLA
DIVIDED WE FALL

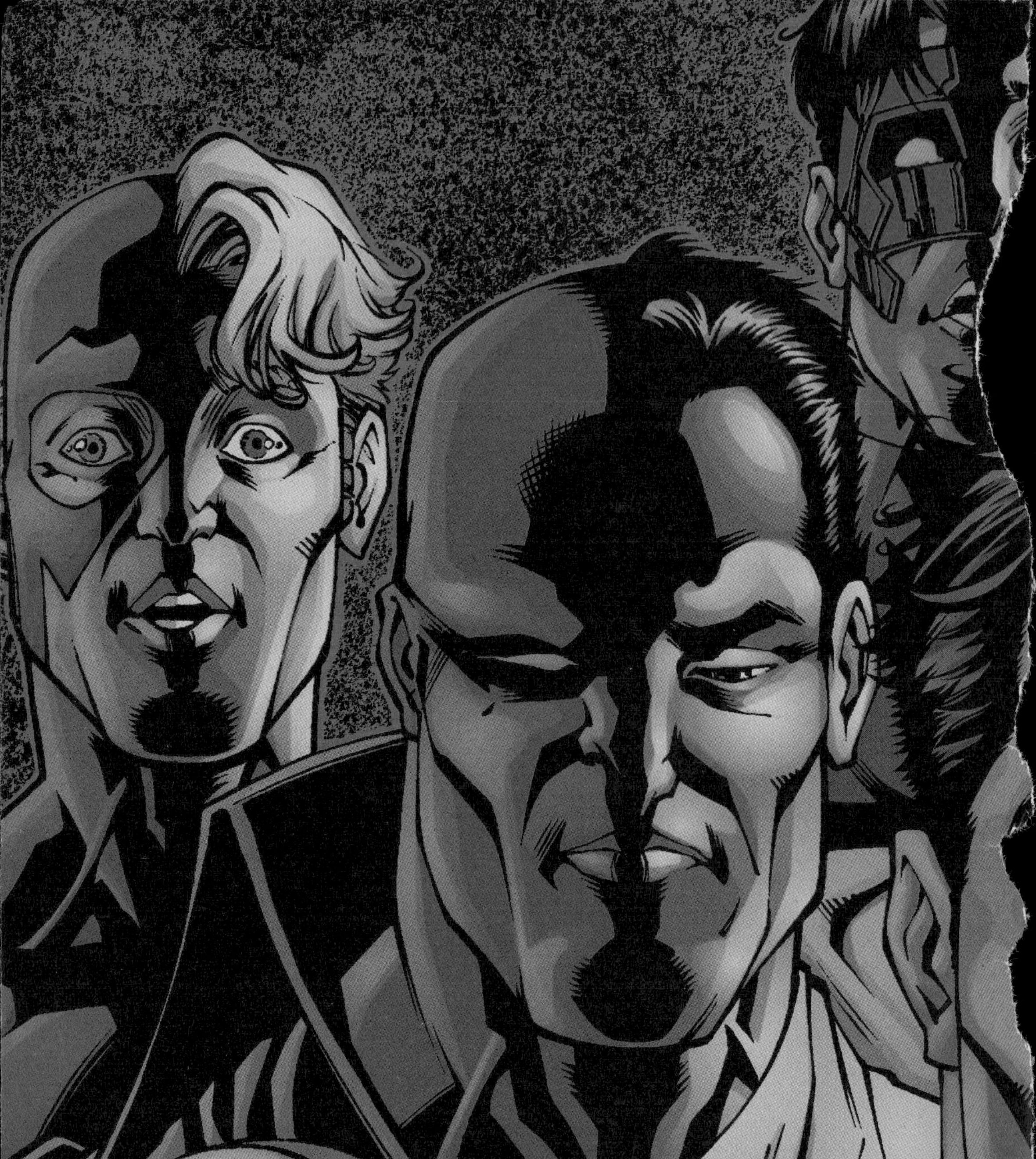

JLA DIVIDED WE FALL

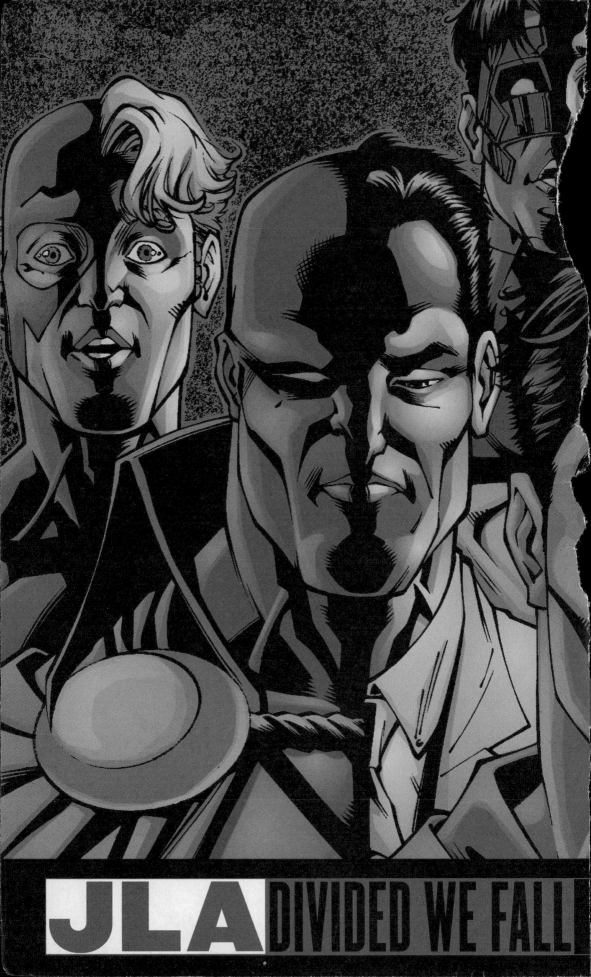

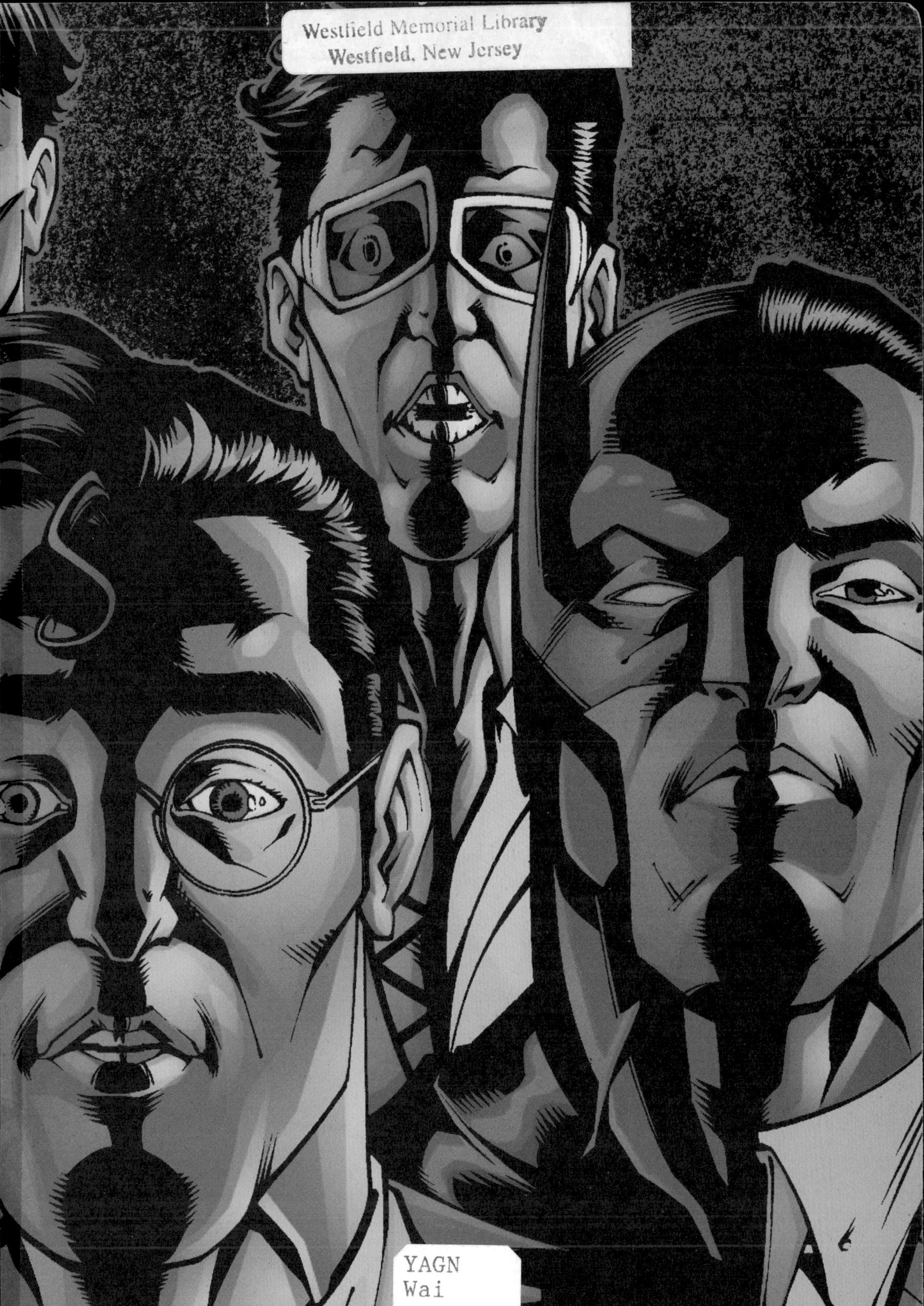

Mark Waid **Writer** Bryan Hitch J.H. Williams III Javier Saltares Phil Jimenez Ty Templeton Doug Mahnke Mark Pajarillo Mike S. Miller **Pencillers** Paul Neary Mick Gray Chris Ivy Kevin Nowlan Drew Geraci Walden Wong Armando Durruthy **Inkers** Laura DePuy John Kalisz **Colorists** Ken Lopez **Letterer** Bryan Hitch & Paul Neary **Original Covers**

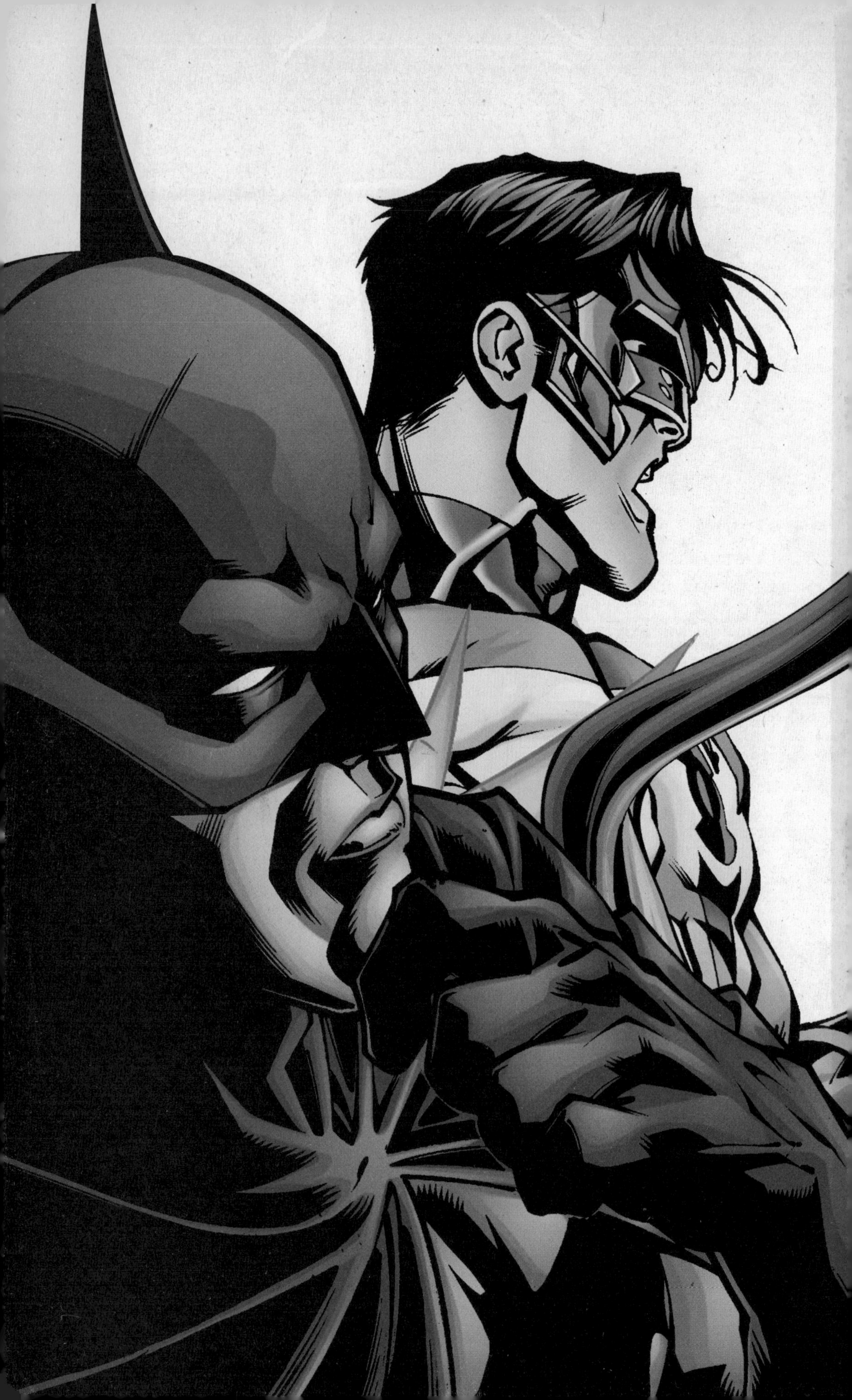

JLA: DIVIDED WE FALL. Published by DC Comics. Cover and compilation copyright © 2001 DC Comics. All Rights Reserved. Originally published in single magazine form as JLA 47-54. Copyright © 2000, 2001 DC Comics. All Rights Reserved. All characters, their distinctive likenesses and related indicia featured in this publication are trademarks of DC Comics. The stories, characters, and incidents featured in this publication are entirely fictional. DC Comics, 1700 Broadway, New York, NY 10019. A division of Warner Bros. — An AOL Time Warner Company. Printed in Canada. First Printing. ISBN: 1-56389-793-8. Cover illustration by Bryan Hitch & Paul Neary. Cover color by Laura DePuy. Publication design by Louis Prandi.

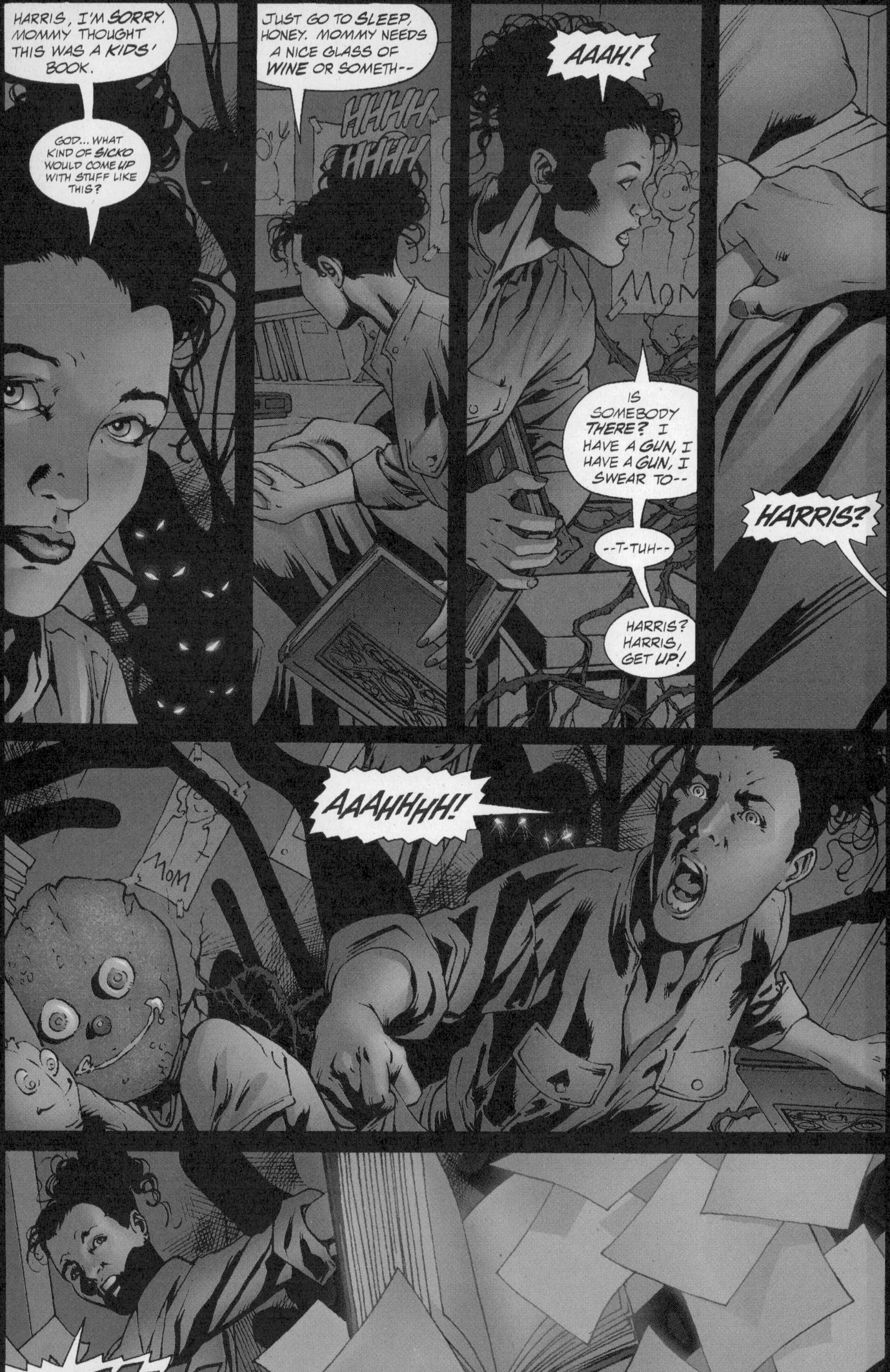
HARRIS, I'M SORRY. MOMMY THOUGHT THIS WAS A KIDS' BOOK.
GOD... WHAT KIND OF SICKO WOULD COME UP WITH STUFF LIKE THIS?
JUST GO TO SLEEP, HONEY. MOMMY NEEDS A NICE GLASS OF WINE OR SOMETH--
HHHH HHHH
AAAH!
MOM
IS SOMEBODY THERE? I HAVE A GUN, I HAVE A GUN, I SWEAR TO--
--T-TUH--
HARRIS? HARRIS, GET UP!
HARRIS?
AAAHHHH!
MOM
NHHAA AAAAAA-

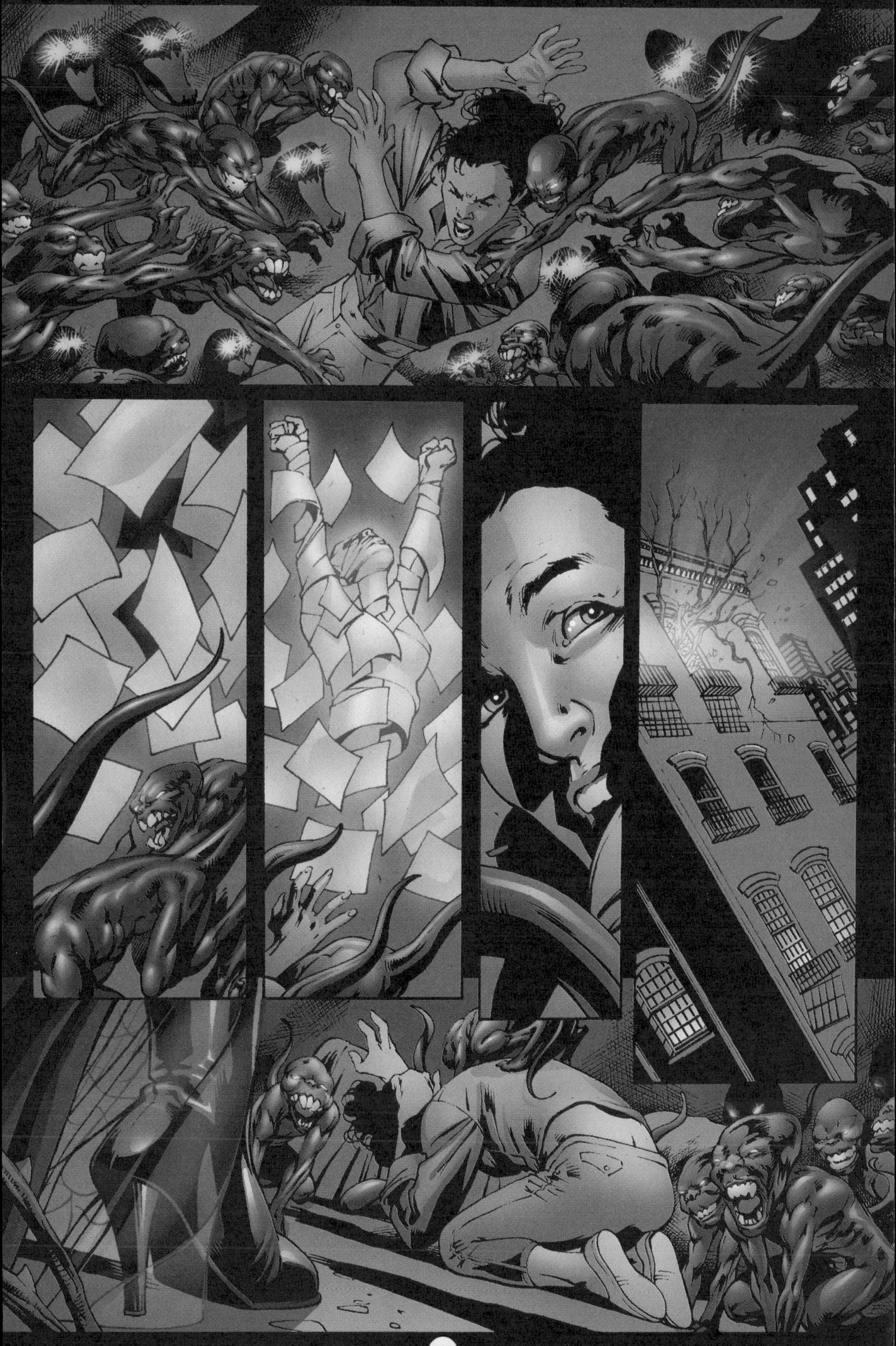

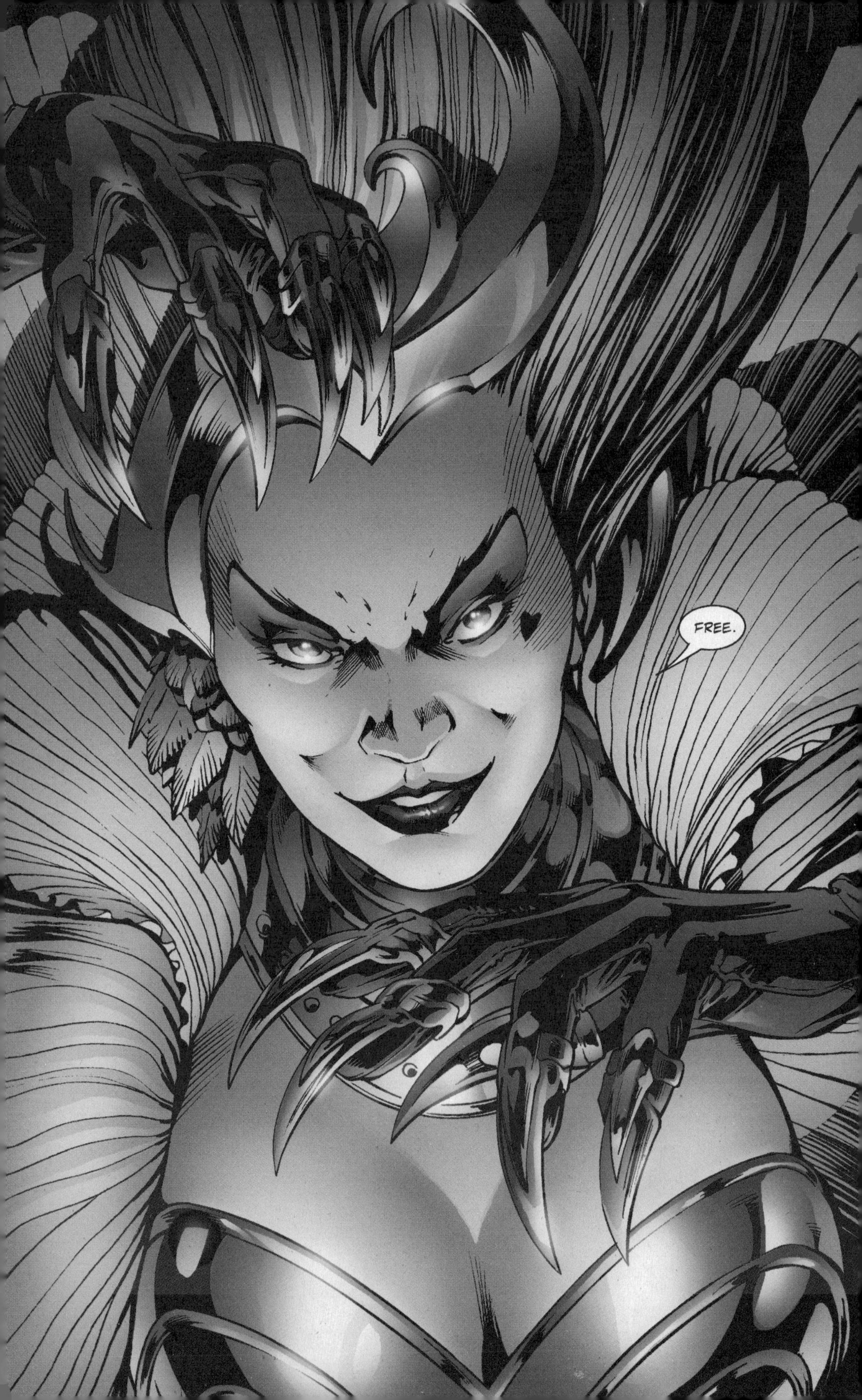
FREE.

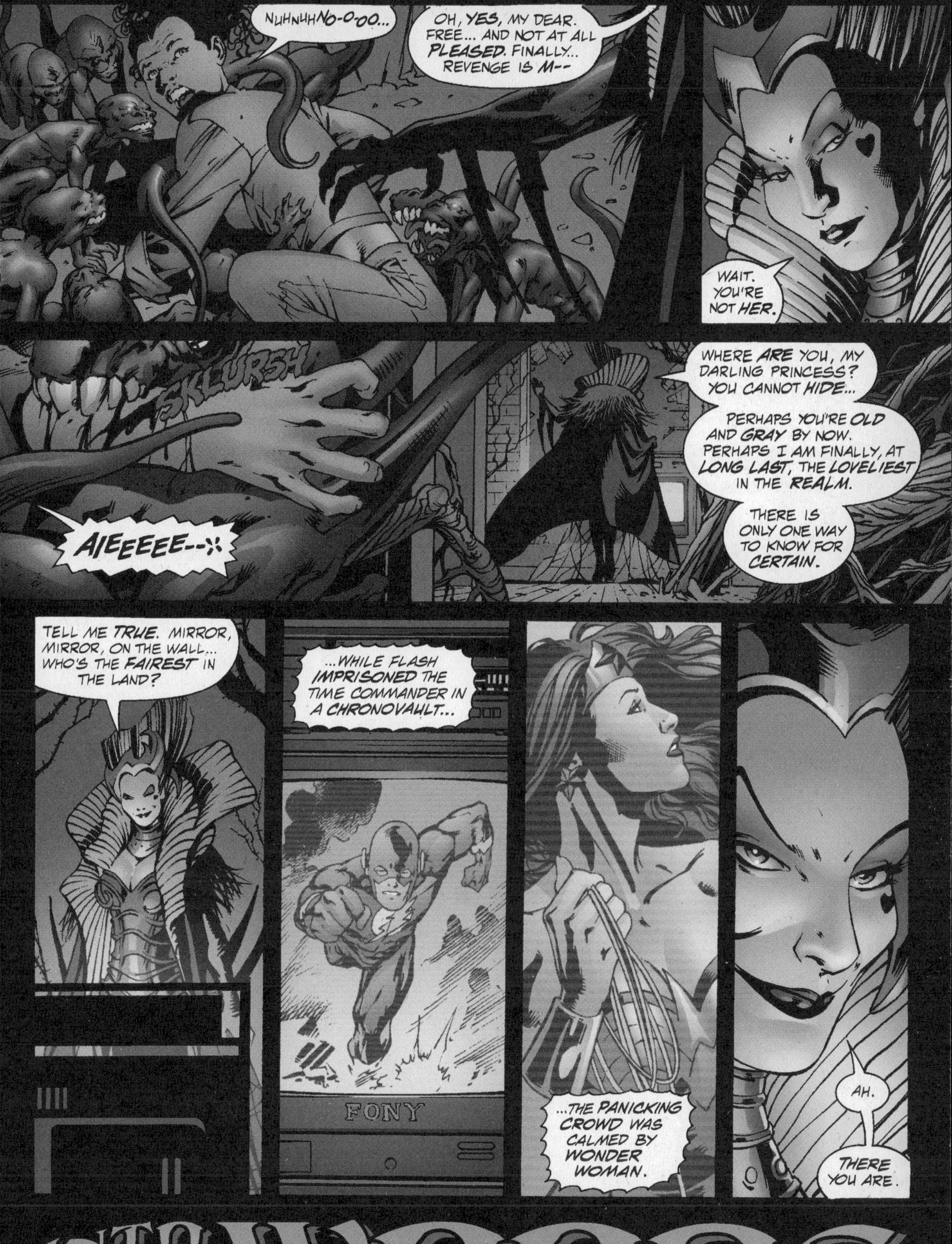
NUHNUHNO-O-OO...
OH, YES, MY DEAR. FREE... AND NOT AT ALL PLEASED. FINALLY... REVENGE IS M--
WAIT. YOU'RE NOT HER.
SKLURSH
AIEEEEE--!
WHERE ARE YOU, MY DARLING PRINCESS? YOU CANNOT HIDE...
PERHAPS YOU'RE OLD AND GRAY BY NOW. PERHAPS I AM FINALLY, AT LONG LAST, THE LOVELIEST IN THE REALM.
THERE IS ONLY ONE WAY TO KNOW FOR CERTAIN.
TELL ME TRUE. MIRROR, MIRROR, ON THE WALL... WHO'S THE FAIREST IN THE LAND?
...WHILE FLASH IMPRISONED THE TIME COMMANDER IN A CHRONOVAULT...
FONY
...THE PANICKING CROWD WAS CALMED BY WONDER WOMAN.
AH.
THERE YOU ARE.

INTO THE WOODS

MARK WAID STORY | BRYAN HITCH PENCILS | PAUL NEARY INKS | KEN LOPEZ LETTERS | LAURA DEPUY COLORS | TONY BEDARD ASSOC. EDITOR | DAN RASPLER EDITOR

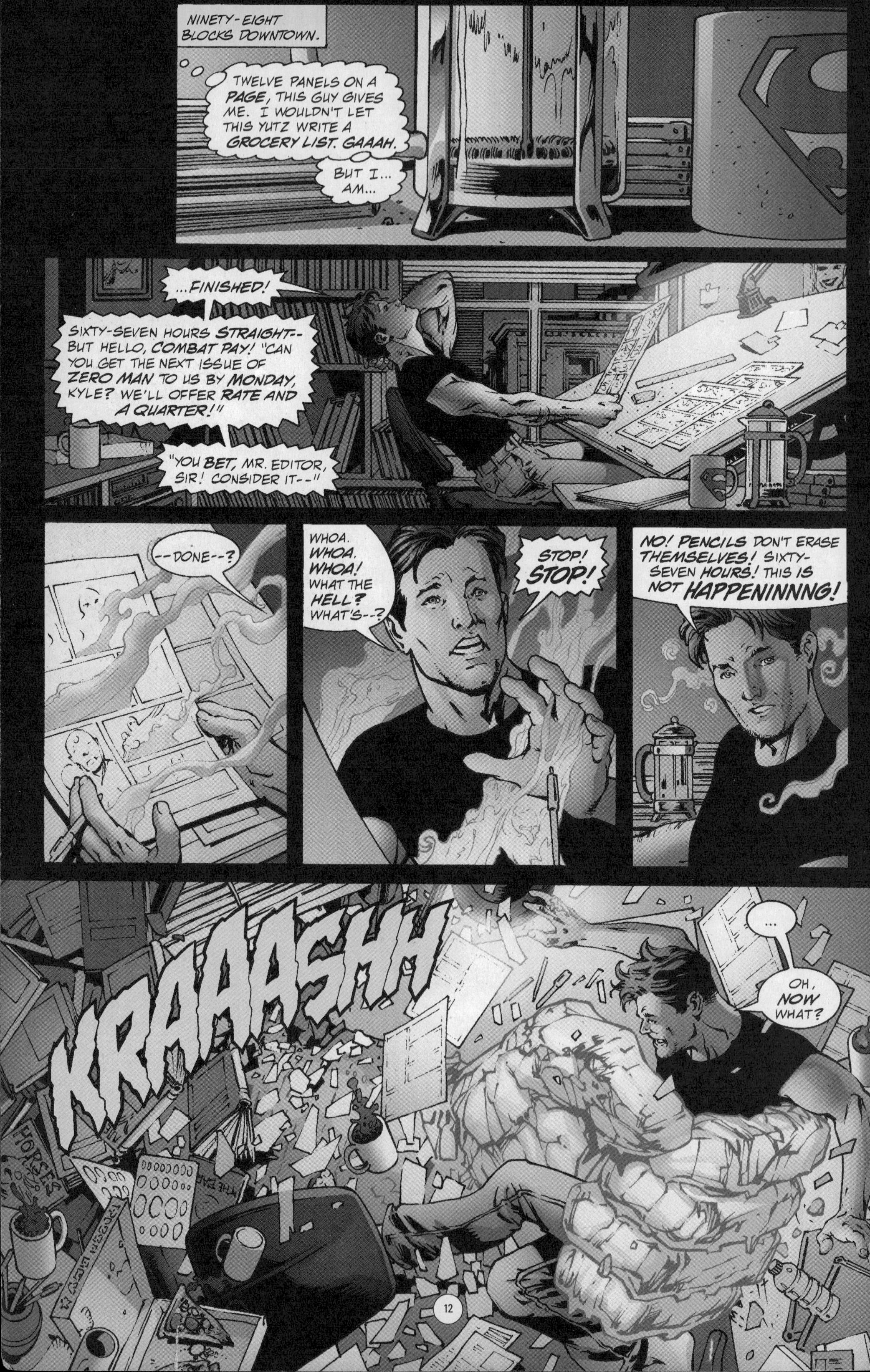

NINETY-EIGHT BLOCKS DOWNTOWN.
TWELVE PANELS ON A PAGE, THIS GUY GIVES ME. I WOULDN'T LET THIS YUTZ WRITE A GROCERY LIST. GAAAH.
BUT I... AM...
...FINISHED!
SIXTY-SEVEN HOURS STRAIGHT-- BUT HELLO, COMBAT PAY! "CAN YOU GET THE NEXT ISSUE OF ZERO MAN TO US BY MONDAY, KYLE? WE'LL OFFER RATE AND A QUARTER!"
"YOU BET, MR. EDITOR, SIR! CONSIDER IT--"
--DONE--?
WHOA. WHOA. WHOA! WHAT THE HELL? WHAT'S--?
STOP! STOP!
NO! PENCILS DON'T ERASE THEMSELVES! SIXTY-SEVEN HOURS! THIS IS NOT HAPPENINNNG!
KRAAASHH
...
OH, NOW WHAT?

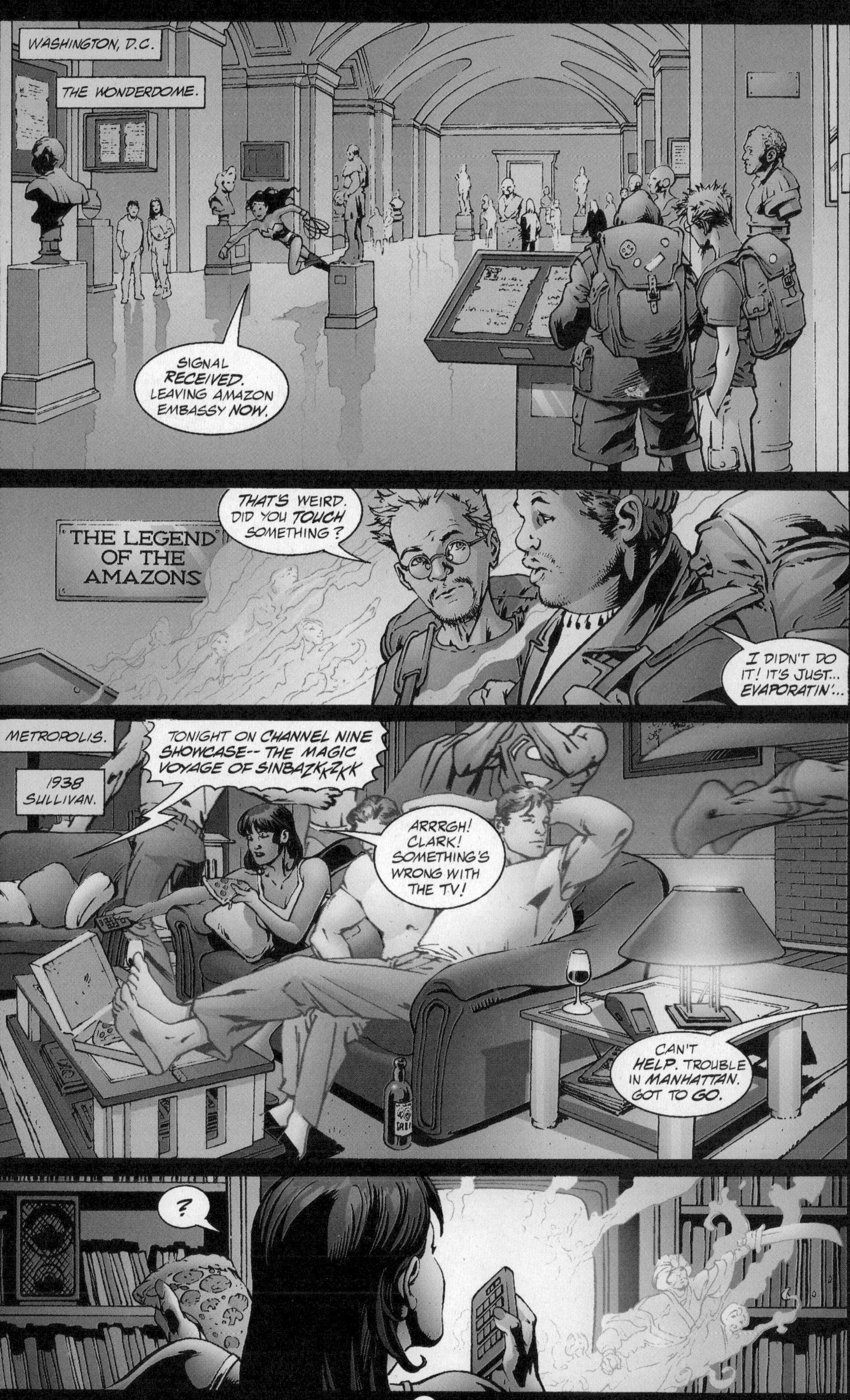

WASHINGTON, D.C.
THE WONDERDOME.
SIGNAL RECEIVED. LEAVING AMAZON EMBASSY NOW.
THE LEGEND OF THE AMAZONS
THAT'S WEIRD. DID YOU TOUCH SOMETHING?
I DIDN'T DO IT! IT'S JUST... EVAPORATIN'...
METROPOLIS.
1938 SULLIVAN.
TONIGHT ON CHANNEL NINE SHOWCASE-- THE MAGIC VOYAGE OF SINBAZKKZKK
ARRRGH! CLARK! SOMETHING'S WRONG WITH THE TV!
CAN'T HELP. TROUBLE IN MANHATTAN. GOT TO GO.
?

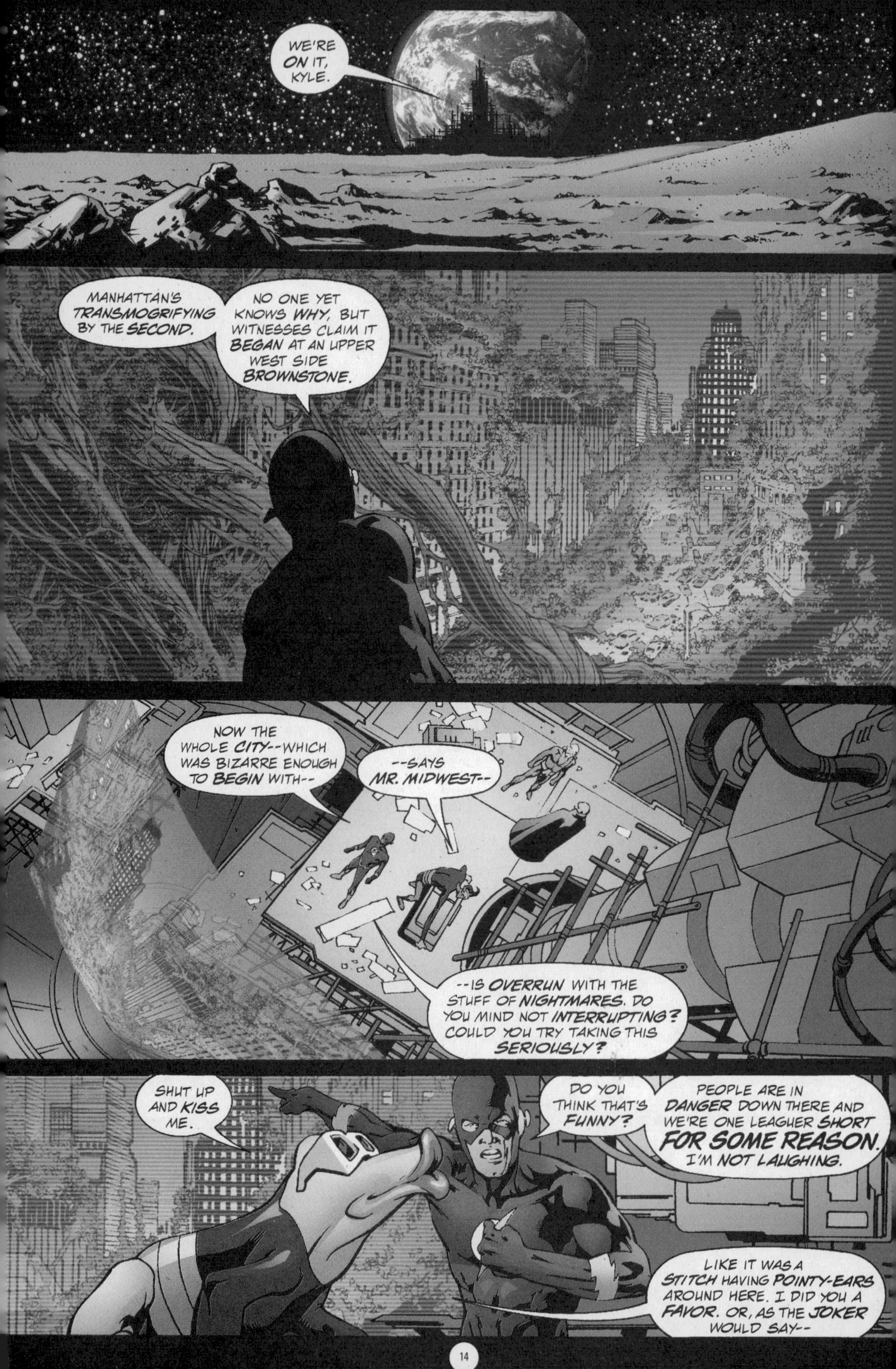
WE'RE ON IT, KYLE.
MANHATTAN'S TRANSMOGRIFYING BY THE SECOND.
NO ONE YET KNOWS WHY, BUT WITNESSES CLAIM IT BEGAN AT AN UPPER WEST SIDE BROWNSTONE.
NOW THE WHOLE CITY--WHICH WAS BIZARRE ENOUGH TO BEGIN WITH--
--SAYS MR. MIDWEST--
--IS OVERRUN WITH THE STUFF OF NIGHTMARES. DO YOU MIND NOT INTERRUPTING? COULD YOU TRY TAKING THIS SERIOUSLY?
SHUT UP AND KISS ME.
DO YOU THINK THAT'S FUNNY?
PEOPLE ARE IN DANGER DOWN THERE AND WE'RE ONE LEAGUER SHORT FOR SOME REASON. I'M NOT LAUGHING.
LIKE IT WAS A STITCH HAVING POINTY-EARS AROUND HERE. I DID YOU A FAVOR. OR, AS THE JOKER WOULD SAY--

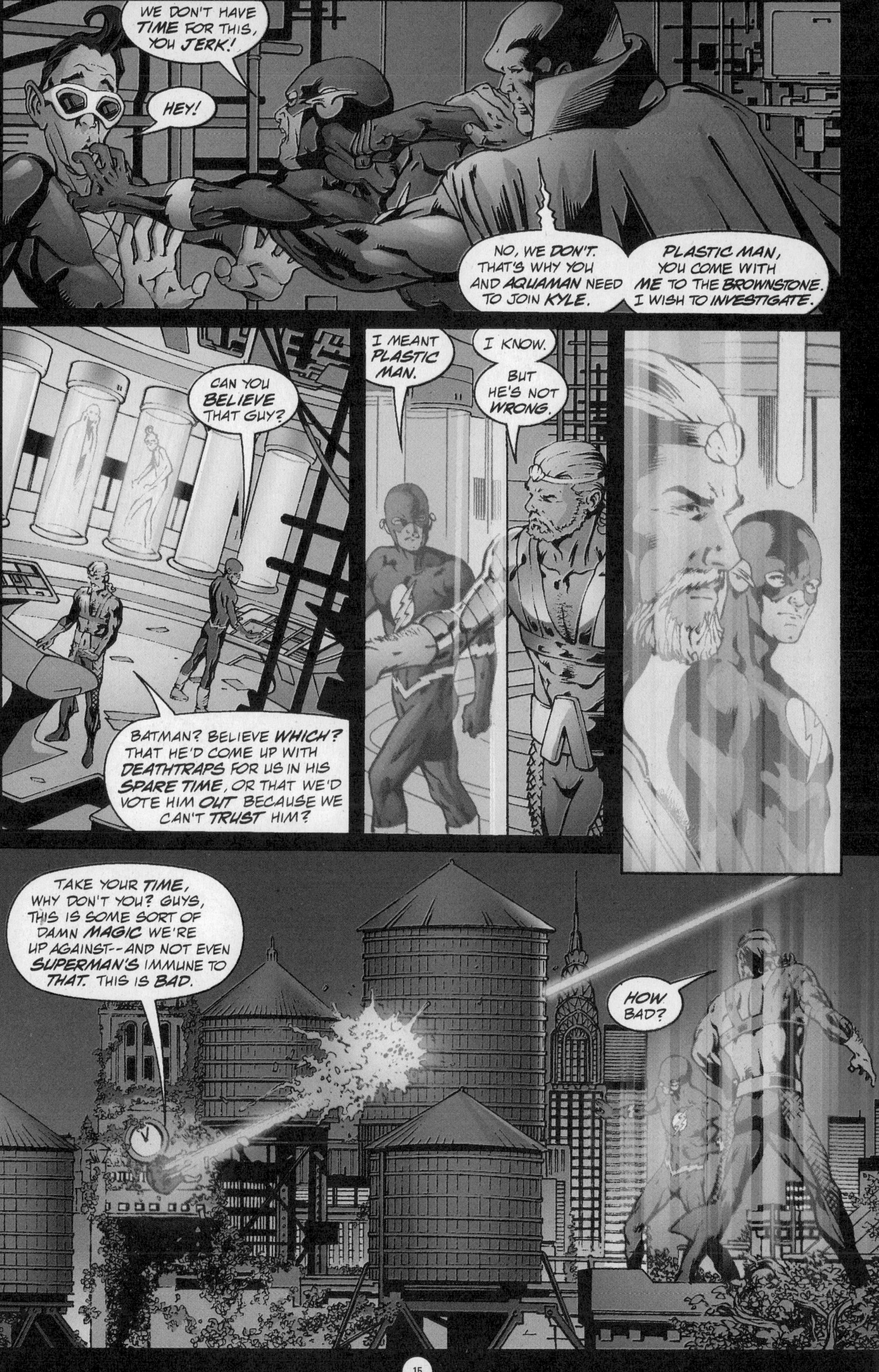
WE DON'T HAVE TIME FOR THIS, YOU JERK!
HEY!
NO, WE DON'T. THAT'S WHY YOU AND AQUAMAN NEED TO JOIN KYLE.
PLASTIC MAN, YOU COME WITH ME TO THE BROWNSTONE. I WISH TO INVESTIGATE.
CAN YOU BELIEVE THAT GUY?
BATMAN? BELIEVE WHICH? THAT HE'D COME UP WITH DEATHTRAPS FOR US IN HIS SPARE TIME, OR THAT WE'D VOTE HIM OUT BECAUSE WE CAN'T TRUST HIM?
I MEANT PLASTIC MAN.
I KNOW.
BUT HE'S NOT WRONG.
TAKE YOUR TIME, WHY DON'T YOU? GUYS, THIS IS SOME SORT OF DAMN MAGIC WE'RE UP AGAINST--AND NOT EVEN SUPERMAN'S IMMUNE TO THAT. THIS IS BAD.
HOW BAD?

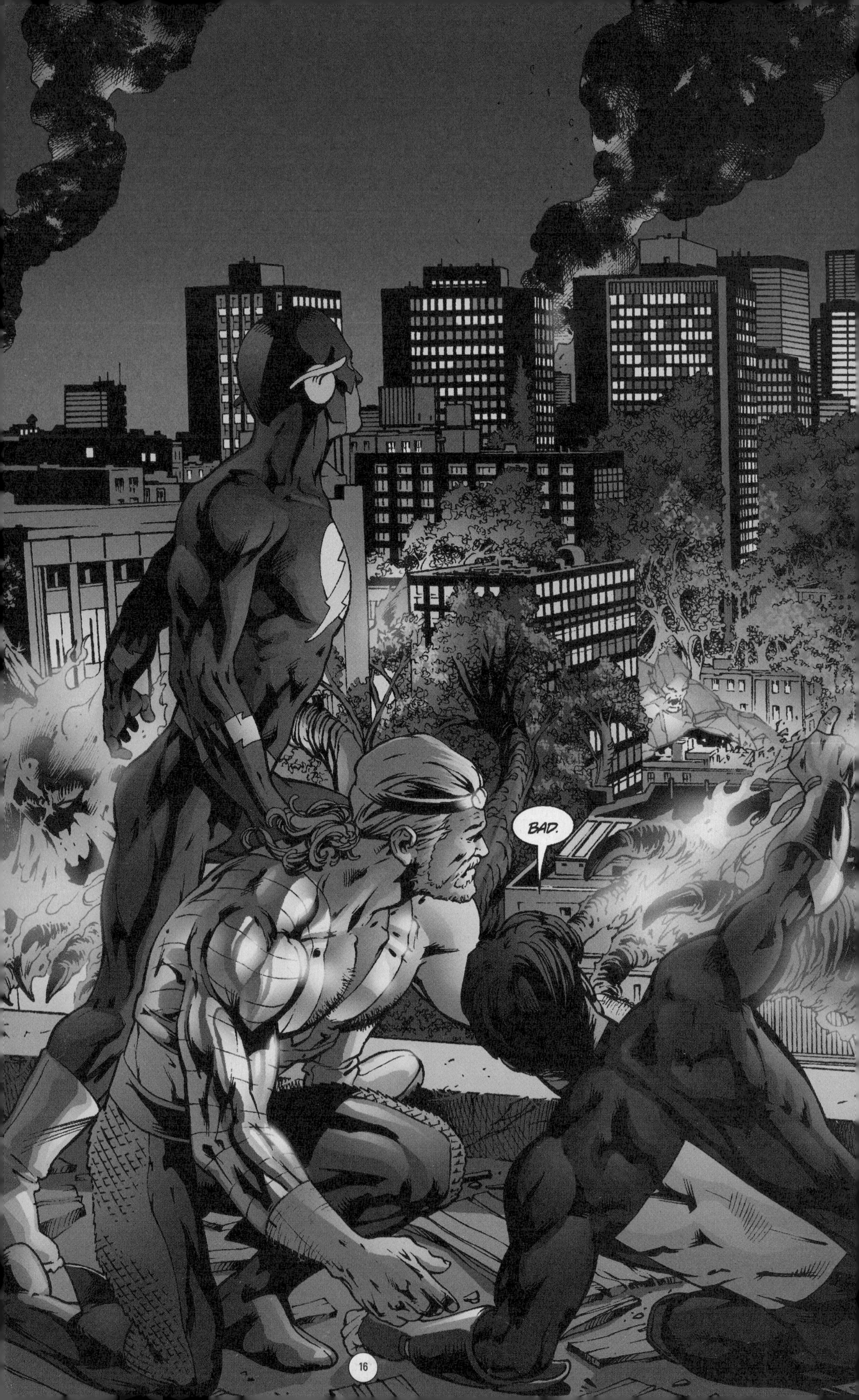
BAD.

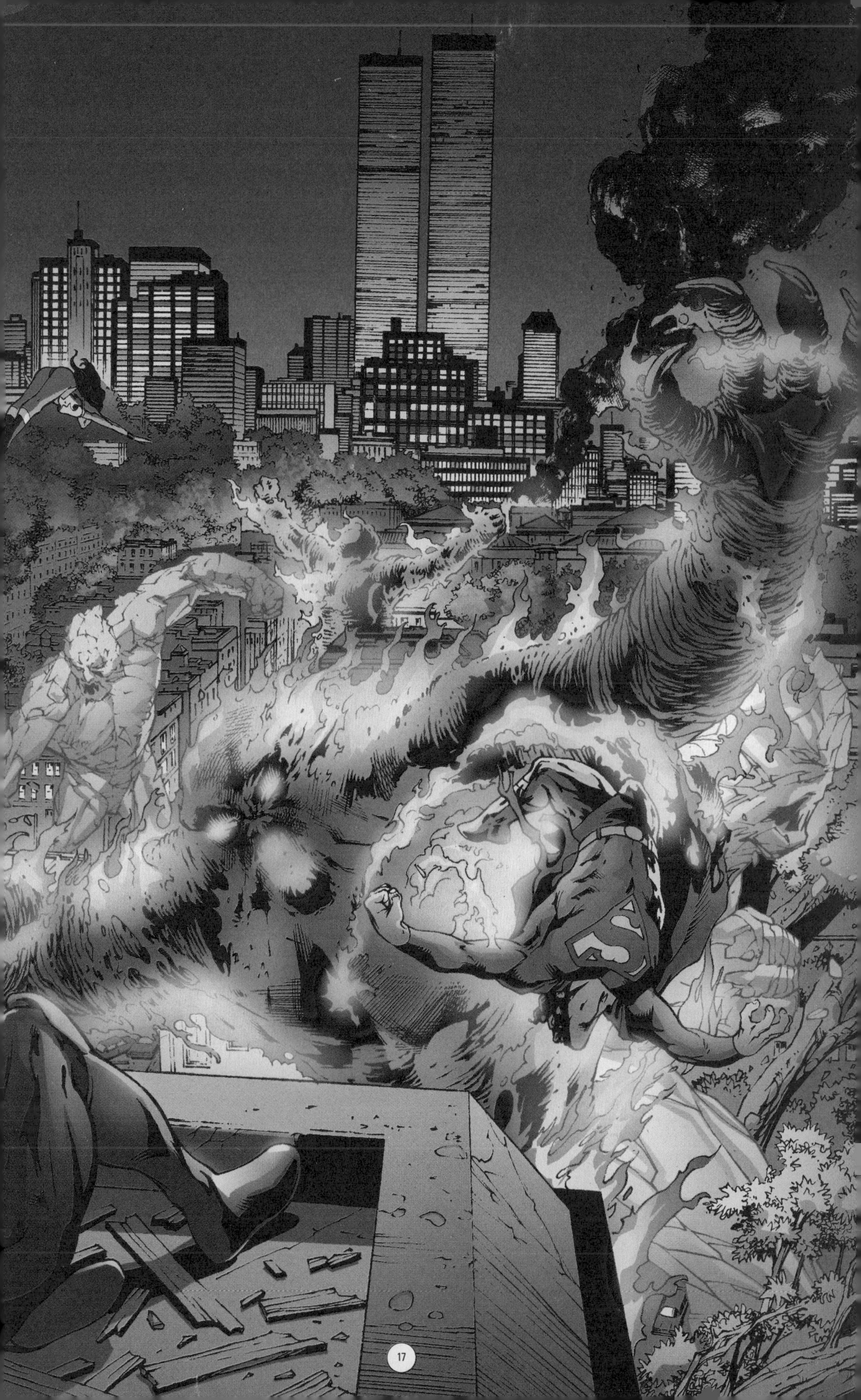

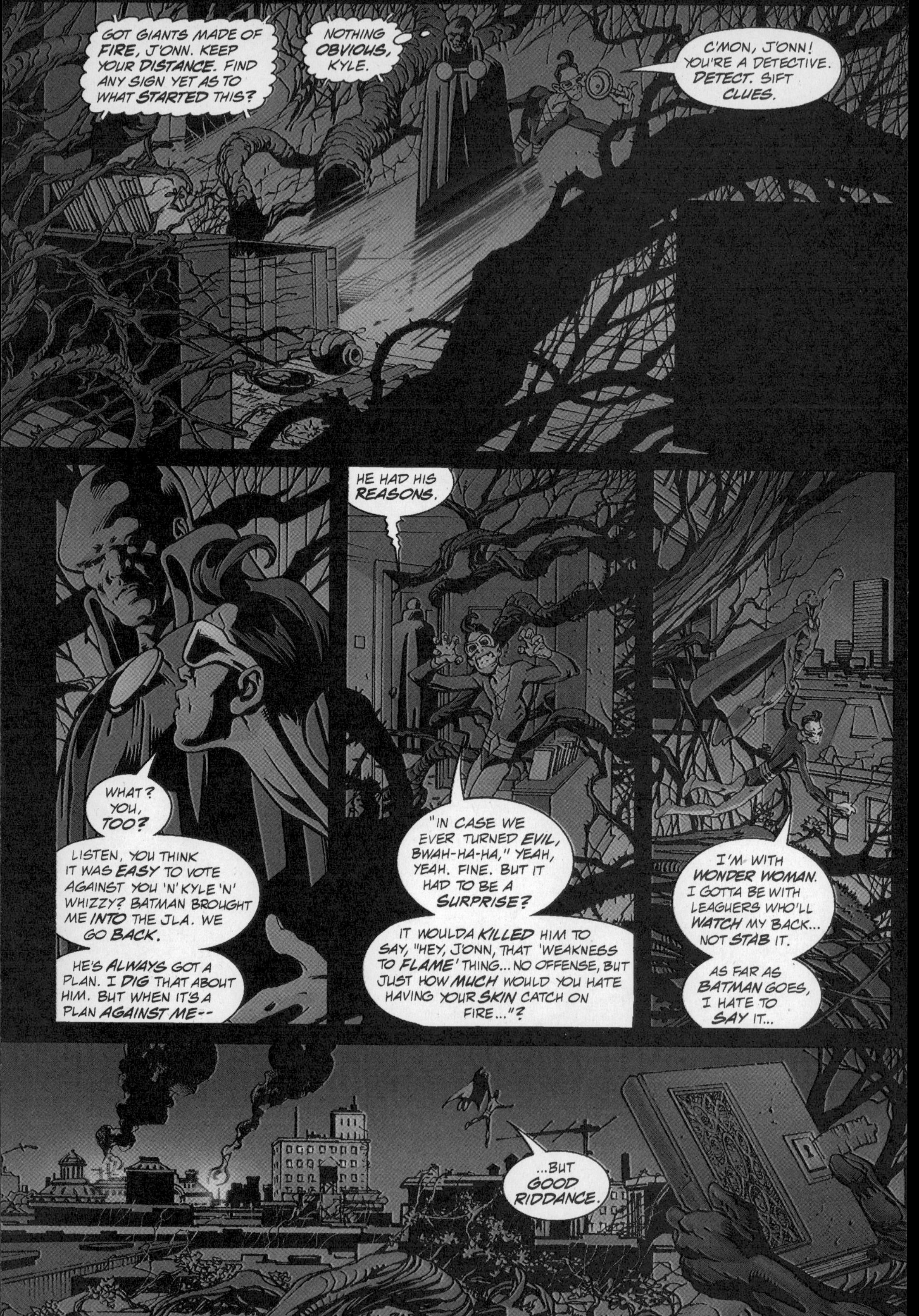
GOT GIANTS MADE OF FIRE, J'ONN. KEEP YOUR DISTANCE. FIND ANY SIGN YET AS TO WHAT STARTED THIS?
NOTHING OBVIOUS, KYLE.
C'MON, J'ONN! YOU'RE A DETECTIVE. DETECT. SIFT CLUES.
WHAT? YOU, TOO?
LISTEN, YOU THINK IT WAS EASY TO VOTE AGAINST YOU 'N' KYLE 'N' WHIZZY? BATMAN BROUGHT ME INTO THE JLA. WE GO BACK.
HE'S ALWAYS GOT A PLAN. I DIG THAT ABOUT HIM. BUT WHEN IT'S A PLAN AGAINST ME--
HE HAD HIS REASONS.
"IN CASE WE EVER TURNED EVIL, BWAH-HA-HA," YEAH, YEAH. FINE. BUT IT HAD TO BE A SURPRISE?
IT WOULDA KILLED HIM TO SAY, "HEY, J'ONN, THAT 'WEAKNESS TO FLAME' THING... NO OFFENSE, BUT JUST HOW MUCH WOULD YOU HATE HAVING YOUR SKIN CATCH ON FIRE..."?
I'M WITH WONDER WOMAN. I GOTTA BE WITH LEAGUERS WHO'LL WATCH MY BACK... NOT STAB IT.
AS FAR AS BATMAN GOES, I HATE TO SAY IT...
...BUT GOOD RIDDANCE.

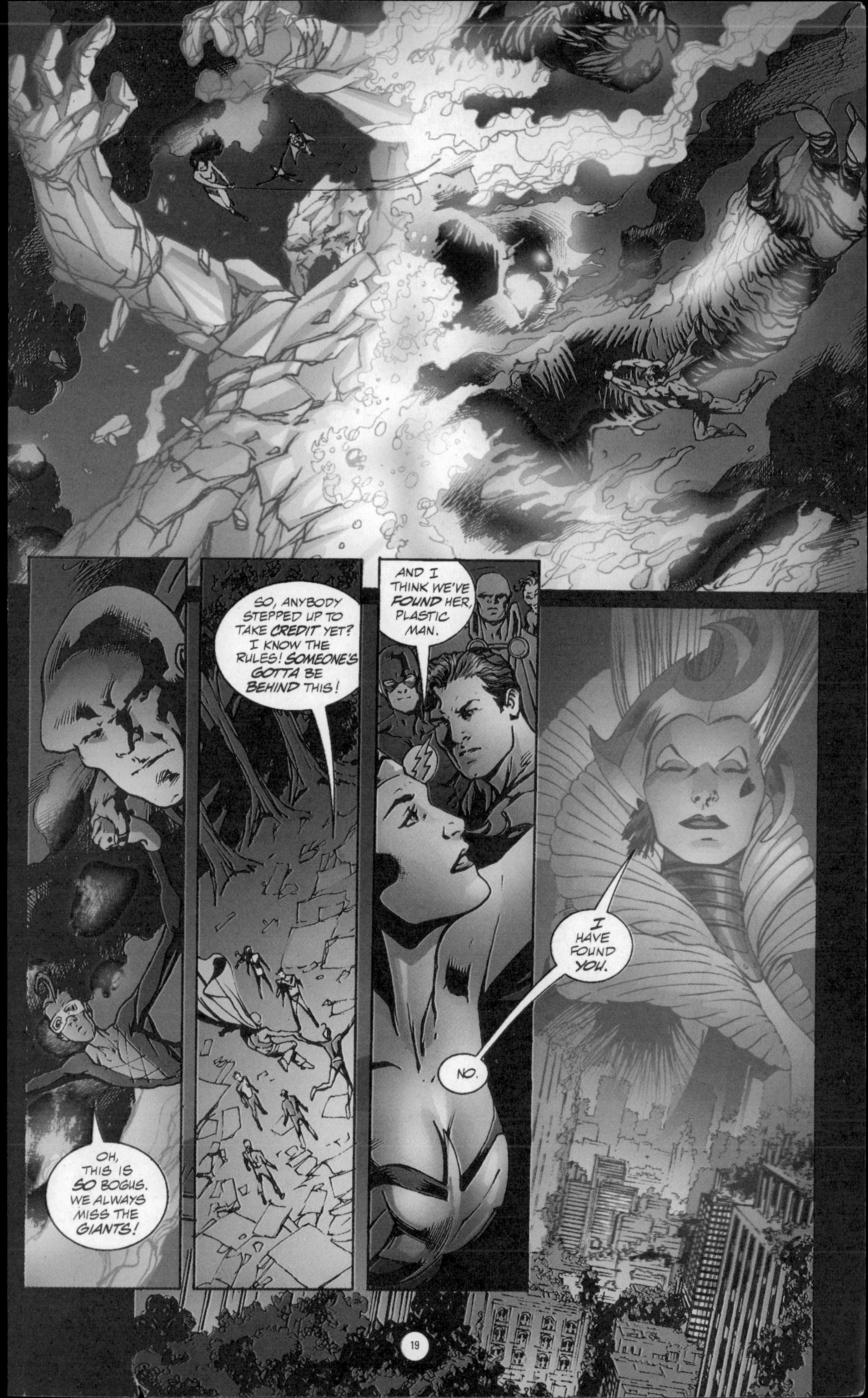

OH, THIS IS SO BOGUS. WE ALWAYS MISS THE GIANTS!
SO, ANYBODY STEPPED UP TO TAKE CREDIT YET? I KNOW THE RULES! SOMEONE'S GOTTA BE BEHIND THIS!
AND I THINK WE'VE FOUND HER, PLASTIC MAN.
I HAVE FOUND YOU.
NO.

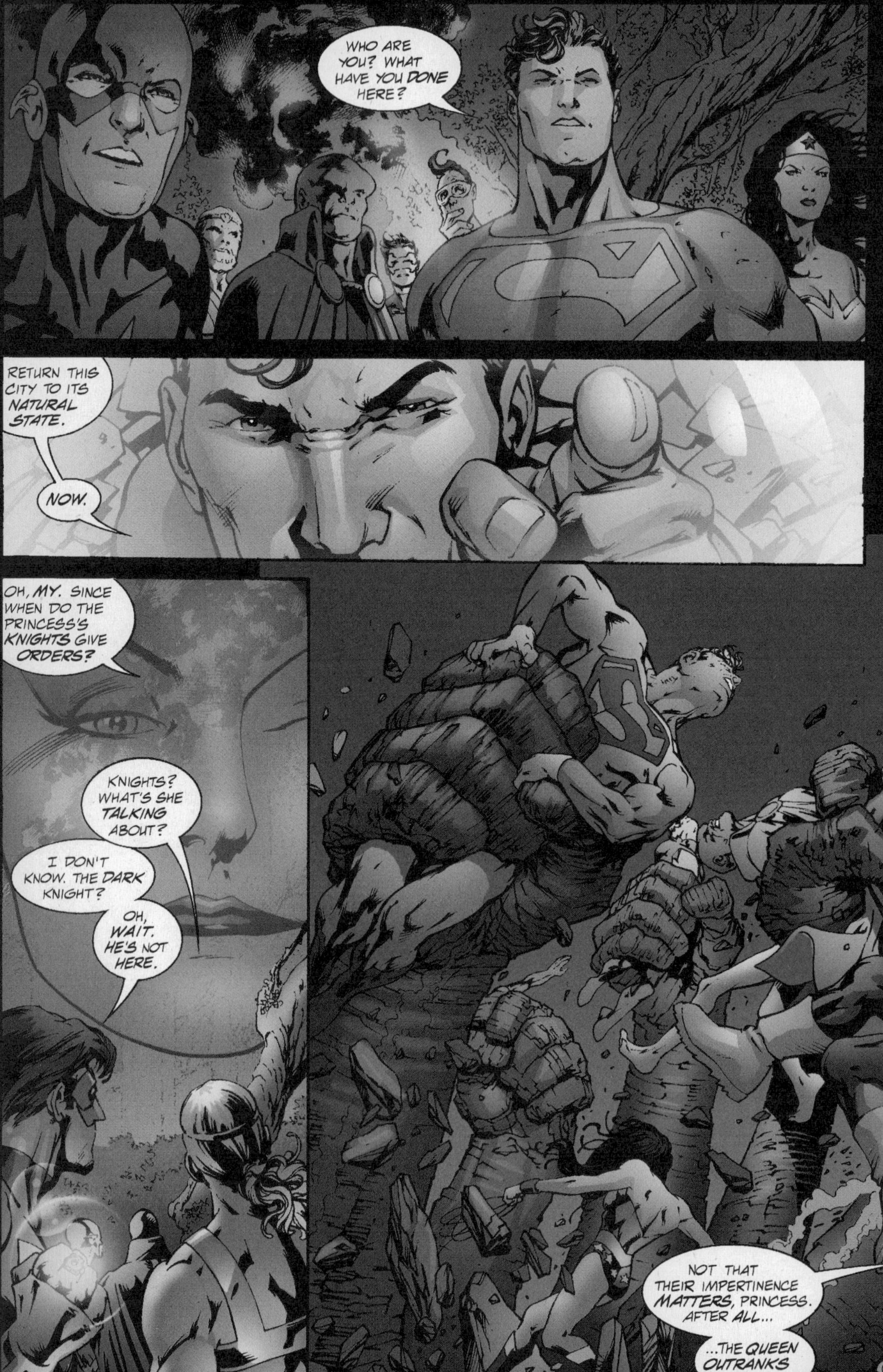
WHO ARE YOU? WHAT HAVE YOU DONE HERE?
RETURN THIS CITY TO ITS NATURAL STATE.
NOW.
OH, MY. SINCE WHEN DO THE PRINCESS'S KNIGHTS GIVE ORDERS?
KNIGHTS? WHAT'S SHE TALKING ABOUT?
I DON'T KNOW. THE DARK KNIGHT?
OH, WAIT. HE'S NOT HERE.
NOT THAT THEIR IMPERTINENCE MATTERS, PRINCESS. AFTER ALL...
...THE QUEEN OUTRANKS YOU.

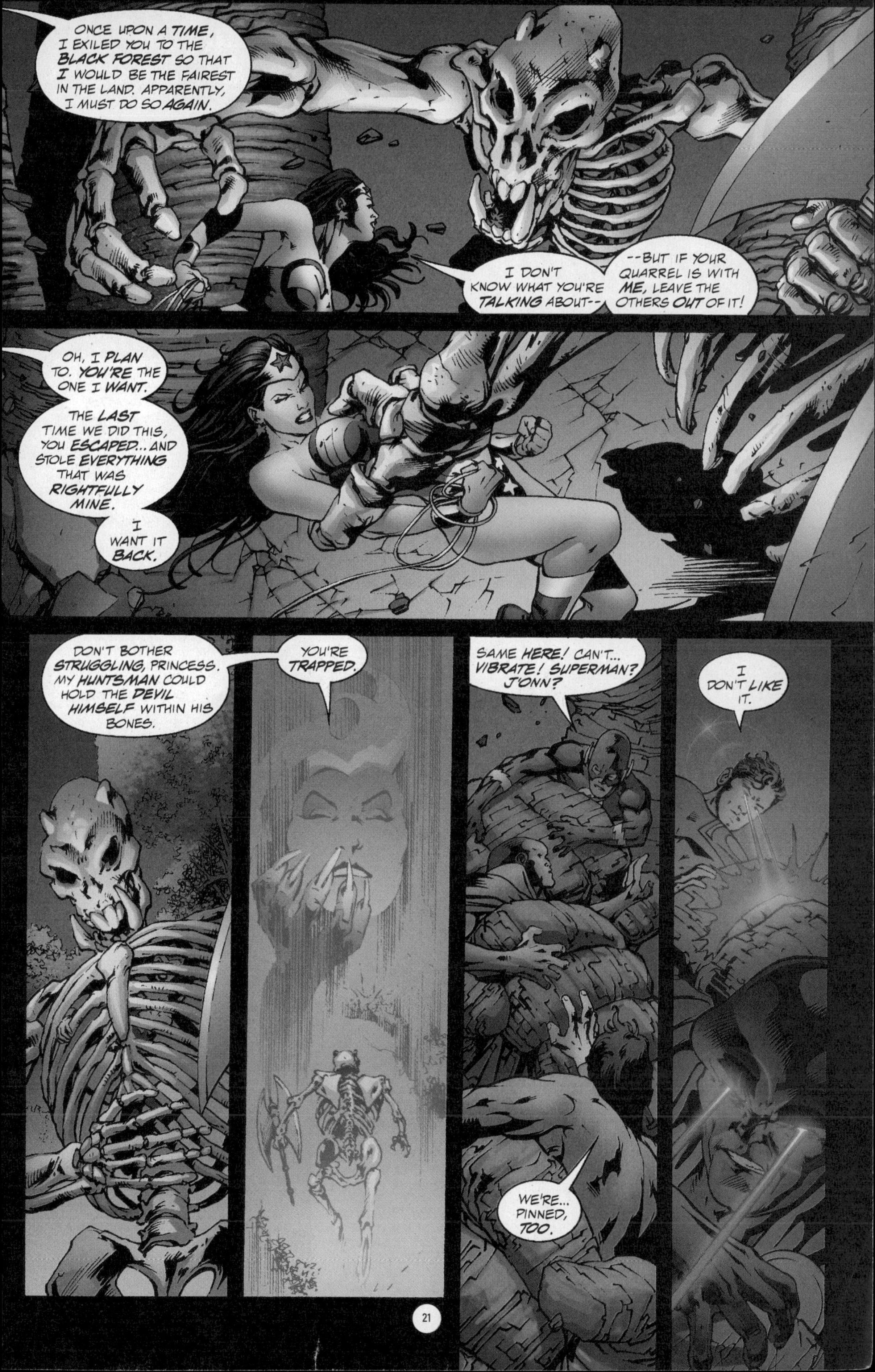
ONCE UPON A TIME, I EXILED YOU TO THE BLACK FOREST SO THAT I WOULD BE THE FAIREST IN THE LAND. APPARENTLY, I MUST DO SO AGAIN.
I DON'T KNOW WHAT YOU'RE TALKING ABOUT--
--BUT IF YOUR QUARREL IS WITH ME, LEAVE THE OTHERS OUT OF IT!
OH, I PLAN TO. YOU'RE THE ONE I WANT.
THE LAST TIME WE DID THIS, YOU ESCAPED... AND STOLE EVERYTHING THAT WAS RIGHTFULLY MINE.
I WANT IT BACK.
DON'T BOTHER STRUGGLING, PRINCESS. MY HUNTSMAN COULD HOLD THE DEVIL HIMSELF WITHIN HIS BONES.
YOU'RE TRAPPED.
SAME HERE! CAN'T... VIBRATE! SUPERMAN? J'ONN?
WE'RE... PINNED, TOO.
I DON'T LIKE IT.

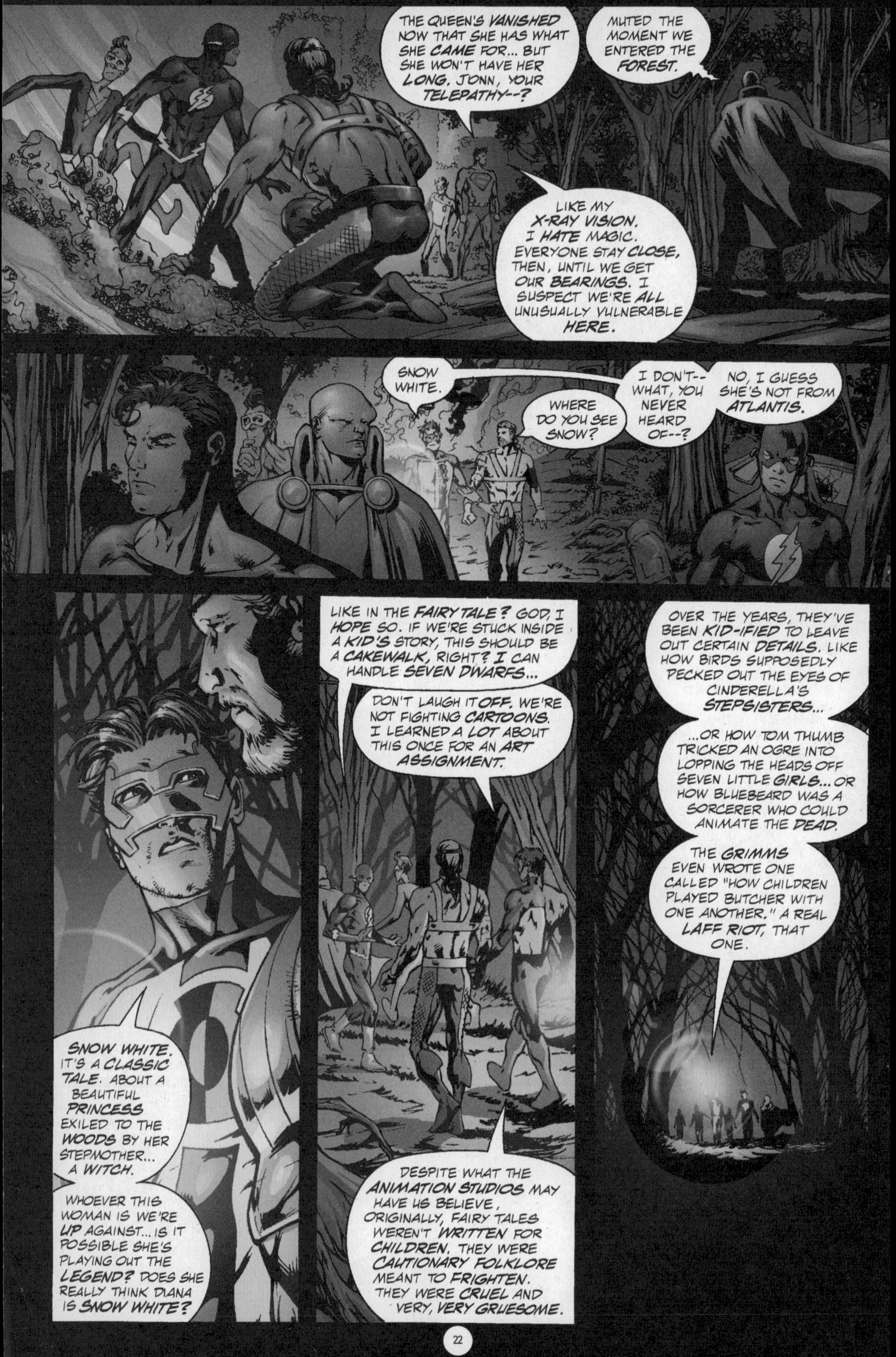
THE QUEEN'S VANISHED NOW THAT SHE HAS WHAT SHE CAME FOR... BUT SHE WON'T HAVE HER LONG. J'ONN, YOUR TELEPATHY--?
MUTED THE MOMENT WE ENTERED THE FOREST.
LIKE MY X-RAY VISION. I HATE MAGIC. EVERYONE STAY CLOSE, THEN, UNTIL WE GET OUR BEARINGS. I SUSPECT WE'RE ALL UNUSUALLY VULNERABLE HERE.
SNOW WHITE.
WHERE DO YOU SEE SNOW?
I DON'T-- WHAT, YOU NEVER HEARD OF--?
NO, I GUESS SHE'S NOT FROM ATLANTIS.
SNOW WHITE. IT'S A CLASSIC TALE. ABOUT A BEAUTIFUL PRINCESS EXILED TO THE WOODS BY HER STEPMOTHER... A WITCH.
WHOEVER THIS WOMAN IS WE'RE UP AGAINST... IS IT POSSIBLE SHE'S PLAYING OUT THE LEGEND? DOES SHE REALLY THINK DIANA IS SNOW WHITE?
LIKE IN THE FAIRY TALE? GOD, I HOPE SO. IF WE'RE STUCK INSIDE A KID'S STORY, THIS SHOULD BE A CAKEWALK, RIGHT? I CAN HANDLE SEVEN DWARFS...
DON'T LAUGH IT OFF. WE'RE NOT FIGHTING CARTOONS. I LEARNED A LOT ABOUT THIS ONCE FOR AN ART ASSIGNMENT.
DESPITE WHAT THE ANIMATION STUDIOS MAY HAVE US BELIEVE, ORIGINALLY, FAIRY TALES WEREN'T WRITTEN FOR CHILDREN. THEY WERE CAUTIONARY FOLKLORE MEANT TO FRIGHTEN. THEY WERE CRUEL AND VERY, VERY GRUESOME.
OVER THE YEARS, THEY'VE BEEN KID-IFIED TO LEAVE OUT CERTAIN DETAILS. LIKE HOW BIRDS SUPPOSEDLY PECKED OUT THE EYES OF CINDERELLA'S STEPSISTERS...
...OR HOW TOM THUMB TRICKED AN OGRE INTO LOPPING THE HEADS OFF SEVEN LITTLE GIRLS... OR HOW BLUEBEARD WAS A SORCERER WHO COULD ANIMATE THE DEAD.
THE GRIMMS EVEN WROTE ONE CALLED "HOW CHILDREN PLAYED BUTCHER WITH ONE ANOTHER." A REAL LAFF RIOT, THAT ONE.

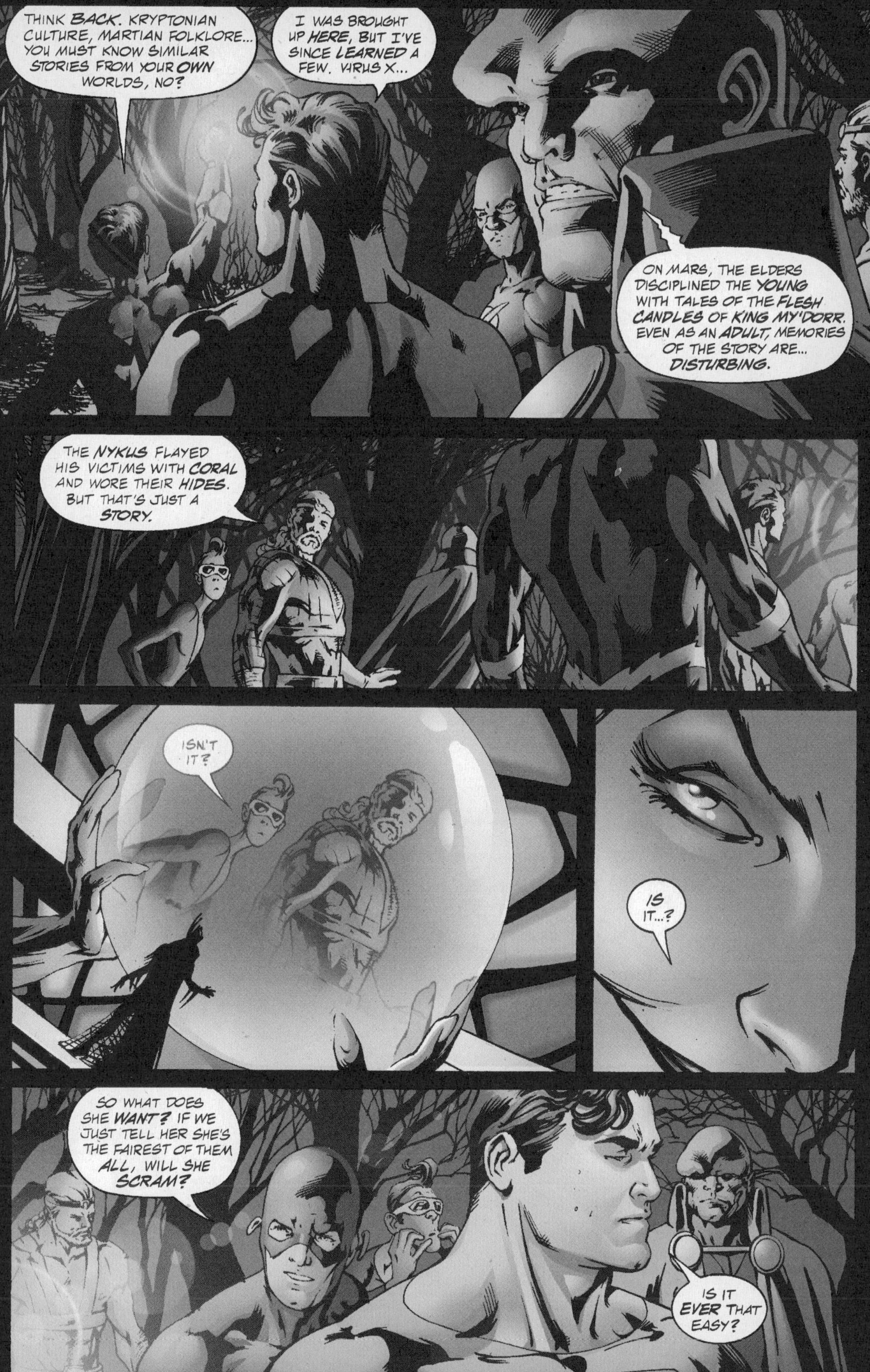
THINK BACK. KRYPTONIAN CULTURE, MARTIAN FOLKLORE... YOU MUST KNOW SIMILAR STORIES FROM YOUR OWN WORLDS, NO?
I WAS BROUGHT UP HERE, BUT I'VE SINCE LEARNED A FEW. VIRUS X...
ON MARS, THE ELDERS DISCIPLINED THE YOUNG WITH TALES OF THE FLESH CANDLES OF KING MY'DORR. EVEN AS AN ADULT, MEMORIES OF THE STORY ARE... DISTURBING.
THE NYKUS FLAYED HIS VICTIMS WITH CORAL AND WORE THEIR HIDES. BUT THAT'S JUST A STORY.
ISN'T IT?
IS IT...?
SO WHAT DOES SHE WANT? IF WE JUST TELL HER SHE'S THE FAIREST OF THEM ALL, WILL SHE SCRAM?
IS IT EVER THAT EASY?

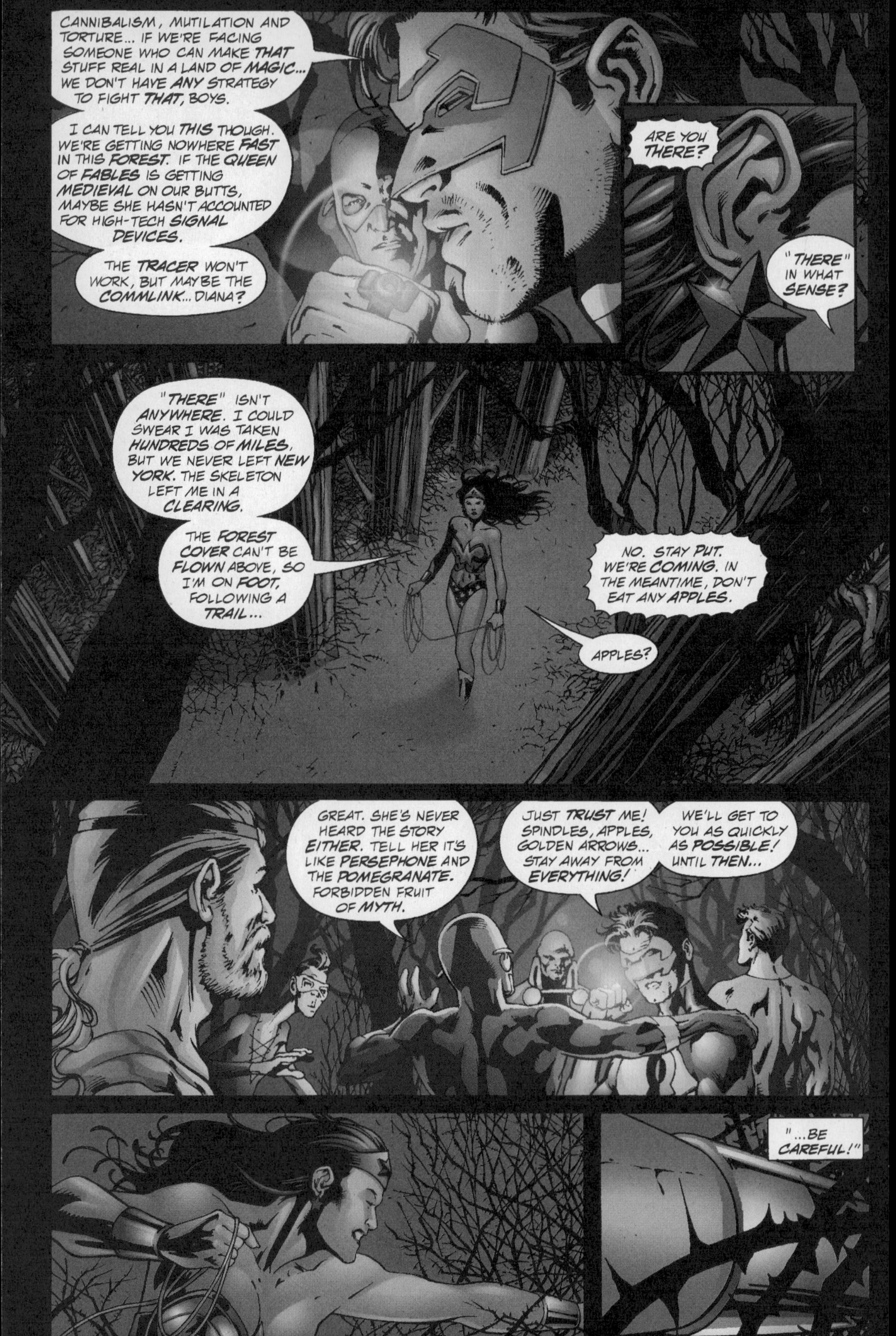
CANNIBALISM, MUTILATION AND TORTURE... IF WE'RE FACING SOMEONE WHO CAN MAKE THAT STUFF REAL IN A LAND OF MAGIC... WE DON'T HAVE ANY STRATEGY TO FIGHT THAT, BOYS.
I CAN TELL YOU THIS THOUGH. WE'RE GETTING NOWHERE FAST IN THIS FOREST. IF THE QUEEN OF FABLES IS GETTING MEDIEVAL ON OUR BUTTS, MAYBE SHE HASN'T ACCOUNTED FOR HIGH-TECH SIGNAL DEVICES.
THE TRACER WON'T WORK, BUT MAYBE THE COMMLINK... DIANA?
ARE YOU THERE?
"THERE" IN WHAT SENSE?
"THERE" ISN'T ANYWHERE. I COULD SWEAR I WAS TAKEN HUNDREDS OF MILES, BUT WE NEVER LEFT NEW YORK. THE SKELETON LEFT ME IN A CLEARING.
THE FOREST COVER CAN'T BE FLOWN ABOVE, SO I'M ON FOOT, FOLLOWING A TRAIL...
NO. STAY PUT. WE'RE COMING. IN THE MEANTIME, DON'T EAT ANY APPLES.
APPLES?
GREAT. SHE'S NEVER HEARD THE STORY EITHER. TELL HER IT'S LIKE PERSEPHONE AND THE POMEGRANATE. FORBIDDEN FRUIT OF MYTH.
JUST TRUST ME! SPINDLES, APPLES, GOLDEN ARROWS... STAY AWAY FROM EVERYTHING!
WE'LL GET TO YOU AS QUICKLY AS POSSIBLE! UNTIL THEN...
"...BE CAREFUL!"

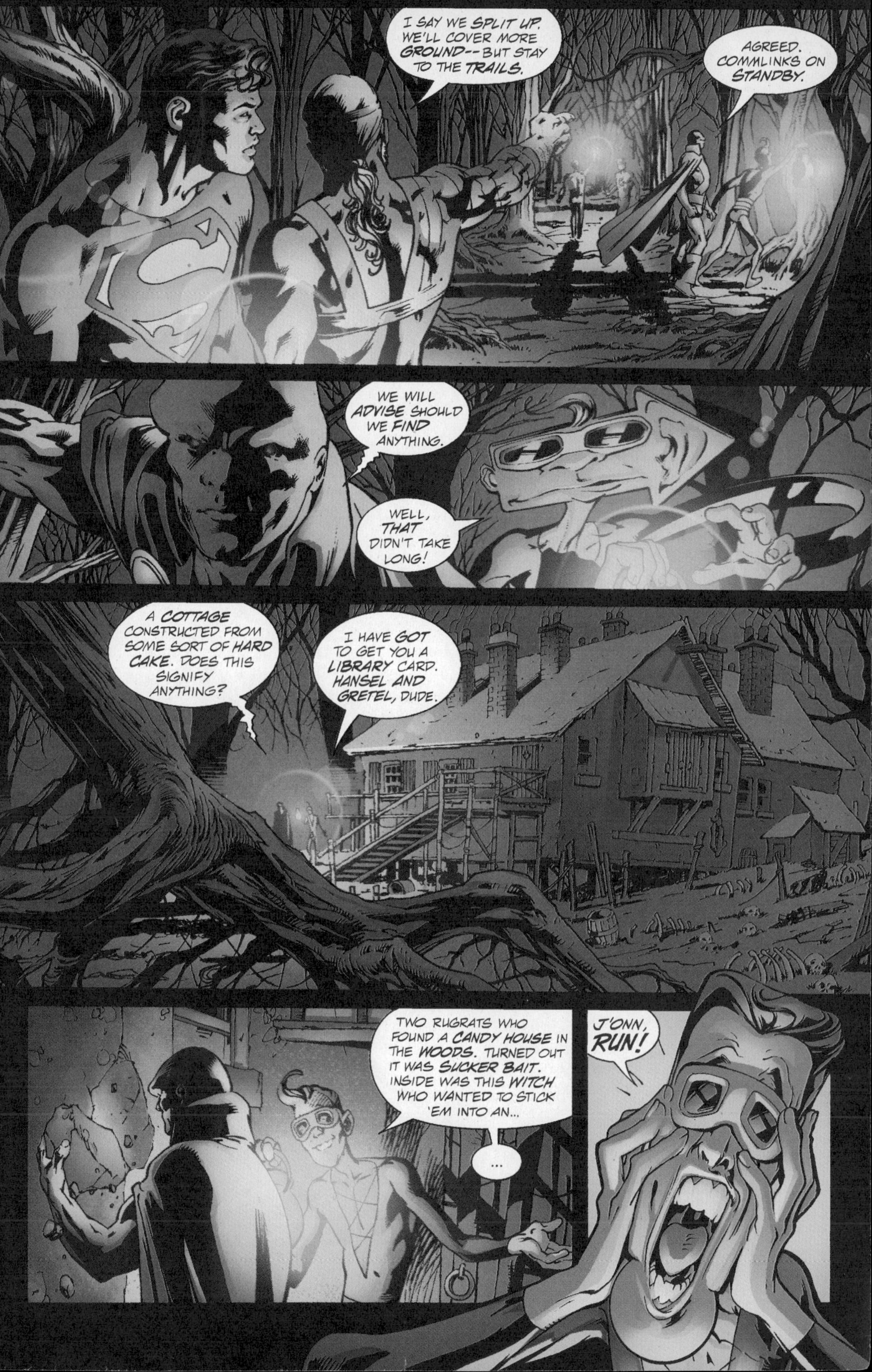
I SAY WE SPLIT UP. WE'LL COVER MORE GROUND-- BUT STAY TO THE TRAILS.
AGREED. COMMLINKS ON STANDBY.
WE WILL ADVISE SHOULD WE FIND ANYTHING.
WELL, THAT DIDN'T TAKE LONG!
A COTTAGE CONSTRUCTED FROM SOME SORT OF HARD CAKE. DOES THIS SIGNIFY ANYTHING?
I HAVE GOT TO GET YOU A LIBRARY CARD. HANSEL AND GRETEL, DUDE.
TWO RUGRATS WHO FOUND A CANDY HOUSE IN THE WOODS. TURNED OUT IT WAS SUCKER BAIT. INSIDE WAS THIS WITCH WHO WANTED TO STICK 'EM INTO AN...
...
J'ONN, RUN!

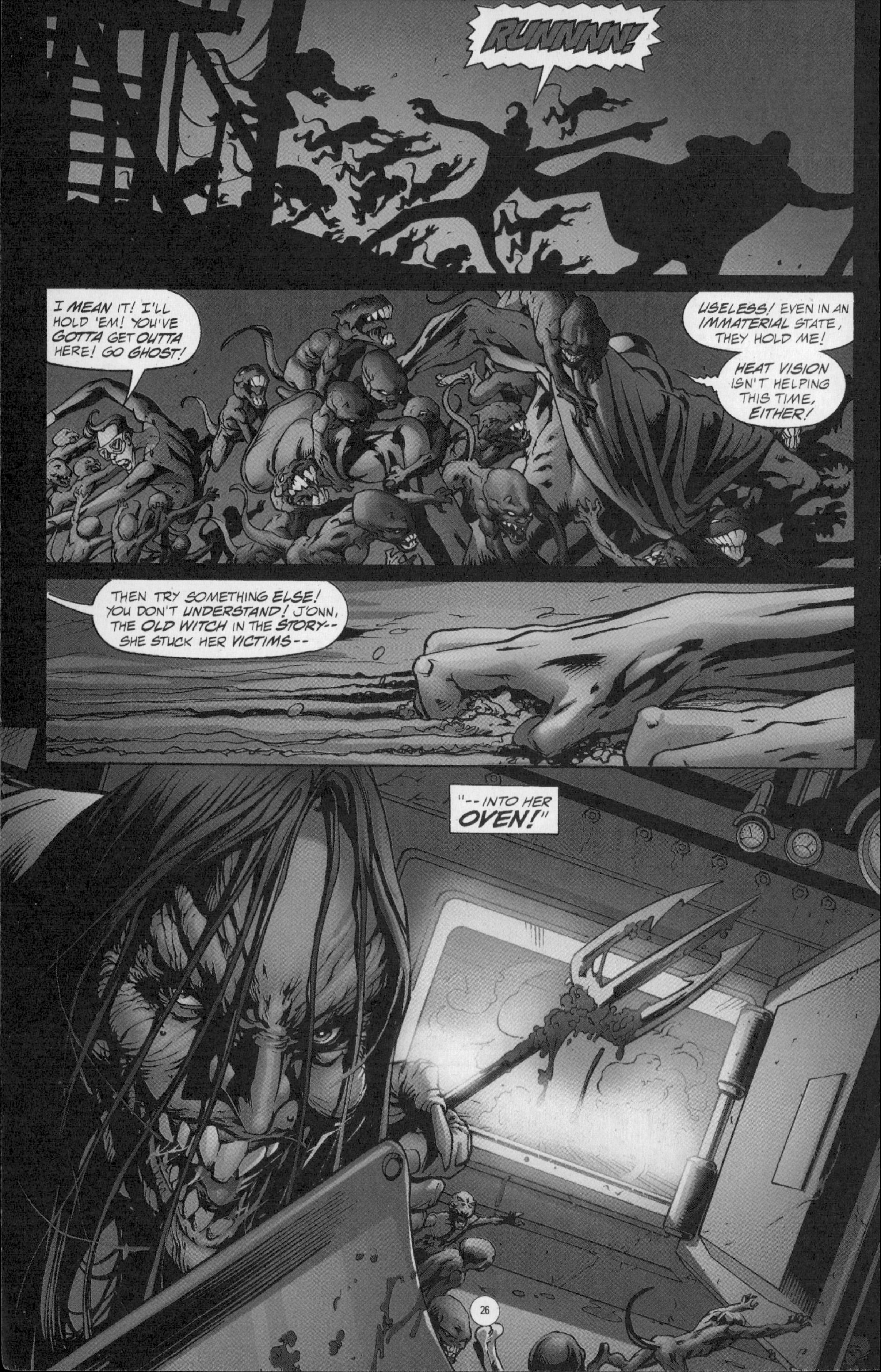
RUNNNN!
I MEAN IT! I'LL HOLD 'EM! YOU'VE GOTTA GET OUTTA HERE! GO GHOST!
USELESS! EVEN IN AN IMMATERIAL STATE, THEY HOLD ME!
HEAT VISION ISN'T HELPING THIS TIME, EITHER!
THEN TRY SOMETHING ELSE! YOU DON'T UNDERSTAND! J'ONN, THE OLD WITCH IN THE STORY-- SHE STUCK HER VICTIMS--
"--INTO HER OVEN!"

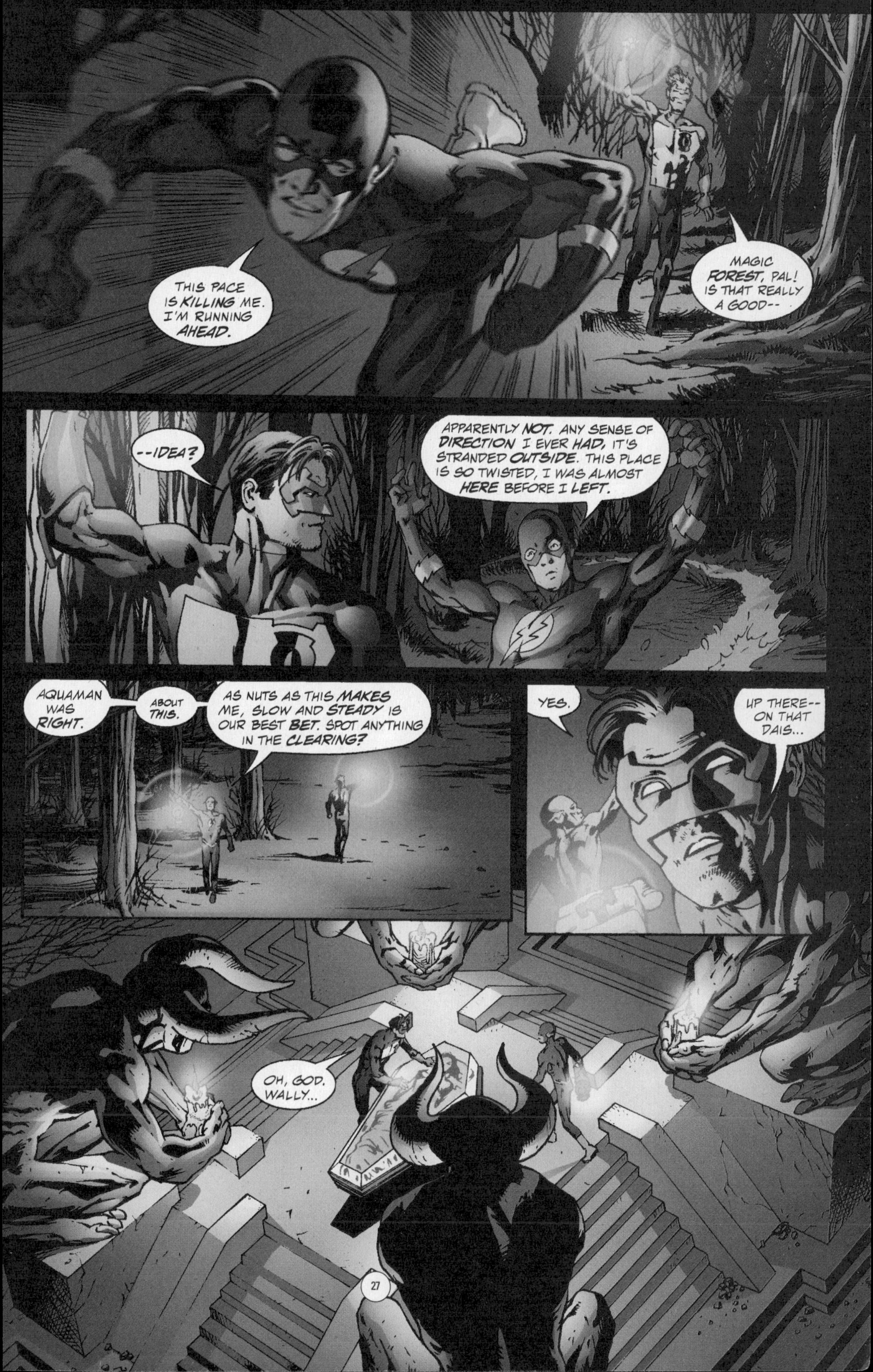
THIS PACE IS KILLING ME. I'M RUNNING AHEAD.
MAGIC FOREST, PAL! IS THAT REALLY A GOOD--
--IDEA?
APPARENTLY NOT. ANY SENSE OF DIRECTION I EVER HAD, IT'S STRANDED OUTSIDE. THIS PLACE IS SO TWISTED, I WAS ALMOST HERE BEFORE I LEFT.
AQUAMAN WAS RIGHT.
ABOUT THIS.
AS NUTS AS THIS MAKES ME, SLOW AND STEADY IS OUR BEST BET. SPOT ANYTHING IN THE CLEARING?
YES.
UP THERE-- ON THAT DAIS...
OH, GOD. WALLY...

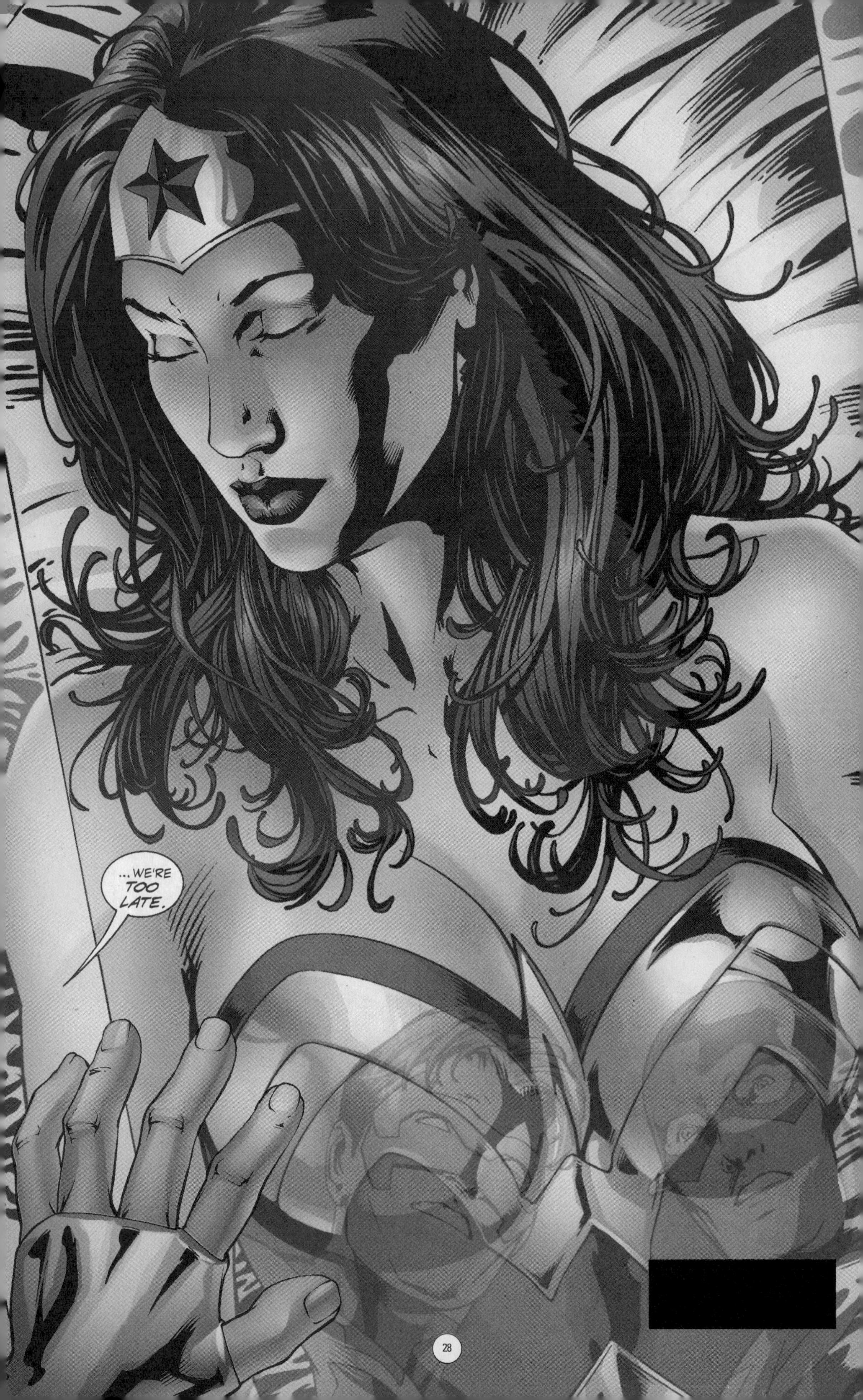
...WE'RE TOO LATE.

[redacted]

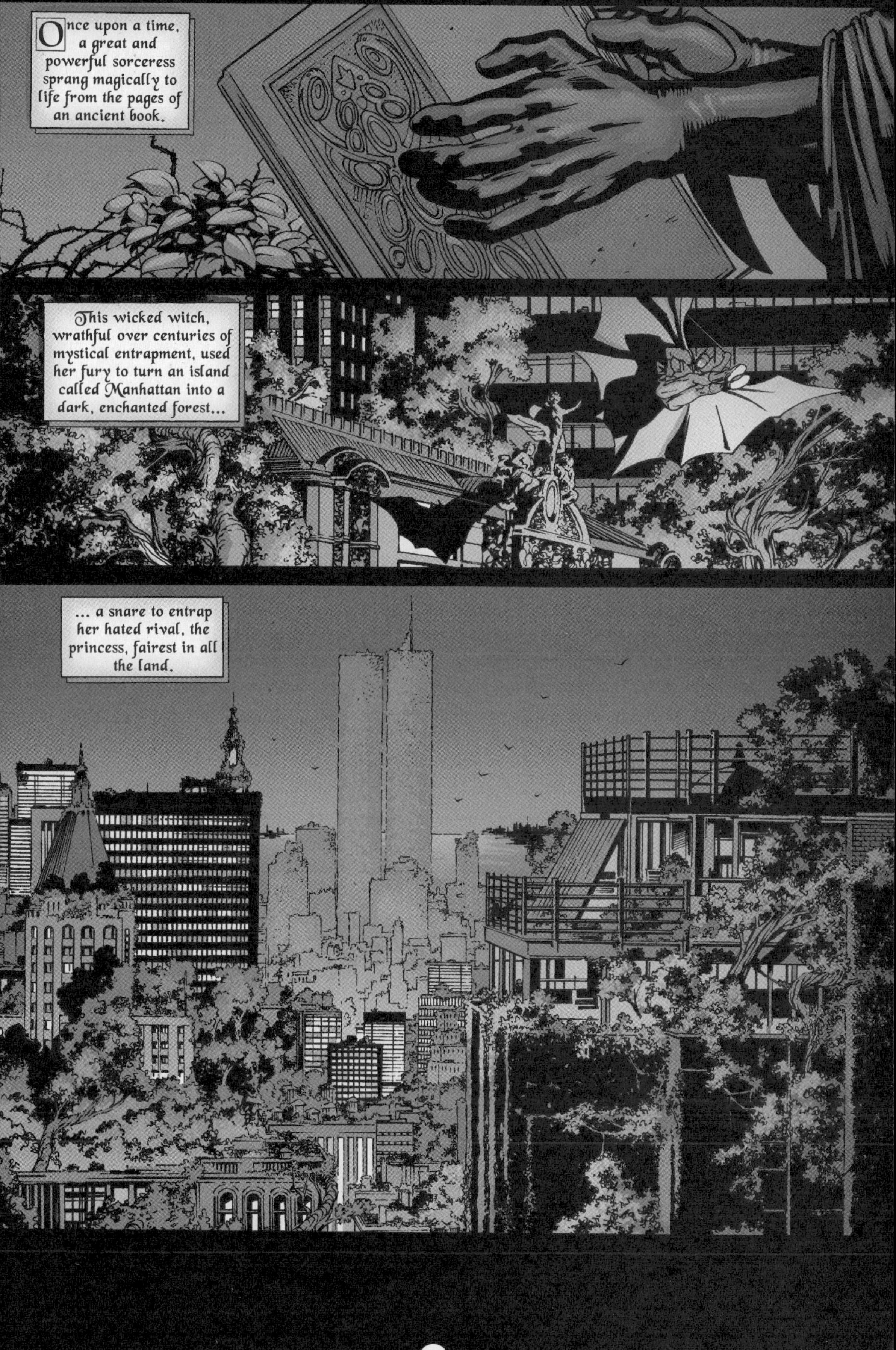
Once upon a time, a great and powerful sorceress sprang magically to life from the pages of an ancient book.
This wicked witch, wrathful over centuries of mystical entrapment, used her fury to turn an island called Manhattan into a dark, enchanted forest...
... a snare to entrap her hated rival, the princess, fairest in all the land.

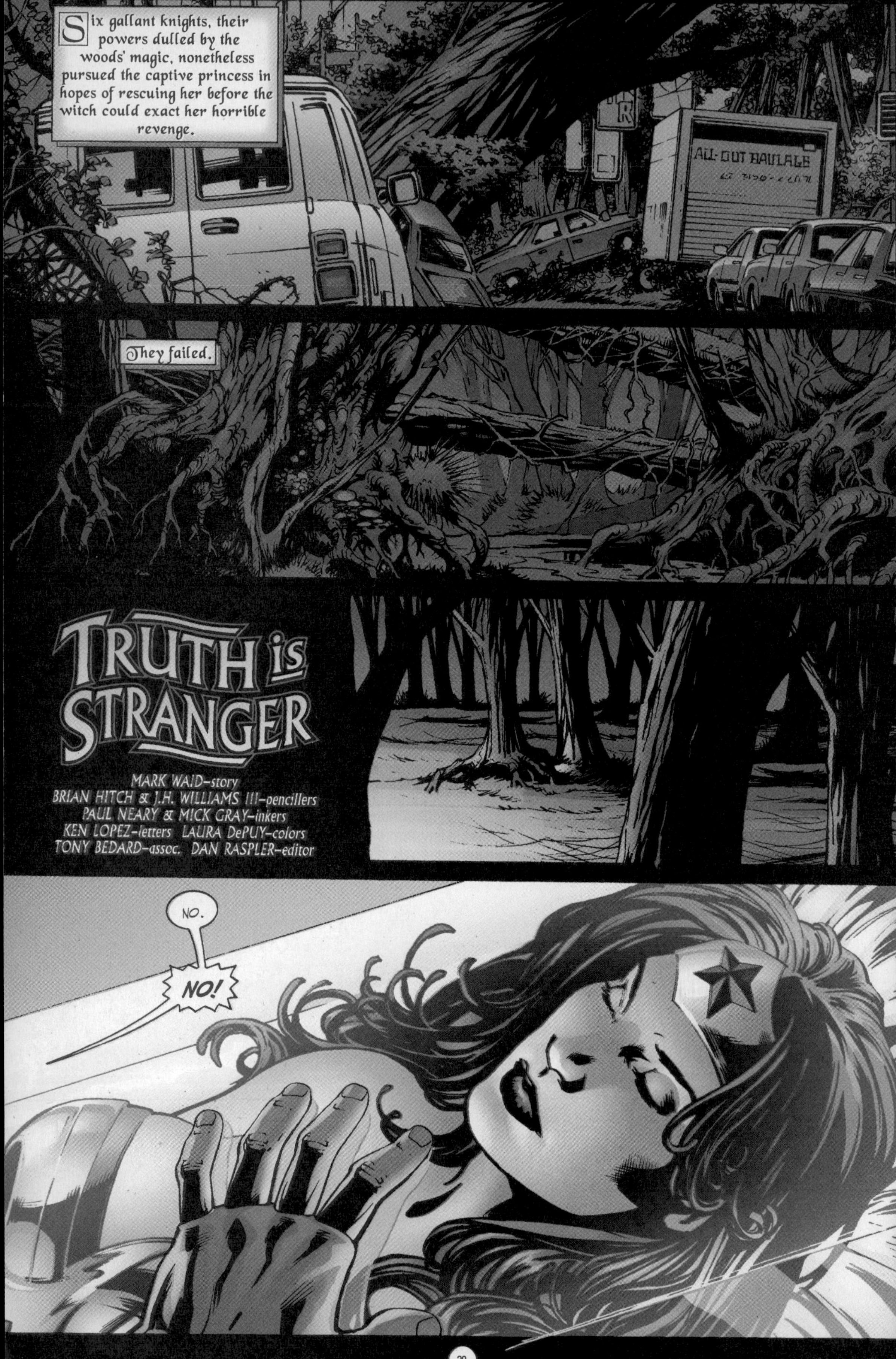

Six gallant knights, their powers dulled by the woods' magic, nonetheless pursued the captive princess in hopes of rescuing her before the witch could exact her horrible revenge.
ALL-OUT HAULAGE
They failed.
TRUTH is STRANGER
MARK WAID–story
BRIAN HITCH & J.H. WILLIAMS III–pencillers
PAUL NEARY & MICK GRAY–inkers
KEN LOPEZ–letters LAURA DePUY–colors
TONY BEDARD–assoc. DAN RASPLER–editor
NO.
NO!

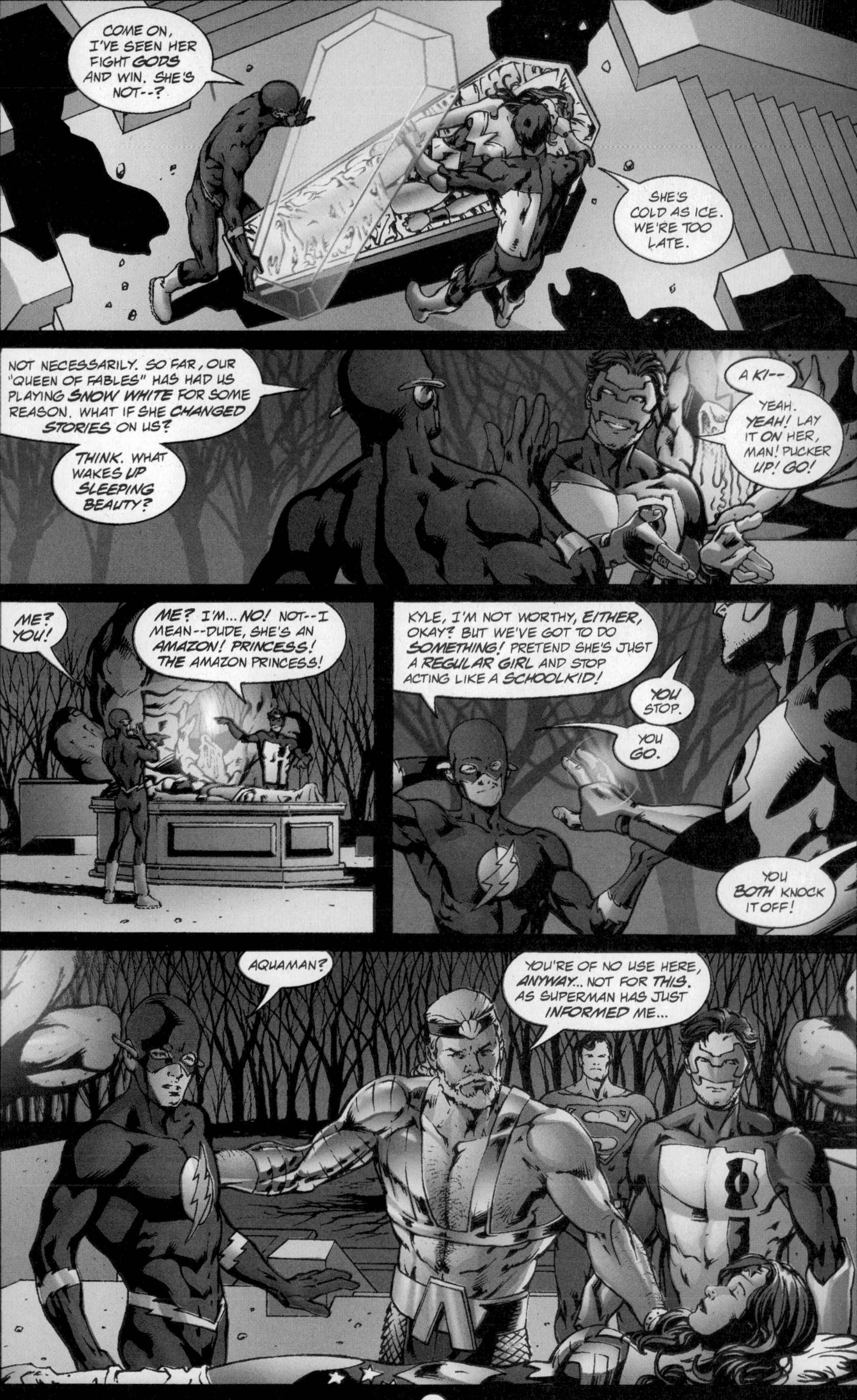
COME ON, I'VE SEEN HER FIGHT GODS AND WIN. SHE'S NOT--?
SHE'S COLD AS ICE. WE'RE TOO LATE.
NOT NECESSARILY. SO FAR, OUR "QUEEN OF FABLES" HAS HAD US PLAYING SNOW WHITE FOR SOME REASON. WHAT IF SHE CHANGED STORIES ON US?
THINK. WHAT WAKES UP SLEEPING BEAUTY?
A KI--
YEAH. YEAH! LAY IT ON HER, MAN! PUCKER UP! GO!
ME? YOU!
ME? I'M... NO! NOT--I MEAN--DUDE, SHE'S AN AMAZON! PRINCESS! THE AMAZON PRINCESS!
KYLE, I'M NOT WORTHY, EITHER, OKAY? BUT WE'VE GOT TO DO SOMETHING! PRETEND SHE'S JUST A REGULAR GIRL AND STOP ACTING LIKE A SCHOOLKID!
YOU STOP.
YOU GO.
YOU BOTH KNOCK IT OFF!
AQUAMAN?
YOU'RE OF NO USE HERE, ANYWAY... NOT FOR THIS. AS SUPERMAN HAS JUST INFORMED ME...

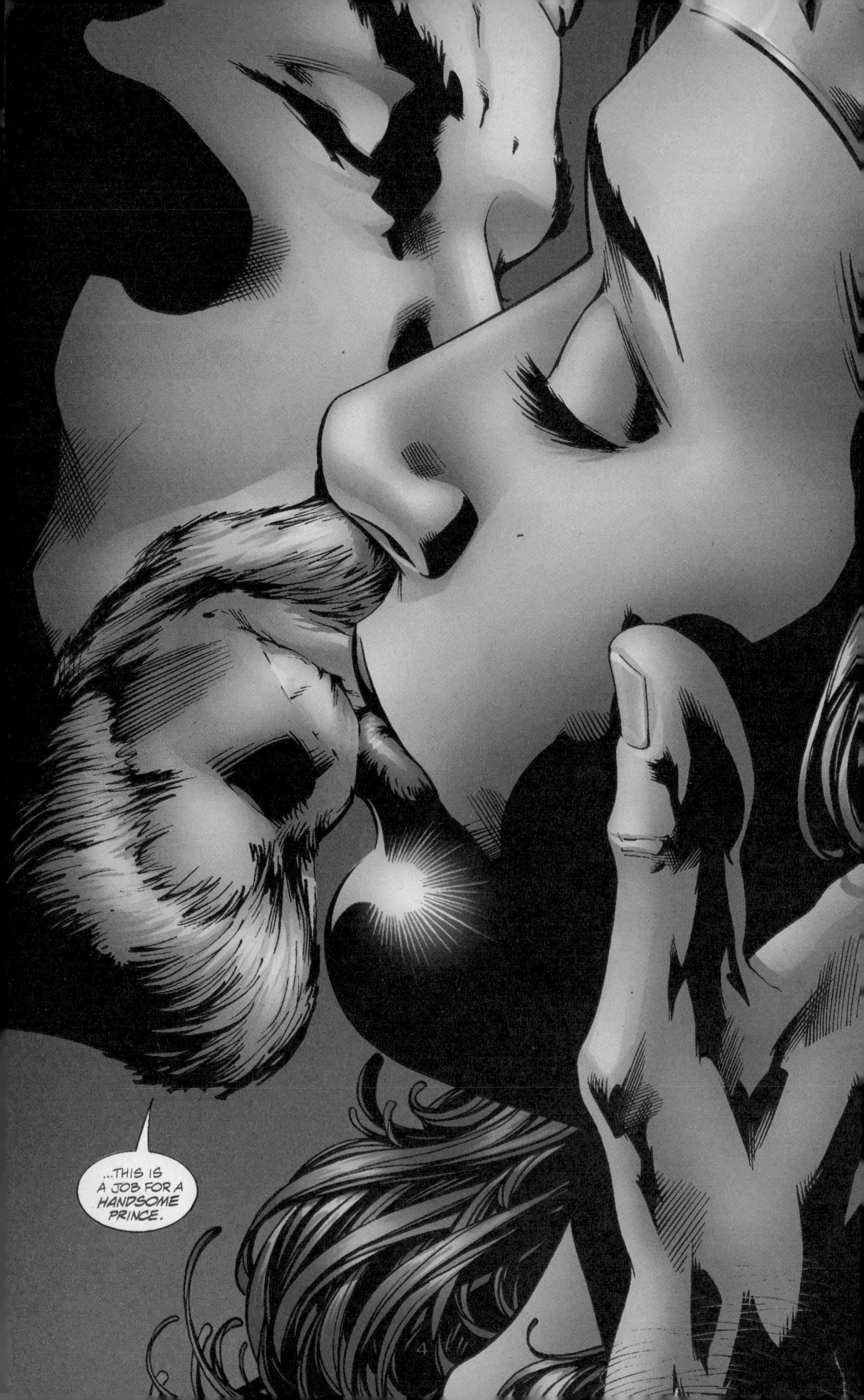
...THIS IS A JOB FOR A HANDSOME PRINCE.

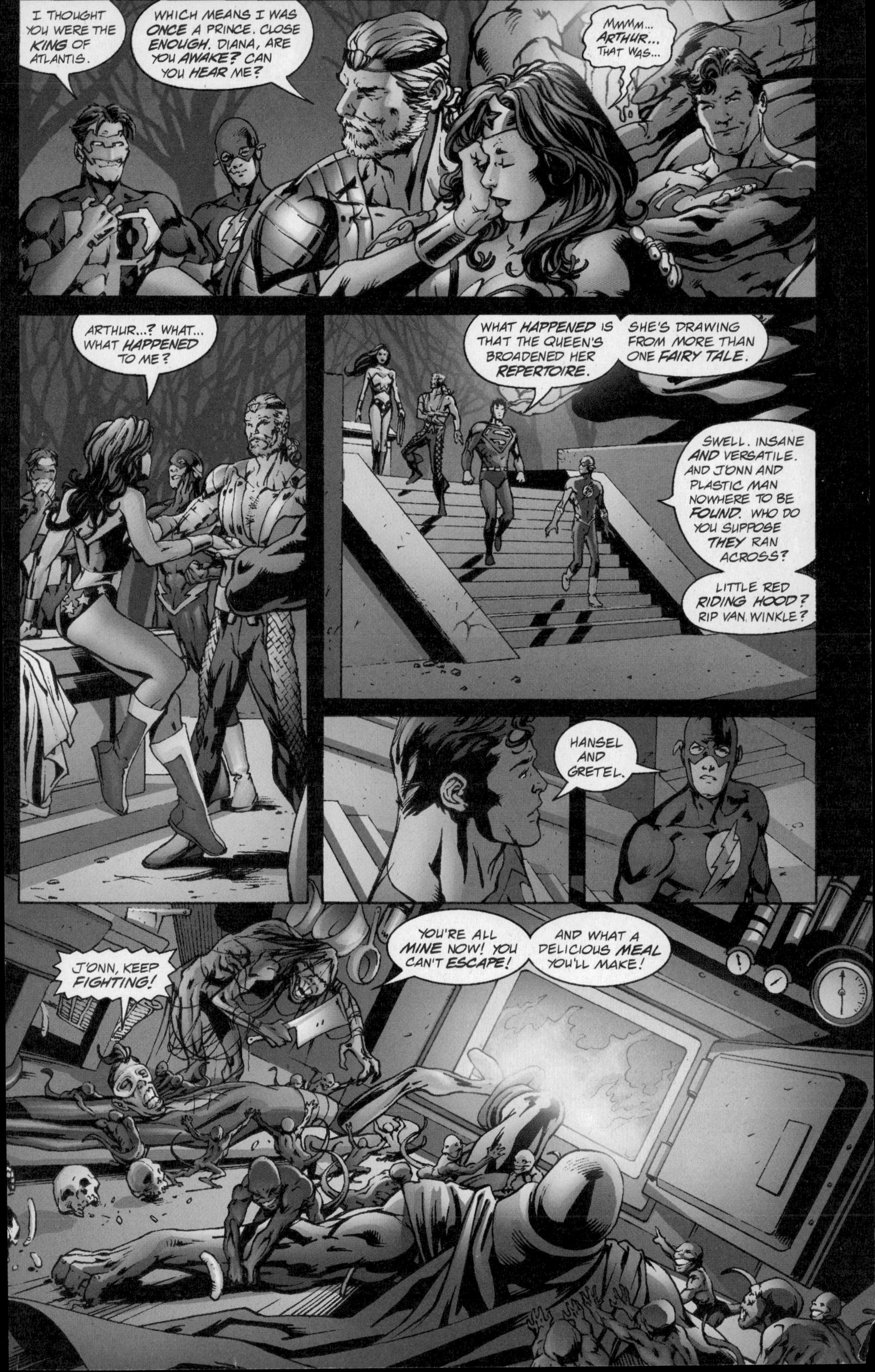
I THOUGHT YOU WERE THE KING OF ATLANTIS.
WHICH MEANS I WAS ONCE A PRINCE. CLOSE ENOUGH. DIANA, ARE YOU AWAKE? CAN YOU HEAR ME?
MMMM... ARTHUR... THAT WAS...
ARTHUR...? WHAT... WHAT HAPPENED TO ME?
WHAT HAPPENED IS THAT THE QUEEN'S BROADENED HER REPERTOIRE.
SHE'S DRAWING FROM MORE THAN ONE FAIRY TALE.
SWELL. INSANE AND VERSATILE. AND J'ONN AND PLASTIC MAN NOWHERE TO BE FOUND. WHO DO YOU SUPPOSE THEY RAN ACROSS?
LITTLE RED RIDING HOOD? RIP VAN WINKLE?
HANSEL AND GRETEL.
J'ONN, KEEP FIGHTING!
YOU'RE ALL MINE NOW! YOU CAN'T ESCAPE!
AND WHAT A DELICIOUS MEAL YOU'LL MAKE!

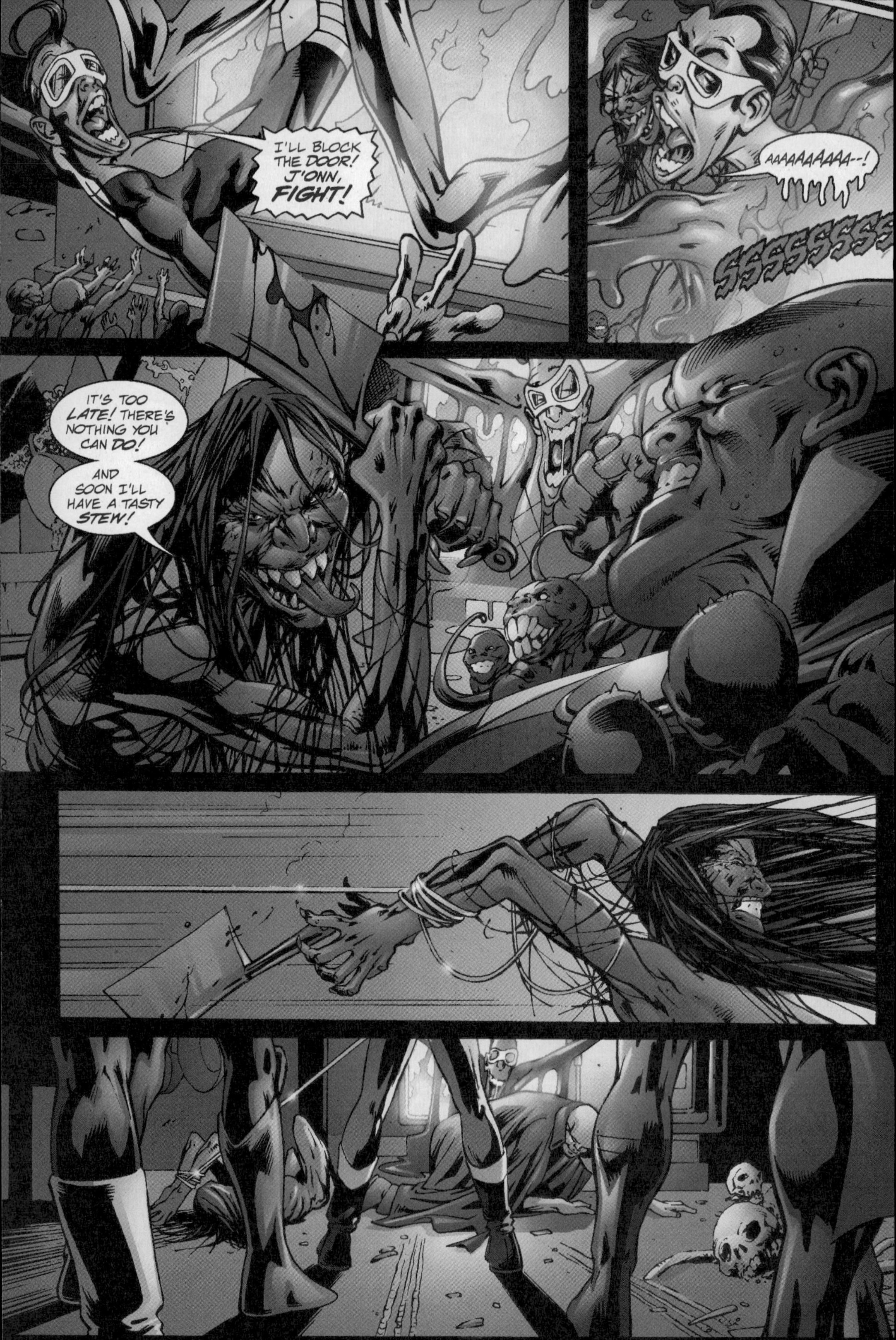
I'LL BLOCK THE DOOR! J'ONN, FIGHT!
AAAAAAAAAA--!
SSSSSSSS
IT'S TOO LATE! THERE'S NOTHING YOU CAN DO!
AND SOON I'LL HAVE A TASTY STEW!

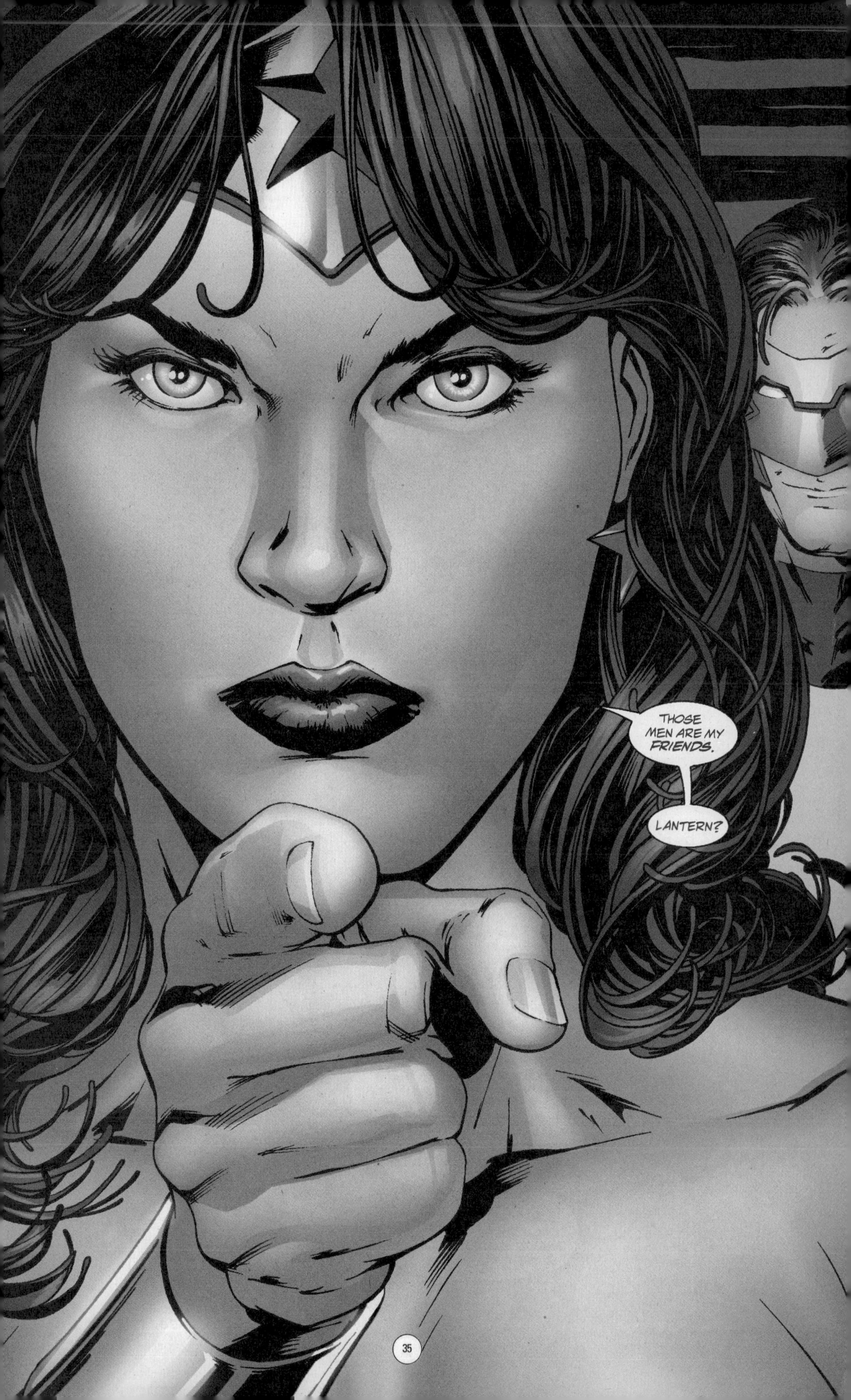
THOSE MEN ARE MY FRIENDS.
LANTERN?

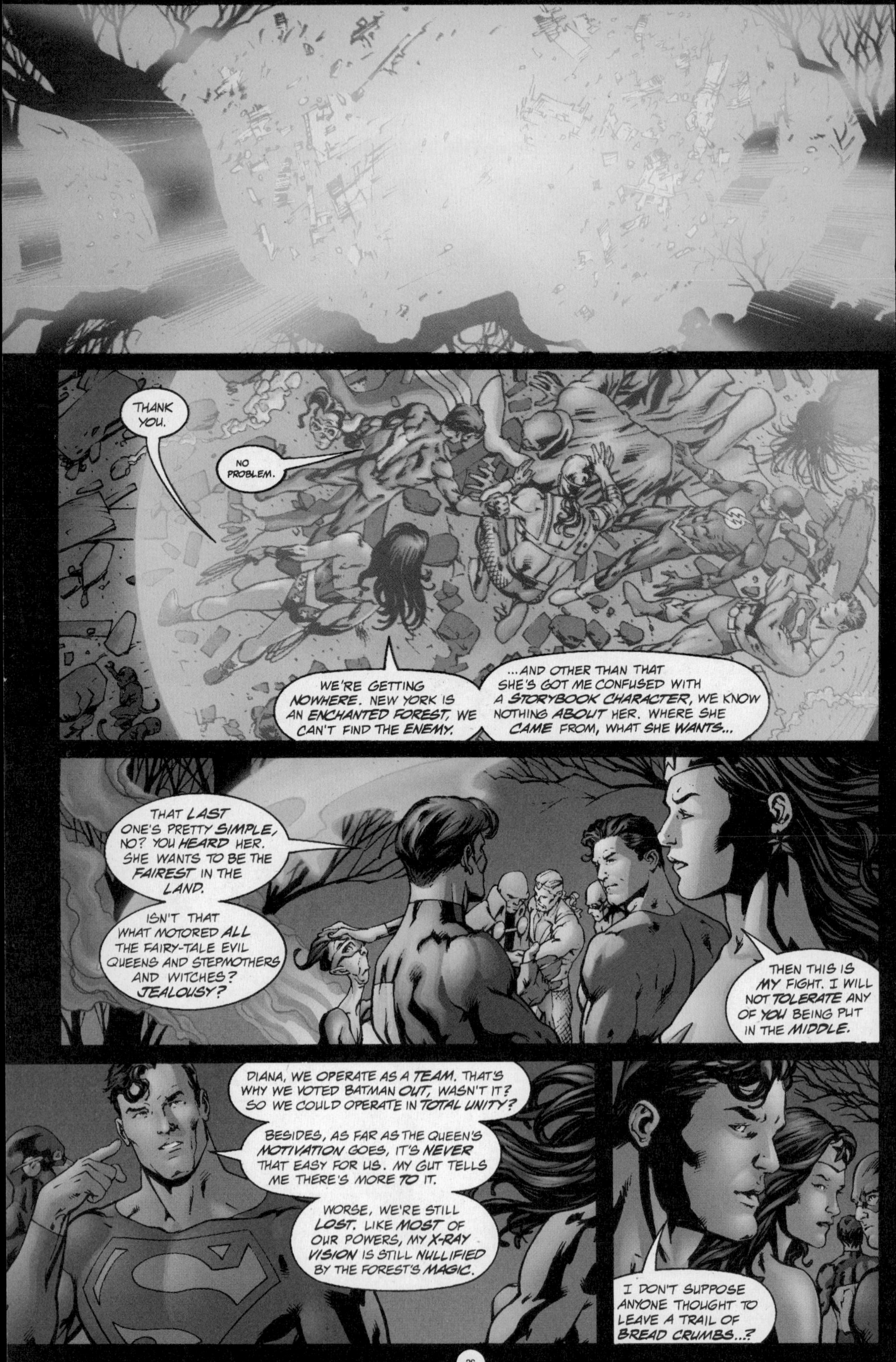
THANK YOU.
NO PROBLEM.
WE'RE GETTING NOWHERE. NEW YORK IS AN ENCHANTED FOREST, WE CAN'T FIND THE ENEMY.
...AND OTHER THAN THAT SHE'S GOT ME CONFUSED WITH A STORYBOOK CHARACTER, WE KNOW NOTHING ABOUT HER. WHERE SHE CAME FROM, WHAT SHE WANTS...
THAT LAST ONE'S PRETTY SIMPLE, NO? YOU HEARD HER. SHE WANTS TO BE THE FAIREST IN THE LAND.
ISN'T THAT WHAT MOTORED ALL THE FAIRY-TALE EVIL QUEENS AND STEPMOTHERS AND WITCHES? JEALOUSY?
THEN THIS IS MY FIGHT. I WILL NOT TOLERATE ANY OF YOU BEING PUT IN THE MIDDLE.
DIANA, WE OPERATE AS A TEAM. THAT'S WHY WE VOTED BATMAN OUT, WASN'T IT? SO WE COULD OPERATE IN TOTAL UNITY?
BESIDES, AS FAR AS THE QUEEN'S MOTIVATION GOES, IT'S NEVER THAT EASY FOR US. MY GUT TELLS ME THERE'S MORE TO IT.
WORSE, WE'RE STILL LOST. LIKE MOST OF OUR POWERS, MY X-RAY VISION IS STILL NULLIFIED BY THE FOREST'S MAGIC.
I DON'T SUPPOSE ANYONE THOUGHT TO LEAVE A TRAIL OF BREAD CRUMBS...?

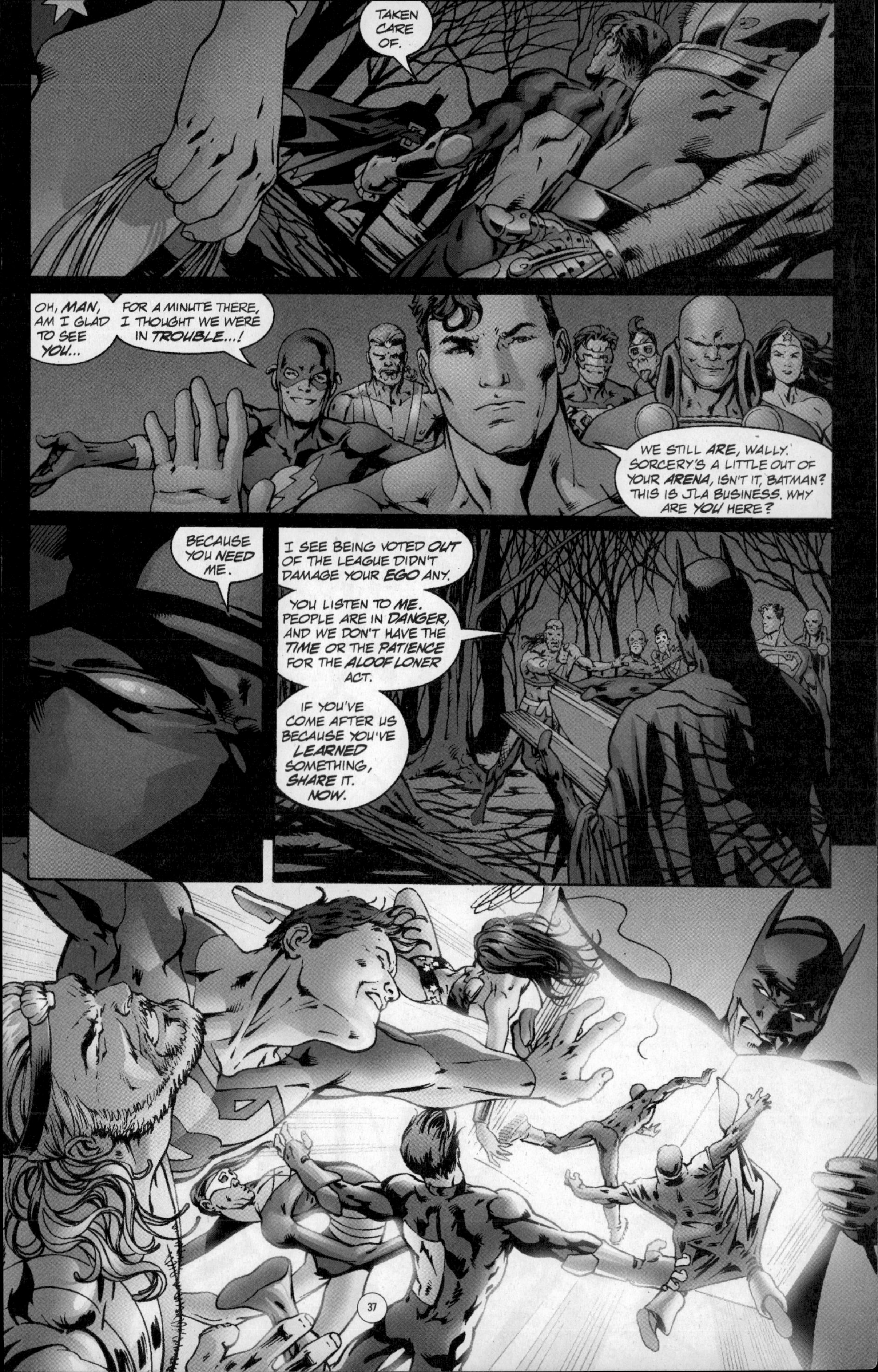
TAKEN CARE OF.
OH, MAN, AM I GLAD TO SEE YOU...
FOR A MINUTE THERE, I THOUGHT WE WERE IN TROUBLE...!
WE STILL ARE, WALLY. SORCERY'S A LITTLE OUT OF YOUR ARENA, ISN'T IT, BATMAN? THIS IS JLA BUSINESS. WHY ARE YOU HERE?
BECAUSE YOU NEED ME.
I SEE BEING VOTED OUT OF THE LEAGUE DIDN'T DAMAGE YOUR EGO ANY.
YOU LISTEN TO ME. PEOPLE ARE IN DANGER, AND WE DON'T HAVE THE TIME OR THE PATIENCE FOR THE ALOOF LONER ACT.
IF YOU'VE COME AFTER US BECAUSE YOU'VE LEARNED SOMETHING, SHARE IT. NOW.

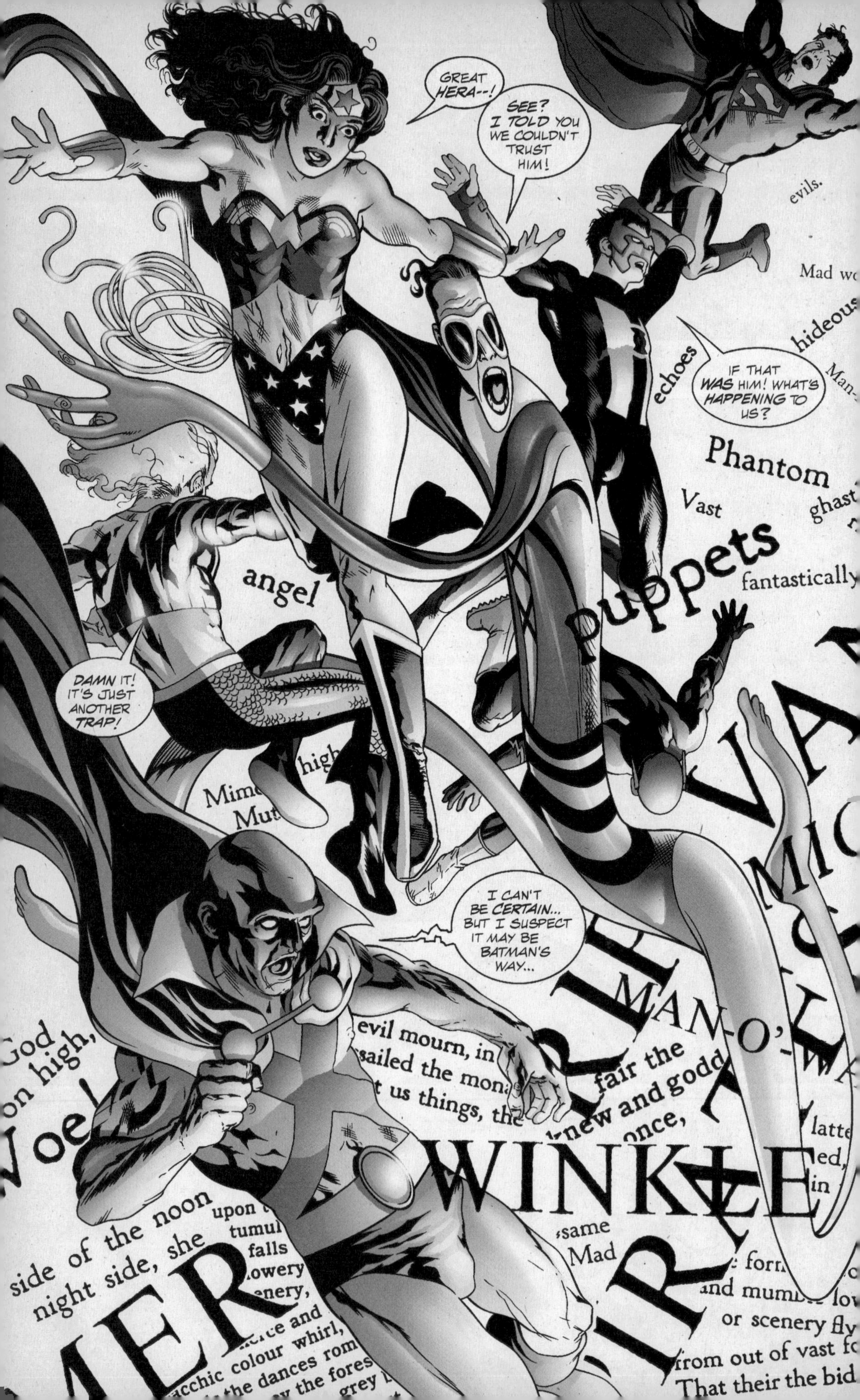
GREAT HERA--!
SEE? I TOLD YOU WE COULDN'T TRUST HIM!
IF THAT WAS HIM! WHAT'S HAPPENING TO US?
DAMN IT! IT'S JUST ANOTHER TRAP!
I CAN'T BE CERTAIN... BUT I SUSPECT IT MAY BE BATMAN'S WAY...

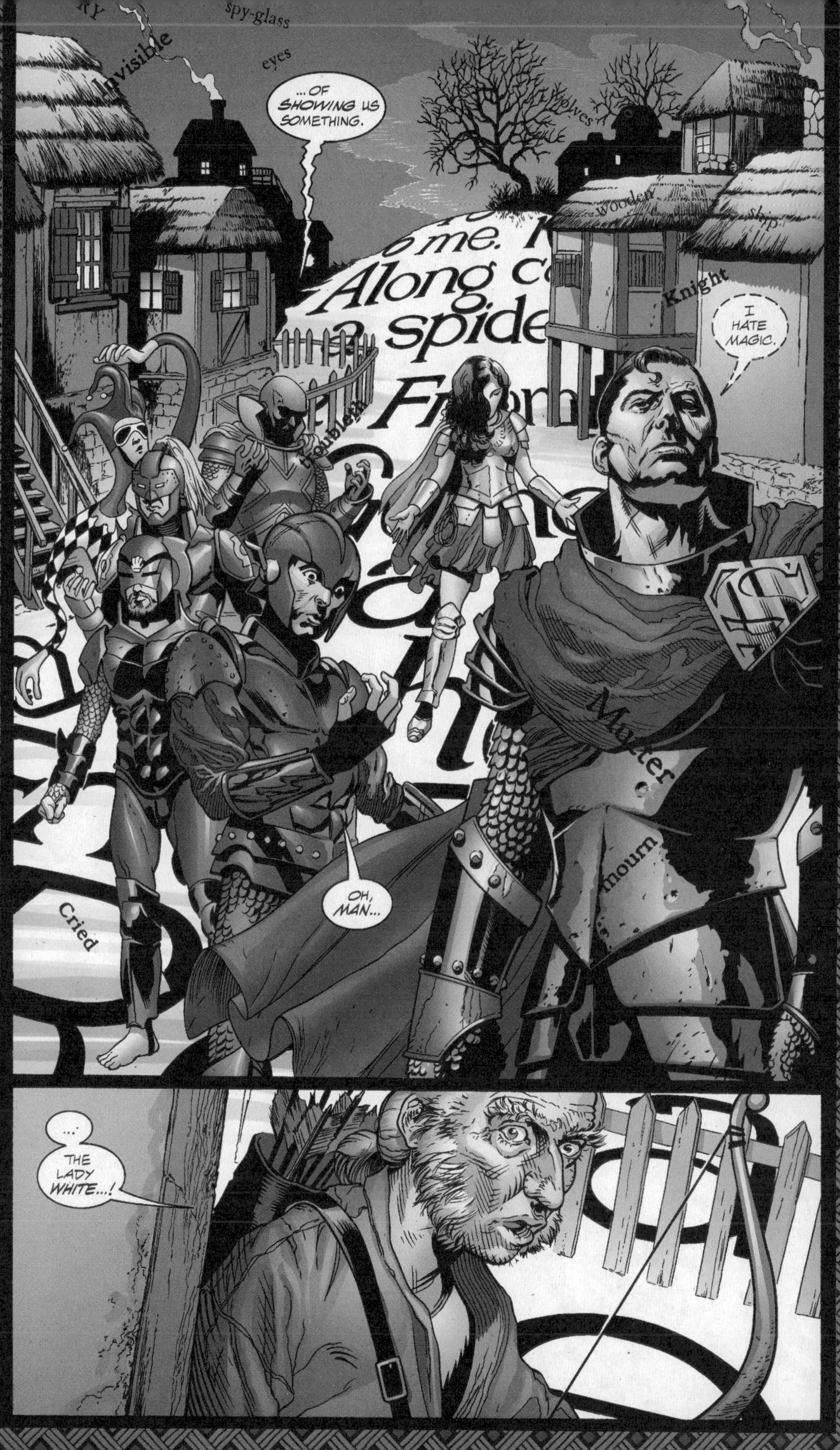
...OF SHOWING US SOMETHING.
I HATE MAGIC.
OH, MAN...
... THE LADY WHITE...!
spy-glass
Invisible
eyes
wolves
wooden
ship
Knight
Doublet
Muster
mourn
Cried

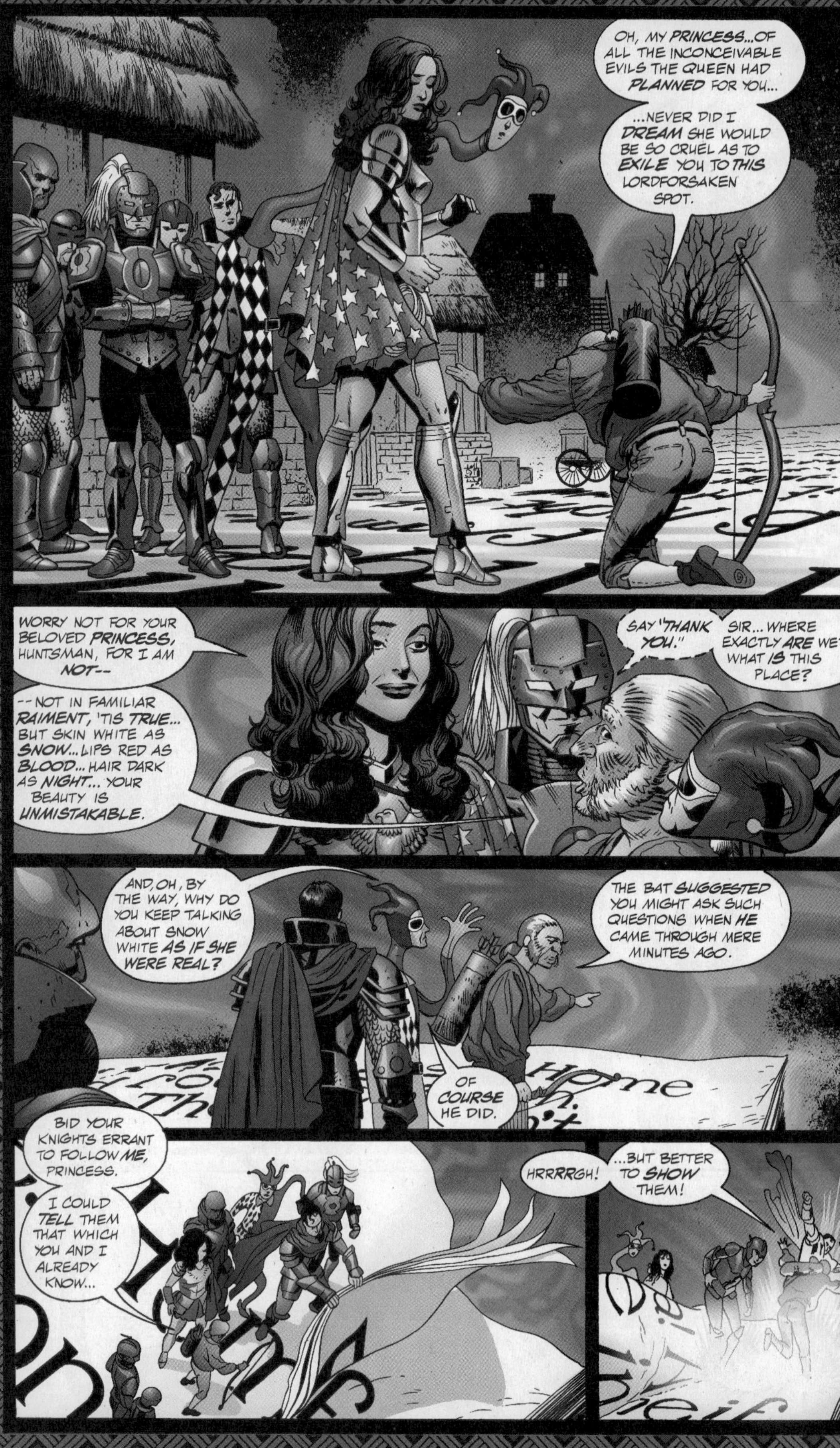
OH, MY PRINCESS...OF ALL THE INCONCEIVABLE EVILS THE QUEEN HAD PLANNED FOR YOU...
...NEVER DID I DREAM SHE WOULD BE SO CRUEL AS TO EXILE YOU TO THIS LORDFORSAKEN SPOT.
WORRY NOT FOR YOUR BELOVED PRINCESS, HUNTSMAN, FOR I AM NOT--
--NOT IN FAMILIAR RAIMENT, 'TIS TRUE... BUT SKIN WHITE AS SNOW...LIPS RED AS BLOOD...HAIR DARK AS NIGHT...YOUR BEAUTY IS UNMISTAKABLE.
SAY "THANK YOU."
SIR...WHERE EXACTLY ARE WE? WHAT IS THIS PLACE?
AND, OH, BY THE WAY, WHY DO YOU KEEP TALKING ABOUT SNOW WHITE AS IF SHE WERE REAL?
THE BAT SUGGESTED YOU MIGHT ASK SUCH QUESTIONS WHEN HE CAME THROUGH MERE MINUTES AGO.
OF COURSE HE DID.
BID YOUR KNIGHTS ERRANT TO FOLLOW ME, PRINCESS.
I COULD TELL THEM THAT WHICH YOU AND I ALREADY KNOW...
HRRRRGH!
...BUT BETTER TO SHOW THEM!

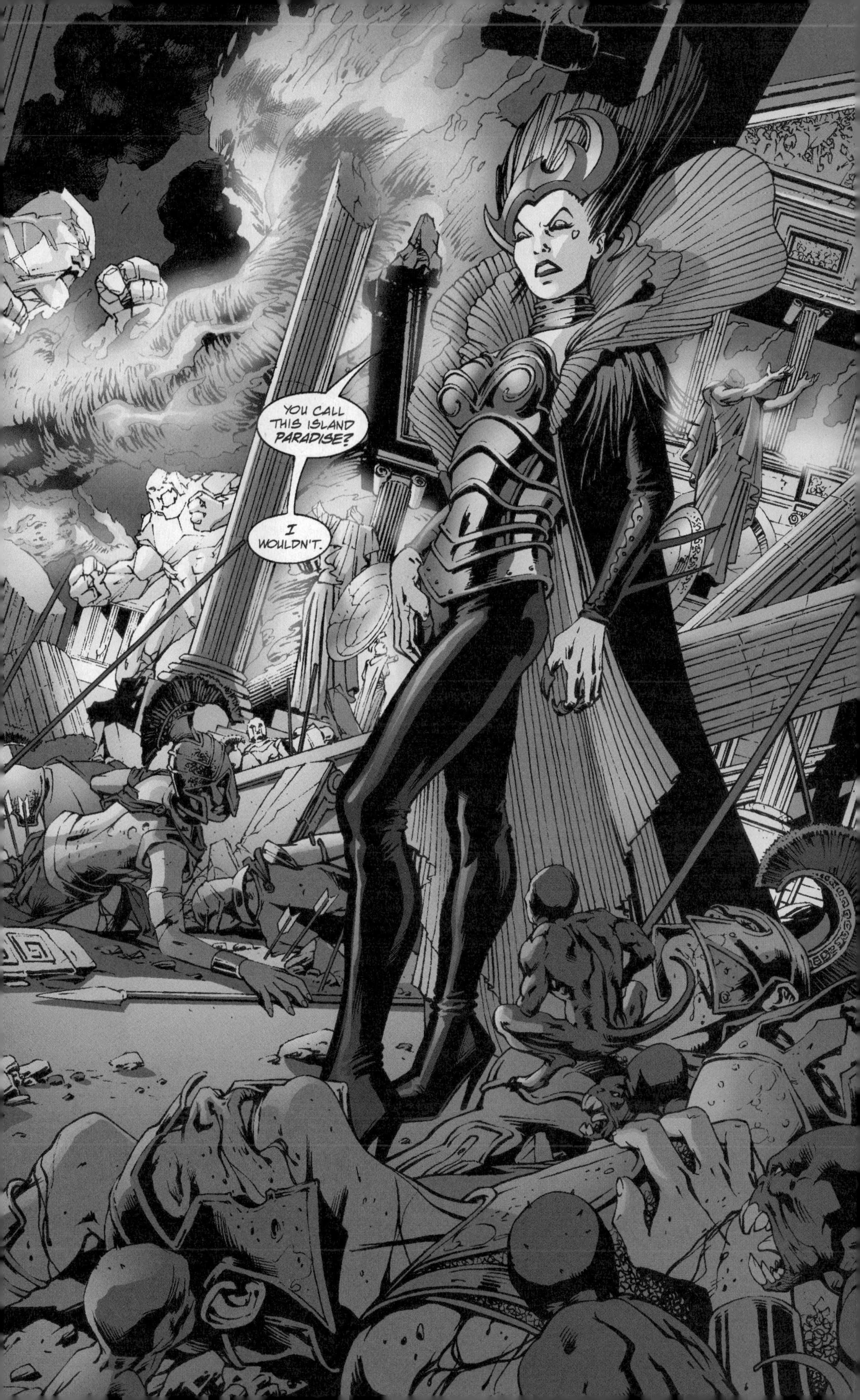
YOU CALL THIS ISLAND *PARADISE?*
I WOULDN'T.

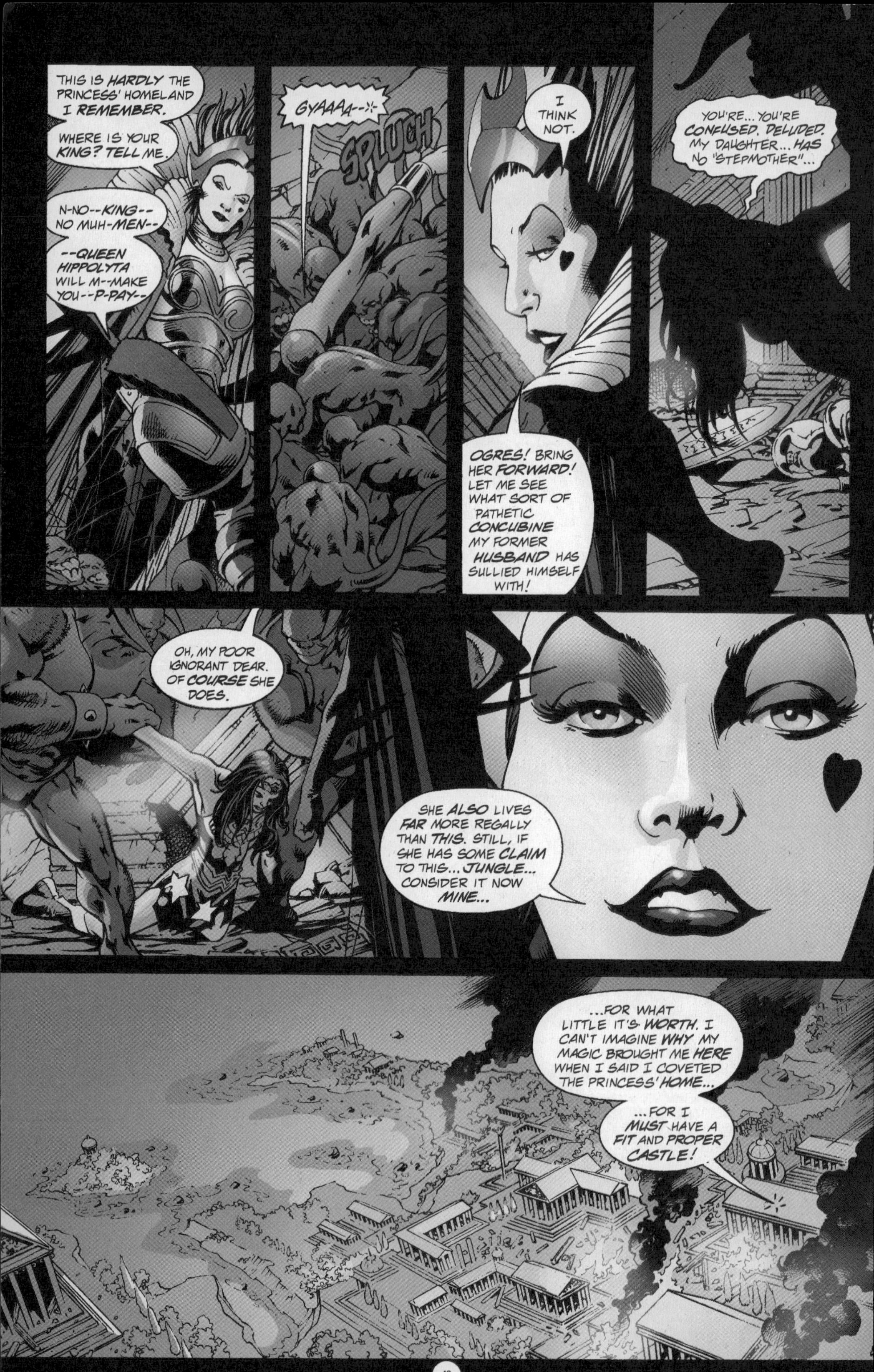
THIS IS HARDLY THE PRINCESS' HOMELAND I REMEMBER.
WHERE IS YOUR KING? TELL ME.
N-NO--KING-- NO MUH-MEN--
--QUEEN HIPPOLYTA WILL M--MAKE YOU--P-PAY--
GYAAAA--
SPLUCH
I THINK NOT.
OGRES! BRING HER FORWARD! LET ME SEE WHAT SORT OF PATHETIC CONCUBINE MY FORMER HUSBAND HAS SULLIED HIMSELF WITH!
YOU'RE... YOU'RE CONFUSED. DELUDED. MY DAUGHTER... HAS NO "STEPMOTHER"...
OH, MY POOR IGNORANT DEAR. OF COURSE SHE DOES.
SHE ALSO LIVES FAR MORE REGALLY THAN THIS. STILL, IF SHE HAS SOME CLAIM TO THIS... JUNGLE... CONSIDER IT NOW MINE...
...FOR WHAT LITTLE IT'S WORTH. I CAN'T IMAGINE WHY MY MAGIC BROUGHT ME HERE WHEN I SAID I COVETED THE PRINCESS' HOME...
...FOR I MUST HAVE A FIT AND PROPER CASTLE!

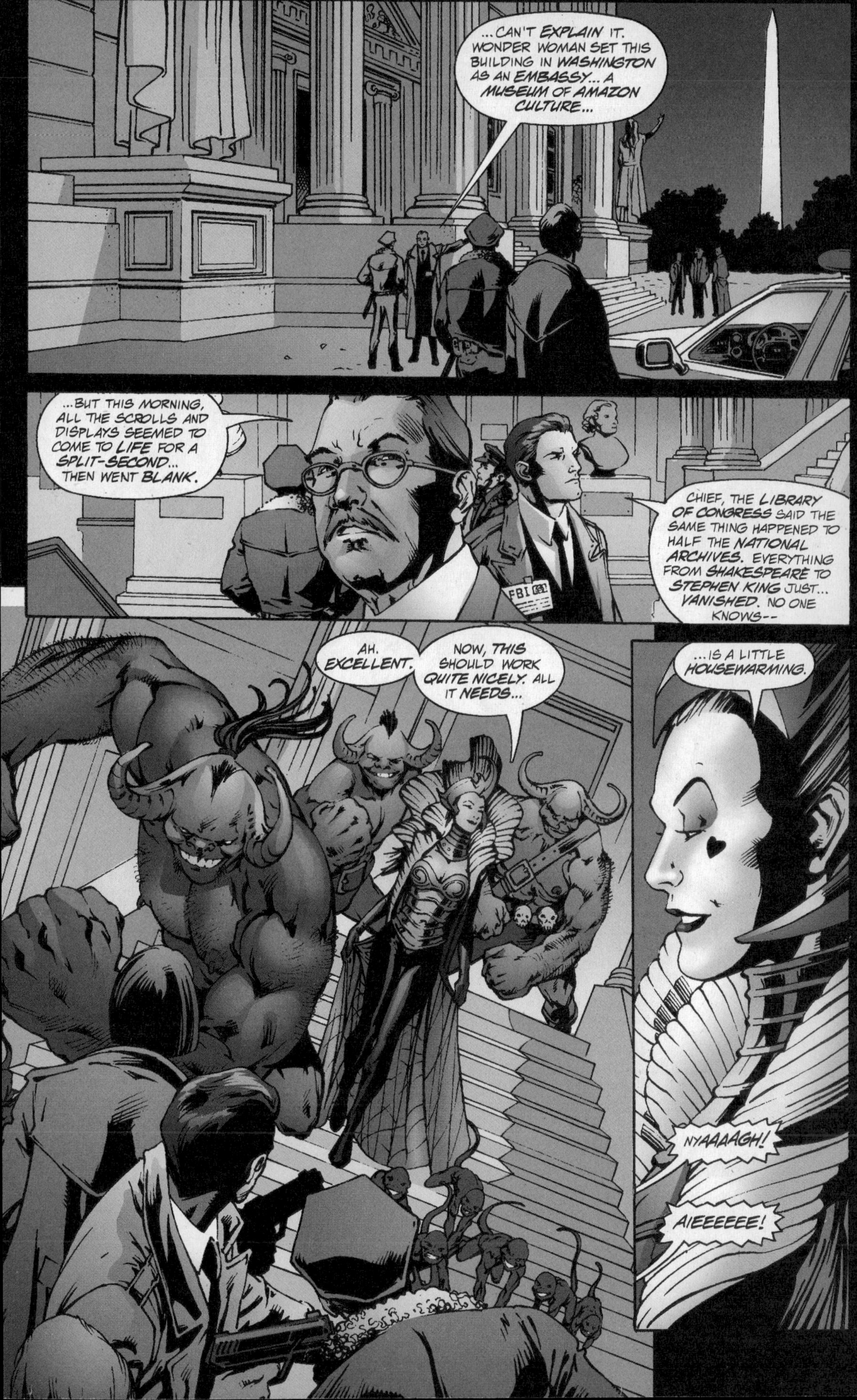
...CAN'T EXPLAIN IT. WONDER WOMAN SET THIS BUILDING IN WASHINGTON AS AN EMBASSY... A MUSEUM OF AMAZON CULTURE...
...BUT THIS MORNING, ALL THE SCROLLS AND DISPLAYS SEEMED TO COME TO LIFE FOR A SPLIT-SECOND... THEN WENT BLANK.
CHIEF, THE LIBRARY OF CONGRESS SAID THE SAME THING HAPPENED TO HALF THE NATIONAL ARCHIVES. EVERYTHING FROM SHAKESPEARE TO STEPHEN KING JUST... VANISHED. NO ONE KNOWS--
FBI
AH. EXCELLENT.
NOW, THIS SHOULD WORK QUITE NICELY. ALL IT NEEDS...
...IS A LITTLE HOUSEWARMING.
NYAAAAGH!
AIEEEEEE!

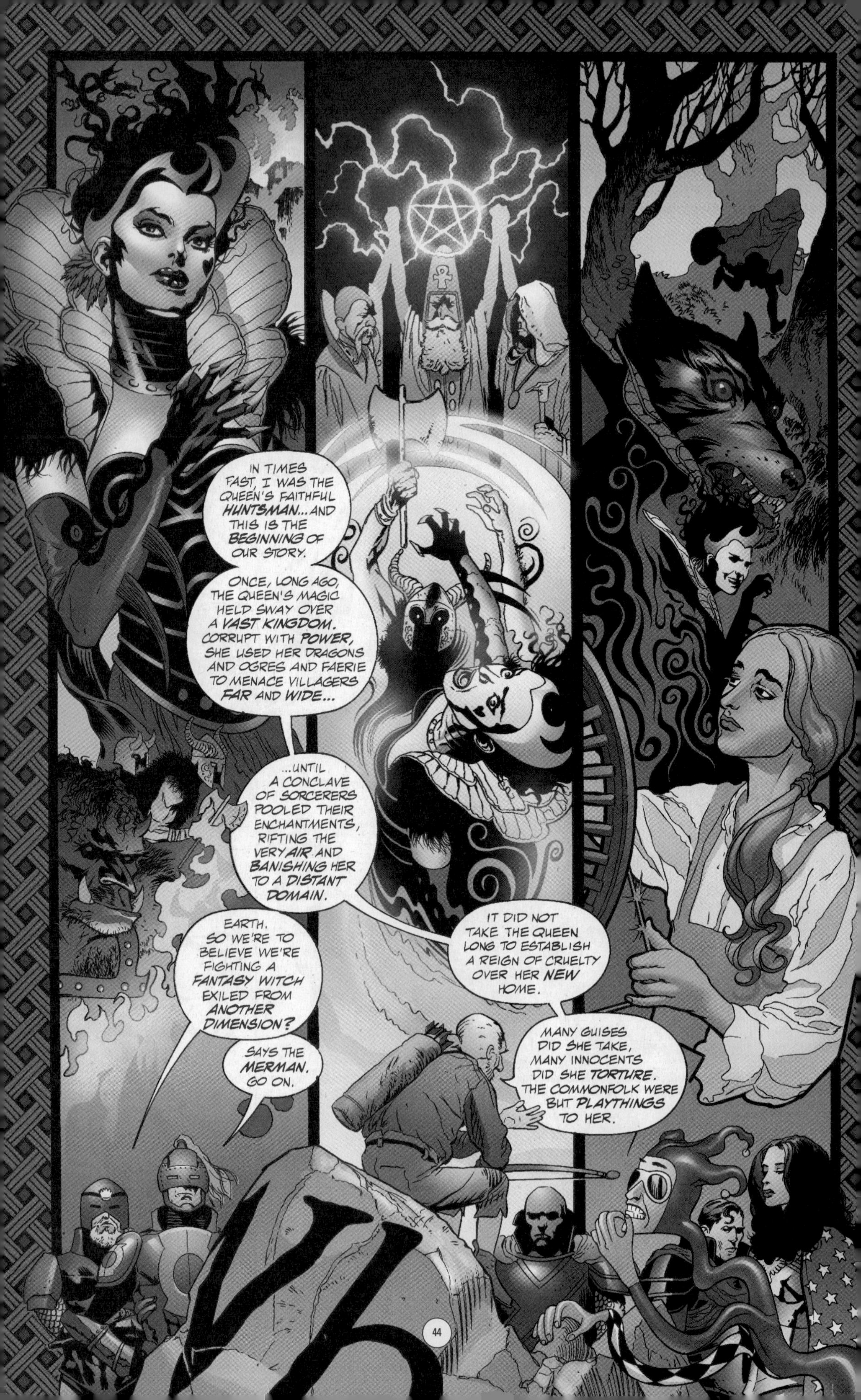
IN TIMES PAST, I WAS THE QUEEN'S FAITHFUL HUNTSMAN... AND THIS IS THE BEGINNING OF OUR STORY.
ONCE, LONG AGO, THE QUEEN'S MAGIC HELD SWAY OVER A VAST KINGDOM. CORRUPT WITH POWER, SHE USED HER DRAGONS AND OGRES AND FAERIE TO MENACE VILLAGERS FAR AND WIDE...
...UNTIL A CONCLAVE OF SORCERERS POOLED THEIR ENCHANTMENTS, RIFTING THE VERY AIR AND BANISHING HER TO A DISTANT DOMAIN.
IT DID NOT TAKE THE QUEEN LONG TO ESTABLISH A REIGN OF CRUELTY OVER HER NEW HOME.
EARTH. SO WE'RE TO BELIEVE WE'RE FIGHTING A FANTASY WITCH EXILED FROM ANOTHER DIMENSION?
SAYS THE MERMAN. GO ON.
MANY GUISES DID SHE TAKE, MANY INNOCENTS DID SHE TORTURE. THE COMMONFOLK WERE BUT PLAYTHINGS TO HER.

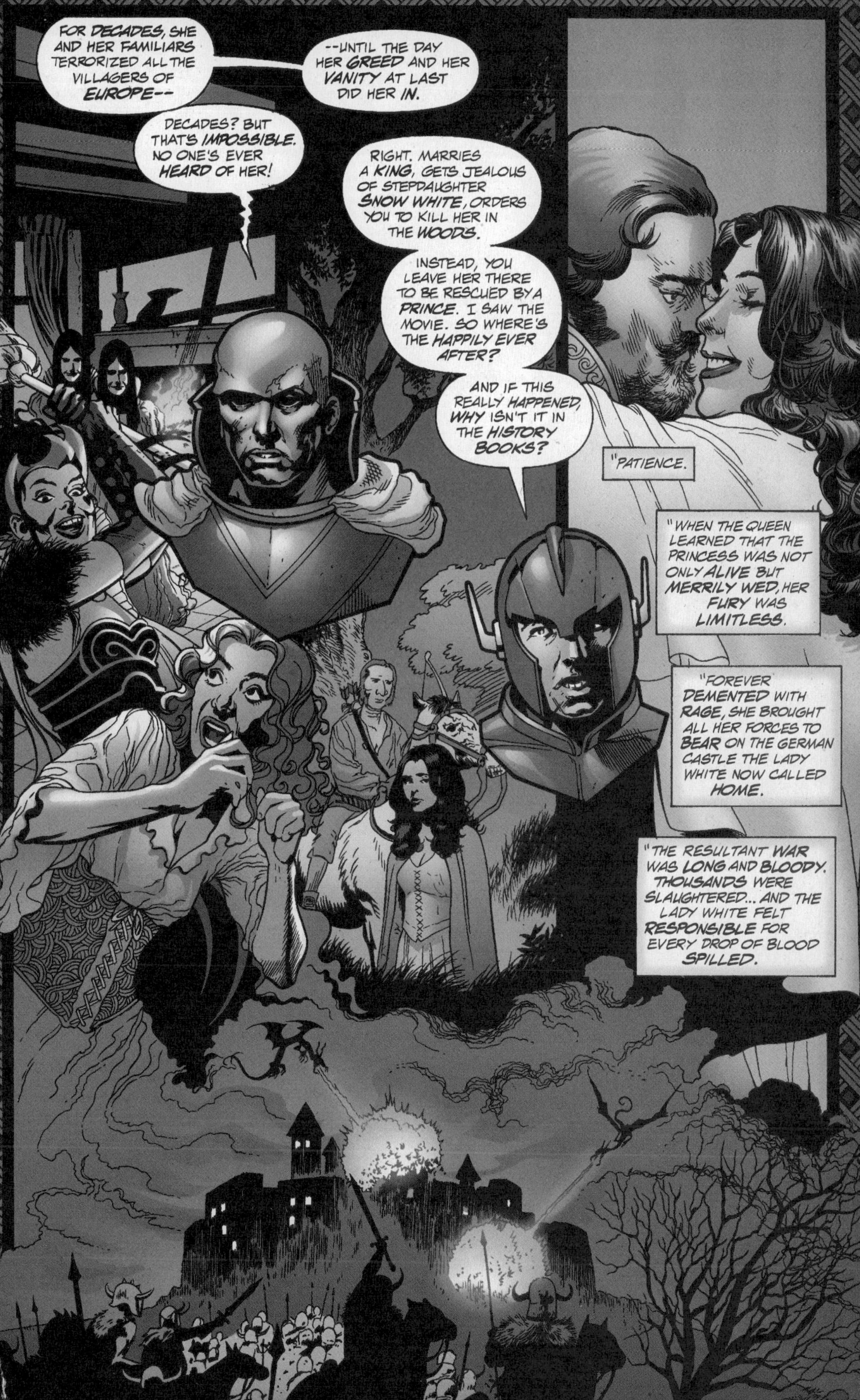

FOR DECADES, SHE AND HER FAMILIARS TERRORIZED ALL THE VILLAGERS OF EUROPE--
--UNTIL THE DAY HER GREED AND HER VANITY AT LAST DID HER IN.
DECADES? BUT THAT'S IMPOSSIBLE. NO ONE'S EVER HEARD OF HER!
RIGHT. MARRIES A KING, GETS JEALOUS OF STEPDAUGHTER SNOW WHITE, ORDERS YOU TO KILL HER IN THE WOODS.
INSTEAD, YOU LEAVE HER THERE TO BE RESCUED BY A PRINCE. I SAW THE MOVIE. SO WHERE'S THE HAPPILY EVER AFTER?
AND IF THIS REALLY HAPPENED, WHY ISN'T IT IN THE HISTORY BOOKS?
"PATIENCE.
"WHEN THE QUEEN LEARNED THAT THE PRINCESS WAS NOT ONLY ALIVE BUT MERRILY WED, HER FURY WAS LIMITLESS.
"FOREVER DEMENTED WITH RAGE, SHE BROUGHT ALL HER FORCES TO BEAR ON THE GERMAN CASTLE THE LADY WHITE NOW CALLED HOME.
"THE RESULTANT WAR WAS LONG AND BLOODY. THOUSANDS WERE SLAUGHTERED... AND THE LADY WHITE FELT RESPONSIBLE FOR EVERY DROP OF BLOOD SPILLED.

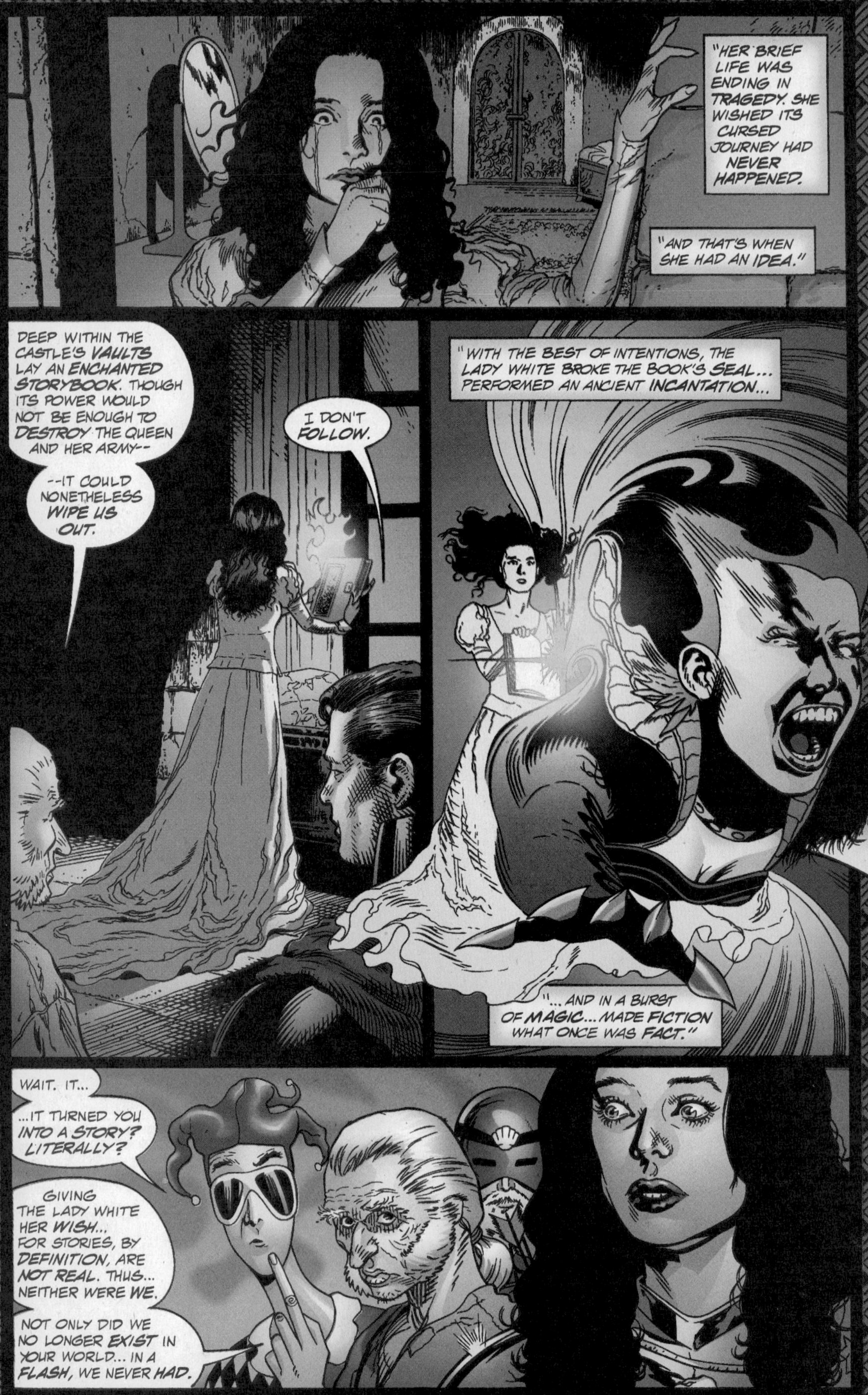
"HER BRIEF LIFE WAS ENDING IN TRAGEDY. SHE WISHED ITS CURSED JOURNEY HAD NEVER HAPPENED.
"AND THAT'S WHEN SHE HAD AN IDEA."
DEEP WITHIN THE CASTLE'S VAULTS LAY AN ENCHANTED STORYBOOK. THOUGH ITS POWER WOULD NOT BE ENOUGH TO DESTROY THE QUEEN AND HER ARMY--
--IT COULD NONETHELESS WIPE US OUT.
I DON'T FOLLOW.
"WITH THE BEST OF INTENTIONS, THE LADY WHITE BROKE THE BOOK'S SEAL... PERFORMED AN ANCIENT INCANTATION...
"...AND IN A BURST OF MAGIC... MADE FICTION WHAT ONCE WAS FACT."
WAIT. IT...
...IT TURNED YOU INTO A STORY? LITERALLY?
GIVING THE LADY WHITE HER WISH... FOR STORIES, BY DEFINITION, ARE NOT REAL. THUS... NEITHER WERE WE.
NOT ONLY DID WE NO LONGER EXIST IN YOUR WORLD... IN A FLASH, WE NEVER HAD.

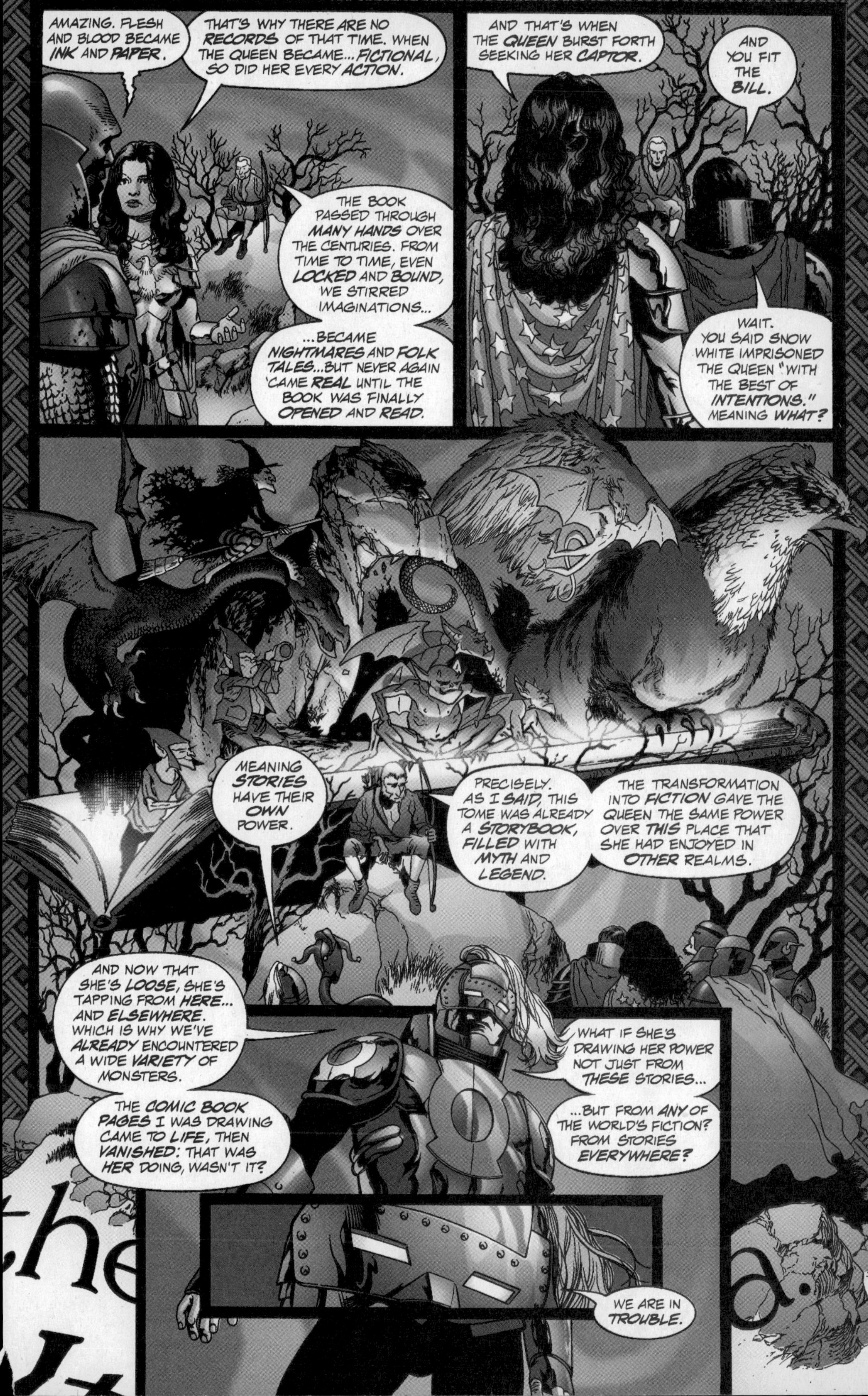
AMAZING. FLESH AND BLOOD BECAME INK AND PAPER.
THAT'S WHY THERE ARE NO RECORDS OF THAT TIME. WHEN THE QUEEN BECAME... FICTIONAL, SO DID HER EVERY ACTION.
THE BOOK PASSED THROUGH MANY HANDS OVER THE CENTURIES. FROM TIME TO TIME, EVEN LOCKED AND BOUND, WE STIRRED IMAGINATIONS...
...BECAME NIGHTMARES AND FOLK TALES... BUT NEVER AGAIN 'CAME REAL UNTIL THE BOOK WAS FINALLY OPENED AND READ.
AND THAT'S WHEN THE QUEEN BURST FORTH SEEKING HER CAPTOR.
AND YOU FIT THE BILL.
WAIT. YOU SAID SNOW WHITE IMPRISONED THE QUEEN "WITH THE BEST OF INTENTIONS." MEANING WHAT?
MEANING STORIES HAVE THEIR OWN POWER.
PRECISELY. AS I SAID, THIS TOME WAS ALREADY A STORYBOOK, FILLED WITH MYTH AND LEGEND.
THE TRANSFORMATION INTO FICTION GAVE THE QUEEN THE SAME POWER OVER THIS PLACE THAT SHE HAD ENJOYED IN OTHER REALMS.
AND NOW THAT SHE'S LOOSE, SHE'S TAPPING FROM HERE... AND ELSEWHERE. WHICH IS WHY WE'VE ALREADY ENCOUNTERED A WIDE VARIETY OF MONSTERS.
THE COMIC BOOK PAGES I WAS DRAWING CAME TO LIFE, THEN VANISHED: THAT WAS HER DOING, WASN'T IT?
WHAT IF SHE'S DRAWING HER POWER NOT JUST FROM THESE STORIES...
...BUT FROM ANY OF THE WORLD'S FICTION? FROM STORIES EVERYWHERE?
WE ARE IN TROUBLE.

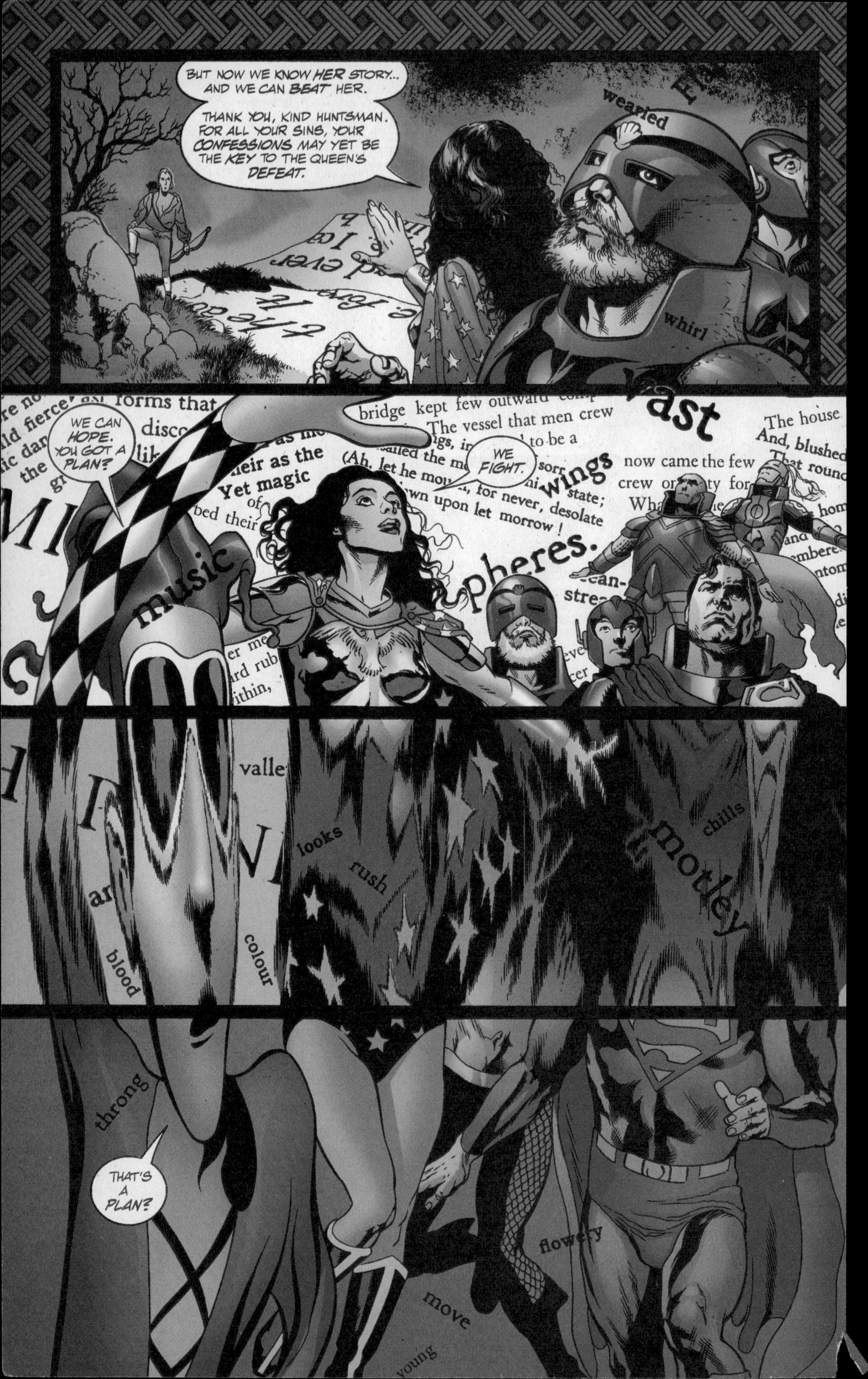

BUT NOW WE KNOW HER STORY... AND WE CAN BEAT HER.
THANK YOU, KIND HUNTSMAN. FOR ALL YOUR SINS, YOUR CONFESSIONS MAY YET BE THE KEY TO THE QUEEN'S DEFEAT.
WE CAN HOPE. YOU GOT A PLAN?
WE FIGHT.
THAT'S A PLAN?

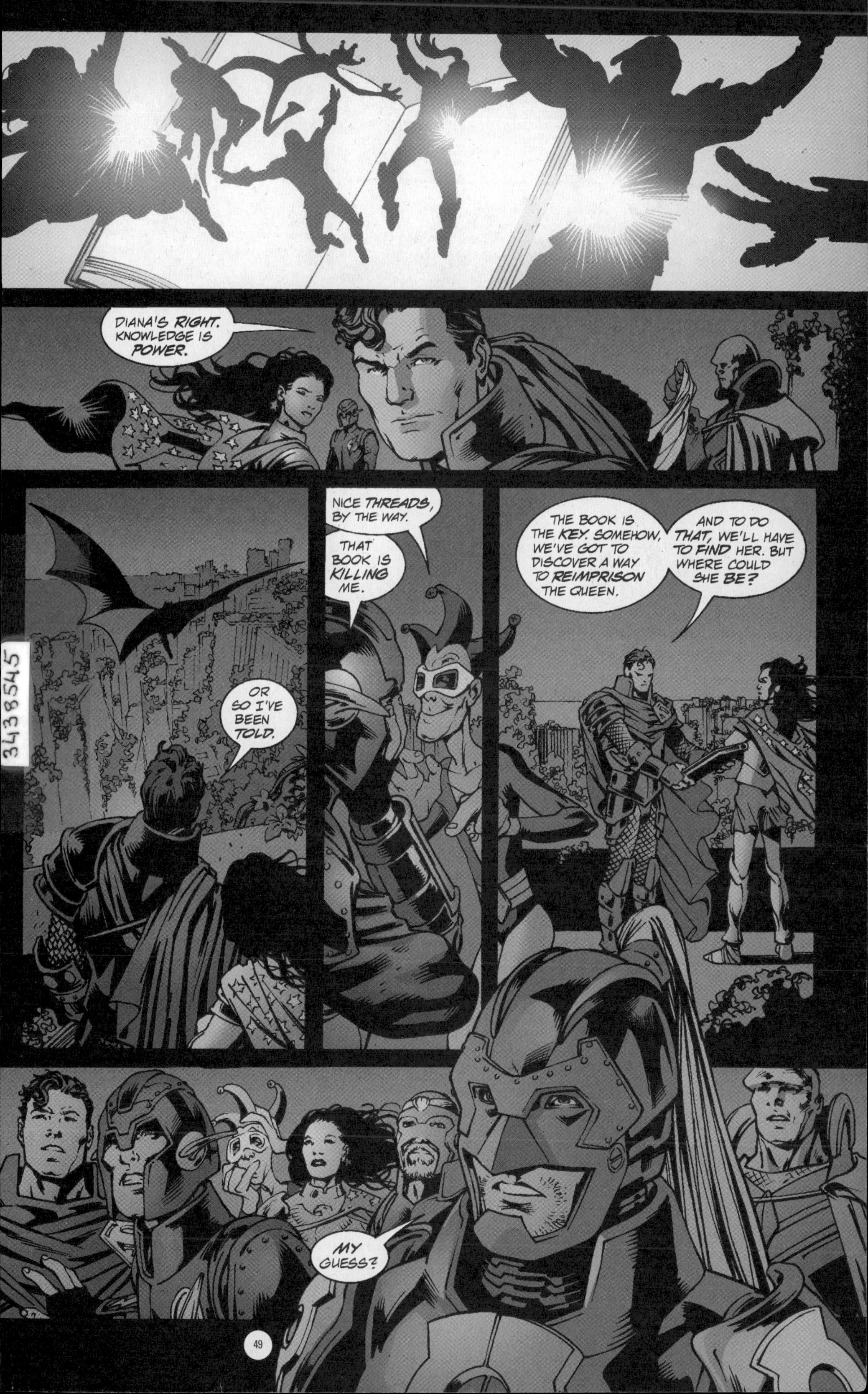
DIANA'S RIGHT. KNOWLEDGE IS POWER.
NICE THREADS, BY THE WAY.
THAT BOOK IS KILLING ME.
OR SO I'VE BEEN TOLD.
THE BOOK IS THE KEY. SOMEHOW, WE'VE GOT TO DISCOVER A WAY TO REIMPRISON THE QUEEN.
AND TO DO THAT, WE'LL HAVE TO FIND HER. BUT WHERE COULD SHE BE?
MY GUESS?

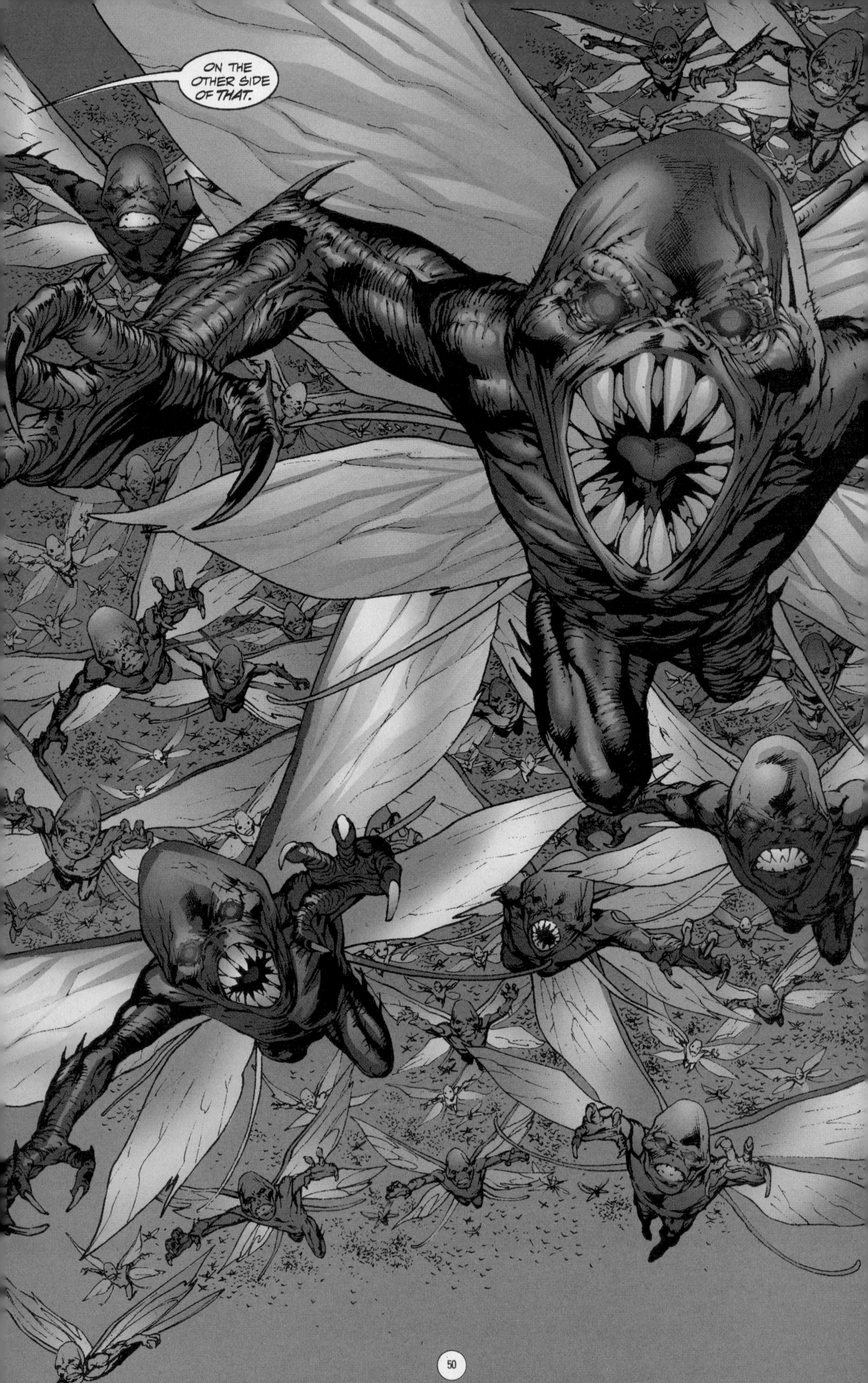
ON THE OTHER SIDE OF THAT.

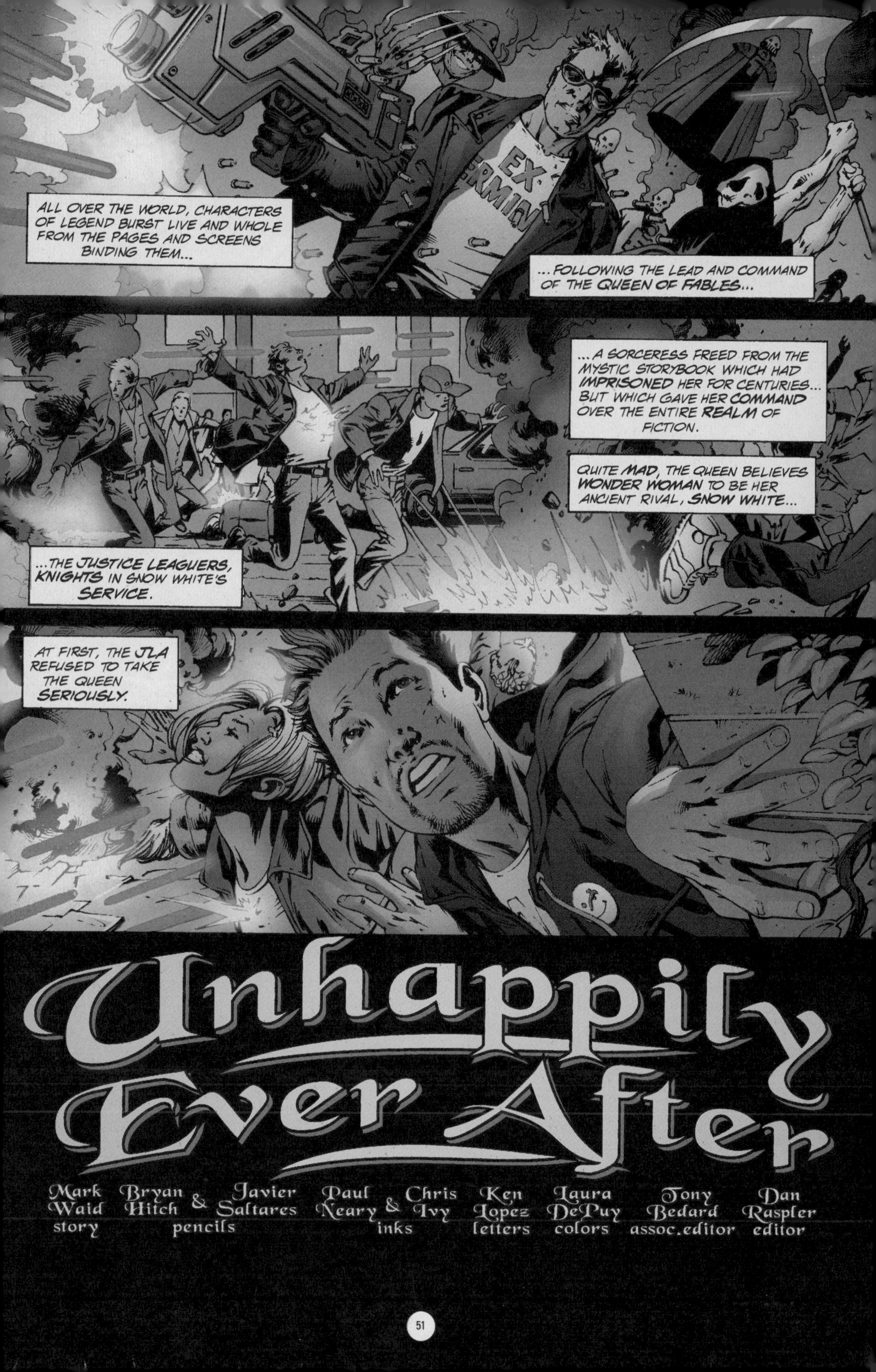
ALL OVER THE WORLD, CHARACTERS OF LEGEND BURST LIVE AND WHOLE FROM THE PAGES AND SCREENS BINDING THEM...
EX TERMIN
...FOLLOWING THE LEAD AND COMMAND OF THE QUEEN OF FABLES...
...A SORCERESS FREED FROM THE MYSTIC STORYBOOK WHICH HAD IMPRISONED HER FOR CENTURIES... BUT WHICH GAVE HER COMMAND OVER THE ENTIRE REALM OF FICTION.
QUITE MAD, THE QUEEN BELIEVES WONDER WOMAN TO BE HER ANCIENT RIVAL, SNOW WHITE...
...THE JUSTICE LEAGUERS, KNIGHTS IN SNOW WHITE'S SERVICE.
AT FIRST, THE JLA REFUSED TO TAKE THE QUEEN SERIOUSLY.

Unhappily Ever After

Mark Waid story · Bryan Hitch & Javier Saltares pencils · Paul Neary & Chris Ivy inks · Ken Lopez letters · Laura DePuy colors · Tony Bedard assoc. editor · Dan Raspler editor

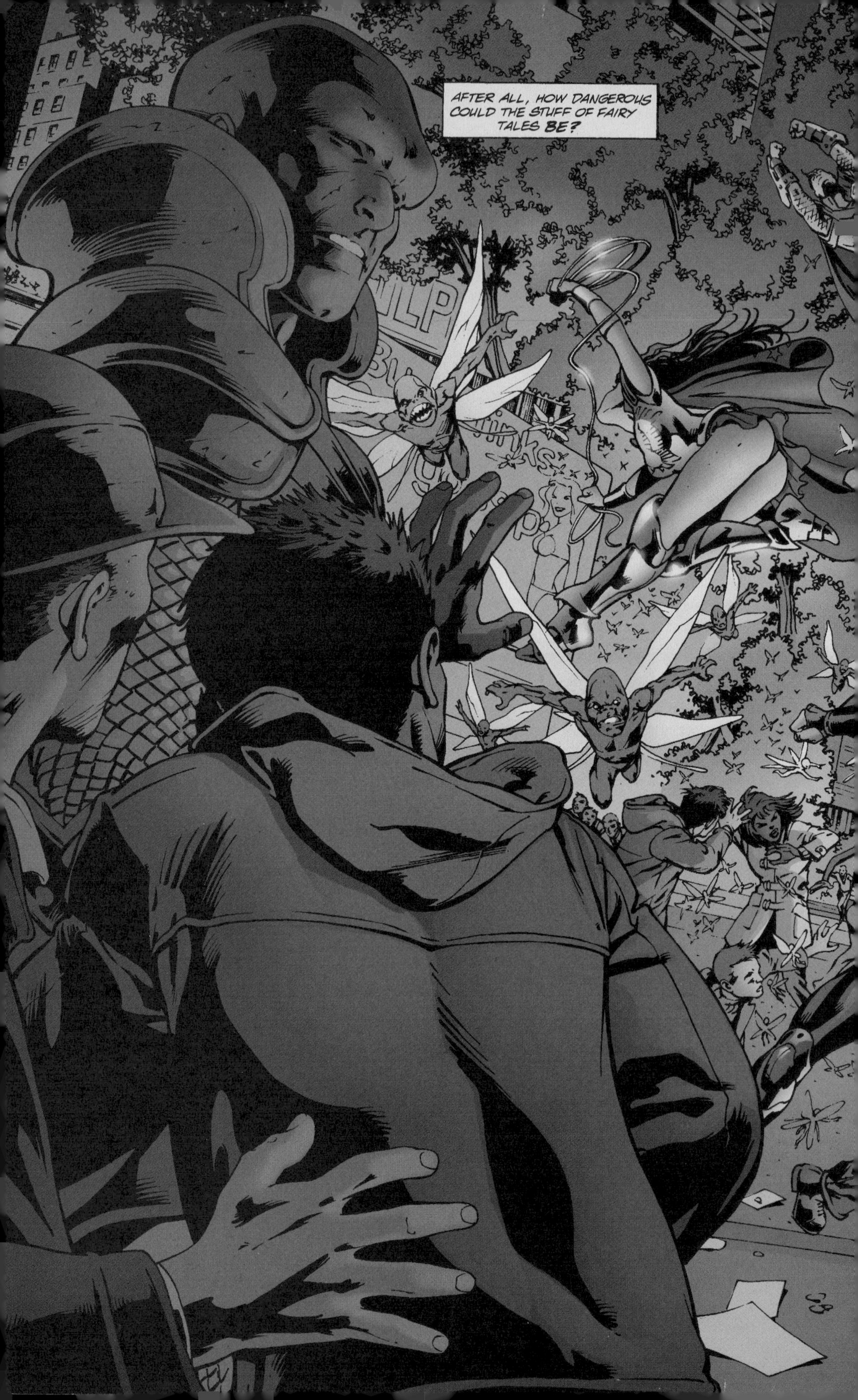
AFTER ALL, HOW DANGEROUS COULD THE STUFF OF FAIRY TALES BE?

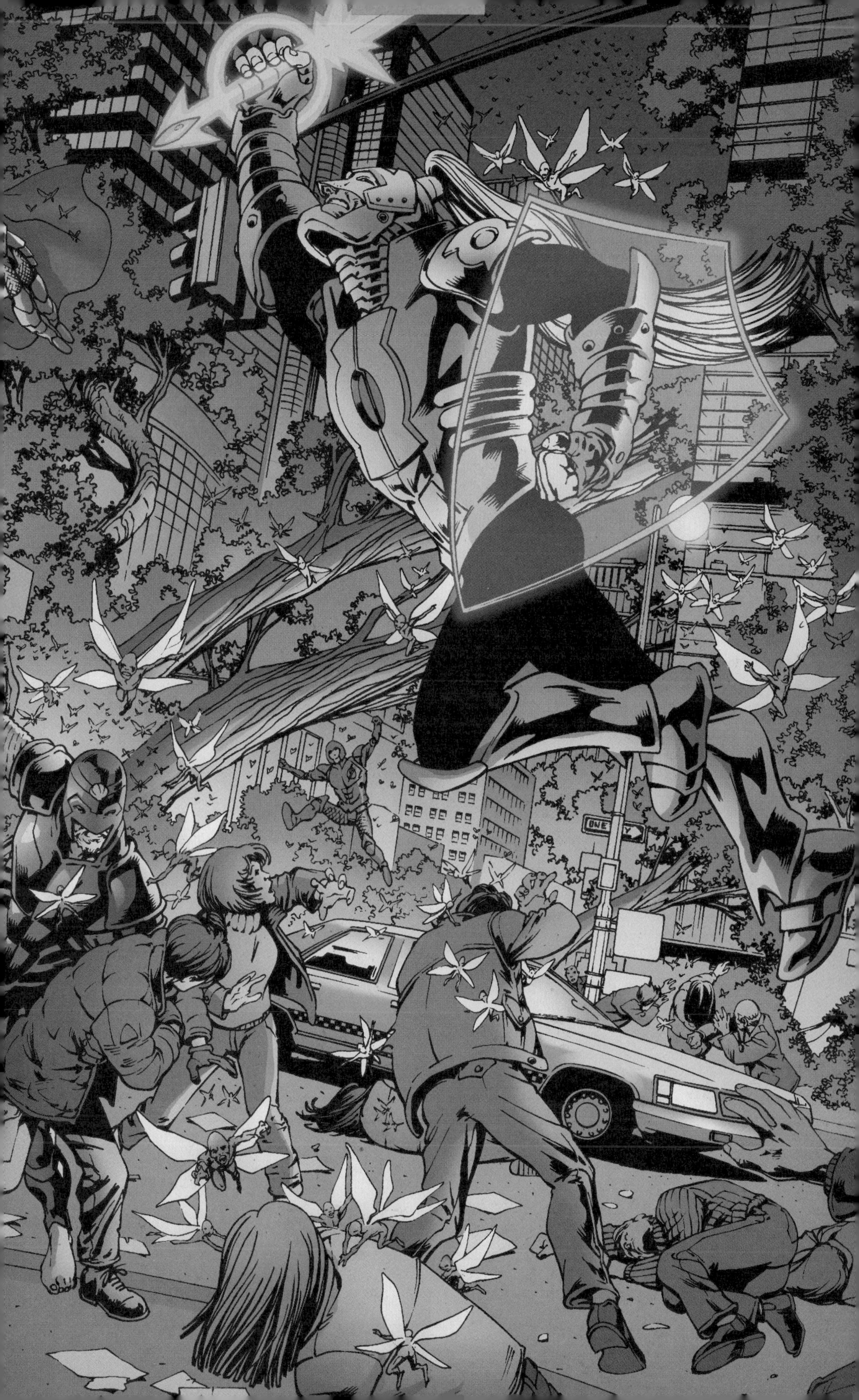
ONE

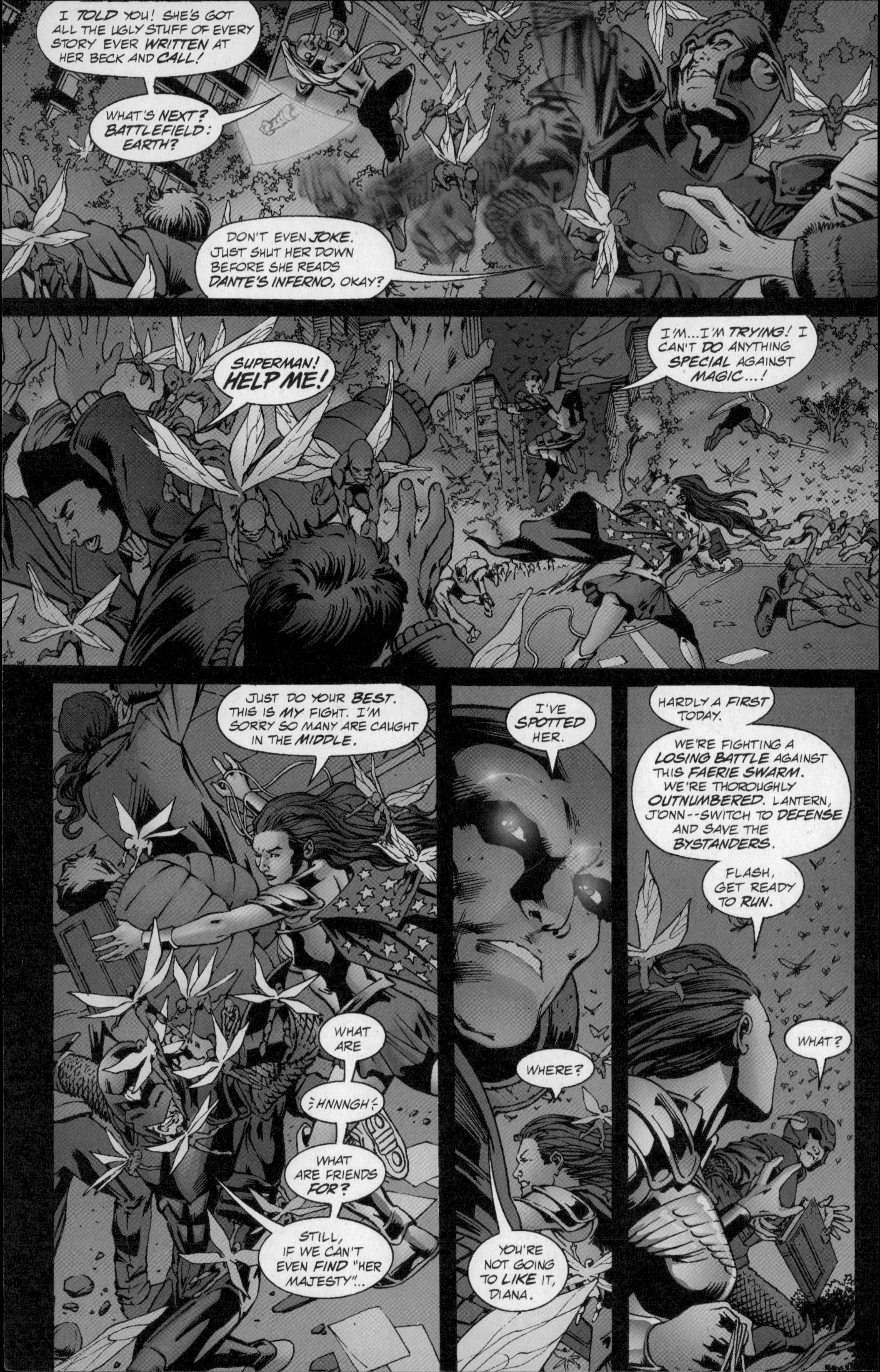
I TOLD YOU! SHE'S GOT ALL THE UGLY STUFF OF EVERY STORY EVER WRITTEN AT HER BECK AND CALL!
WHAT'S NEXT? BATTLEFIELD: EARTH?
DON'T EVEN JOKE. JUST SHUT HER DOWN BEFORE SHE READS DANTE'S INFERNO, OKAY?
SUPERMAN! HELP ME!
I'M...I'M TRYING! I CAN'T DO ANYTHING SPECIAL AGAINST MAGIC...!
JUST DO YOUR BEST. THIS IS MY FIGHT. I'M SORRY SO MANY ARE CAUGHT IN THE MIDDLE.
WHAT ARE
HNNNGH
WHAT ARE FRIENDS FOR?
STILL, IF WE CAN'T EVEN FIND "HER MAJESTY"...
I'VE SPOTTED HER.
WHERE?
YOU'RE NOT GOING TO LIKE IT, DIANA.
HARDLY A FIRST TODAY.
WE'RE FIGHTING A LOSING BATTLE AGAINST THIS FAERIE SWARM. WE'RE THOROUGHLY OUTNUMBERED. LANTERN, J'ONN--SWITCH TO DEFENSE AND SAVE THE BYSTANDERS.
FLASH, GET READY TO RUN.
WHAT?

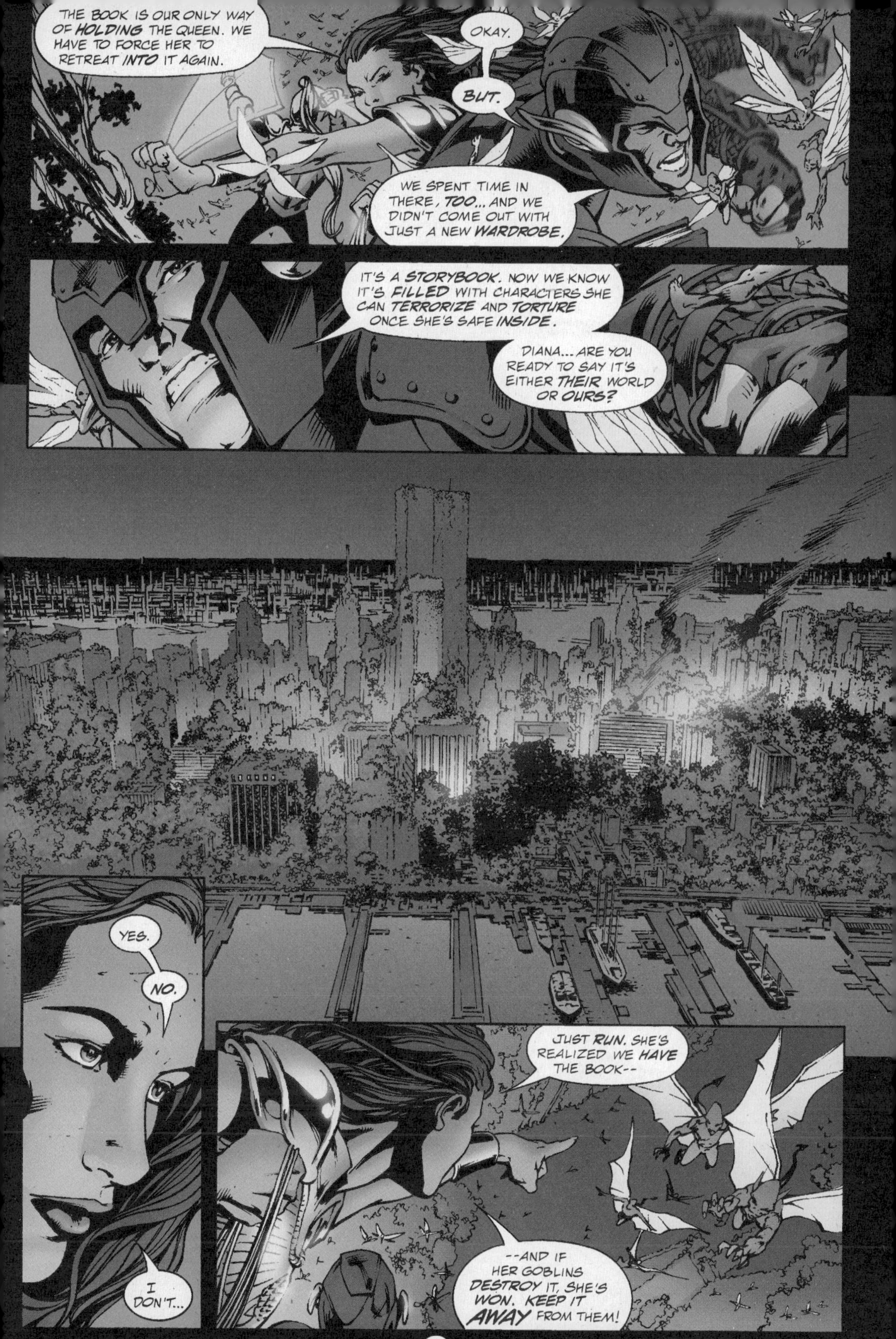
THE BOOK IS OUR ONLY WAY OF HOLDING THE QUEEN. WE HAVE TO FORCE HER TO RETREAT INTO IT AGAIN.
OKAY.
BUT.
WE SPENT TIME IN THERE, TOO... AND WE DIDN'T COME OUT WITH JUST A NEW WARDROBE.
IT'S A STORYBOOK. NOW WE KNOW IT'S FILLED WITH CHARACTERS SHE CAN TERRORIZE AND TORTURE ONCE SHE'S SAFE INSIDE.
DIANA... ARE YOU READY TO SAY IT'S EITHER THEIR WORLD OR OURS?
YES.
NO.
I DON'T...
JUST RUN. SHE'S REALIZED WE HAVE THE BOOK--
--AND IF HER GOBLINS DESTROY IT, SHE'S WON. KEEP IT AWAY FROM THEM!

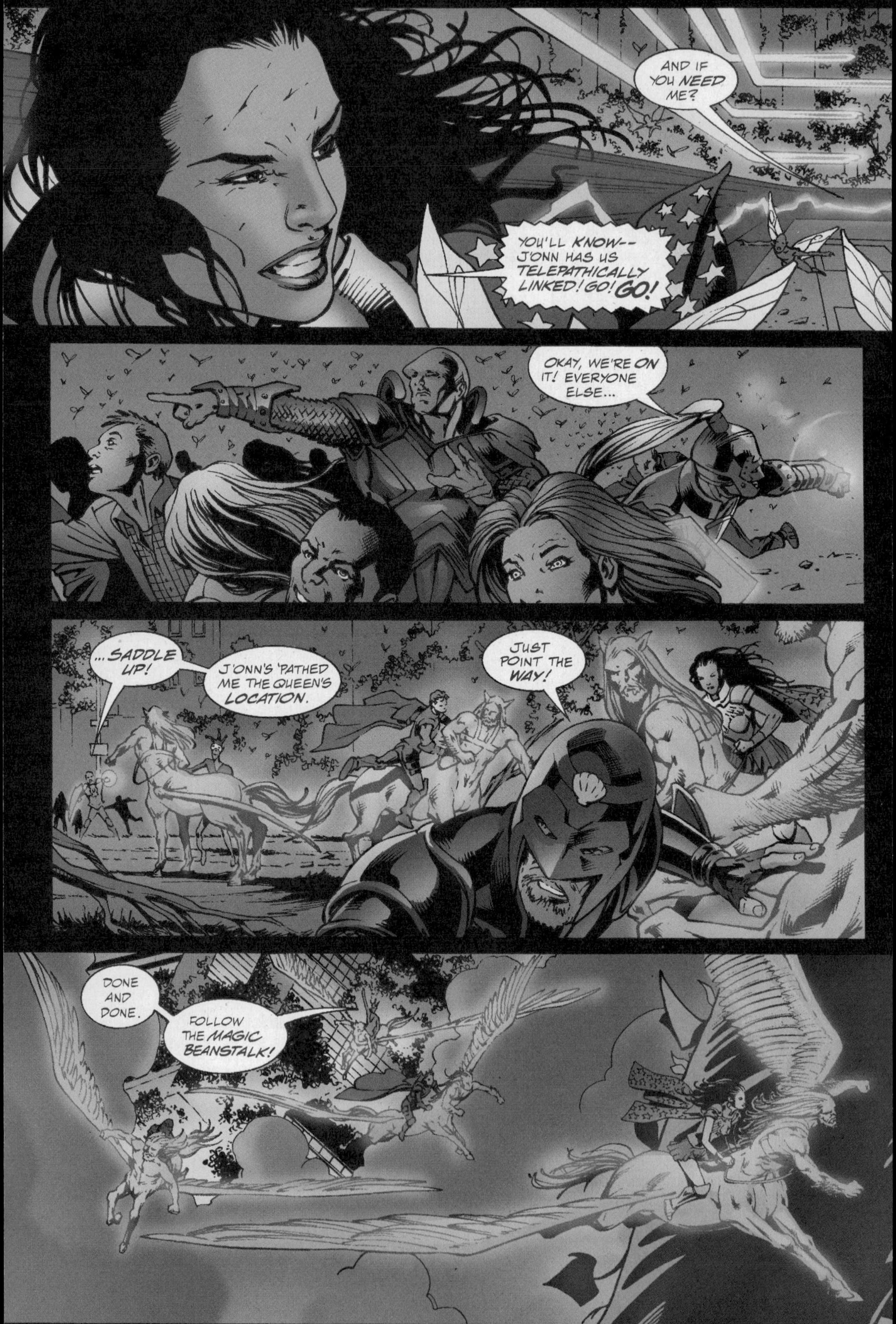
AND IF YOU NEED ME?
YOU'LL KNOW-- J'ONN HAS US TELEPATHICALLY LINKED! GO! GO!
OKAY, WE'RE ON IT! EVERYONE ELSE...
...SADDLE UP!
J'ONN'S 'PATHED ME THE QUEEN'S LOCATION.
JUST POINT THE WAY!
DONE AND DONE.
FOLLOW THE MAGIC BEANSTALK!

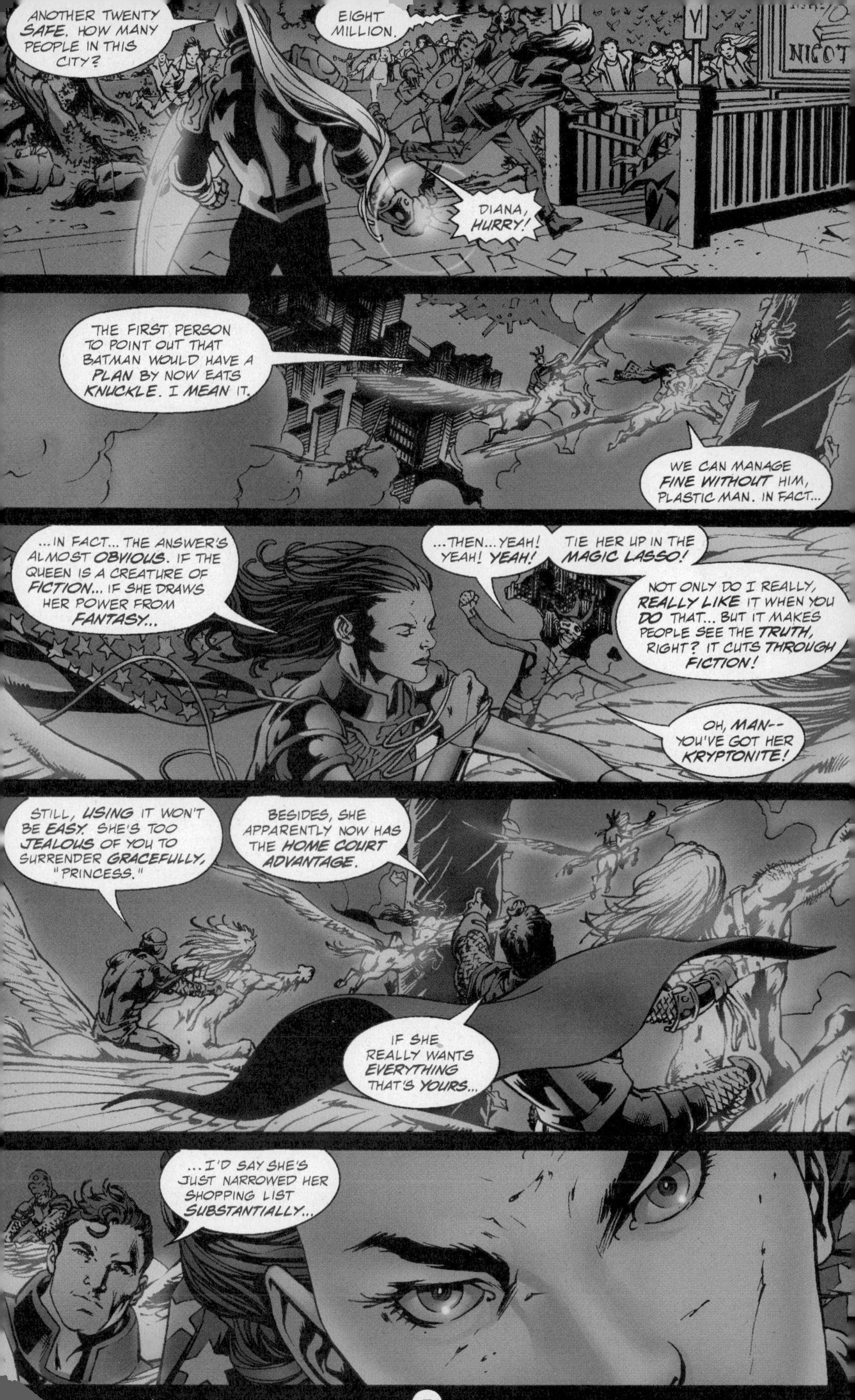
ANOTHER TWENTY SAFE. HOW MANY PEOPLE IN THIS CITY?
EIGHT MILLION.
DIANA, HURRY!
THE FIRST PERSON TO POINT OUT THAT BATMAN WOULD HAVE A PLAN BY NOW EATS KNUCKLE. I MEAN IT.
WE CAN MANAGE FINE WITHOUT HIM, PLASTIC MAN. IN FACT...
...IN FACT... THE ANSWER'S ALMOST OBVIOUS. IF THE QUEEN IS A CREATURE OF FICTION... IF SHE DRAWS HER POWER FROM FANTASY...
...THEN...YEAH! YEAH! YEAH!
TIE HER UP IN THE MAGIC LASSO!
NOT ONLY DO I REALLY, REALLY LIKE IT WHEN YOU DO THAT... BUT IT MAKES PEOPLE SEE THE TRUTH, RIGHT? IT CUTS THROUGH FICTION!
OH, MAN-- YOU'VE GOT HER KRYPTONITE!
STILL, USING IT WON'T BE EASY. SHE'S TOO JEALOUS OF YOU TO SURRENDER GRACEFULLY, "PRINCESS."
BESIDES, SHE APPARENTLY NOW HAS THE HOME COURT ADVANTAGE.
IF SHE REALLY WANTS EVERYTHING THAT'S YOURS...
...I'D SAY SHE'S JUST NARROWED HER SHOPPING LIST SUBSTANTIALLY...

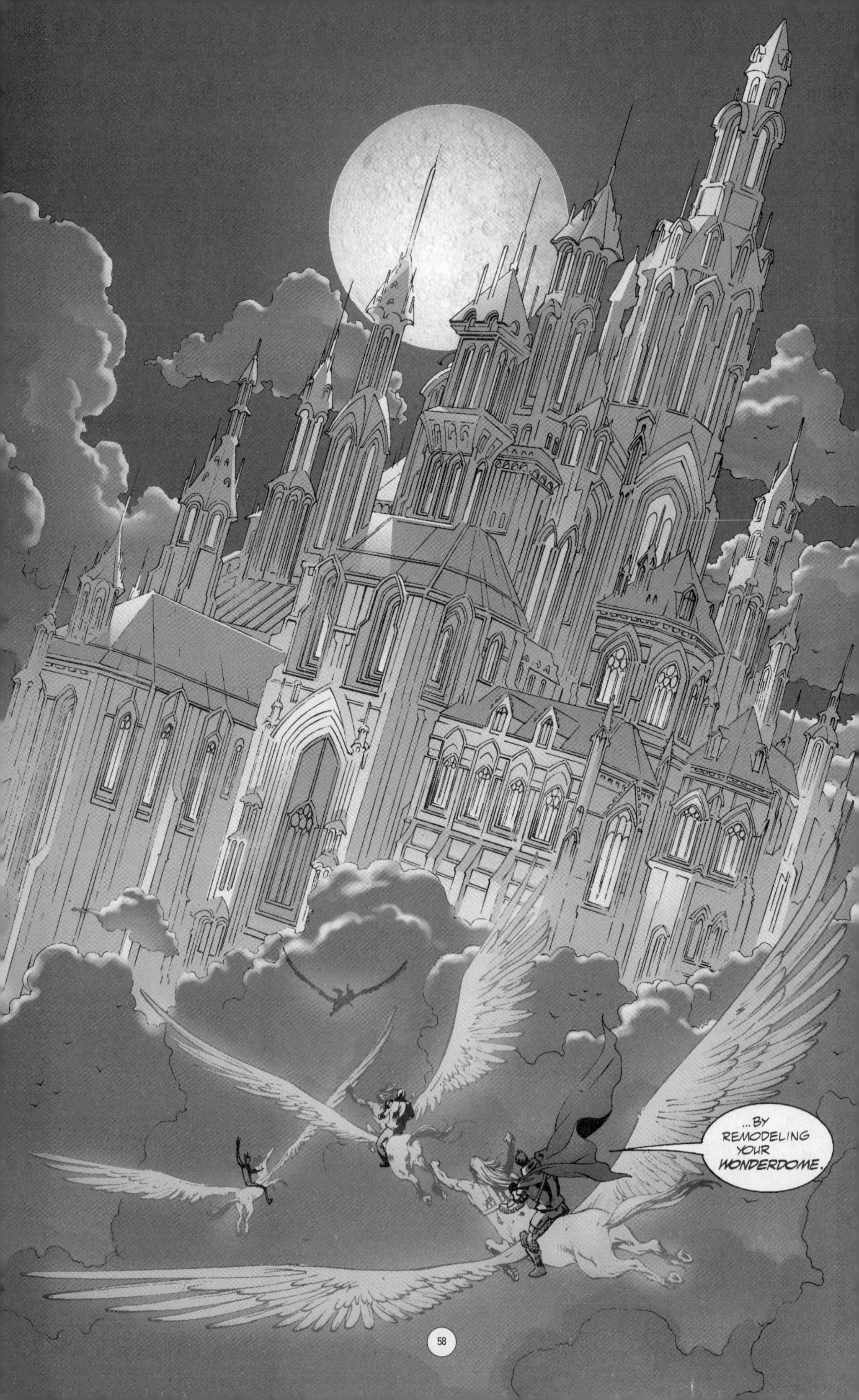
...BY
REMODELING
YOUR
WONDERDOME.

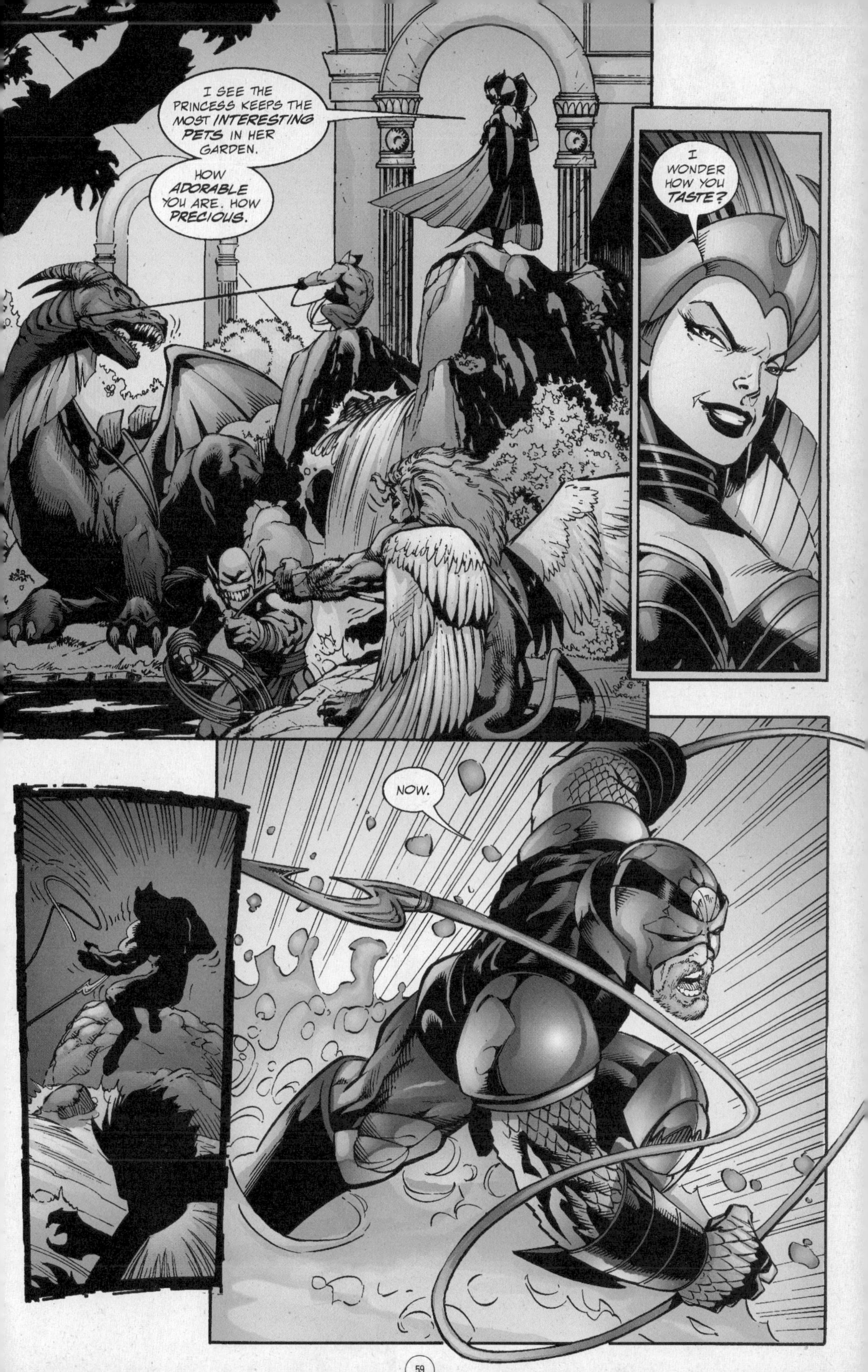
I SEE THE PRINCESS KEEPS THE MOST INTERESTING PETS IN HER GARDEN.
HOW ADORABLE YOU ARE. HOW PRECIOUS.
I WONDER HOW YOU TASTE?
NOW.

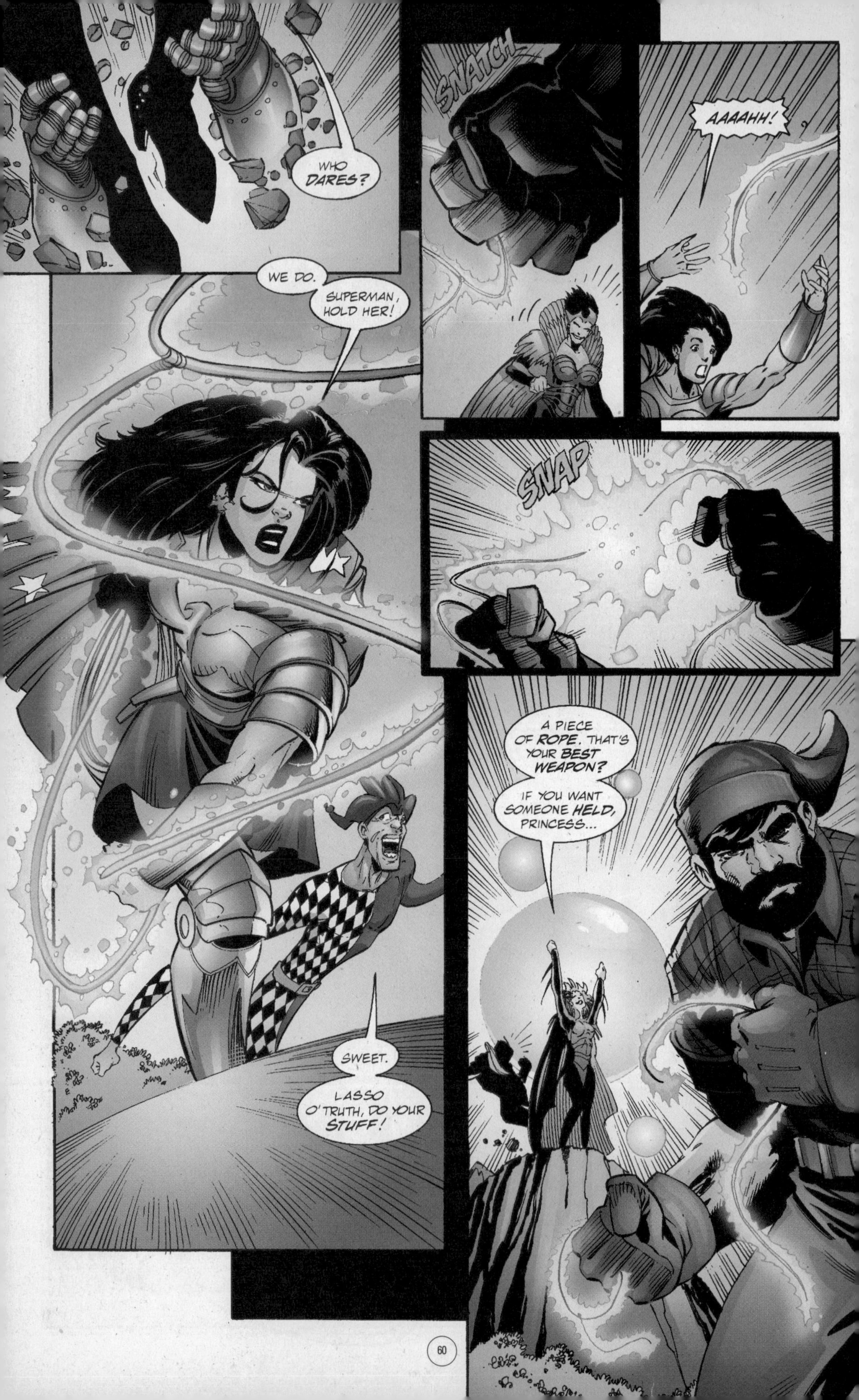
WHO DARES?
SNATCH
AAAAHH!
WE DO.
SUPERMAN, HOLD HER!
SNAP
SWEET.
LASSO O' TRUTH, DO YOUR STUFF!
A PIECE OF ROPE. THAT'S YOUR BEST WEAPON?
IF YOU WANT SOMEONE HELD, PRINCESS...

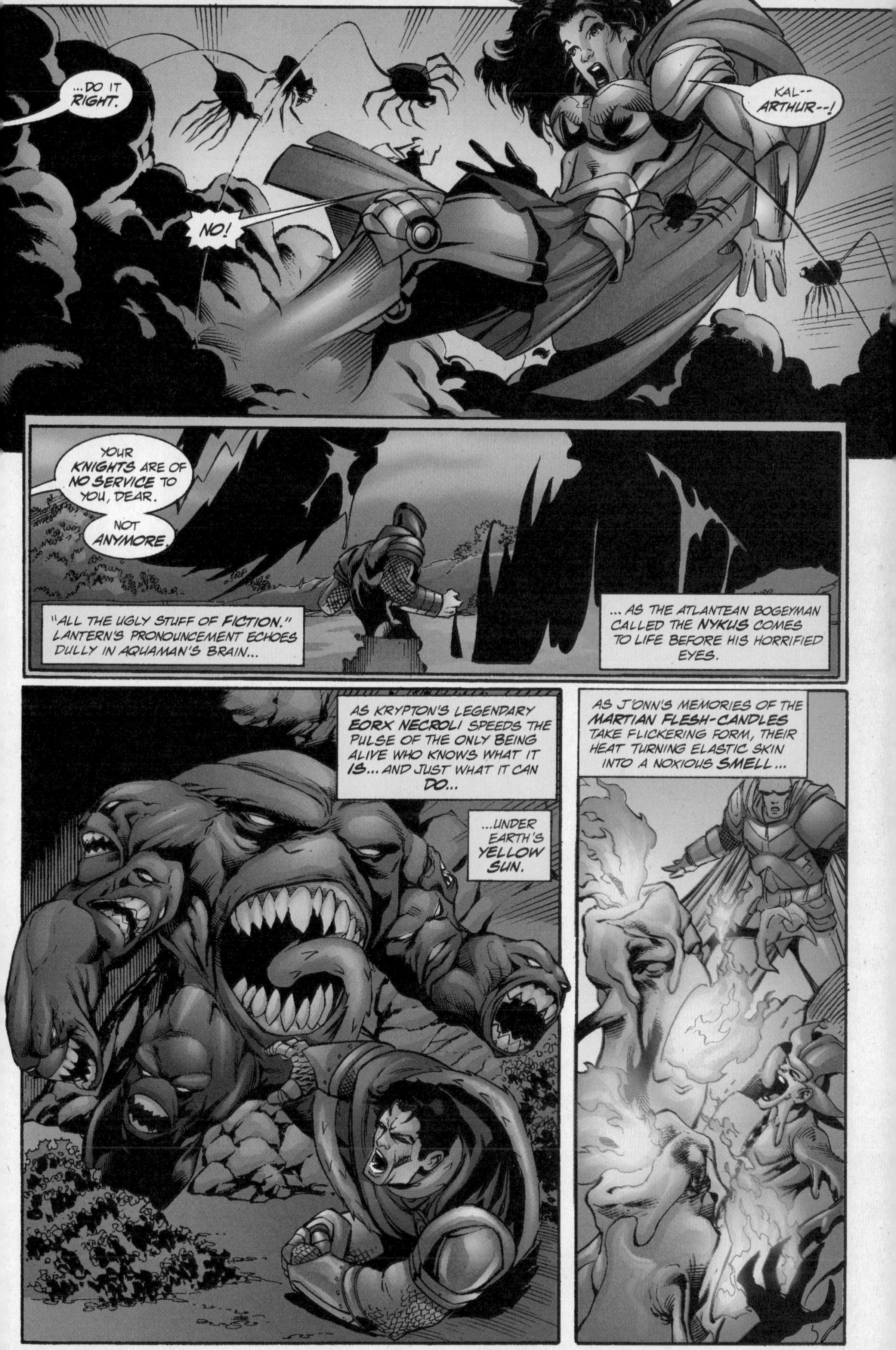
...DO IT RIGHT.
NO!
KAL-- ARTHUR--!
YOUR KNIGHTS ARE OF NO SERVICE TO YOU, DEAR.
NOT ANYMORE.
"ALL THE UGLY STUFF OF FICTION." LANTERN'S PRONOUNCEMENT ECHOES DULLY IN AQUAMAN'S BRAIN...
...AS THE ATLANTEAN BOGEYMAN CALLED THE NYKUS COMES TO LIFE BEFORE HIS HORRIFIED EYES.
AS KRYPTON'S LEGENDARY EORX NECROLI SPEEDS THE PULSE OF THE ONLY BEING ALIVE WHO KNOWS WHAT IT IS... AND JUST WHAT IT CAN DO...
...UNDER EARTH'S YELLOW SUN.
AS J'ONN'S MEMORIES OF THE MARTIAN FLESH-CANDLES TAKE FLICKERING FORM, THEIR HEAT TURNING ELASTIC SKIN INTO A NOXIOUS SMELL...

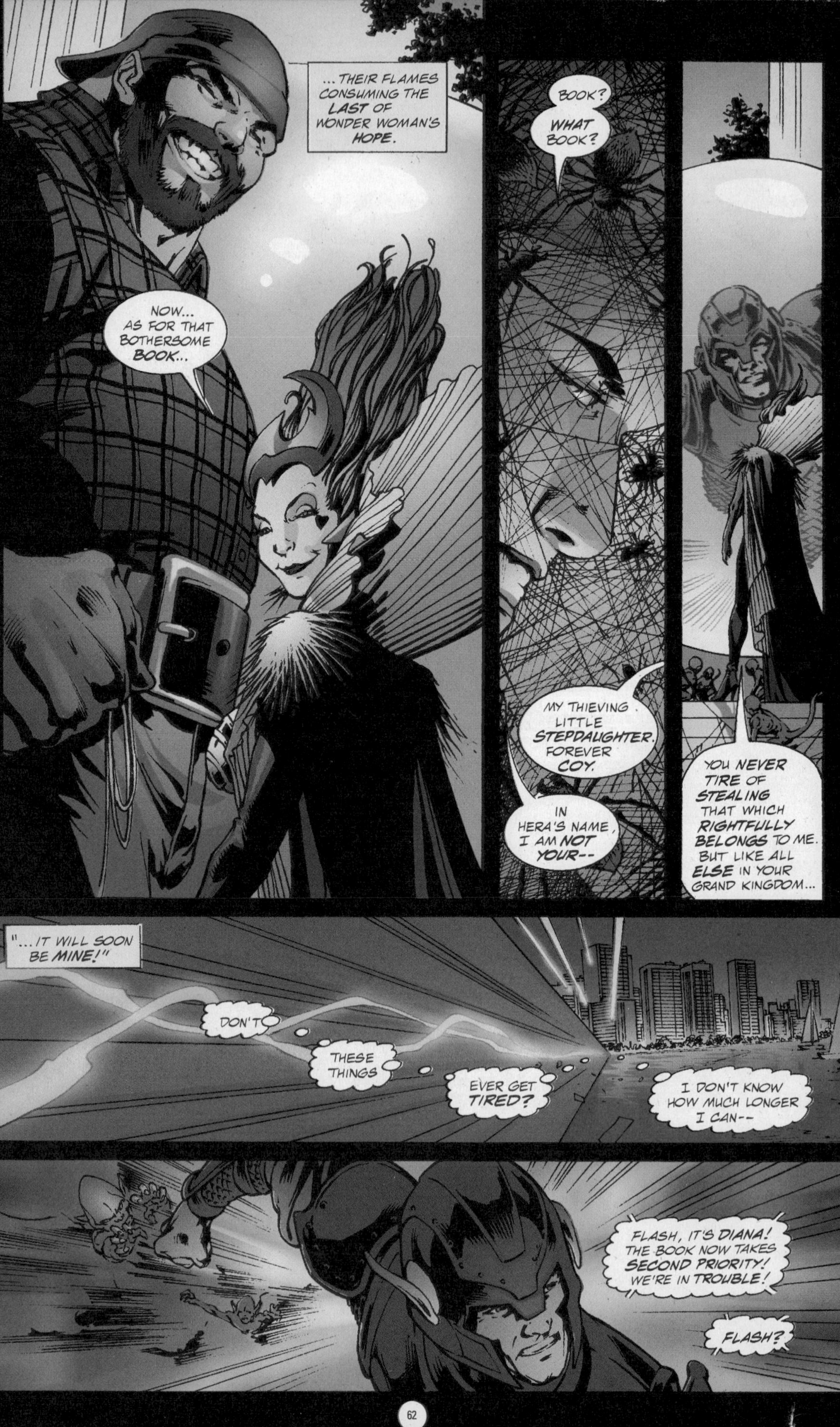
...THEIR FLAMES CONSUMING THE LAST OF WONDER WOMAN'S HOPE.
NOW... AS FOR THAT BOTHERSOME BOOK...
BOOK?
WHAT BOOK?
MY THIEVING LITTLE STEPDAUGHTER. FOREVER COY.
IN HERA'S NAME, I AM NOT YOUR--
YOU NEVER TIRE OF STEALING THAT WHICH RIGHTFULLY BELONGS TO ME. BUT LIKE ALL ELSE IN YOUR GRAND KINGDOM...
"...IT WILL SOON BE MINE!"
DON'T
THESE THINGS
EVER GET TIRED?
I DON'T KNOW HOW MUCH LONGER I CAN--
FLASH, IT'S DIANA! THE BOOK NOW TAKES SECOND PRIORITY! WE'RE IN TROUBLE!
FLASH?

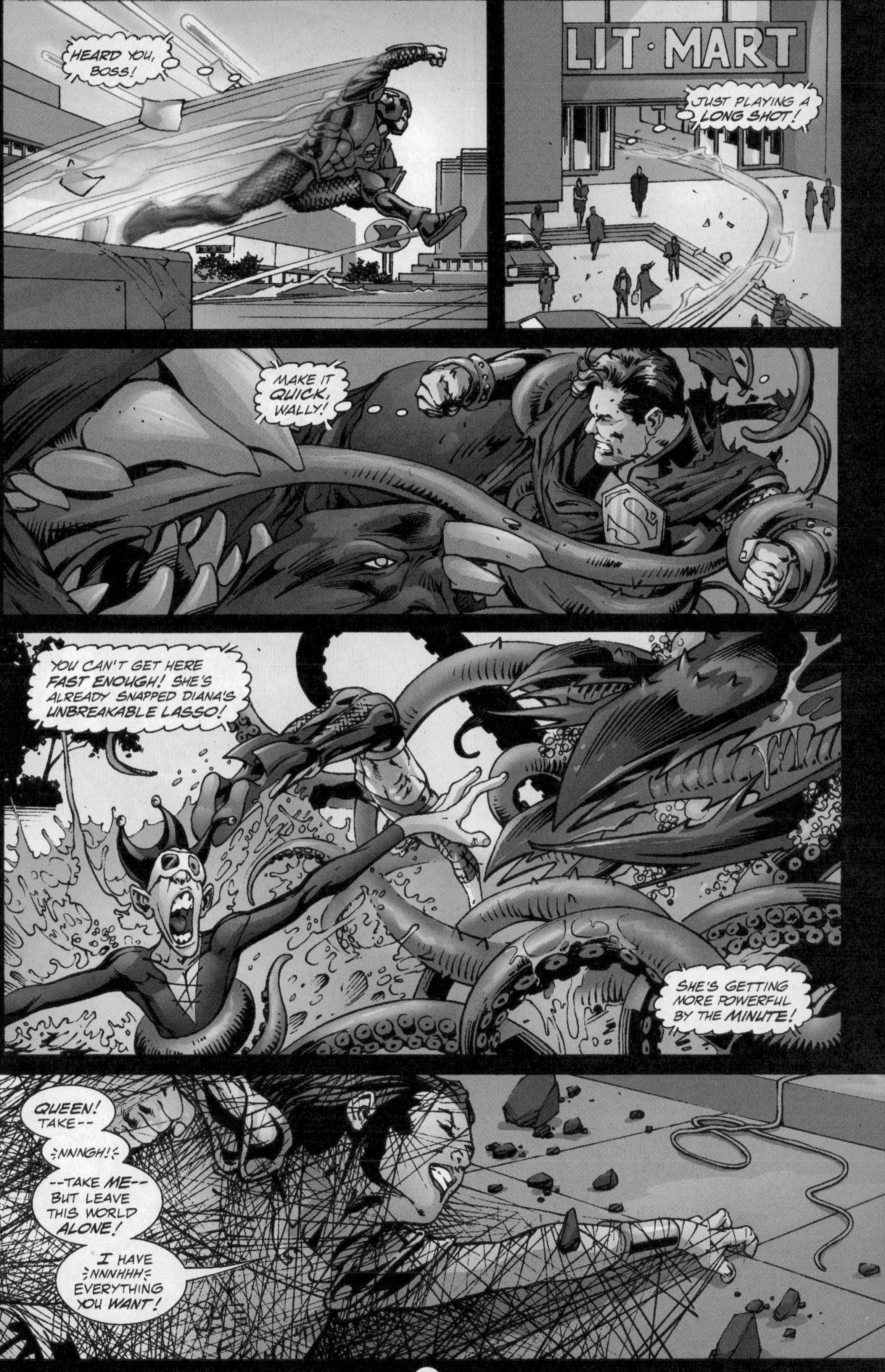
HEARD YOU, BOSS!
LIT·MART
JUST PLAYING A LONG SHOT!
MAKE IT QUICK, WALLY!
YOU CAN'T GET HERE FAST ENOUGH! SHE'S ALREADY SNAPPED DIANA'S UNBREAKABLE LASSO!
SHE'S GETTING MORE POWERFUL BY THE MINUTE!
QUEEN! TAKE--
NNNGH!
--TAKE ME-- BUT LEAVE THIS WORLD ALONE!
I HAVE
NNNHHH
EVERYTHING YOU WANT!

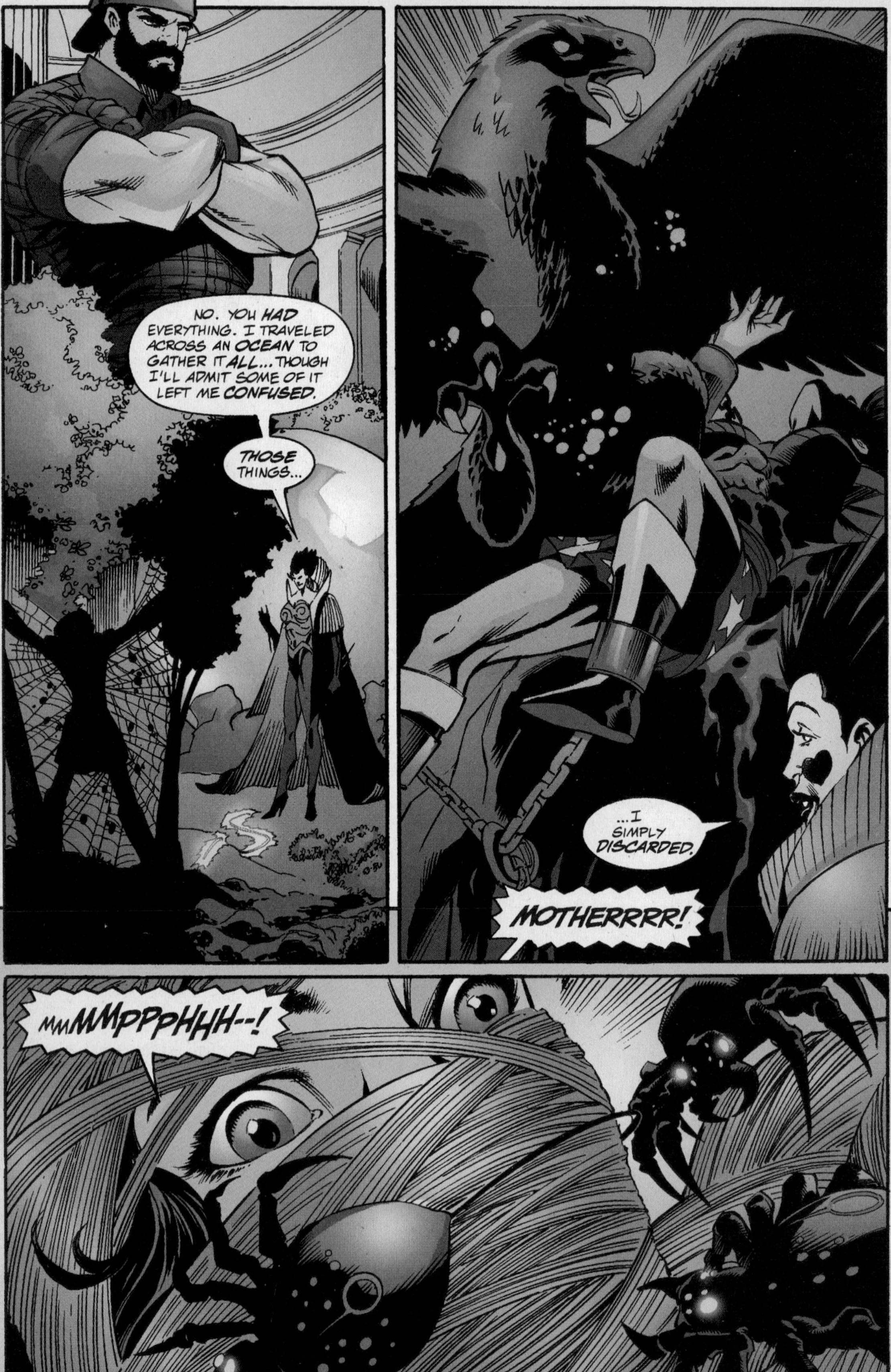
NO. YOU HAD EVERYTHING. I TRAVELED ACROSS AN OCEAN TO GATHER IT ALL... THOUGH I'LL ADMIT SOME OF IT LEFT ME CONFUSED.
THOSE THINGS...
...I SIMPLY DISCARDED.
MOTHERRRR!
MMMMPPPHHH--!

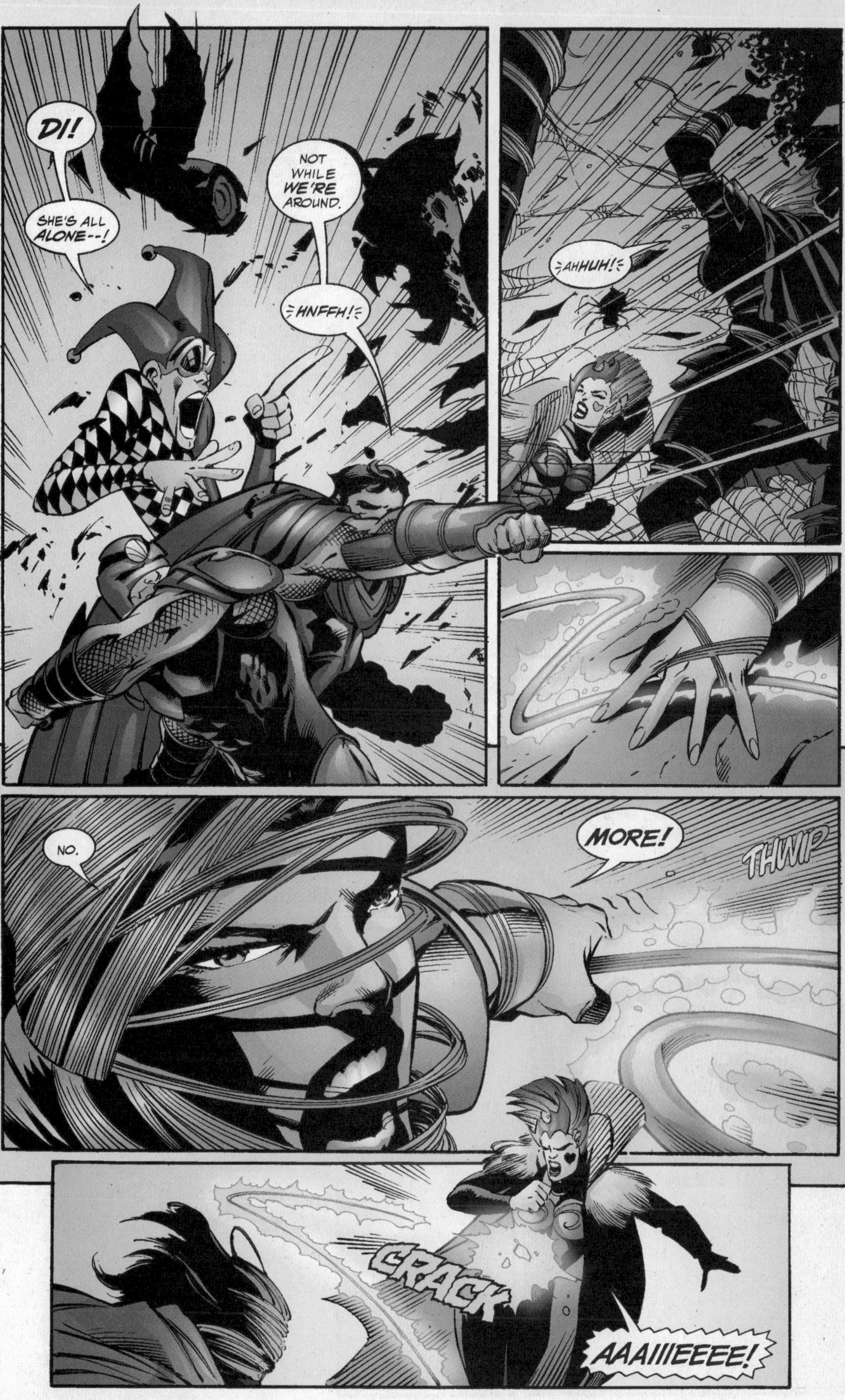
DI!
SHE'S ALL ALONE--!
NOT WHILE WE'RE AROUND.
HNFFH!
AHHUH!
NO.
MORE!
THWIP
CRACK
AAAIIIEEEE!

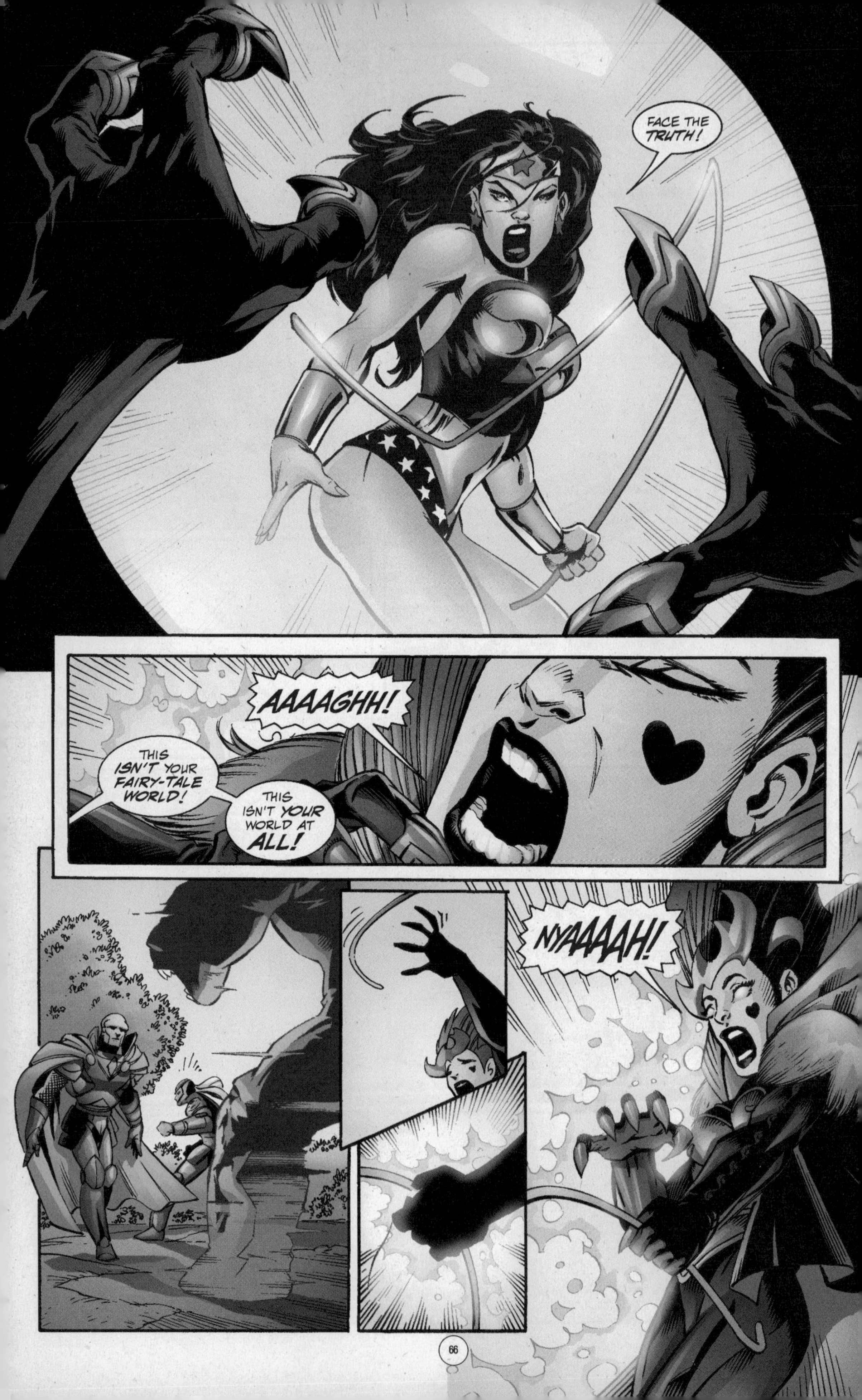
FACE THE TRUTH!
AAAAGHH!
THIS ISN'T YOUR FAIRY-TALE WORLD!
THIS ISN'T YOUR WORLD AT ALL!
NYAAAAH!

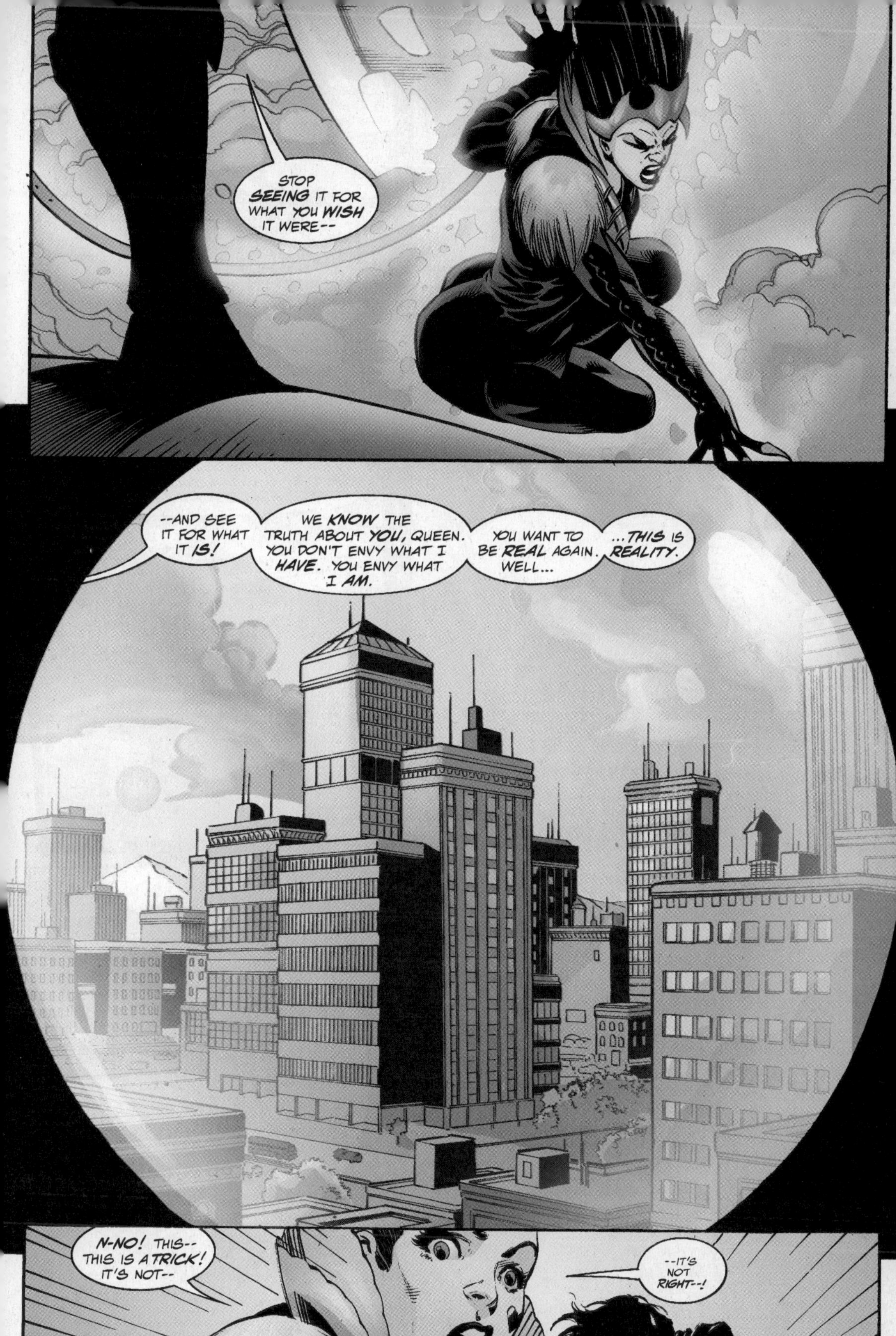
STOP SEEING IT FOR WHAT YOU WISH IT WERE--
--AND SEE IT FOR WHAT IT IS!
WE KNOW THE TRUTH ABOUT YOU, QUEEN. YOU DON'T ENVY WHAT I HAVE. YOU ENVY WHAT I AM.
YOU WANT TO BE REAL AGAIN. WELL...
...THIS IS REALITY.
N-NO! THIS-- THIS IS A TRICK! IT'S NOT--
--IT'S NOT RIGHT--!

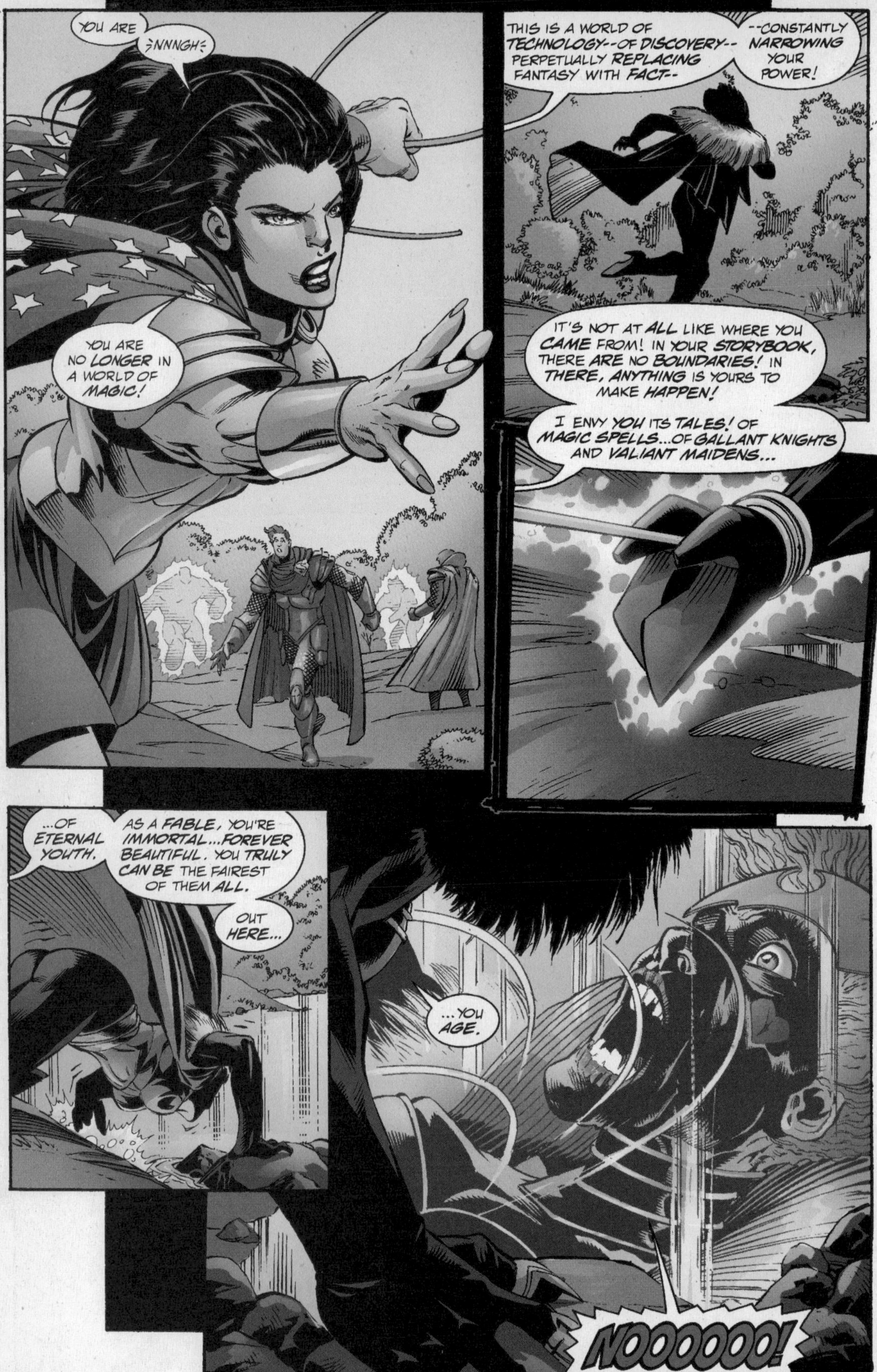
YOU ARE
=NNNGH=
YOU ARE NO LONGER IN A WORLD OF MAGIC!
THIS IS A WORLD OF TECHNOLOGY--OF DISCOVERY-- PERPETUALLY REPLACING FANTASY WITH FACT--
--CONSTANTLY NARROWING YOUR POWER!
IT'S NOT AT ALL LIKE WHERE YOU CAME FROM! IN YOUR STORYBOOK, THERE ARE NO BOUNDARIES! IN THERE, ANYTHING IS YOURS TO MAKE HAPPEN!
I ENVY YOU ITS TALES! OF MAGIC SPELLS...OF GALLANT KNIGHTS AND VALIANT MAIDENS...
...OF ETERNAL YOUTH.
AS A FABLE, YOU'RE IMMORTAL...FOREVER BEAUTIFUL. YOU TRULY CAN BE THE FAIREST OF THEM ALL.
OUT HERE...
...YOU AGE.
NOOOOOO!

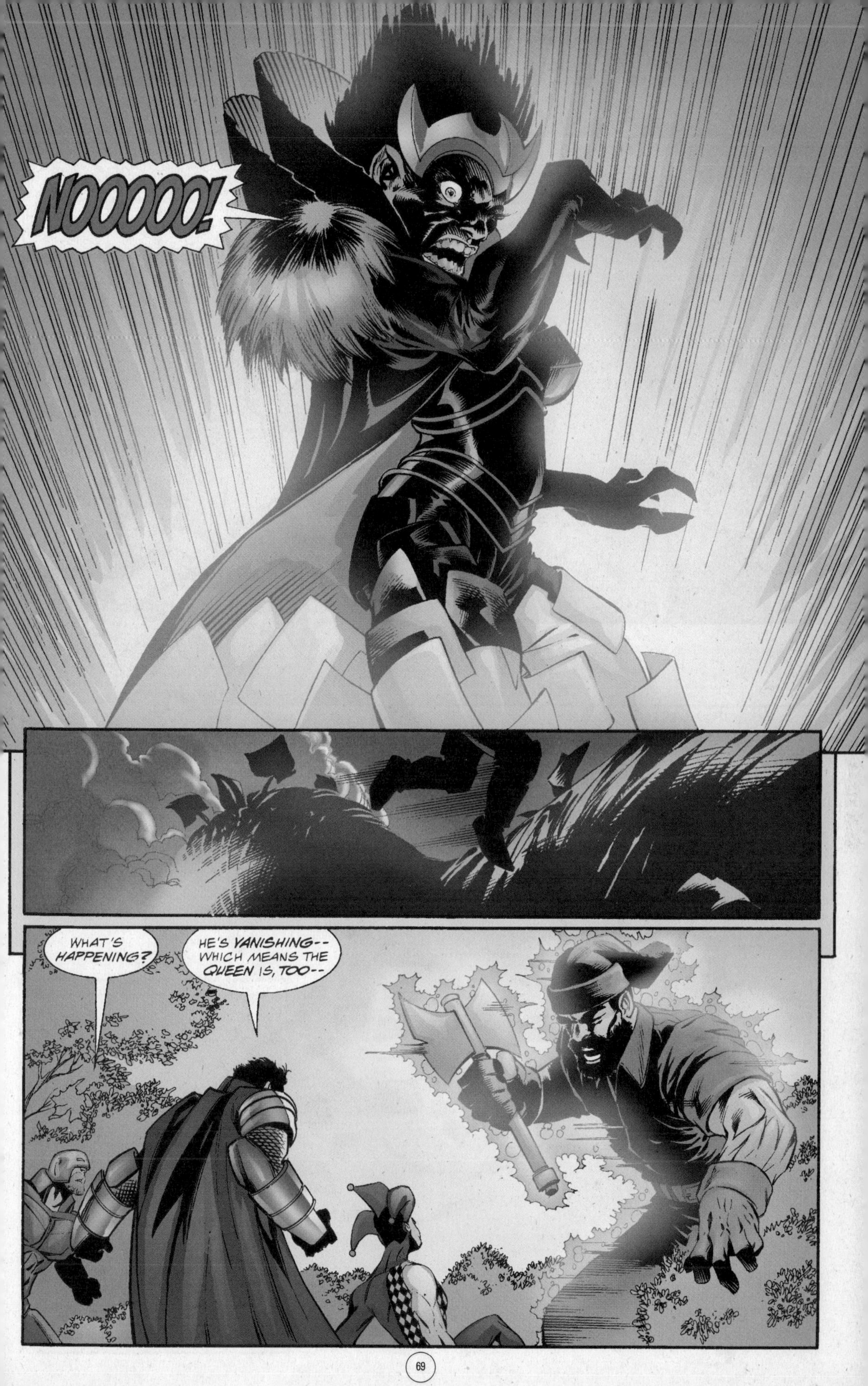
NOOOOO!
WHAT'S HAPPENING?
HE'S *VANISHING*-- WHICH MEANS THE *QUEEN* IS, *TOO*--

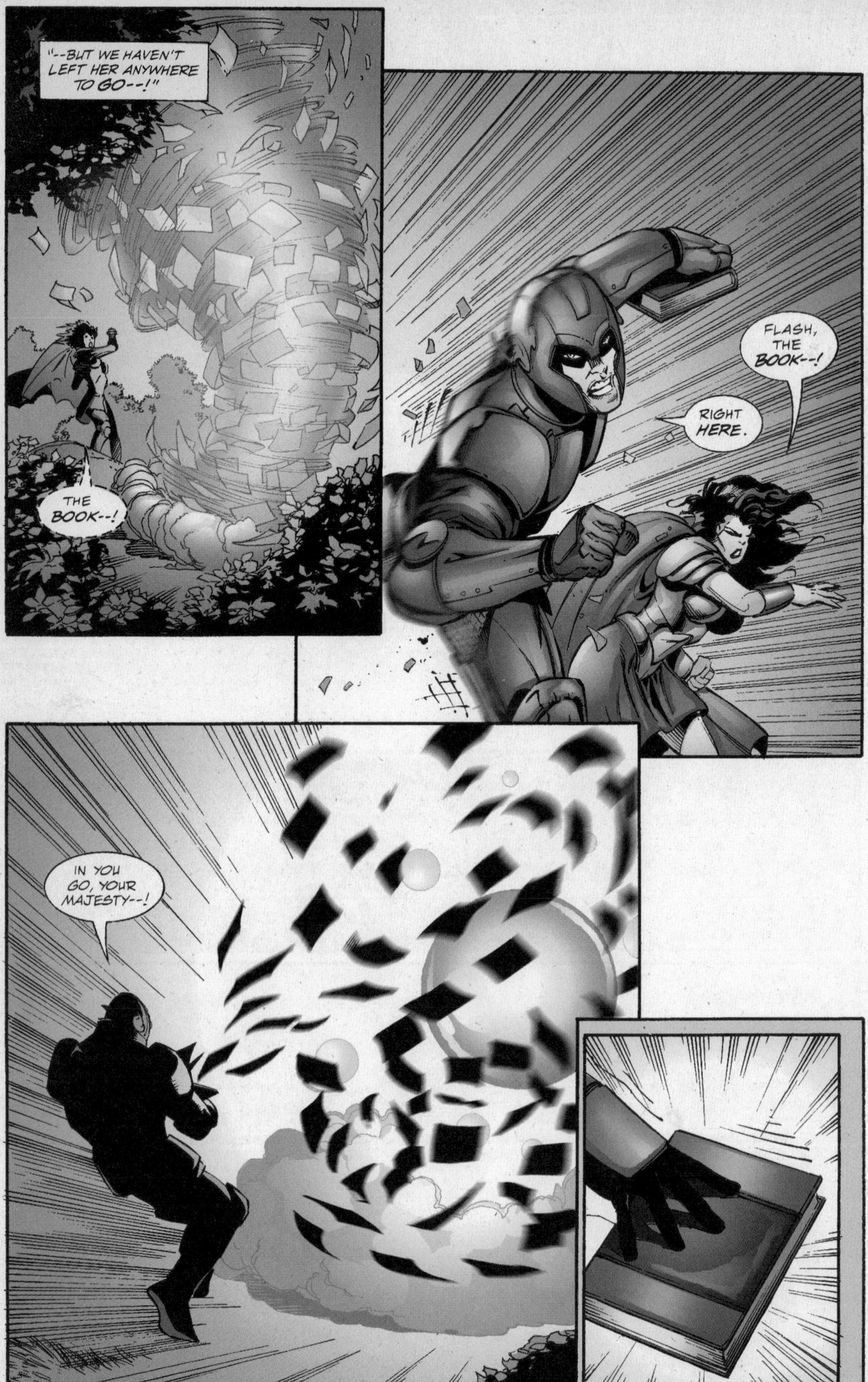
"--BUT WE HAVEN'T LEFT HER ANYWHERE TO GO--!"
THE BOOK--!
FLASH, THE BOOK--!
RIGHT HERE.
IN YOU GO, YOUR MAJESTY--!

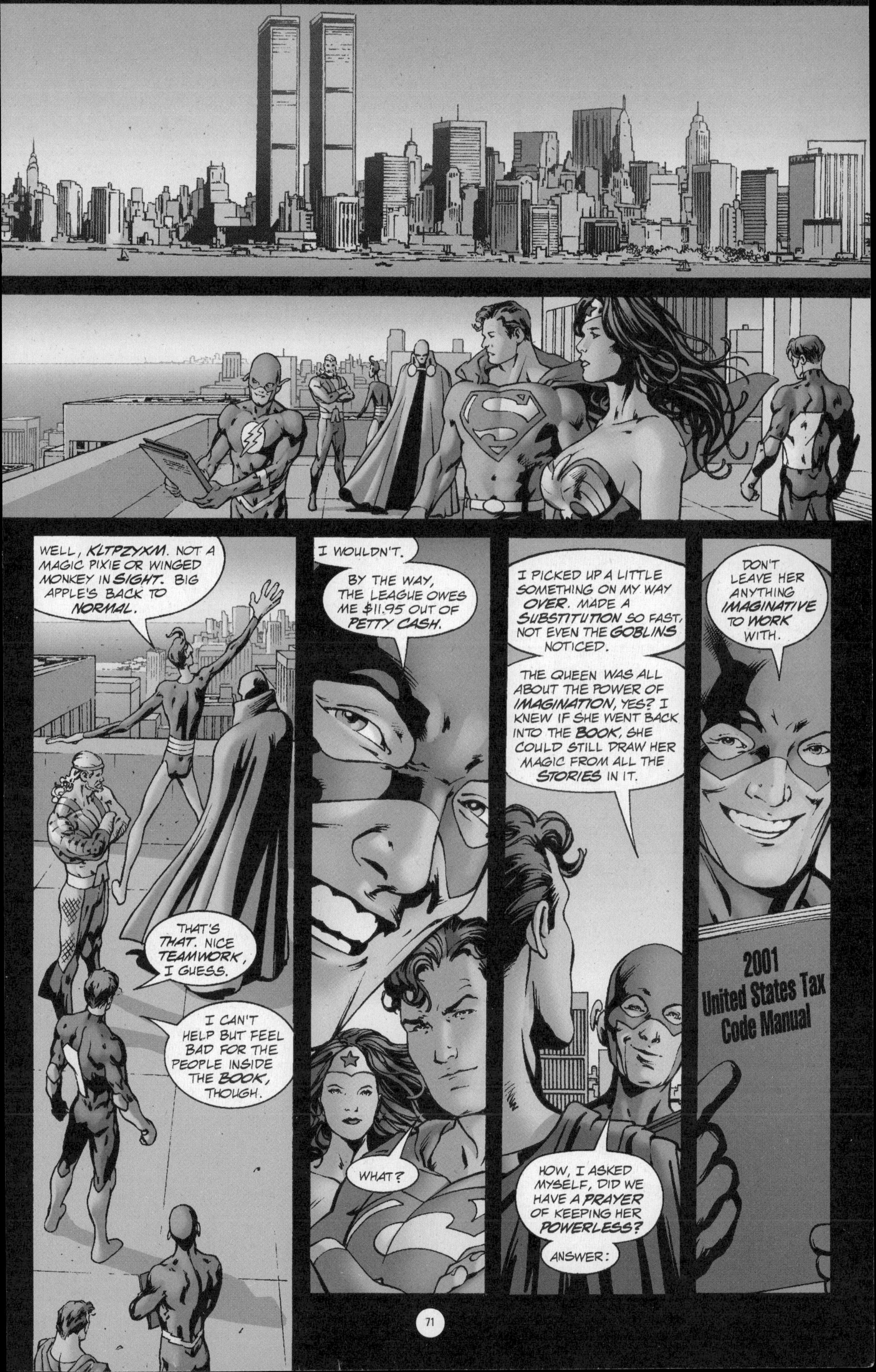
WELL, KLTPZYXM. NOT A MAGIC PIXIE OR WINGED MONKEY IN SIGHT. BIG APPLE'S BACK TO NORMAL.
THAT'S THAT. NICE TEAMWORK, I GUESS.
I CAN'T HELP BUT FEEL BAD FOR THE PEOPLE INSIDE THE BOOK, THOUGH.
I WOULDN'T.
BY THE WAY, THE LEAGUE OWES ME $11.95 OUT OF PETTY CASH.
WHAT?
I PICKED UP A LITTLE SOMETHING ON MY WAY OVER. MADE A SUBSTITUTION SO FAST, NOT EVEN THE GOBLINS NOTICED.
THE QUEEN WAS ALL ABOUT THE POWER OF IMAGINATION, YES? I KNEW IF SHE WENT BACK INTO THE BOOK, SHE COULD STILL DRAW HER MAGIC FROM ALL THE STORIES IN IT.
HOW, I ASKED MYSELF, DID WE HAVE A PRAYER OF KEEPING HER POWERLESS?
ANSWER:
DON'T LEAVE HER ANYTHING IMAGINATIVE TO WORK WITH.
2001 United States Tax Code Manual

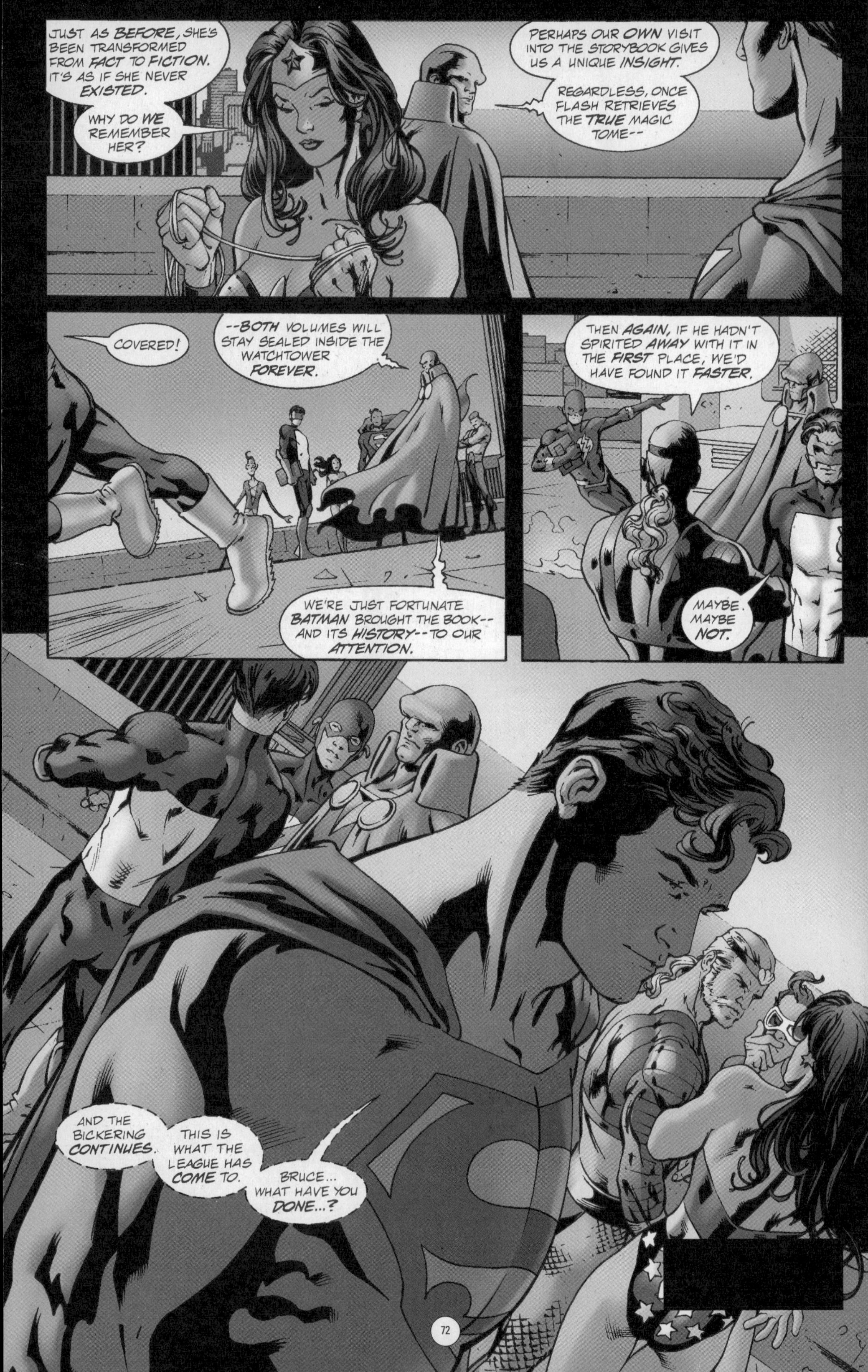
JUST AS BEFORE, SHE'S BEEN TRANSFORMED FROM FACT TO FICTION. IT'S AS IF SHE NEVER EXISTED.
WHY DO WE REMEMBER HER?
PERHAPS OUR OWN VISIT INTO THE STORYBOOK GIVES US A UNIQUE INSIGHT.
REGARDLESS, ONCE FLASH RETRIEVES THE TRUE MAGIC TOME--
COVERED!
--BOTH VOLUMES WILL STAY SEALED INSIDE THE WATCHTOWER FOREVER.
WE'RE JUST FORTUNATE BATMAN BROUGHT THE BOOK--AND ITS HISTORY--TO OUR ATTENTION.
THEN AGAIN, IF HE HADN'T SPIRITED AWAY WITH IT IN THE FIRST PLACE, WE'D HAVE FOUND IT FASTER.
MAYBE. MAYBE NOT.
AND THE BICKERING CONTINUES.
THIS IS WHAT THE LEAGUE HAS COME TO.
BRUCE... WHAT HAVE YOU DONE...?
[redacted]

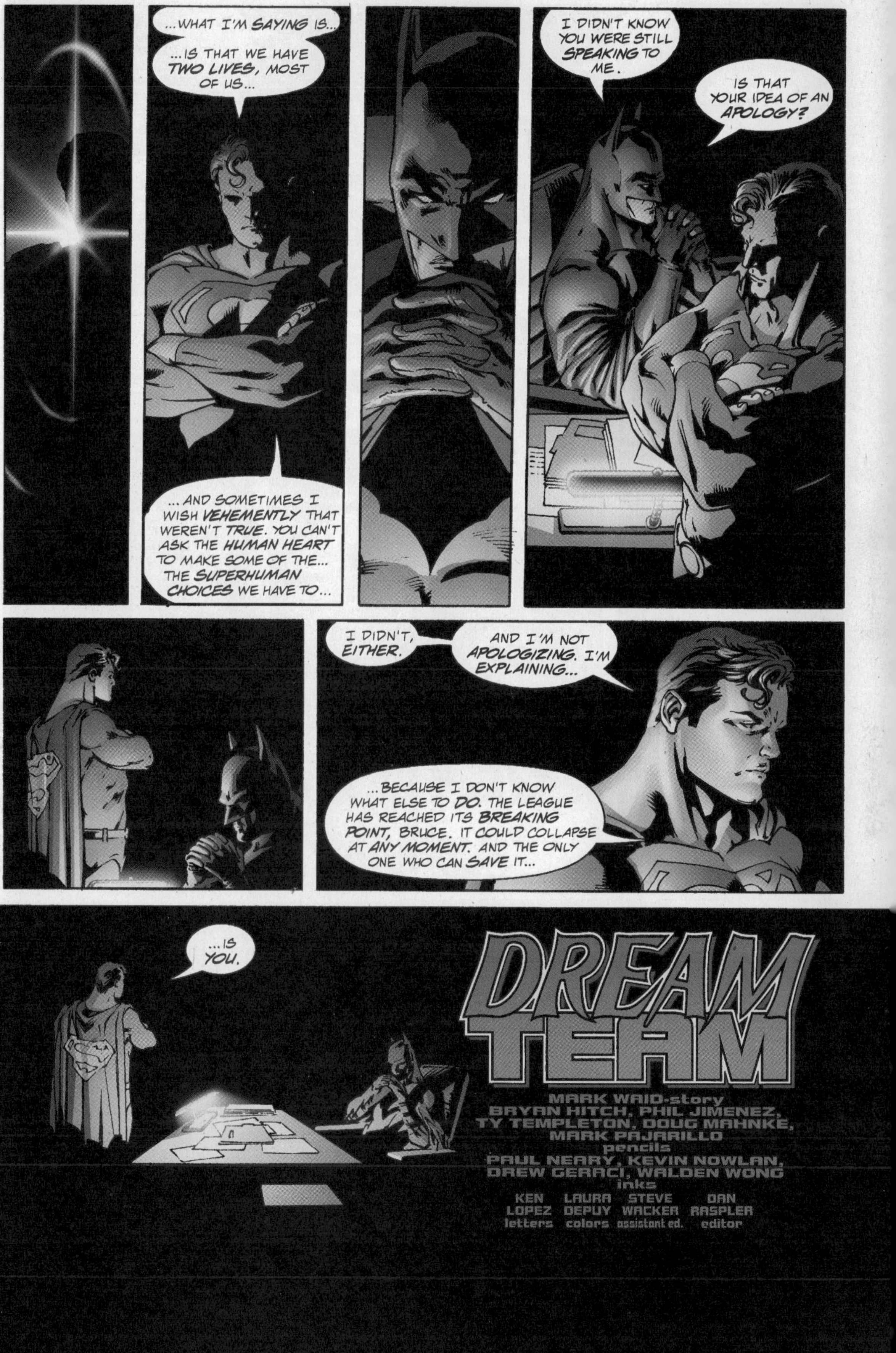
...WHAT I'M SAYING IS...
...IS THAT WE HAVE TWO LIVES, MOST OF US...
...AND SOMETIMES I WISH VEHEMENTLY THAT WEREN'T TRUE. YOU CAN'T ASK THE HUMAN HEART TO MAKE SOME OF THE... THE SUPERHUMAN CHOICES WE HAVE TO...
I DIDN'T KNOW YOU WERE STILL SPEAKING TO ME.
IS THAT YOUR IDEA OF AN APOLOGY?
I DIDN'T, EITHER.
AND I'M NOT APOLOGIZING. I'M EXPLAINING...
...BECAUSE I DON'T KNOW WHAT ELSE TO DO. THE LEAGUE HAS REACHED ITS BREAKING POINT, BRUCE. IT COULD COLLAPSE AT ANY MOMENT. AND THE ONLY ONE WHO CAN SAVE IT...
...IS YOU.
DREAM TEAM
MARK WAID-story
BRYAN HITCH, PHIL JIMENEZ, TY TEMPLETON, DOUG MAHNKE, MARK PAJARILLO
pencils
PAUL NEARY, KEVIN NOWLAN, DREW GERACI, WALDEN WONG
inks
KEN LOPEZ letters
LAURA DEPUY colors
STEVE WACKER assistant ed.
DAN RASPLER editor

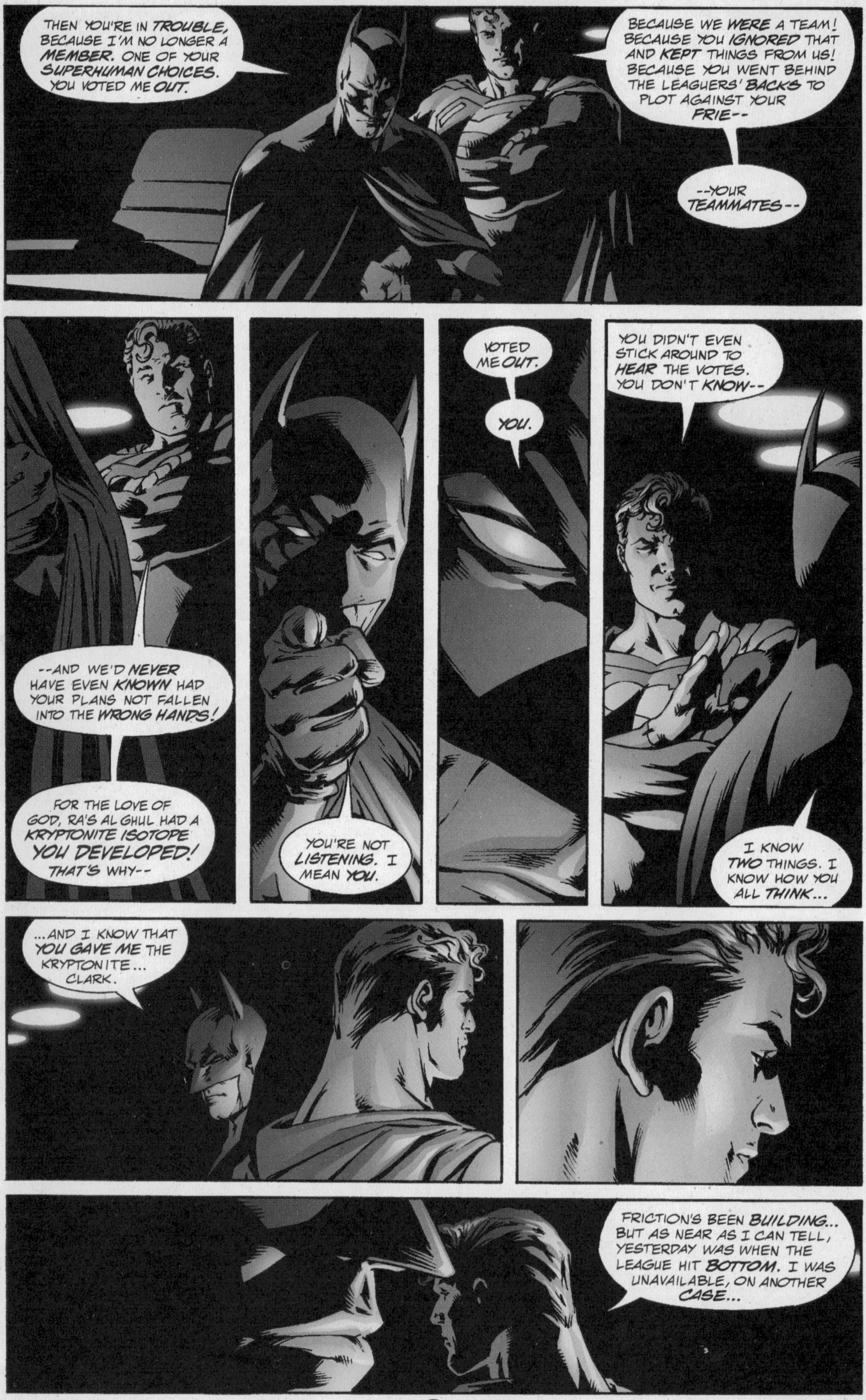
THEN YOU'RE IN TROUBLE, BECAUSE I'M NO LONGER A MEMBER. ONE OF YOUR SUPERHUMAN CHOICES. YOU VOTED ME OUT.
BECAUSE WE WERE A TEAM! BECAUSE YOU IGNORED THAT AND KEPT THINGS FROM US! BECAUSE YOU WENT BEHIND THE LEAGUERS' BACKS TO PLOT AGAINST YOUR FRIE--
--YOUR TEAMMATES--
--AND WE'D NEVER HAVE EVEN KNOWN HAD YOUR PLANS NOT FALLEN INTO THE WRONG HANDS!
FOR THE LOVE OF GOD, RA'S AL GHUL HAD A KRYPTONITE ISOTOPE YOU DEVELOPED! THAT'S WHY--
YOU'RE NOT LISTENING. I MEAN YOU.
VOTED ME OUT.
YOU.
YOU DIDN'T EVEN STICK AROUND TO HEAR THE VOTES. YOU DON'T KNOW--
I KNOW TWO THINGS. I KNOW HOW YOU ALL THINK...
...AND I KNOW THAT YOU GAVE ME THE KRYPTONITE... CLARK.
FRICTION'S BEEN BUILDING... BUT AS NEAR AS I CAN TELL, YESTERDAY WAS WHEN THE LEAGUE HIT BOTTOM. I WAS UNAVAILABLE, ON ANOTHER CASE...

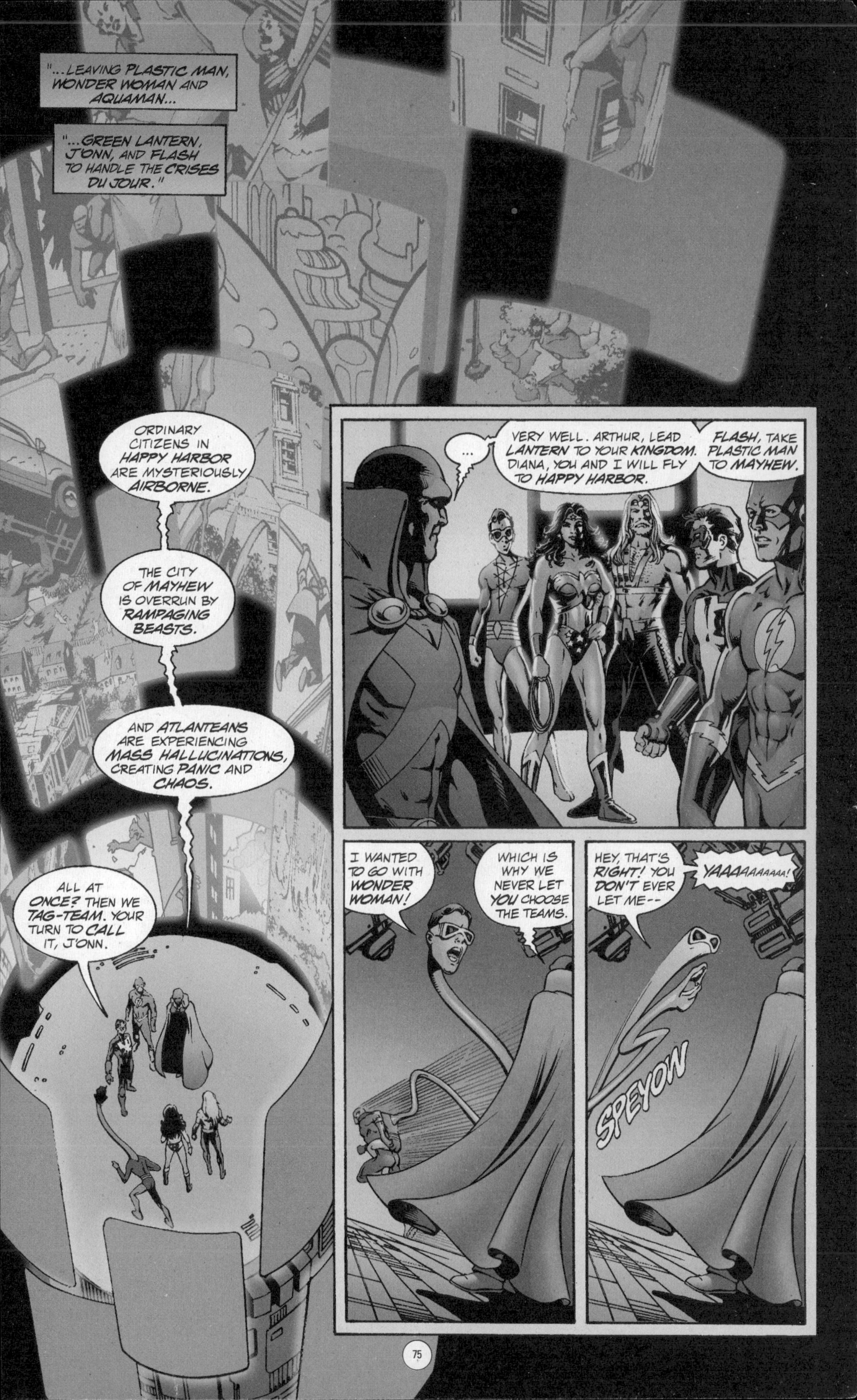
"...LEAVING PLASTIC MAN, WONDER WOMAN AND AQUAMAN...
"...GREEN LANTERN, J'ONN, AND FLASH TO HANDLE THE CRISES DU JOUR."
ORDINARY CITIZENS IN HAPPY HARBOR ARE MYSTERIOUSLY AIRBORNE.
THE CITY OF MAYHEW IS OVERRUN BY RAMPAGING BEASTS.
AND ATLANTEANS ARE EXPERIENCING MASS HALLUCINATIONS, CREATING PANIC AND CHAOS.
ALL AT ONCE? THEN WE TAG-TEAM. YOUR TURN TO CALL IT, J'ONN.
...
VERY WELL. ARTHUR, LEAD LANTERN TO YOUR KINGDOM. DIANA, YOU AND I WILL FLY TO HAPPY HARBOR.
FLASH, TAKE PLASTIC MAN TO MAYHEW.
I WANTED TO GO WITH WONDER WOMAN!
WHICH IS WHY WE NEVER LET YOU CHOOSE THE TEAMS.
HEY, THAT'S RIGHT! YOU DON'T EVER LET ME--
YAAAAaaaaaa!
SPEYOW

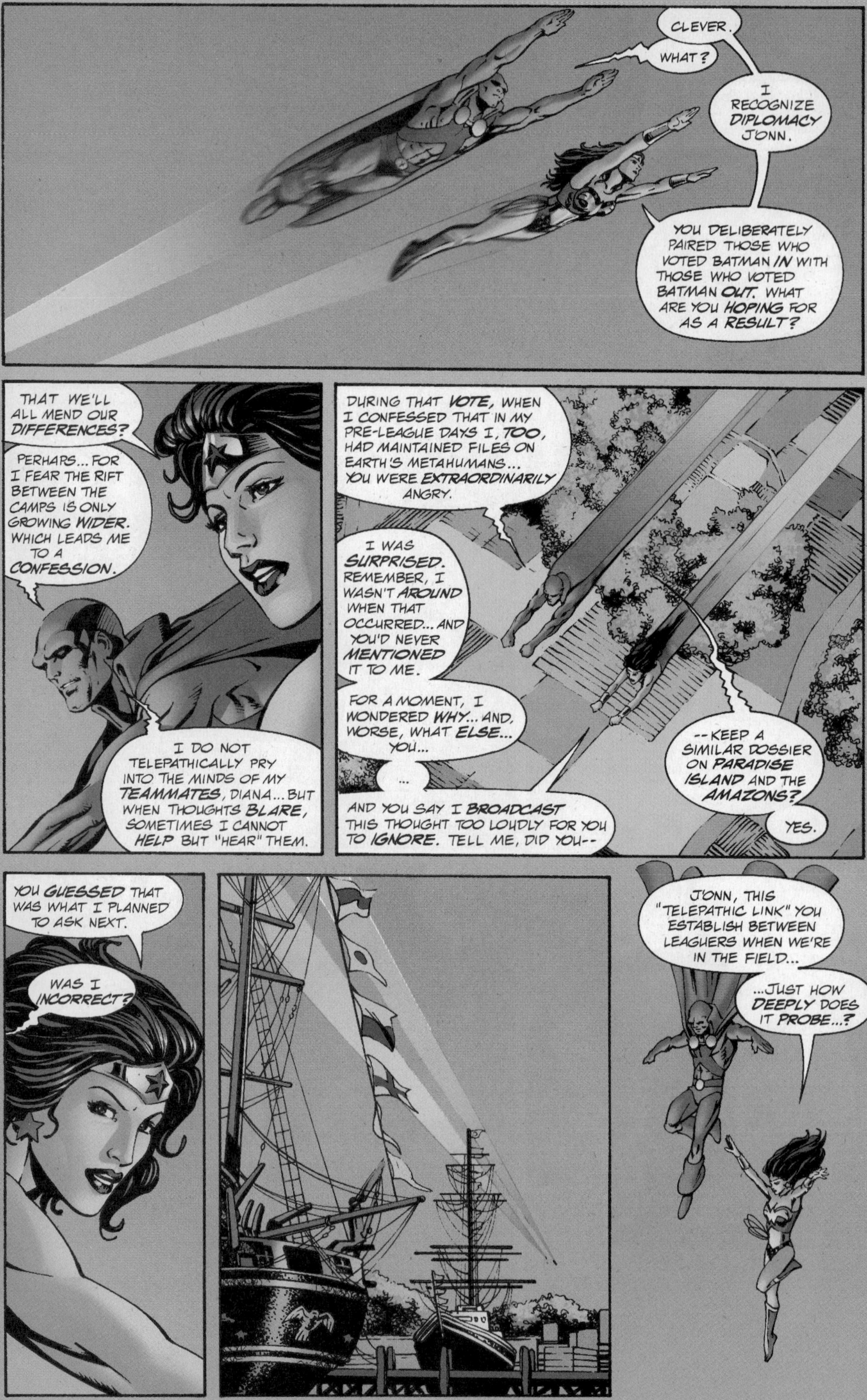
CLEVER.
WHAT?
I RECOGNIZE DIPLOMACY J'ONN.
YOU DELIBERATELY PAIRED THOSE WHO VOTED BATMAN IN WITH THOSE WHO VOTED BATMAN OUT. WHAT ARE YOU HOPING FOR AS A RESULT?
THAT WE'LL ALL MEND OUR DIFFERENCES?
PERHAPS... FOR I FEAR THE RIFT BETWEEN THE CAMPS IS ONLY GROWING WIDER. WHICH LEADS ME TO A CONFESSION.
I DO NOT TELEPATHICALLY PRY INTO THE MINDS OF MY TEAMMATES, DIANA... BUT WHEN THOUGHTS BLARE, SOMETIMES I CANNOT HELP BUT "HEAR" THEM.
DURING THAT VOTE, WHEN I CONFESSED THAT IN MY PRE-LEAGUE DAYS I, TOO, HAD MAINTAINED FILES ON EARTH'S METAHUMANS... YOU WERE EXTRAORDINARILY ANGRY.
I WAS SURPRISED. REMEMBER, I WASN'T AROUND WHEN THAT OCCURRED... AND YOU'D NEVER MENTIONED IT TO ME.
FOR A MOMENT, I WONDERED WHY... AND, WORSE, WHAT ELSE... YOU...
...
AND YOU SAY I BROADCAST THIS THOUGHT TOO LOUDLY FOR YOU TO IGNORE. TELL ME, DID YOU--
--KEEP A SIMILAR DOSSIER ON PARADISE ISLAND AND THE AMAZONS?
YES.
YOU GUESSED THAT WAS WHAT I PLANNED TO ASK NEXT.
WAS I INCORRECT?
J'ONN, THIS "TELEPATHIC LINK" YOU ESTABLISH BETWEEN LEAGUERS WHEN WE'RE IN THE FIELD...
...JUST HOW DEEPLY DOES IT PROBE...?

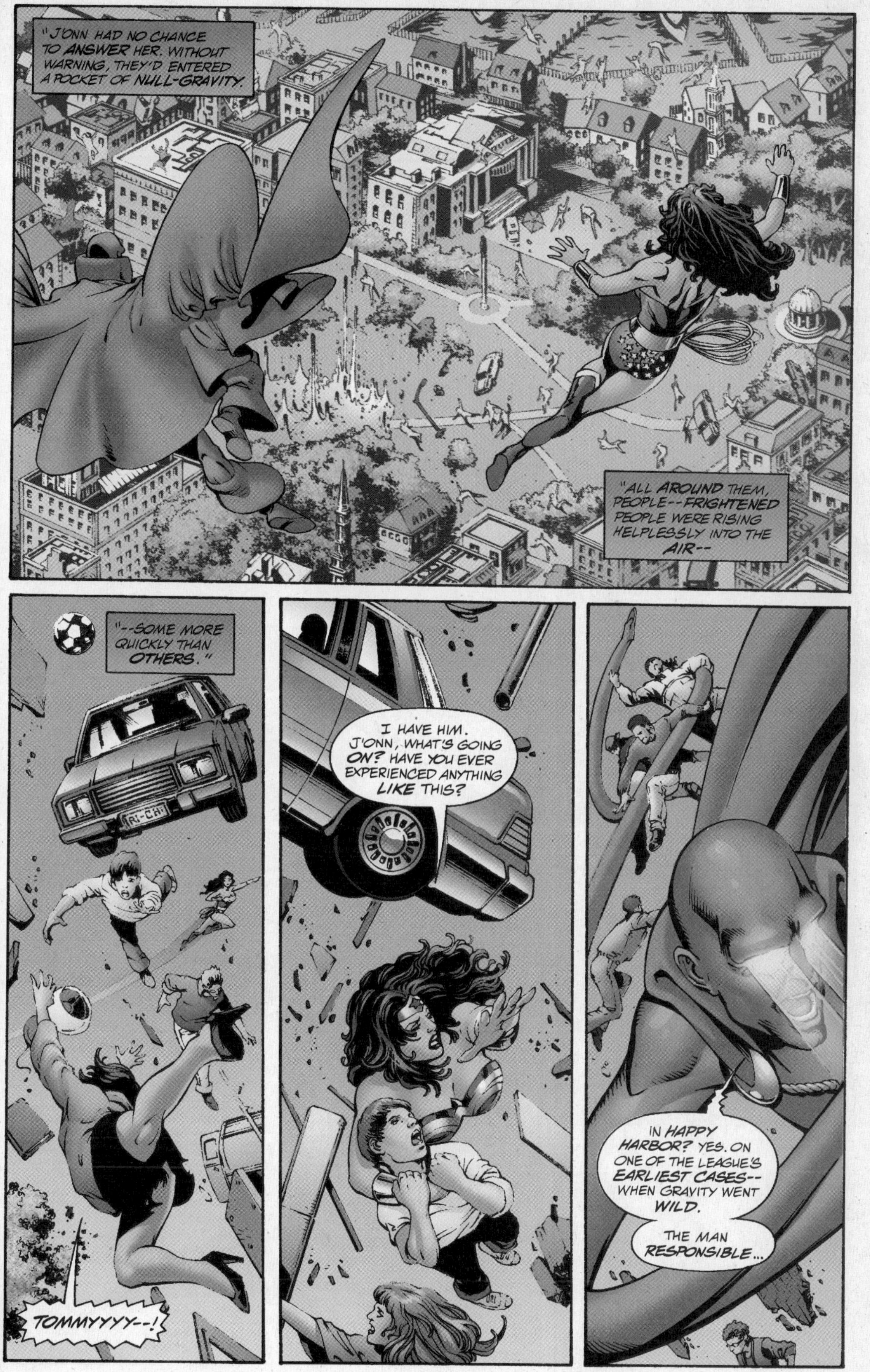
"J'ONN HAD NO CHANCE TO ANSWER HER. WITHOUT WARNING, THEY'D ENTERED A POCKET OF NULL-GRAVITY.
"ALL AROUND THEM, PEOPLE--FRIGHTENED PEOPLE WERE RISING HELPLESSLY INTO THE AIR--
"--SOME MORE QUICKLY THAN OTHERS."
RI-CHI
TOMMYYYY--!
I HAVE HIM. J'ONN, WHAT'S GOING ON? HAVE YOU EVER EXPERIENCED ANYTHING LIKE THIS?
IN HAPPY HARBOR? YES. ON ONE OF THE LEAGUE'S EARLIEST CASES--WHEN GRAVITY WENT WILD.
THE MAN RESPONSIBLE...

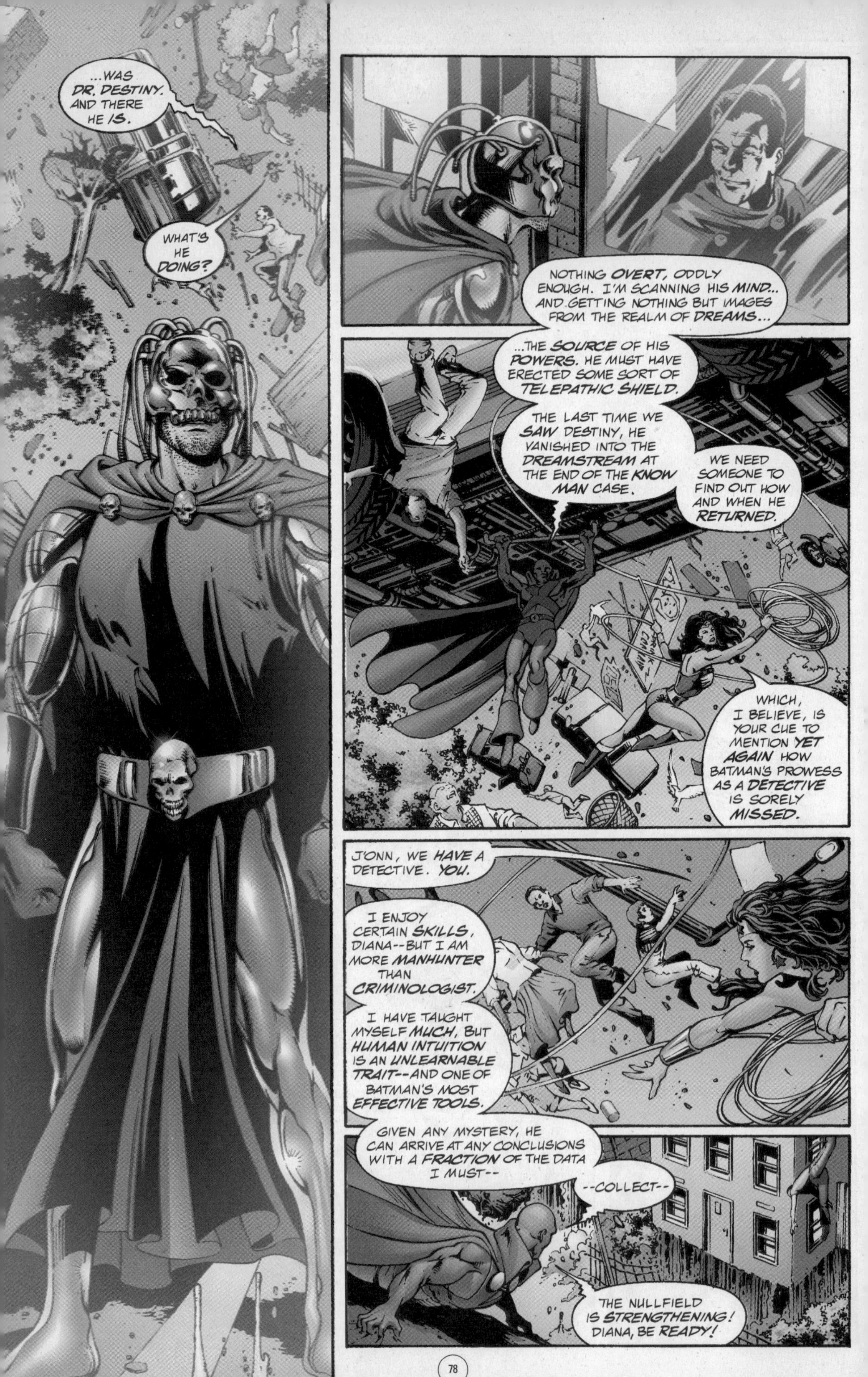
...WAS DR. DESTINY. AND THERE HE IS.
WHAT'S HE DOING?
NOTHING OVERT, ODDLY ENOUGH. I'M SCANNING HIS MIND... AND GETTING NOTHING BUT IMAGES FROM THE REALM OF DREAMS...
...THE SOURCE OF HIS POWERS. HE MUST HAVE ERECTED SOME SORT OF TELEPATHIC SHIELD.
THE LAST TIME WE SAW DESTINY, HE VANISHED INTO THE DREAMSTREAM AT THE END OF THE KNOW MAN CASE.
WE NEED SOMEONE TO FIND OUT HOW AND WHEN HE RETURNED.
WHICH, I BELIEVE, IS YOUR CUE TO MENTION YET AGAIN HOW BATMAN'S PROWESS AS A DETECTIVE IS SORELY MISSED.
J'ONN, WE HAVE A DETECTIVE. YOU.
I ENJOY CERTAIN SKILLS, DIANA--BUT I AM MORE MANHUNTER THAN CRIMINOLOGIST.
I HAVE TAUGHT MYSELF MUCH, BUT HUMAN INTUITION IS AN UNLEARNABLE TRAIT--AND ONE OF BATMAN'S MOST EFFECTIVE TOOLS.
GIVEN ANY MYSTERY, HE CAN ARRIVE AT ANY CONCLUSIONS WITH A FRACTION OF THE DATA I MUST--
--COLLECT--
THE NULLFIELD IS STRENGTHENING! DIANA, BE READY!

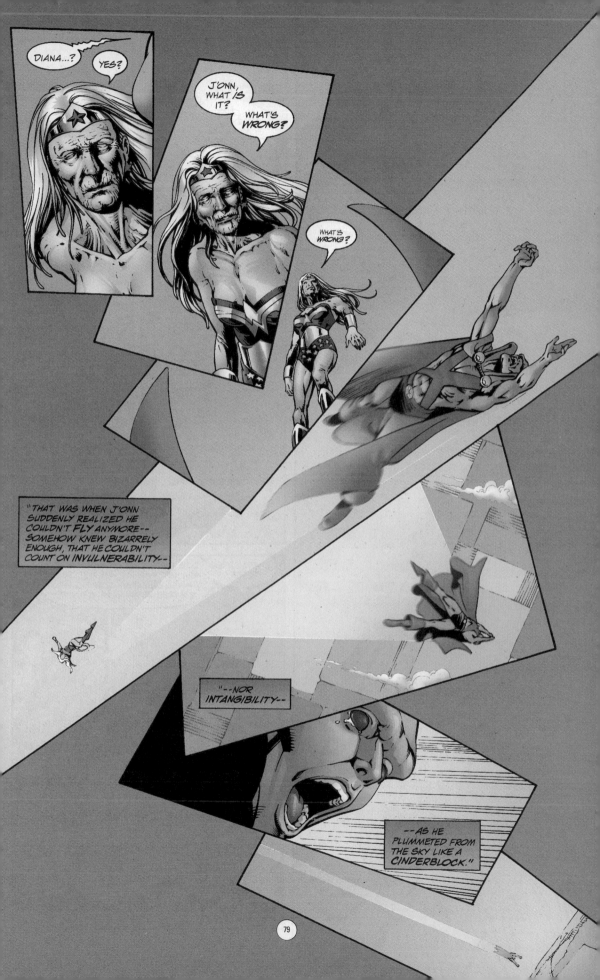

DIANA...?

YES?

J'ONN, WHAT **IS** IT? WHAT'S **WRONG?**

WHAT'S WRONG?

"THAT WAS WHEN J'ONN SUDDENLY REALIZED HE COULDN'T FLY ANYMORE-- SOMEHOW KNEW BIZARRELY ENOUGH, THAT HE COULDN'T COUNT ON INVULNERABILITY--

"--NOR INTANGIBILITY--

--AS HE PLUMMETED FROM THE SKY LIKE A **CINDERBLOCK.**"

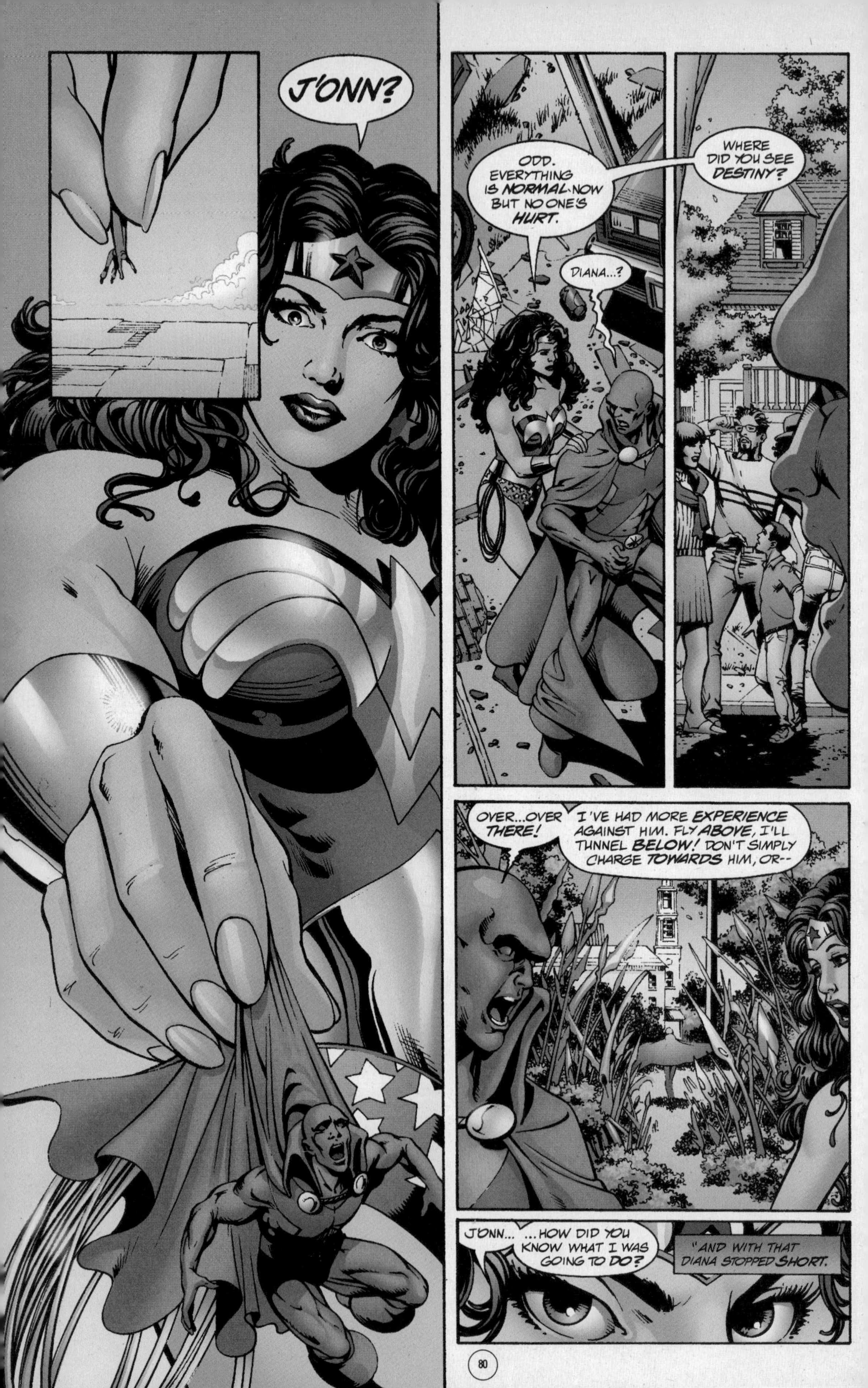
J'ONN?
ODD. EVERYTHING IS NORMAL NOW BUT NO ONE'S HURT.
WHERE DID YOU SEE DESTINY?
DIANA...?
OVER...OVER THERE!
I'VE HAD MORE EXPERIENCE AGAINST HIM. FLY ABOVE, I'LL TUNNEL BELOW! DON'T SIMPLY CHARGE TOWARDS HIM, OR--
J'ONN...
...HOW DID YOU KNOW WHAT I WAS GOING TO DO?
"AND WITH THAT DIANA STOPPED SHORT.

"SHE HESITATED ONLY A SPLIT-SECOND--"

DIANA, IT WAS SPECULATION! I DIDN'T SCAN YOUR--

"--BUT THAT ONE CLOCKTICK COST THEM.

--MAAAAAAAGH!

J'ONN!

"HORRIBLY."

DIA... WAAA... AAA

HH-- HELLLP-PP

NNN NNN EEE

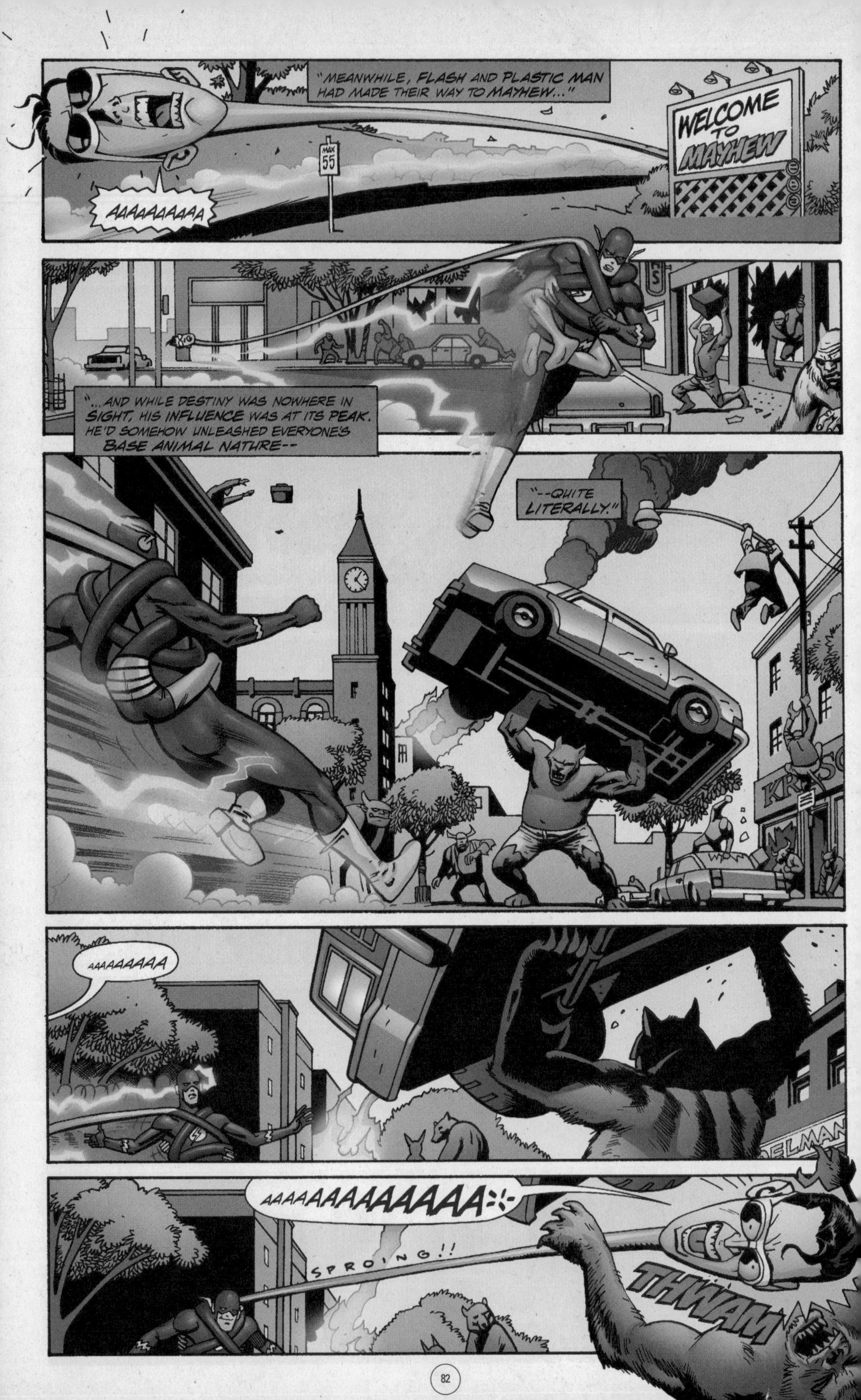
"MEANWHILE, FLASH AND PLASTIC MAN HAD MADE THEIR WAY TO MAYHEW..."
MAX 55
WELCOME TO MAYHEW
AAAAAAAAAA
"...AND WHILE DESTINY WAS NOWHERE IN SIGHT, HIS INFLUENCE WAS AT ITS PEAK. HE'D SOMEHOW UNLEASHED EVERYONE'S BASE ANIMAL NATURE--
"--QUITE LITERALLY."
AAAAAAAAA
AAAAAAAAAAAAAAA
SPROING!!
THWAM

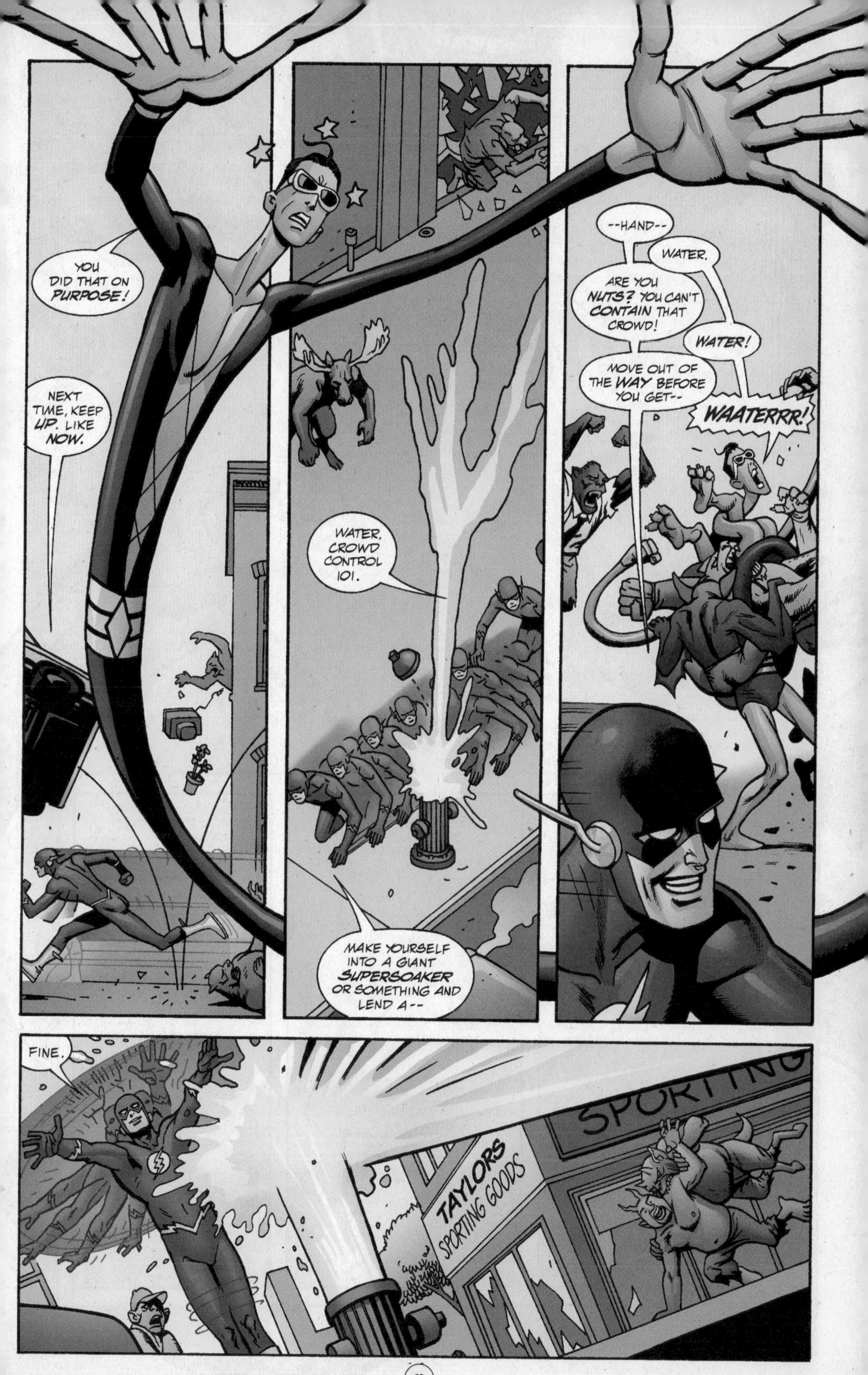

YOU DID THAT ON PURPOSE!
NEXT TIME, KEEP UP. LIKE NOW.
WATER. CROWD CONTROL 101.
MAKE YOURSELF INTO A GIANT SUPERSOAKER OR SOMETHING AND LEND A--
--HAND--
ARE YOU NUTS? YOU CAN'T CONTAIN THAT CROWD!
MOVE OUT OF THE WAY BEFORE YOU GET--
WATER.
WATER!
WAATERRR!
FINE.
SPORTING
TAYLORS SPORTING GOODS

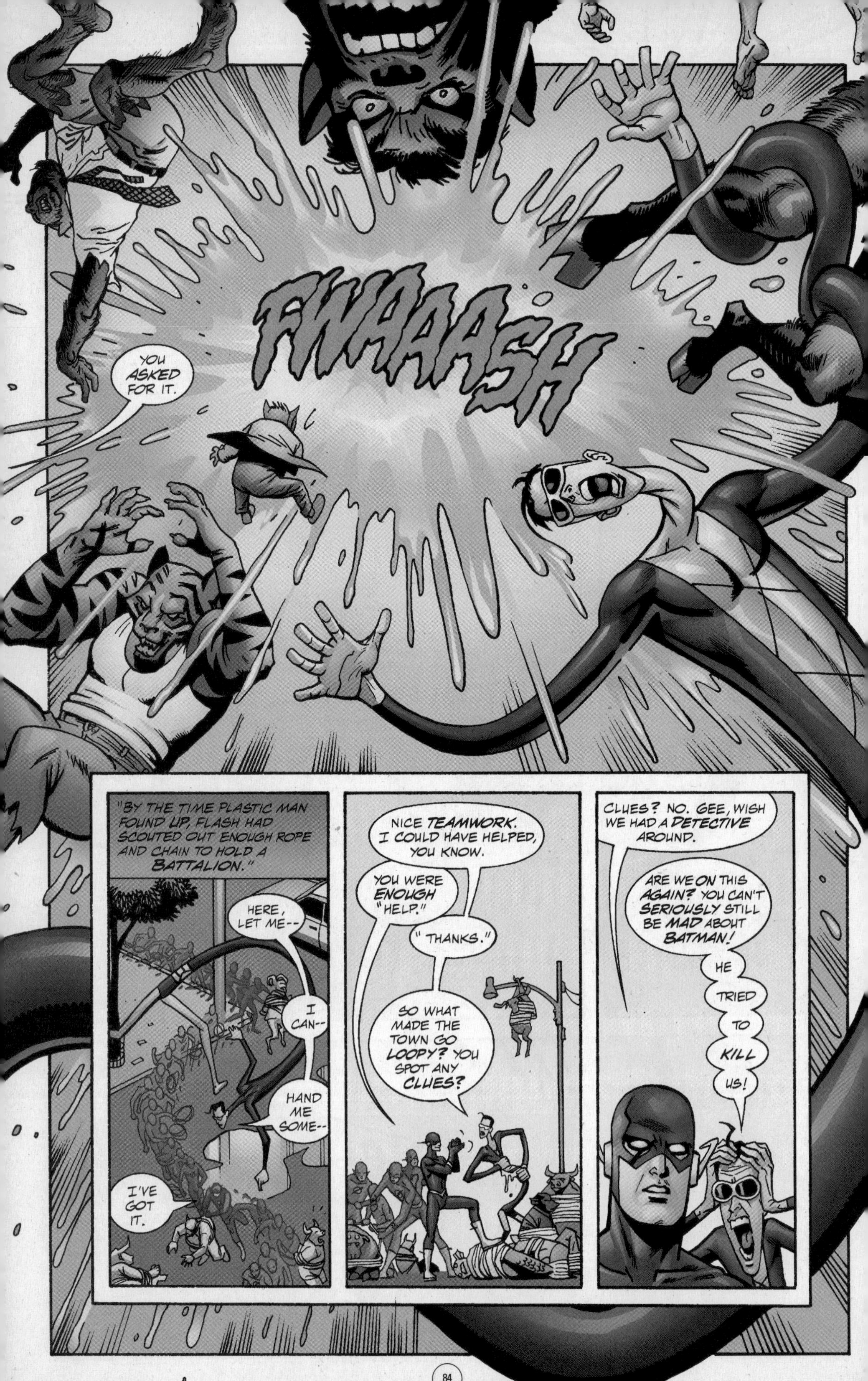
FWAAASH
YOU ASKED FOR IT.
"BY THE TIME PLASTIC MAN FOUND UP, FLASH HAD SCOUTED OUT ENOUGH ROPE AND CHAIN TO HOLD A BATTALION."
HERE, LET ME--
I CAN--
HAND ME SOME--
I'VE GOT IT.
NICE TEAMWORK. I COULD HAVE HELPED, YOU KNOW.
YOU WERE ENOUGH "HELP."
"THANKS."
SO WHAT MADE THE TOWN GO LOOPY? YOU SPOT ANY CLUES?
CLUES? NO. GEE, WISH WE HAD A DETECTIVE AROUND.
ARE WE ON THIS AGAIN? YOU CAN'T SERIOUSLY STILL BE MAD ABOUT BATMAN!
HE TRIED TO KILL US!

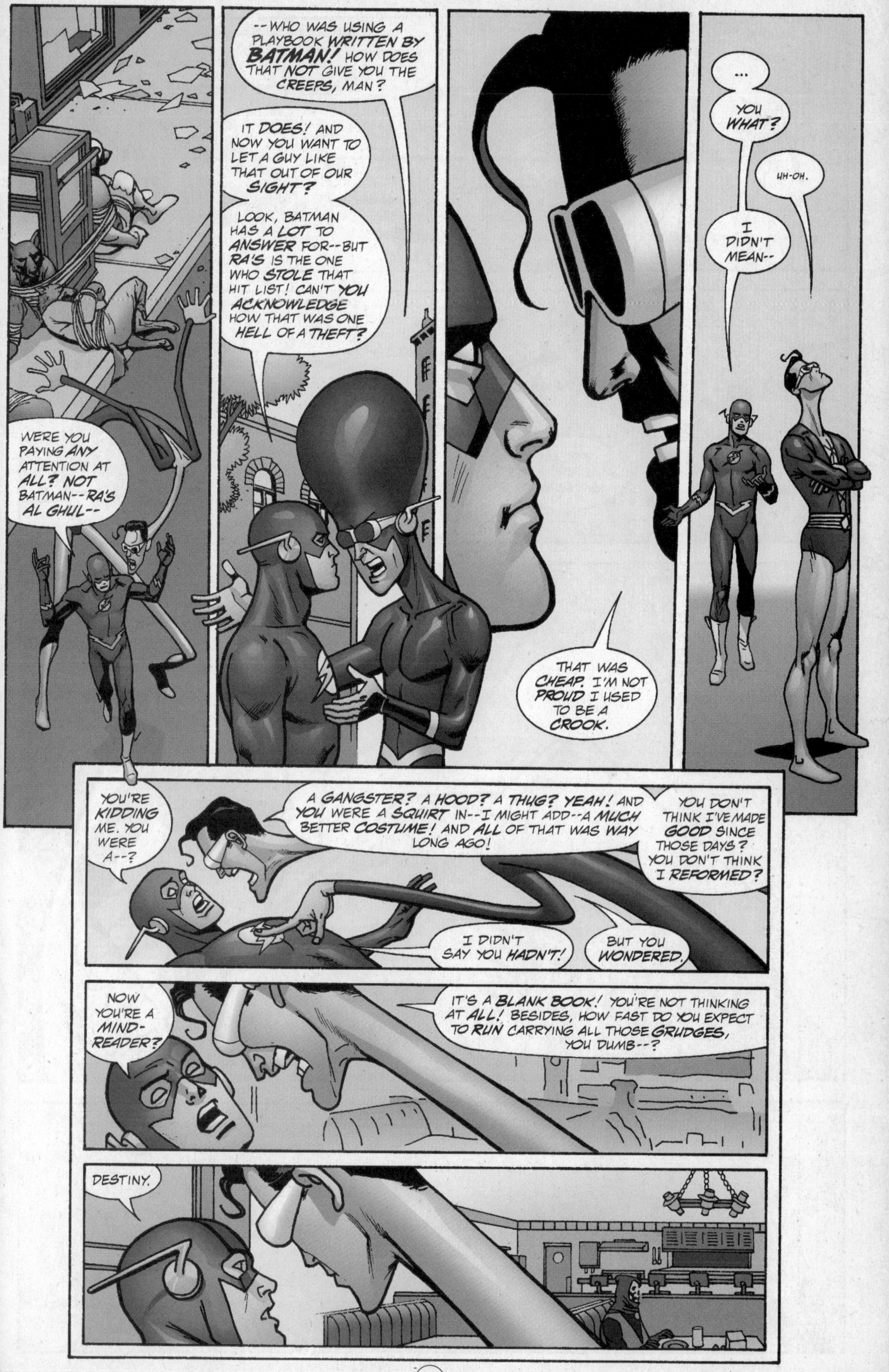

--WHO WAS USING A PLAYBOOK WRITTEN BY BATMAN! HOW DOES THAT NOT GIVE YOU THE CREEPS, MAN?
IT DOES! AND NOW YOU WANT TO LET A GUY LIKE THAT OUT OF OUR SIGHT?
LOOK, BATMAN HAS A LOT TO ANSWER FOR--BUT RA'S IS THE ONE WHO STOLE THAT HIT LIST! CAN'T YOU ACKNOWLEDGE HOW THAT WAS ONE HELL OF A THEFT?
WERE YOU PAYING ANY ATTENTION AT ALL? NOT BATMAN--RA'S AL GHUL--
THAT WAS CHEAP. I'M NOT PROUD I USED TO BE A CROOK.
...
YOU WHAT?
UH-OH.
I DIDN'T MEAN--
YOU'RE KIDDING ME. YOU WERE A--?
A GANGSTER? A HOOD? A THUG? YEAH! AND YOU WERE A SQUIRT IN--I MIGHT ADD--A MUCH BETTER COSTUME! AND ALL OF THAT WAS WAY LONG AGO!
YOU DON'T THINK I'VE MADE GOOD SINCE THOSE DAYS? YOU DON'T THINK I REFORMED?
I DIDN'T SAY YOU HADN'T!
BUT YOU WONDERED.
NOW YOU'RE A MIND-READER?
IT'S A BLANK BOOK! YOU'RE NOT THINKING AT ALL! BESIDES, HOW FAST DO YOU EXPECT TO RUN CARRYING ALL THOSE GRUDGES, YOU DUMB--?
DESTINY.

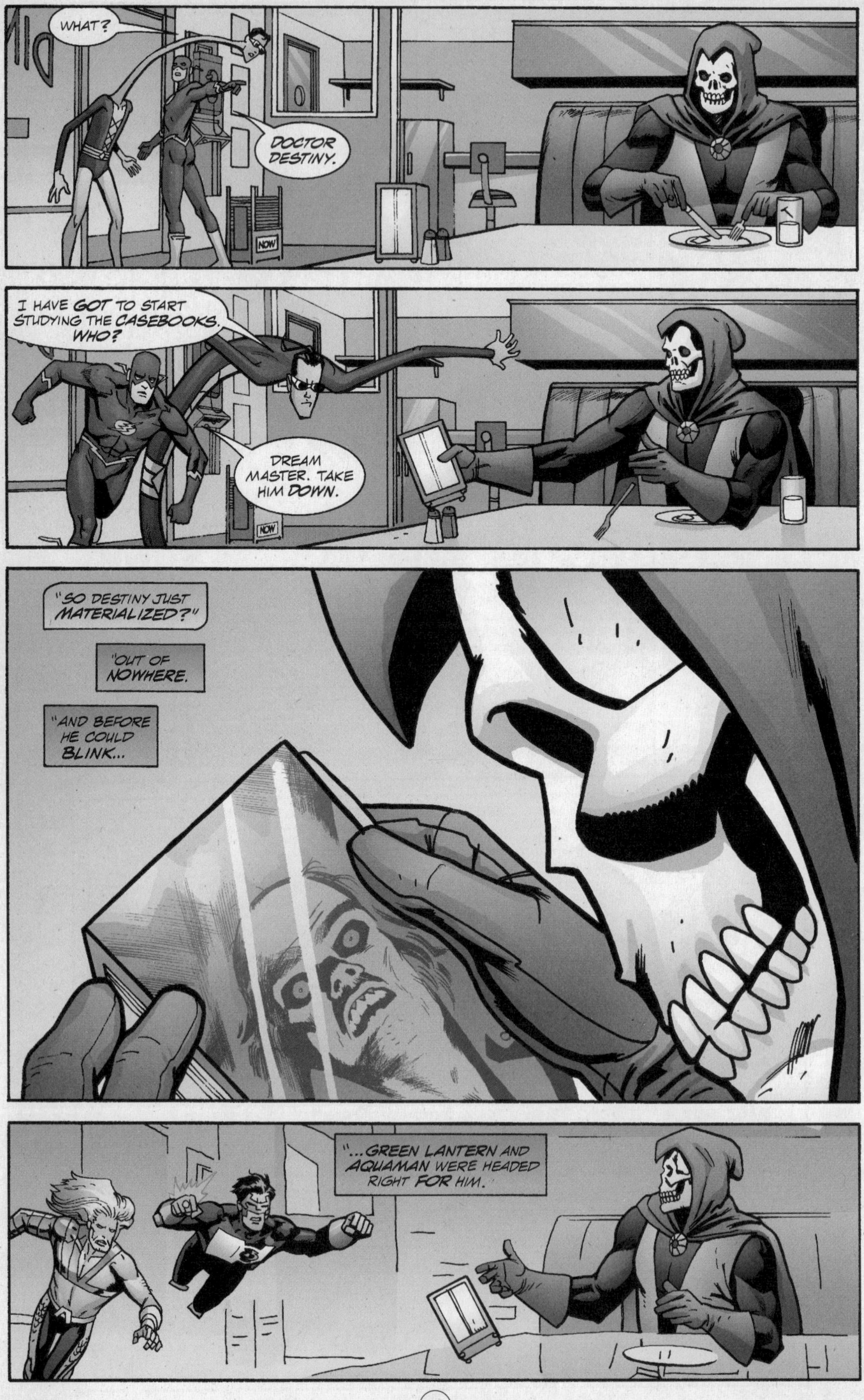
WHAT?
DOCTOR DESTINY.
NOW
I HAVE GOT TO START STUDYING THE CASEBOOKS. WHO?
DREAM MASTER. TAKE HIM DOWN.
NOW
"SO DESTINY JUST MATERIALIZED?"
"OUT OF NOWHERE.
"AND BEFORE HE COULD BLINK...
"...GREEN LANTERN AND AQUAMAN WERE HEADED RIGHT FOR HIM.

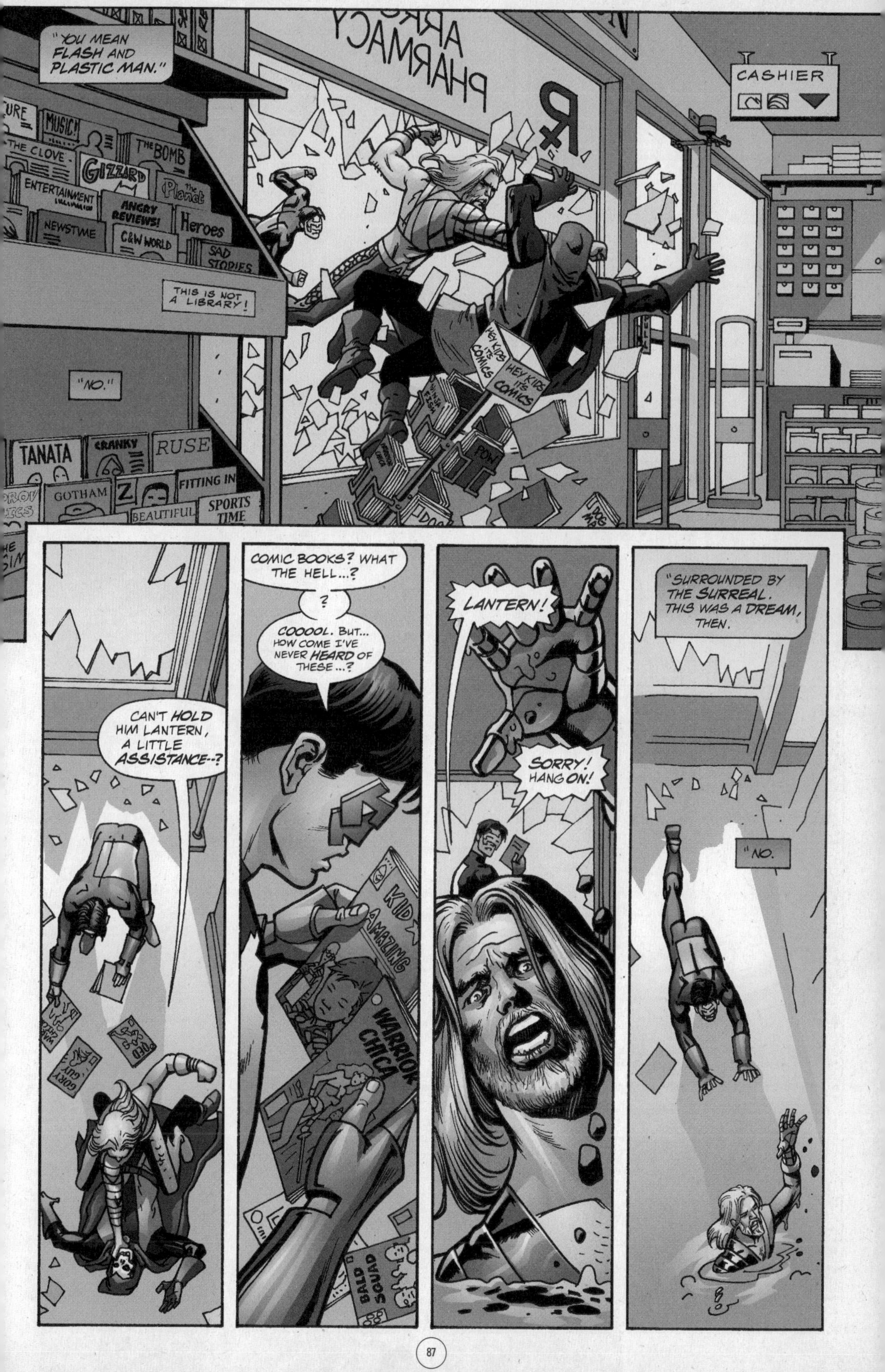
"YOU MEAN FLASH AND PLASTIC MAN."
"NO."
CAN'T HOLD HIM LANTERN, A LITTLE ASSISTANCE--?
COMIC BOOKS? WHAT THE HELL...?
?
COOOOL. BUT... HOW COME I'VE NEVER HEARD OF THESE...?
LANTERN!
SORRY! HANG ON!
"SURROUNDED BY THE SURREAL. THIS WAS A DREAM, THEN.
"NO.

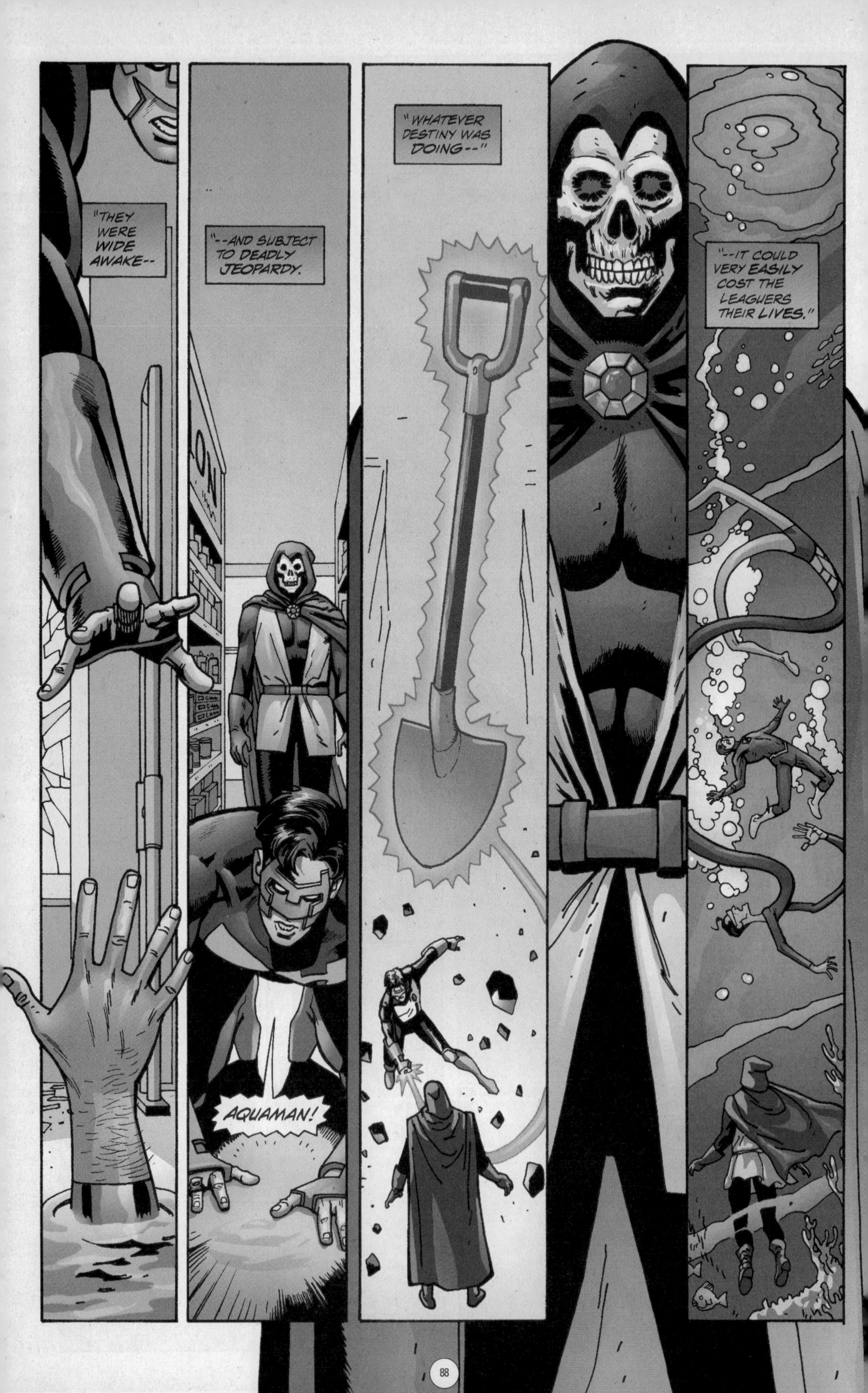
"THEY WERE WIDE AWAKE--
"--AND SUBJECT TO DEADLY JEOPARDY.
AQUAMAN!
"WHATEVER DESTINY WAS DOING--"
"--IT COULD VERY EASILY COST THE LEAGUERS THEIR LIVES."

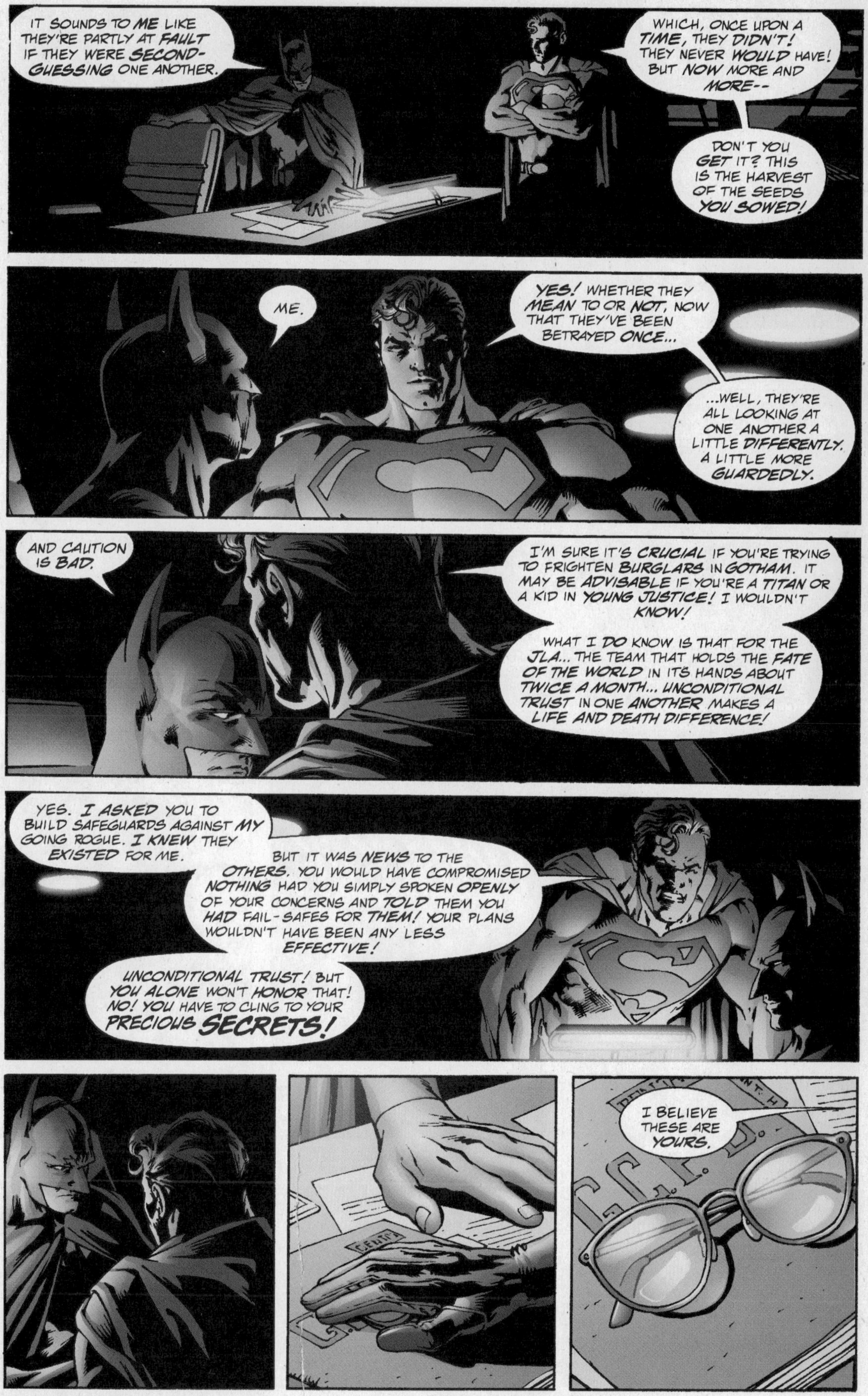
IT SOUNDS TO ME LIKE THEY'RE PARTLY AT FAULT IF THEY WERE SECOND-GUESSING ONE ANOTHER.
WHICH, ONCE UPON A TIME, THEY DIDN'T! THEY NEVER WOULD HAVE! BUT NOW MORE AND MORE--
DON'T YOU GET IT? THIS IS THE HARVEST OF THE SEEDS YOU SOWED!
ME.
YES! WHETHER THEY MEAN TO OR NOT, NOW THAT THEY'VE BEEN BETRAYED ONCE...
...WELL, THEY'RE ALL LOOKING AT ONE ANOTHER A LITTLE DIFFERENTLY. A LITTLE MORE GUARDEDLY.
AND CAUTION IS BAD.
I'M SURE IT'S CRUCIAL IF YOU'RE TRYING TO FRIGHTEN BURGLARS IN GOTHAM. IT MAY BE ADVISABLE IF YOU'RE A TITAN OR A KID IN YOUNG JUSTICE! I WOULDN'T KNOW!
WHAT I DO KNOW IS THAT FOR THE JLA... THE TEAM THAT HOLDS THE FATE OF THE WORLD IN ITS HANDS ABOUT TWICE A MONTH... UNCONDITIONAL TRUST IN ONE ANOTHER MAKES A LIFE AND DEATH DIFFERENCE!
YES. I ASKED YOU TO BUILD SAFEGUARDS AGAINST MY GOING ROGUE. I KNEW THEY EXISTED FOR ME.
BUT IT WAS NEWS TO THE OTHERS. YOU WOULD HAVE COMPROMISED NOTHING HAD YOU SIMPLY SPOKEN OPENLY OF YOUR CONCERNS AND TOLD THEM YOU HAD FAIL-SAFES FOR THEM! YOUR PLANS WOULDN'T HAVE BEEN ANY LESS EFFECTIVE!
UNCONDITIONAL TRUST! BUT YOU ALONE WON'T HONOR THAT! NO! YOU HAVE TO CLING TO YOUR PRECIOUS SECRETS!
I BELIEVE THESE ARE YOURS.

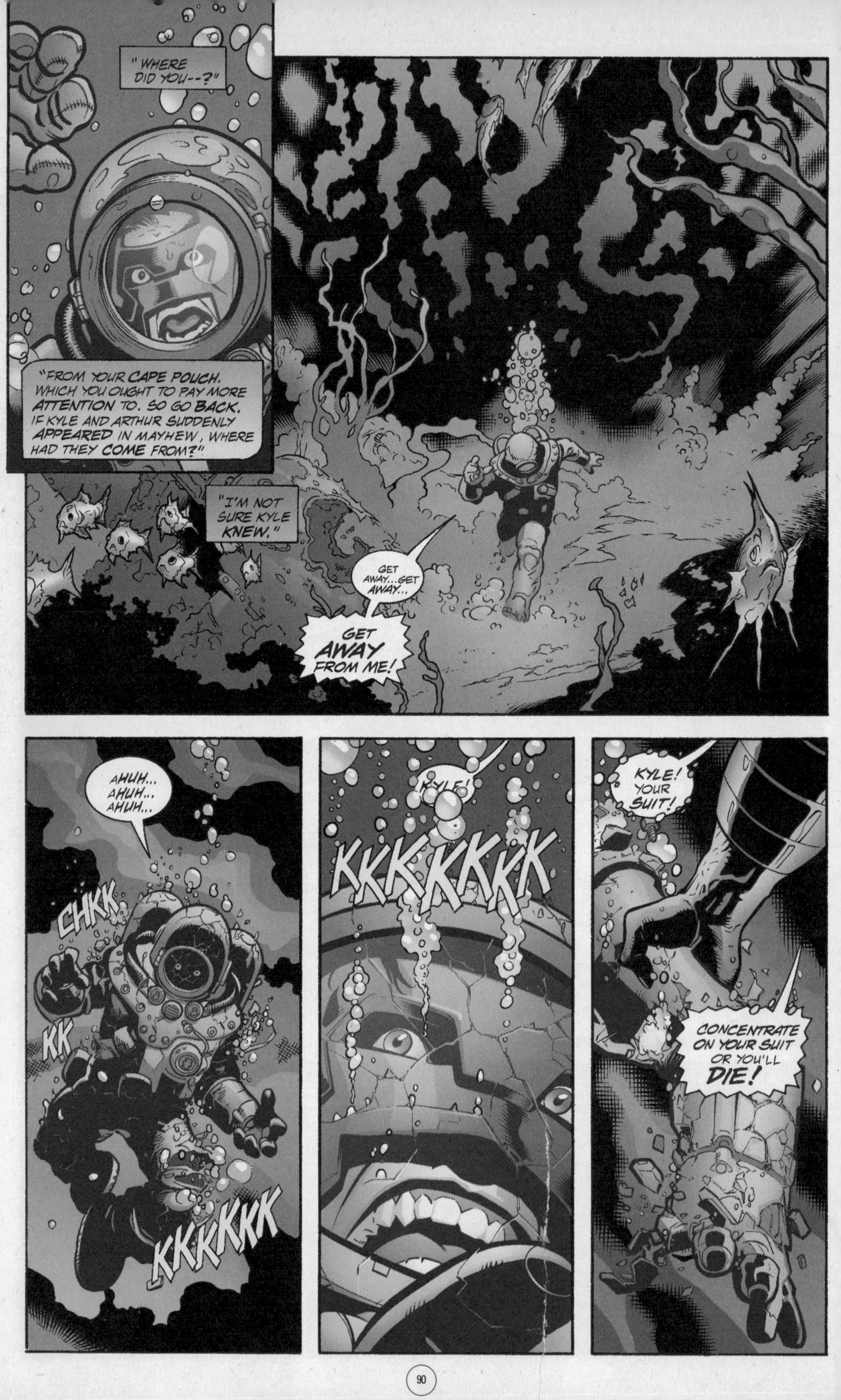
"WHERE DID YOU--?"
"FROM YOUR CAPE POUCH. WHICH YOU OUGHT TO PAY MORE ATTENTION TO. SO GO BACK. IF KYLE AND ARTHUR SUDDENLY APPEARED IN MAYHEW, WHERE HAD THEY COME FROM?"
"I'M NOT SURE KYLE KNEW."
GET AWAY...GET AWAY...
GET AWAY FROM ME!
AHUH... AHUH... AHUH...
CHKK
KK
KKKKKK
KYLE!
KKKKKKK
KYLE! YOUR SUIT!
CONCENTRATE ON YOUR SUIT OR YOU'LL DIE!

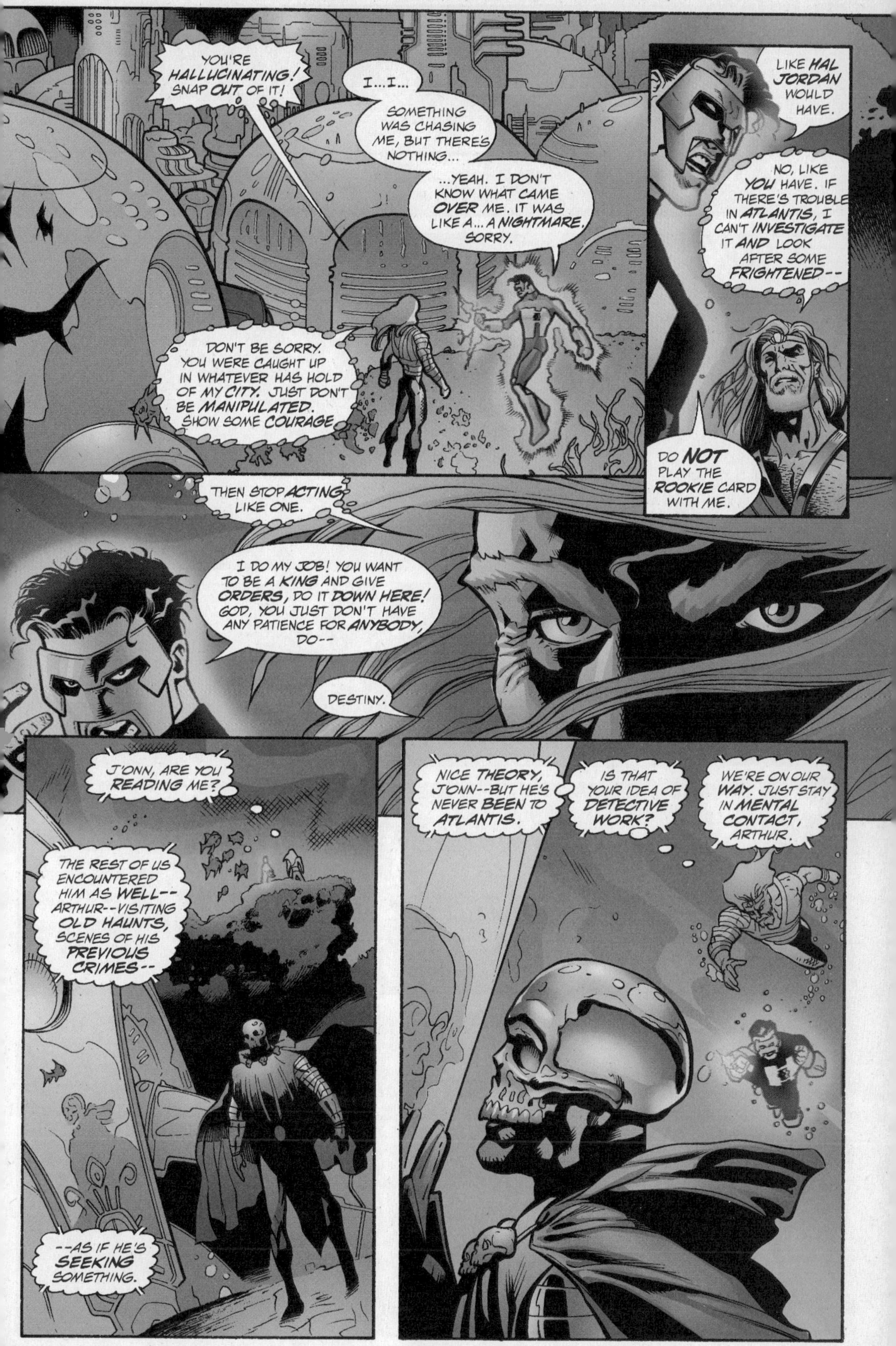
YOU'RE HALLUCINATING! SNAP OUT OF IT!
I...I...
SOMETHING WAS CHASING ME, BUT THERE'S NOTHING...
...YEAH. I DON'T KNOW WHAT CAME OVER ME. IT WAS LIKE A... A NIGHTMARE. SORRY.
DON'T BE SORRY. YOU WERE CAUGHT UP IN WHATEVER HAS HOLD OF MY CITY. JUST DON'T BE MANIPULATED. SHOW SOME COURAGE.
LIKE HAL JORDAN WOULD HAVE.
NO, LIKE YOU HAVE. IF THERE'S TROUBLE IN ATLANTIS, I CAN'T INVESTIGATE IT AND LOOK AFTER SOME FRIGHTENED--
DO NOT PLAY THE ROOKIE CARD WITH ME.
THEN STOP ACTING LIKE ONE.
I DO MY JOB! YOU WANT TO BE A KING AND GIVE ORDERS, DO IT DOWN HERE! GOD, YOU JUST DON'T HAVE ANY PATIENCE FOR ANYBODY, DO--
DESTINY.
J'ONN, ARE YOU READING ME?
THE REST OF US ENCOUNTERED HIM AS WELL--ARTHUR--VISITING OLD HAUNTS, SCENES OF HIS PREVIOUS CRIMES--
--AS IF HE'S SEEKING SOMETHING.
NICE THEORY, J'ONN--BUT HE'S NEVER BEEN TO ATLANTIS.
IS THAT YOUR IDEA OF DETECTIVE WORK?
WE'RE ON OUR WAY. JUST STAY IN MENTAL CONTACT, ARTHUR.

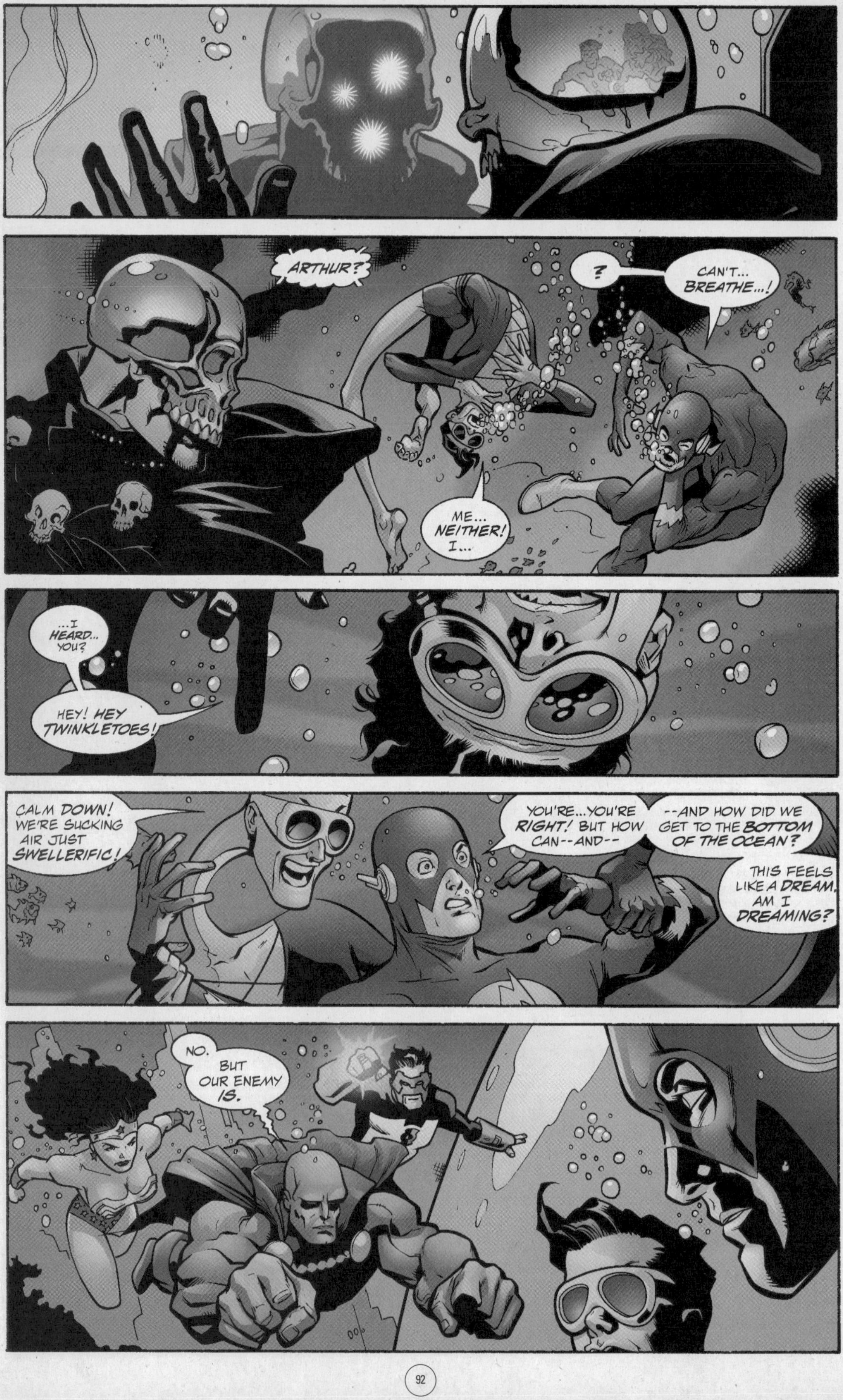
ARTHUR?
?
CAN'T... BREATHE...!
ME... NEITHER! I...
...I HEARD... YOU?
HEY! HEY TWINKLETOES!
CALM DOWN! WE'RE SUCKING AIR JUST SWELLERIFIC!
YOU'RE... YOU'RE RIGHT! BUT HOW CAN--AND--
--AND HOW DID WE GET TO THE BOTTOM OF THE OCEAN?
THIS FEELS LIKE A DREAM. AM I DREAMING?
NO.
BUT OUR ENEMY IS.

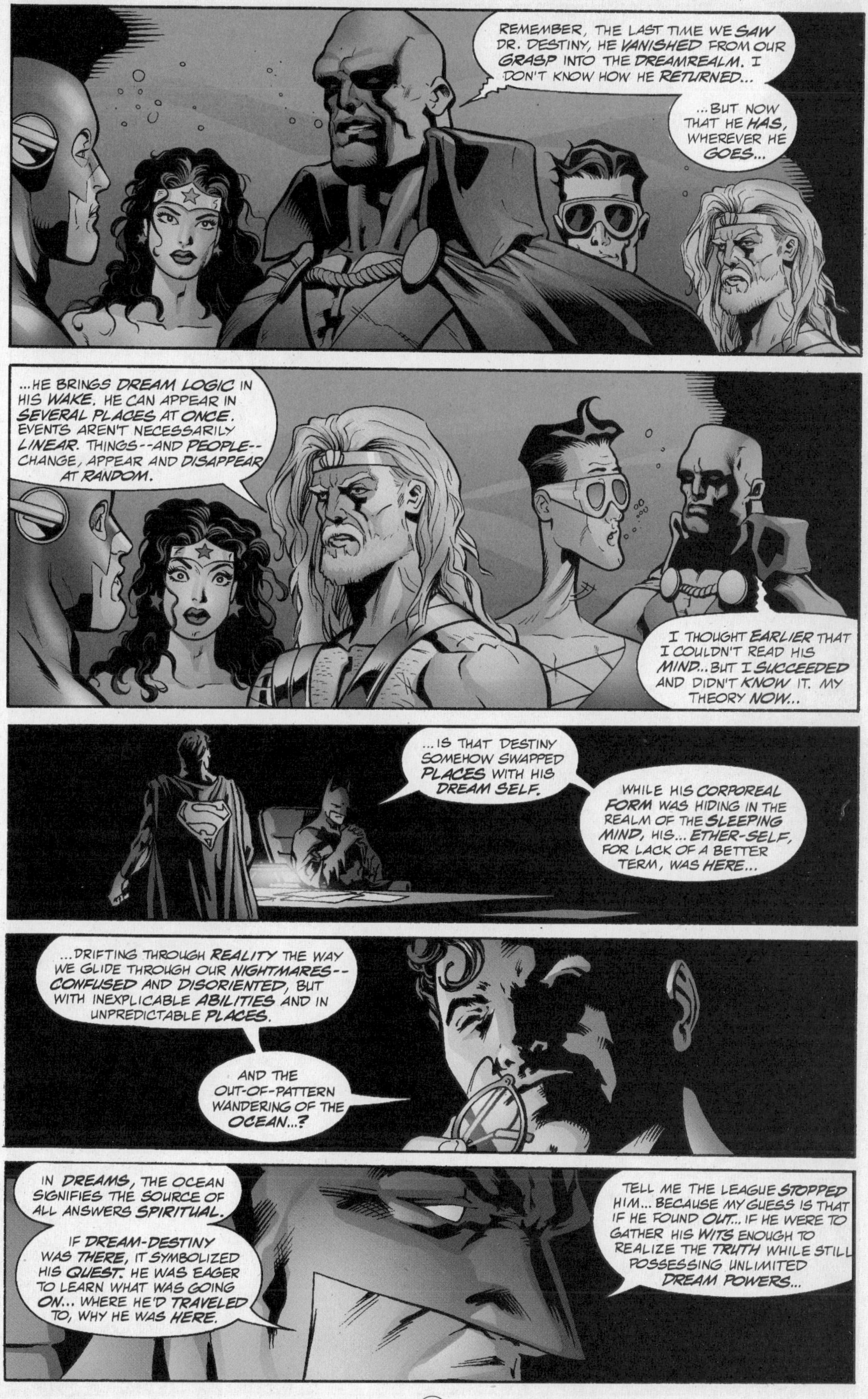
REMEMBER, THE LAST TIME WE SAW DR. DESTINY, HE VANISHED FROM OUR GRASP INTO THE DREAMREALM. I DON'T KNOW HOW HE RETURNED...
...BUT NOW THAT HE HAS, WHEREVER HE GOES...
...HE BRINGS DREAM LOGIC IN HIS WAKE. HE CAN APPEAR IN SEVERAL PLACES AT ONCE. EVENTS AREN'T NECESSARILY LINEAR. THINGS--AND PEOPLE--CHANGE, APPEAR AND DISAPPEAR AT RANDOM.
I THOUGHT EARLIER THAT I COULDN'T READ HIS MIND...BUT I SUCCEEDED AND DIDN'T KNOW IT. MY THEORY NOW...
...IS THAT DESTINY SOMEHOW SWAPPED PLACES WITH HIS DREAM SELF.
WHILE HIS CORPOREAL FORM WAS HIDING IN THE REALM OF THE SLEEPING MIND, HIS... ETHER-SELF, FOR LACK OF A BETTER TERM, WAS HERE...
...DRIFTING THROUGH REALITY THE WAY WE GLIDE THROUGH OUR NIGHTMARES--CONFUSED AND DISORIENTED, BUT WITH INEXPLICABLE ABILITIES AND IN UNPREDICTABLE PLACES.
AND THE OUT-OF-PATTERN WANDERING OF THE OCEAN...?
IN DREAMS, THE OCEAN SIGNIFIES THE SOURCE OF ALL ANSWERS SPIRITUAL.
IF DREAM-DESTINY WAS THERE, IT SYMBOLIZED HIS QUEST. HE WAS EAGER TO LEARN WHAT WAS GOING ON... WHERE HE'D TRAVELED TO, WHY HE WAS HERE.
TELL ME THE LEAGUE STOPPED HIM... BECAUSE MY GUESS IS THAT IF HE FOUND OUT... IF HE WERE TO GATHER HIS WITS ENOUGH TO REALIZE THE TRUTH WHILE STILL POSSESSING UNLIMITED DREAM POWERS...

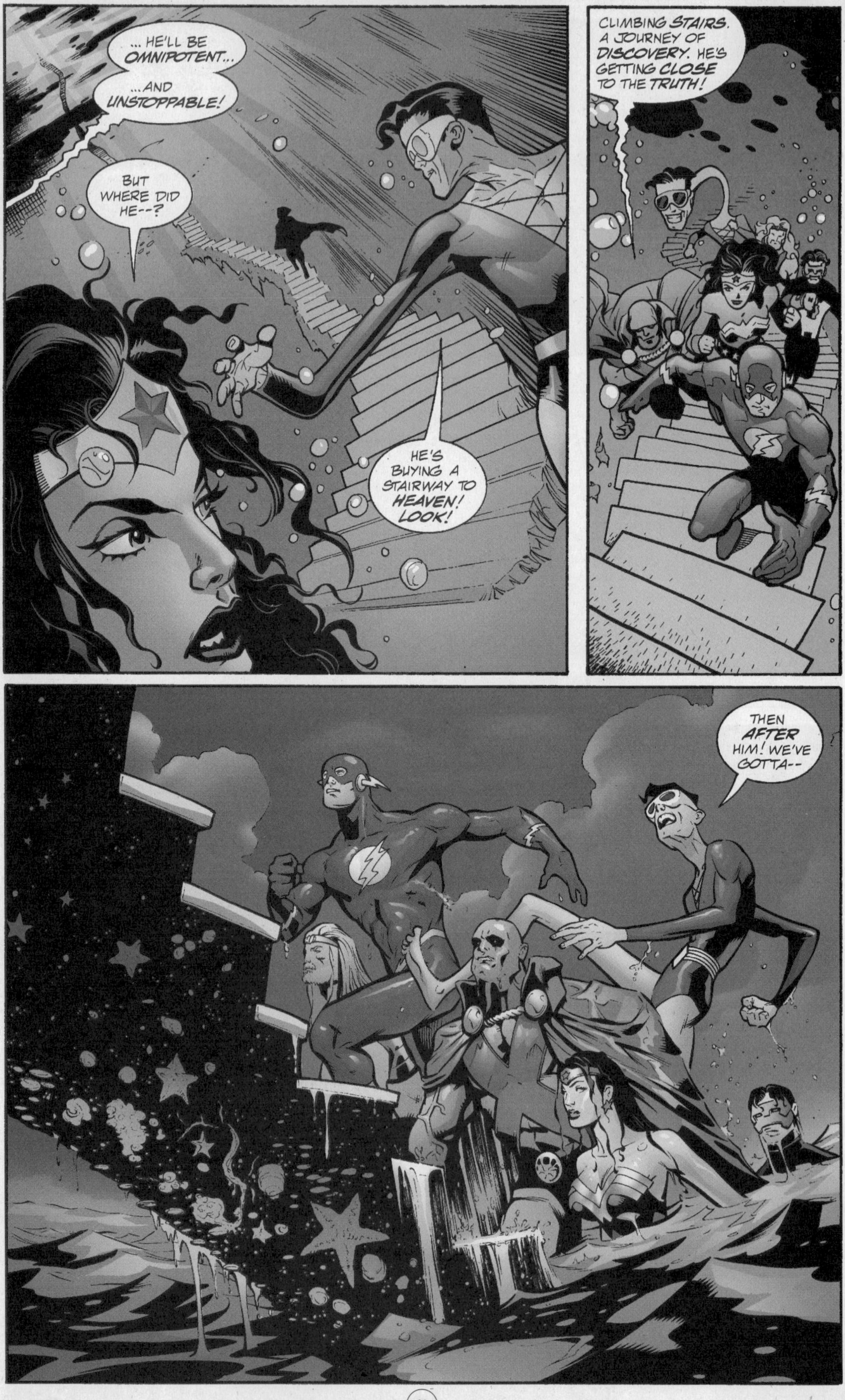
... HE'LL BE OMNIPOTENT...
...AND UNSTOPPABLE!
BUT WHERE DID HE--?
HE'S BUYING A STAIRWAY TO HEAVEN! LOOK!
CLIMBING STAIRS. A JOURNEY OF DISCOVERY. HE'S GETTING CLOSE TO THE TRUTH!
THEN AFTER HIM! WE'VE GOTTA--

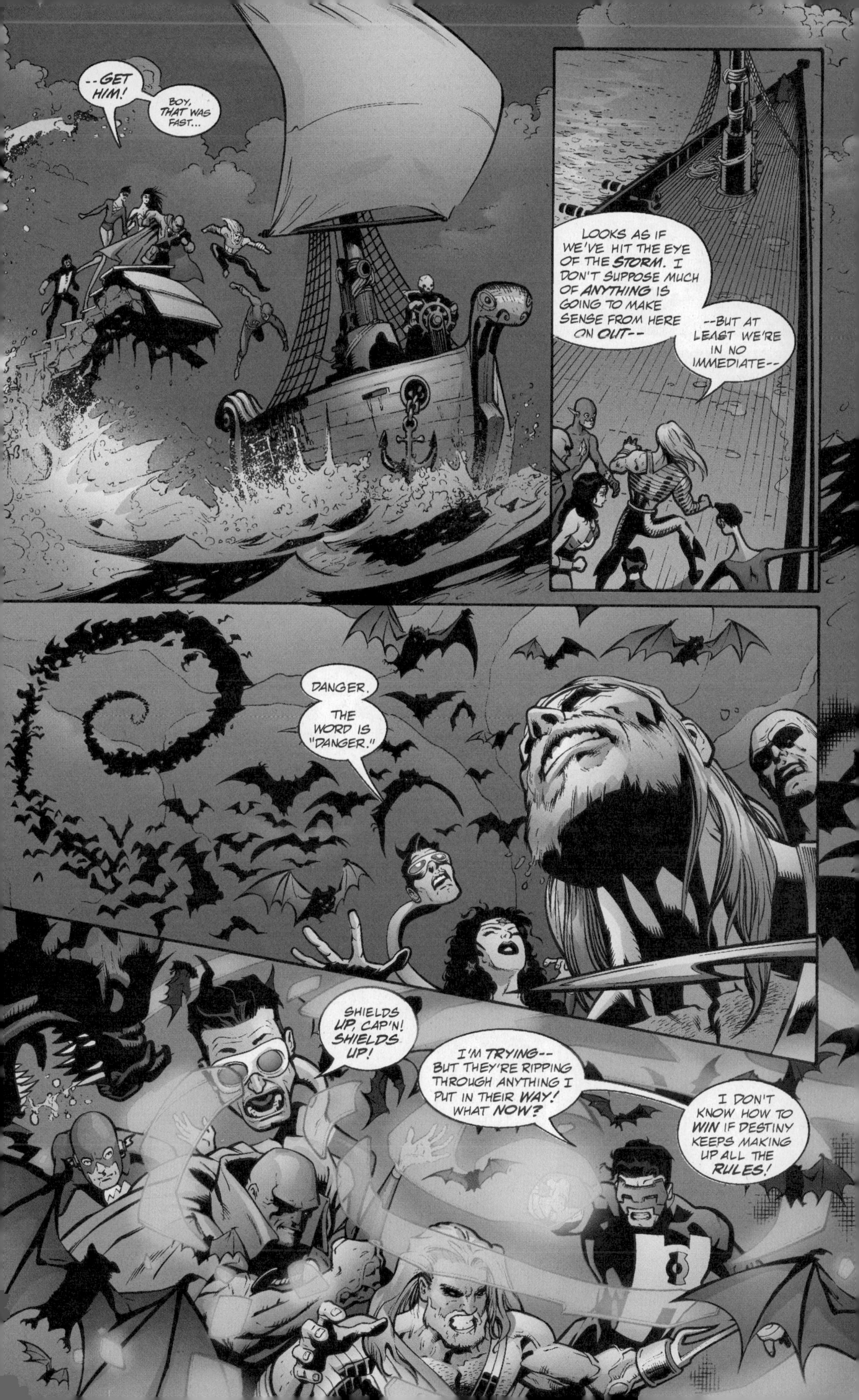
--GET HIM!
BOY, THAT WAS FAST...
LOOKS AS IF WE'VE HIT THE EYE OF THE STORM. I DON'T SUPPOSE MUCH OF ANYTHING IS GOING TO MAKE SENSE FROM HERE ON OUT--
--BUT AT LEAST WE'RE IN NO IMMEDIATE--
DANGER.
THE WORD IS "DANGER."
SHIELDS UP, CAP'N! SHIELDS UP!
I'M TRYING-- BUT THEY'RE RIPPING THROUGH ANYTHING I PUT IN THEIR WAY! WHAT NOW?
I DON'T KNOW HOW TO WIN IF DESTINY KEEPS MAKING UP ALL THE RULES!

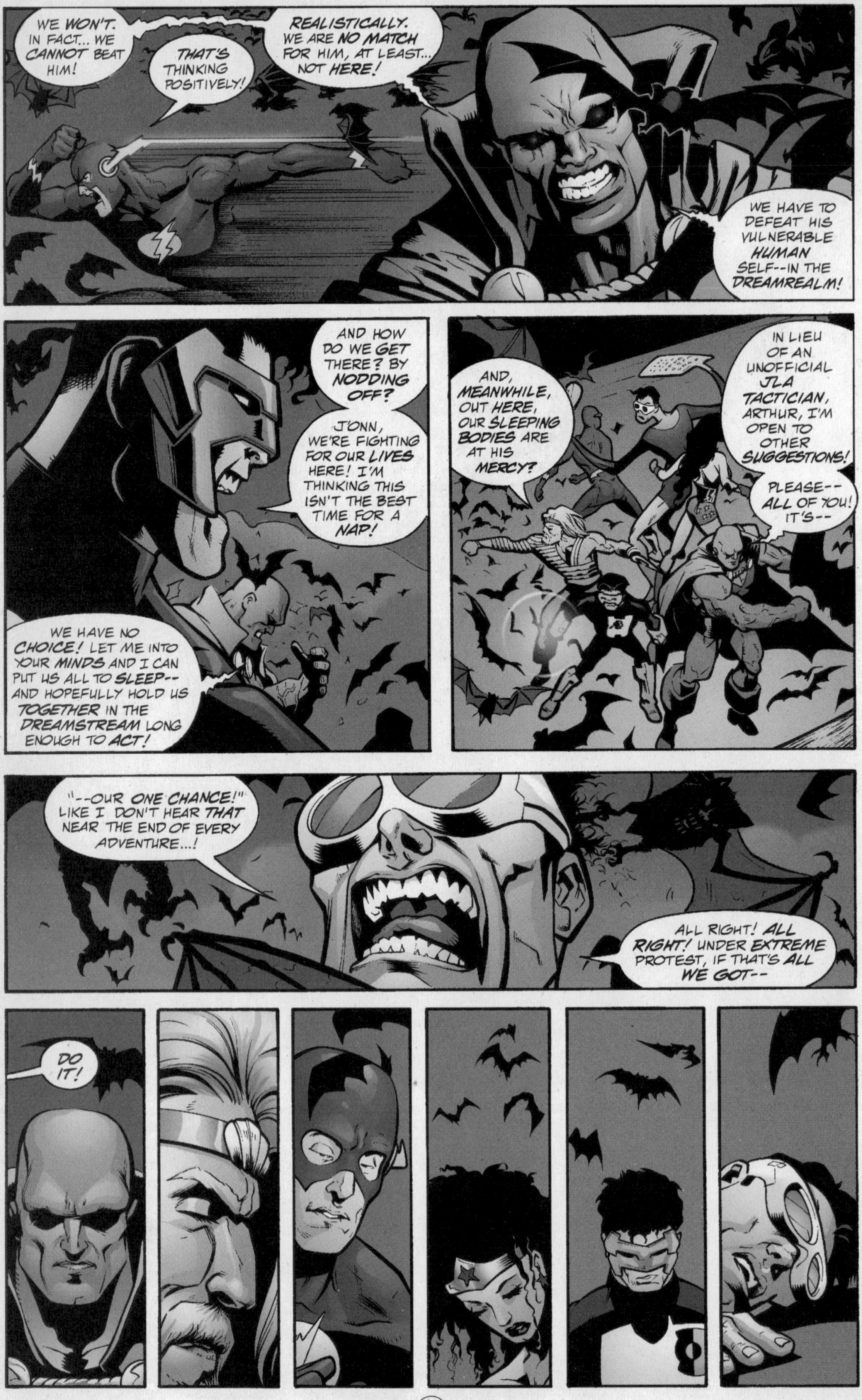
WE WON'T. IN FACT... WE CANNOT BEAT HIM!
THAT'S THINKING POSITIVELY!
REALISTICALLY. WE ARE NO MATCH FOR HIM, AT LEAST... NOT HERE!
WE HAVE TO DEFEAT HIS VULNERABLE HUMAN SELF--IN THE DREAMREALM!
AND HOW DO WE GET THERE? BY NODDING OFF?
J'ONN, WE'RE FIGHTING FOR OUR LIVES HERE! I'M THINKING THIS ISN'T THE BEST TIME FOR A NAP!
WE HAVE NO CHOICE! LET ME INTO YOUR MINDS AND I CAN PUT US ALL TO SLEEP-- AND HOPEFULLY HOLD US TOGETHER IN THE DREAMSTREAM LONG ENOUGH TO ACT!
AND, MEANWHILE, OUT HERE, OUR SLEEPING BODIES ARE AT HIS MERCY?
IN LIEU OF AN UNOFFICIAL JLA TACTICIAN, ARTHUR, I'M OPEN TO OTHER SUGGESTIONS!
PLEASE-- ALL OF YOU! IT'S--
"--OUR ONE CHANCE!" LIKE I DON'T HEAR THAT NEAR THE END OF EVERY ADVENTURE...!
ALL RIGHT! ALL RIGHT! UNDER EXTREME PROTEST, IF THAT'S ALL WE GOT--
DO IT!

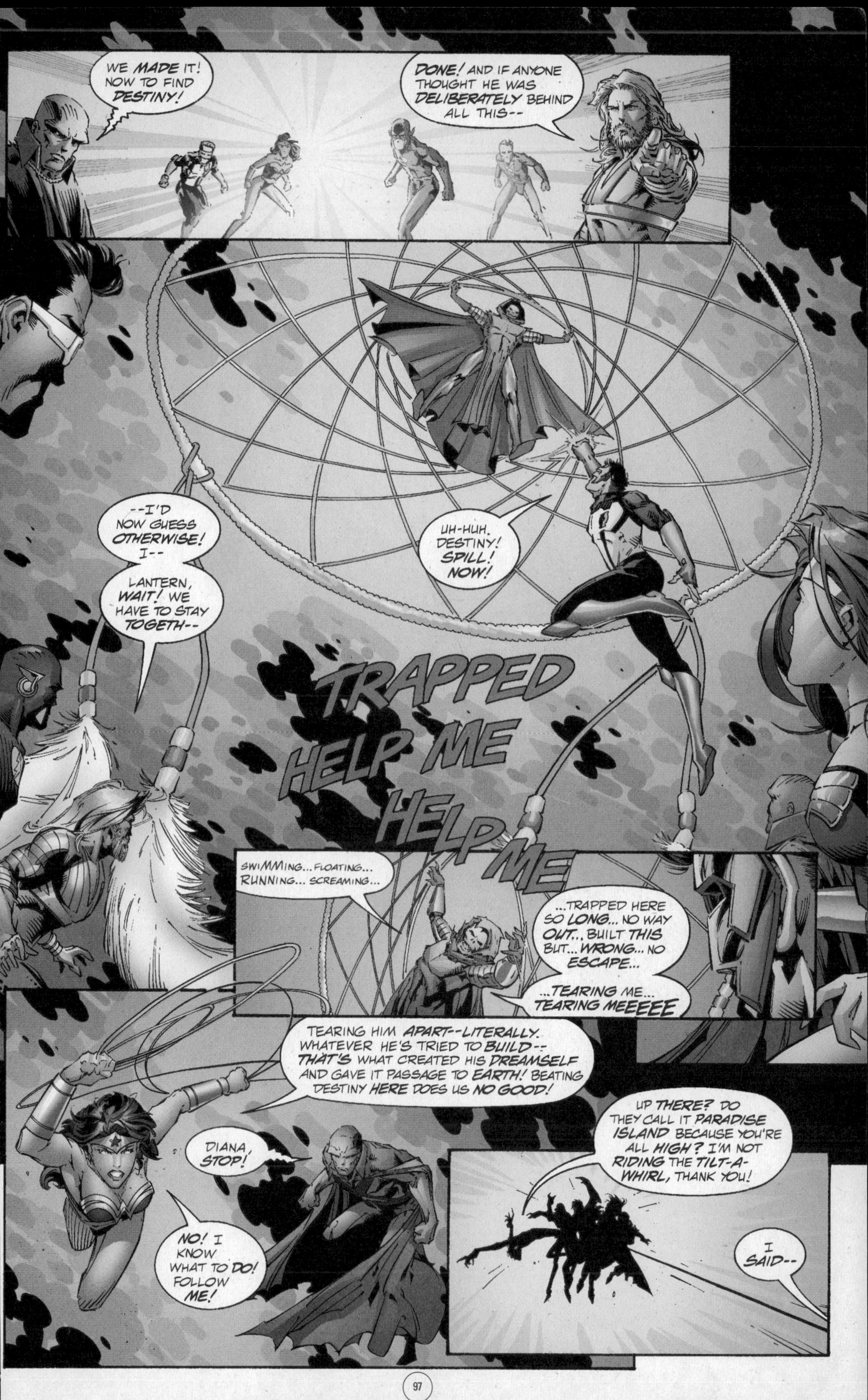

WE MADE IT! NOW TO FIND DESTINY!
DONE! AND IF ANYONE THOUGHT HE WAS DELIBERATELY BEHIND ALL THIS--
--I'D NOW GUESS OTHERWISE! I--
LANTERN, WAIT! WE HAVE TO STAY TOGETH--
UH-HUH. DESTINY! SPILL! NOW!
TRAPPED
HELP ME
HELP ME
SWIMMING... FLOATING... RUNNING... SCREAMING...
...TRAPPED HERE SO LONG... NO WAY OUT... BUILT THIS BUT... WRONG... NO ESCAPE...
...TEARING ME... TEARING MEEEEE
TEARING HIM APART--LITERALLY. WHATEVER HE'S TRIED TO BUILD-- THAT'S WHAT CREATED HIS DREAMSELF AND GAVE IT PASSAGE TO EARTH! BEATING DESTINY HERE DOES US NO GOOD!
DIANA, STOP!
NO! I KNOW WHAT TO DO! FOLLOW ME!
UP THERE? DO THEY CALL IT PARADISE ISLAND BECAUSE YOU'RE ALL HIGH? I'M NOT RIDING THE TILT-A-WHIRL, THANK YOU!
I SAID--

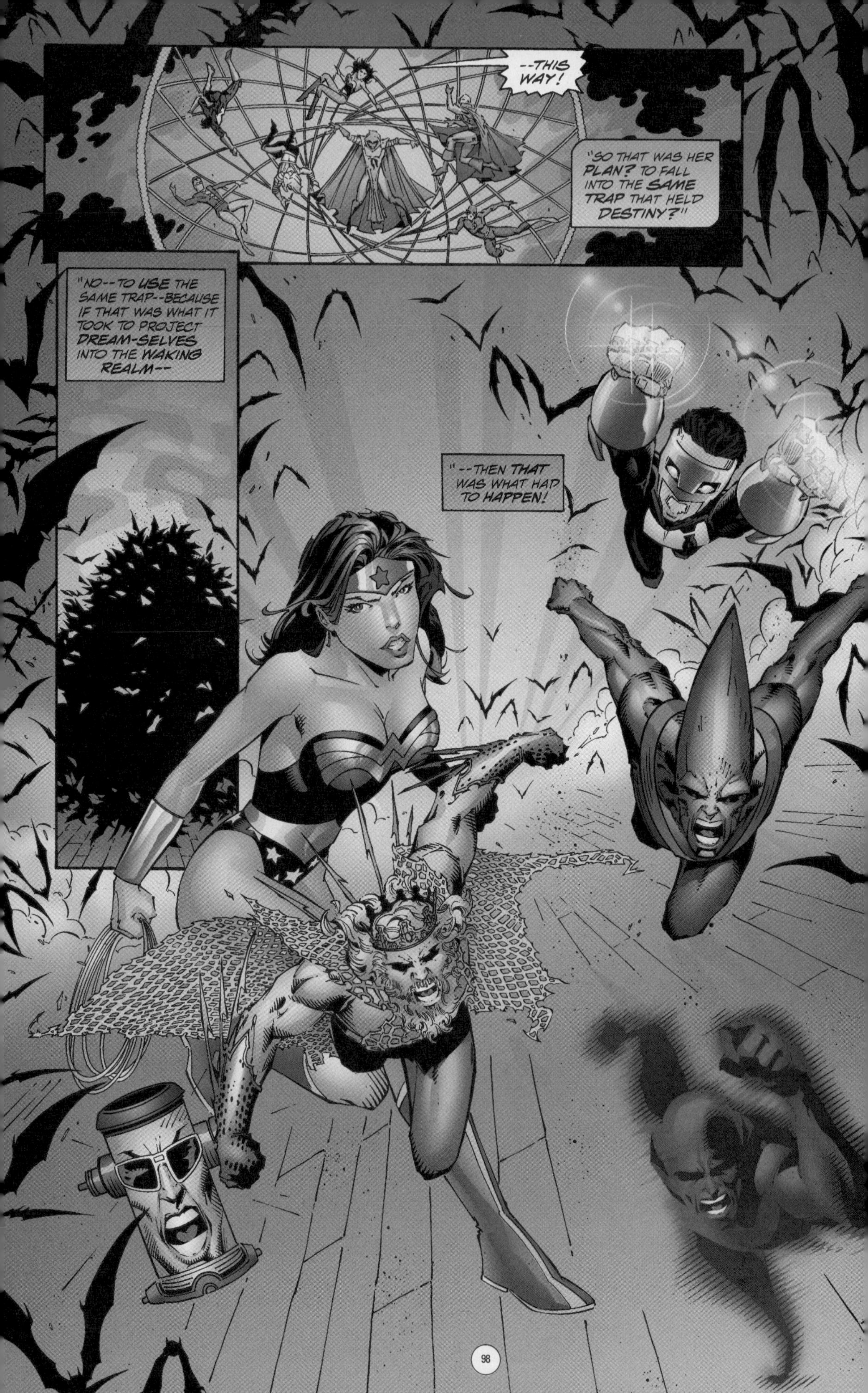
--THIS WAY!
"SO THAT WAS HER PLAN? TO FALL INTO THE SAME TRAP THAT HELD DESTINY?"
"NO--TO USE THE SAME TRAP--BECAUSE IF THAT WAS WHAT IT TOOK TO PROJECT DREAM-SELVES INTO THE WAKING REALM--
"--THEN THAT WAS WHAT HAD TO HAPPEN!

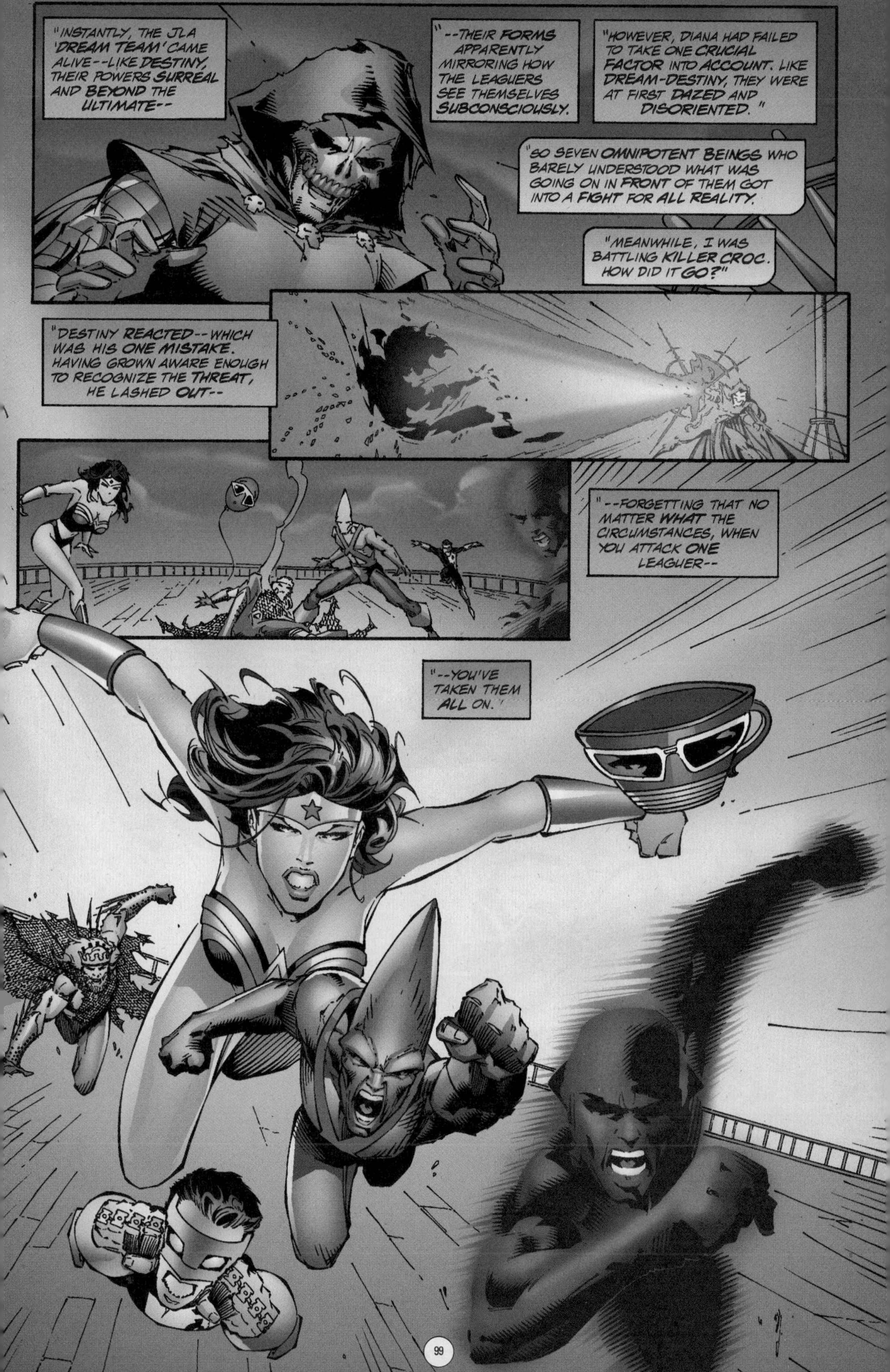
"INSTANTLY, THE JLA 'DREAM TEAM' CAME ALIVE--LIKE DESTINY, THEIR POWERS SURREAL AND BEYOND THE ULTIMATE--
--THEIR FORMS APPARENTLY MIRRORING HOW THE LEAGUERS SEE THEMSELVES SUBCONSCIOUSLY.
"HOWEVER, DIANA HAD FAILED TO TAKE ONE CRUCIAL FACTOR INTO ACCOUNT. LIKE DREAM-DESTINY, THEY WERE AT FIRST DAZED AND DISORIENTED."
"SO SEVEN OMNIPOTENT BEINGS WHO BARELY UNDERSTOOD WHAT WAS GOING ON IN FRONT OF THEM GOT INTO A FIGHT FOR ALL REALITY.
"MEANWHILE, I WAS BATTLING KILLER CROC. HOW DID IT GO?"
"DESTINY REACTED--WHICH WAS HIS ONE MISTAKE. HAVING GROWN AWARE ENOUGH TO RECOGNIZE THE THREAT, HE LASHED OUT--
"--FORGETTING THAT NO MATTER WHAT THE CIRCUMSTANCES, WHEN YOU ATTACK ONE LEAGUER--
"--YOU'VE TAKEN THEM ALL ON."

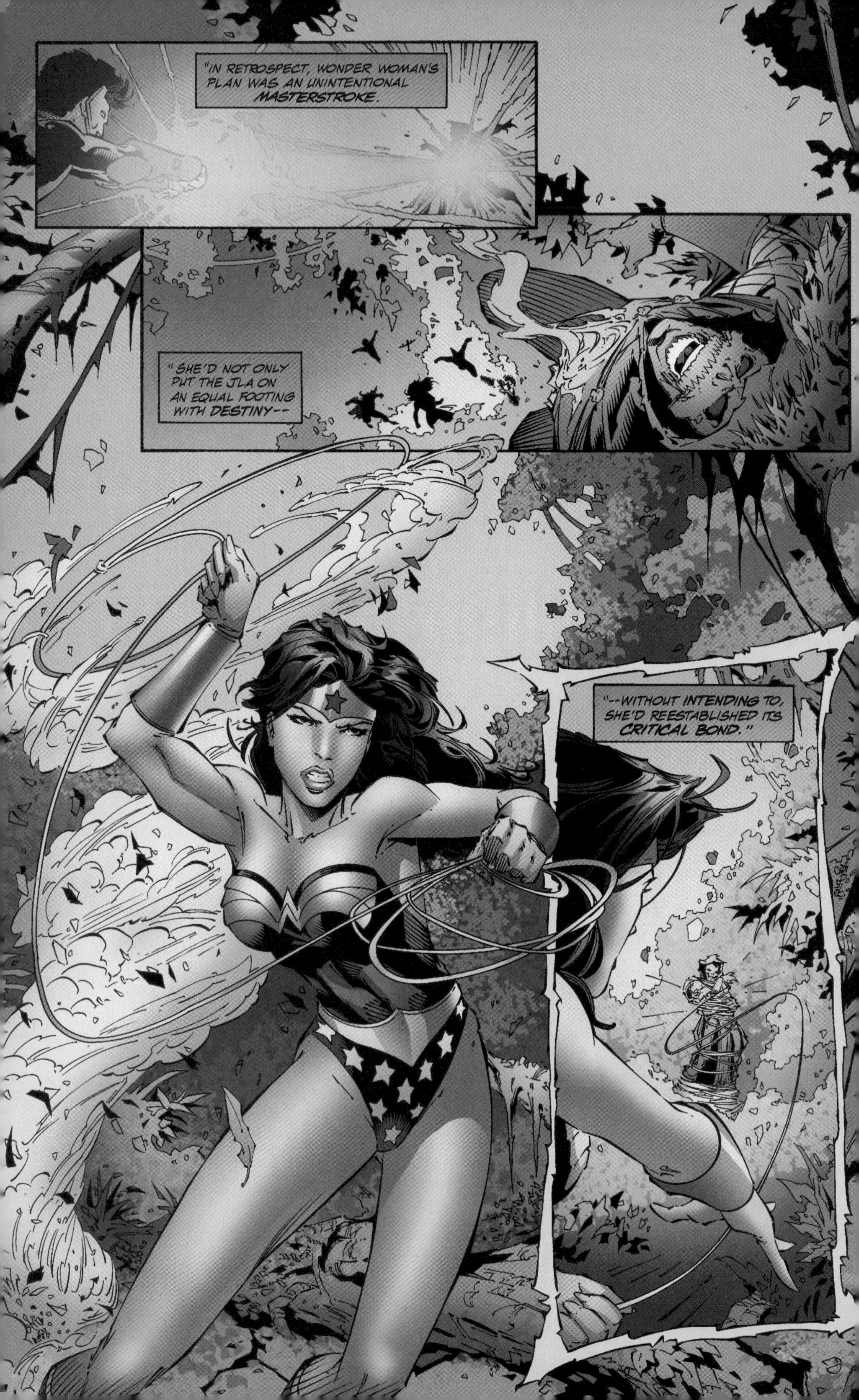
"IN RETROSPECT, WONDER WOMAN'S PLAN WAS AN UNINTENTIONAL MASTERSTROKE.
"SHE'D NOT ONLY PUT THE JLA ON AN EQUAL FOOTING WITH DESTINY--
"--WITHOUT INTENDING TO, SHE'D REESTABLISHED ITS CRITICAL BOND."

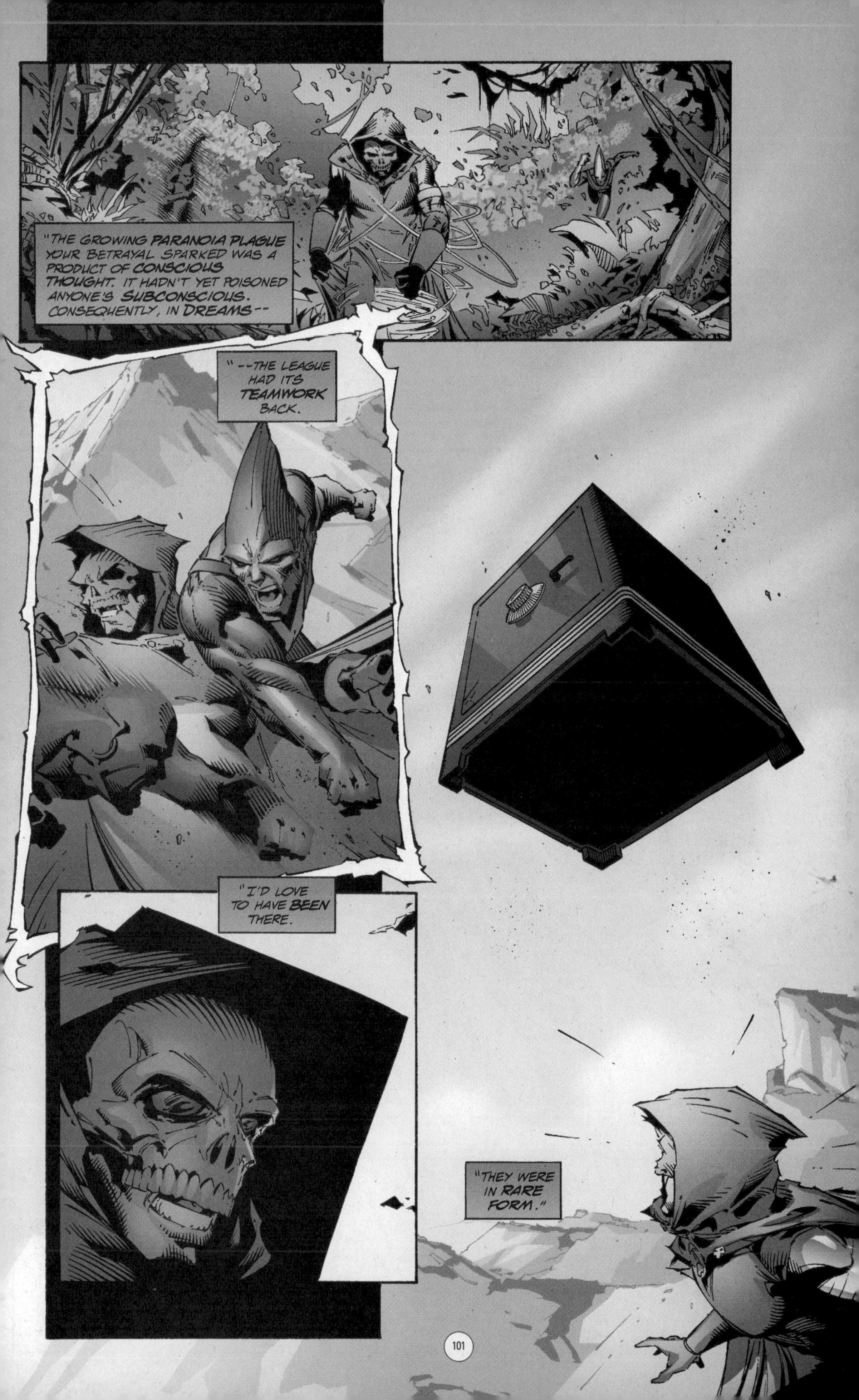
"THE GROWING PARANOIA PLAGUE YOUR BETRAYAL SPARKED WAS A PRODUCT OF CONSCIOUS THOUGHT. IT HADN'T YET POISONED ANYONE'S SUBCONSCIOUS. CONSEQUENTLY, IN DREAMS--
"--THE LEAGUE HAD ITS TEAMWORK BACK.
"I'D LOVE TO HAVE BEEN THERE.
"THEY WERE IN RARE FORM."

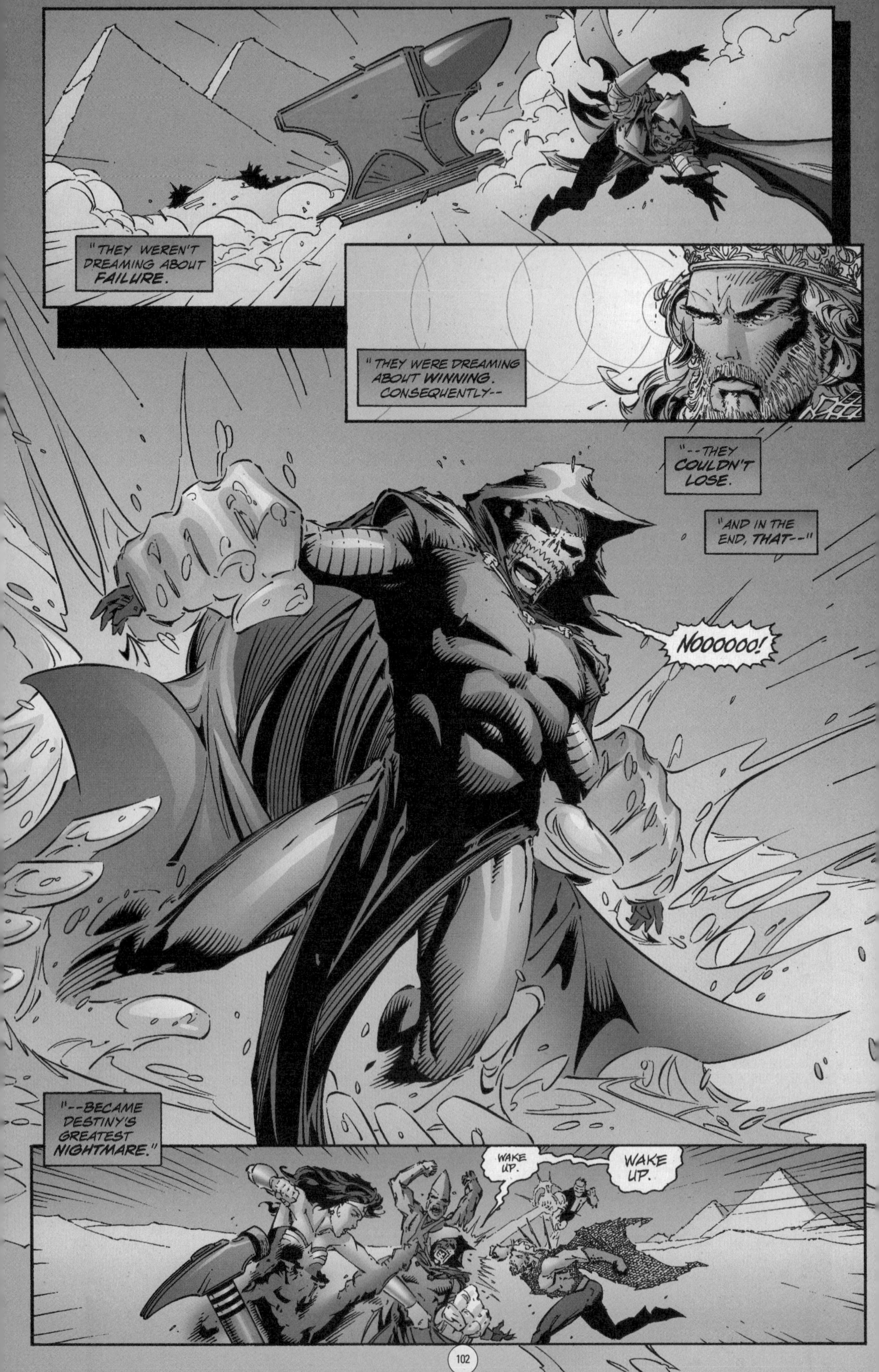
"THEY WEREN'T DREAMING ABOUT FAILURE.
"THEY WERE DREAMING ABOUT WINNING. CONSEQUENTLY--
"--THEY COULDN'T LOSE.
"AND IN THE END, THAT--"
NOOOOOO!
"--BECAME DESTINY'S GREATEST NIGHTMARE."
WAKE UP.
WAKE UP.

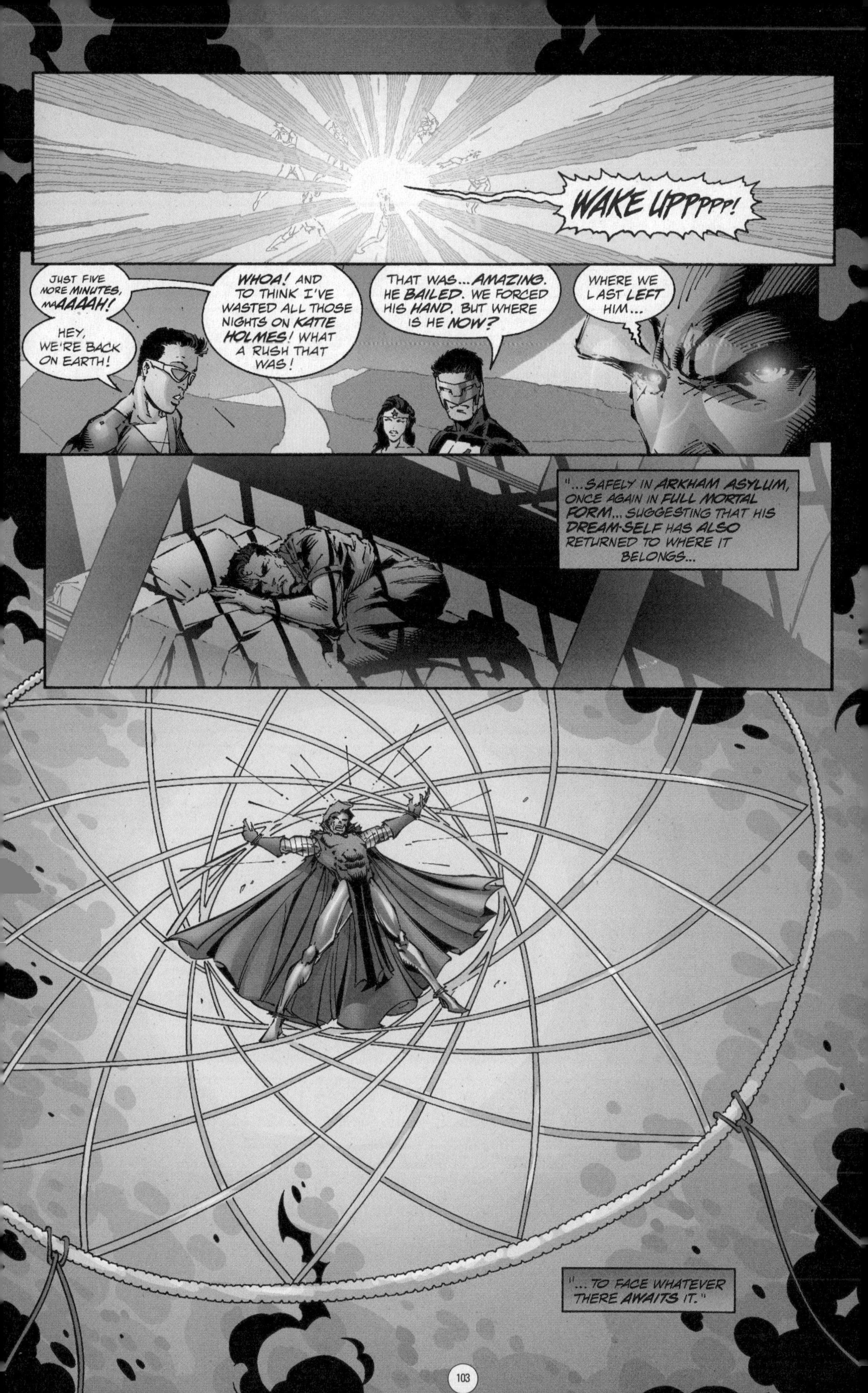
WAKE UPPPPP!
JUST FIVE MORE MINUTES, MAAAAAH!
HEY, WE'RE BACK ON EARTH!
WHOA! AND TO THINK I'VE WASTED ALL THOSE NIGHTS ON KATIE HOLMES! WHAT A RUSH THAT WAS!
THAT WAS... AMAZING. HE BAILED. WE FORCED HIS HAND. BUT WHERE IS HE NOW?
WHERE WE LAST LEFT HIM...
"...SAFELY IN ARKHAM ASYLUM, ONCE AGAIN IN FULL MORTAL FORM... SUGGESTING THAT HIS DREAM-SELF HAS ALSO RETURNED TO WHERE IT BELONGS...
"...TO FACE WHATEVER THERE AWAITS IT."

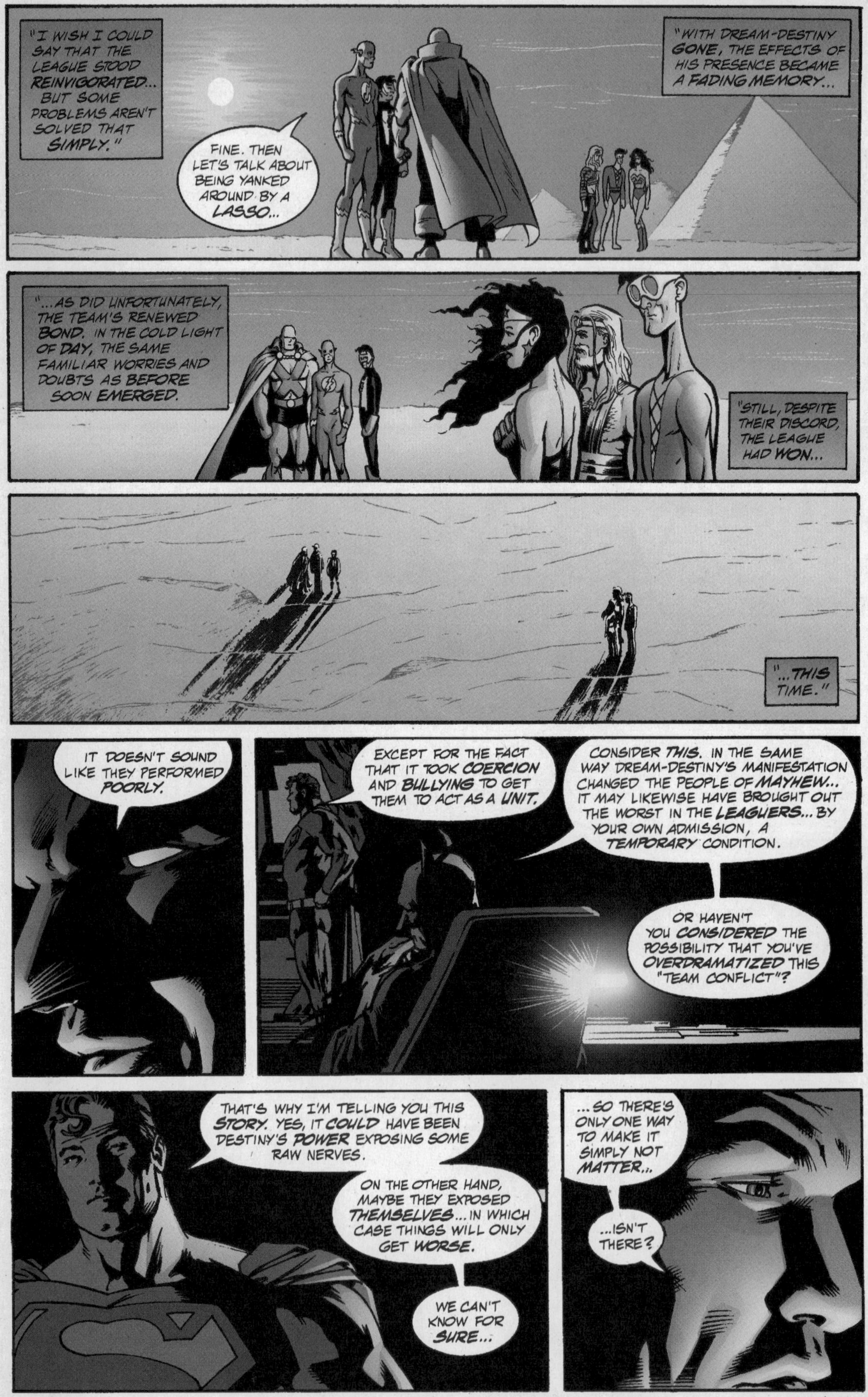
"I WISH I COULD SAY THAT THE LEAGUE STOOD REINVIGORATED... BUT SOME PROBLEMS AREN'T SOLVED THAT SIMPLY."
FINE. THEN LET'S TALK ABOUT BEING YANKED AROUND BY A LASSO...
"WITH DREAM-DESTINY GONE, THE EFFECTS OF HIS PRESENCE BECAME A FADING MEMORY...
"...AS DID UNFORTUNATELY, THE TEAM'S RENEWED BOND. IN THE COLD LIGHT OF DAY, THE SAME FAMILIAR WORRIES AND DOUBTS AS BEFORE SOON EMERGED.
"STILL, DESPITE THEIR DISCORD, THE LEAGUE HAD WON...
"...THIS TIME."
IT DOESN'T SOUND LIKE THEY PERFORMED POORLY.
EXCEPT FOR THE FACT THAT IT TOOK COERCION AND BULLYING TO GET THEM TO ACT AS A UNIT.
CONSIDER THIS. IN THE SAME WAY DREAM-DESTINY'S MANIFESTATION CHANGED THE PEOPLE OF MAYHEW... IT MAY LIKEWISE HAVE BROUGHT OUT THE WORST IN THE LEAGUERS... BY YOUR OWN ADMISSION, A TEMPORARY CONDITION.
OR HAVEN'T YOU CONSIDERED THE POSSIBILITY THAT YOU'VE OVERDRAMATIZED THIS "TEAM CONFLICT"?
THAT'S WHY I'M TELLING YOU THIS STORY. YES, IT COULD HAVE BEEN DESTINY'S POWER EXPOSING SOME RAW NERVES.
ON THE OTHER HAND, MAYBE THEY EXPOSED THEMSELVES... IN WHICH CASE THINGS WILL ONLY GET WORSE.
WE CAN'T KNOW FOR SURE...
...SO THERE'S ONLY ONE WAY TO MAKE IT SIMPLY NOT MATTER...
...ISN'T THERE?

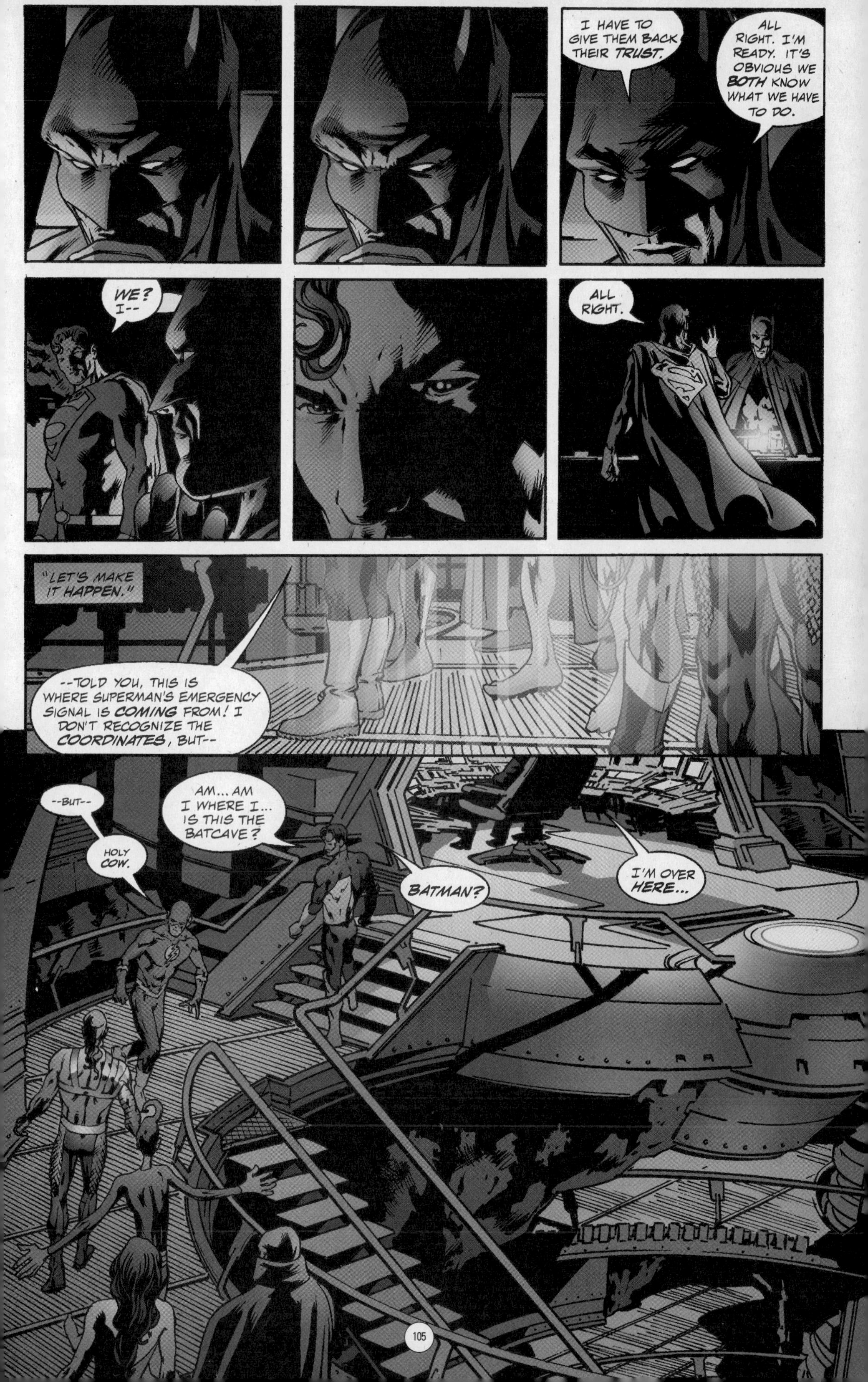
I HAVE TO GIVE THEM BACK THEIR TRUST.
ALL RIGHT. I'M READY. IT'S OBVIOUS WE BOTH KNOW WHAT WE HAVE TO DO.
WE? I--
ALL RIGHT.
"LET'S MAKE IT HAPPEN."
--TOLD YOU, THIS IS WHERE SUPERMAN'S EMERGENCY SIGNAL IS COMING FROM! I DON'T RECOGNIZE THE COORDINATES, BUT--
--BUT--
HOLY COW.
AM... AM I WHERE I... IS THIS THE BATCAVE?
BATMAN?
I'M OVER HERE...

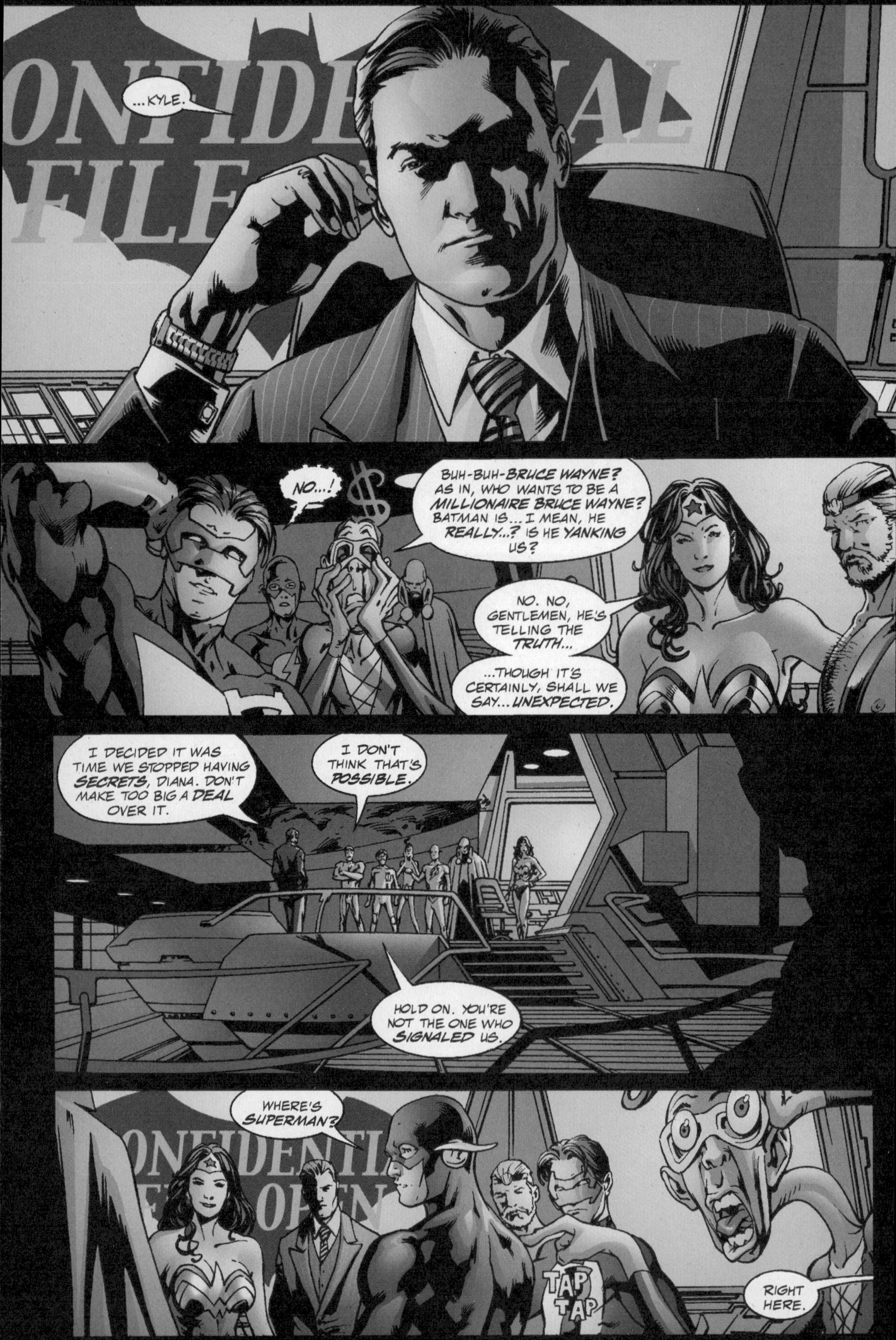

ONFIDENTIAL FILE
...KYLE.
NO...!
$
BUH-BUH-BRUCE WAYNE? AS IN, WHO WANTS TO BE A MILLIONAIRE BRUCE WAYNE? BATMAN IS... I MEAN, HE REALLY...? IS HE YANKING US?
NO. NO, GENTLEMEN, HE'S TELLING THE TRUTH...
...THOUGH IT'S CERTAINLY, SHALL WE SAY... UNEXPECTED.
I DECIDED IT WAS TIME WE STOPPED HAVING SECRETS, DIANA. DON'T MAKE TOO BIG A DEAL OVER IT.
I DON'T THINK THAT'S POSSIBLE.
HOLD ON. YOU'RE NOT THE ONE WHO SIGNALED US.
WHERE'S SUPERMAN?
TAP TAP
RIGHT HERE.

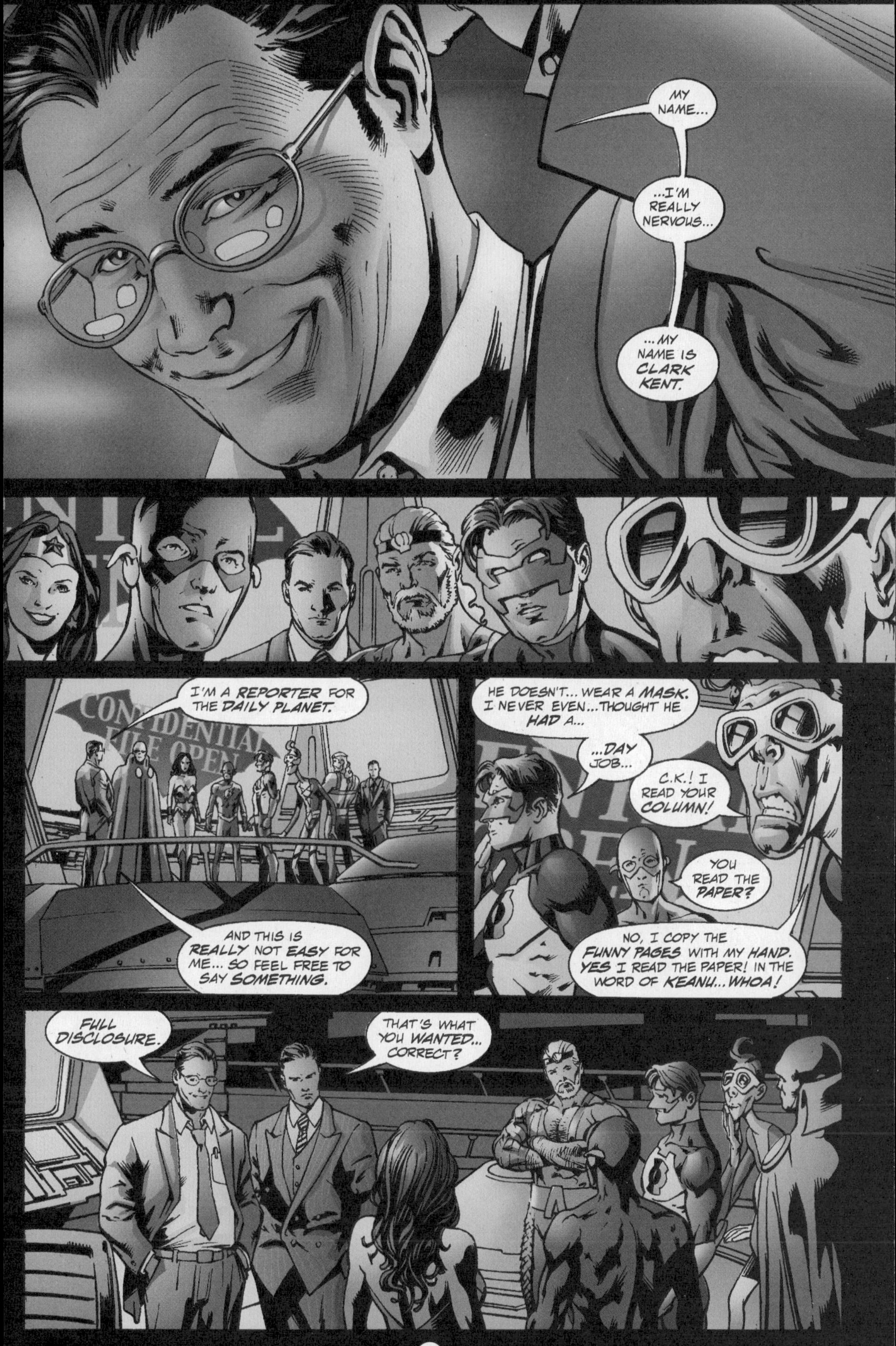
MY NAME...
...I'M REALLY NERVOUS...
...MY NAME IS CLARK KENT.
I'M A REPORTER FOR THE DAILY PLANET.
CONFIDENTIAL FILE OPEN
AND THIS IS REALLY NOT EASY FOR ME... SO FEEL FREE TO SAY SOMETHING.
HE DOESN'T... WEAR A MASK. I NEVER EVEN...THOUGHT HE HAD A...
...DAY JOB...
C.K.! I READ YOUR COLUMN!
YOU READ THE PAPER?
NO, I COPY THE FUNNY PAGES WITH MY HAND. YES I READ THE PAPER! IN THE WORD OF KEANU...WHOA!
FULL DISCLOSURE.
THAT'S WHAT YOU WANTED... CORRECT?

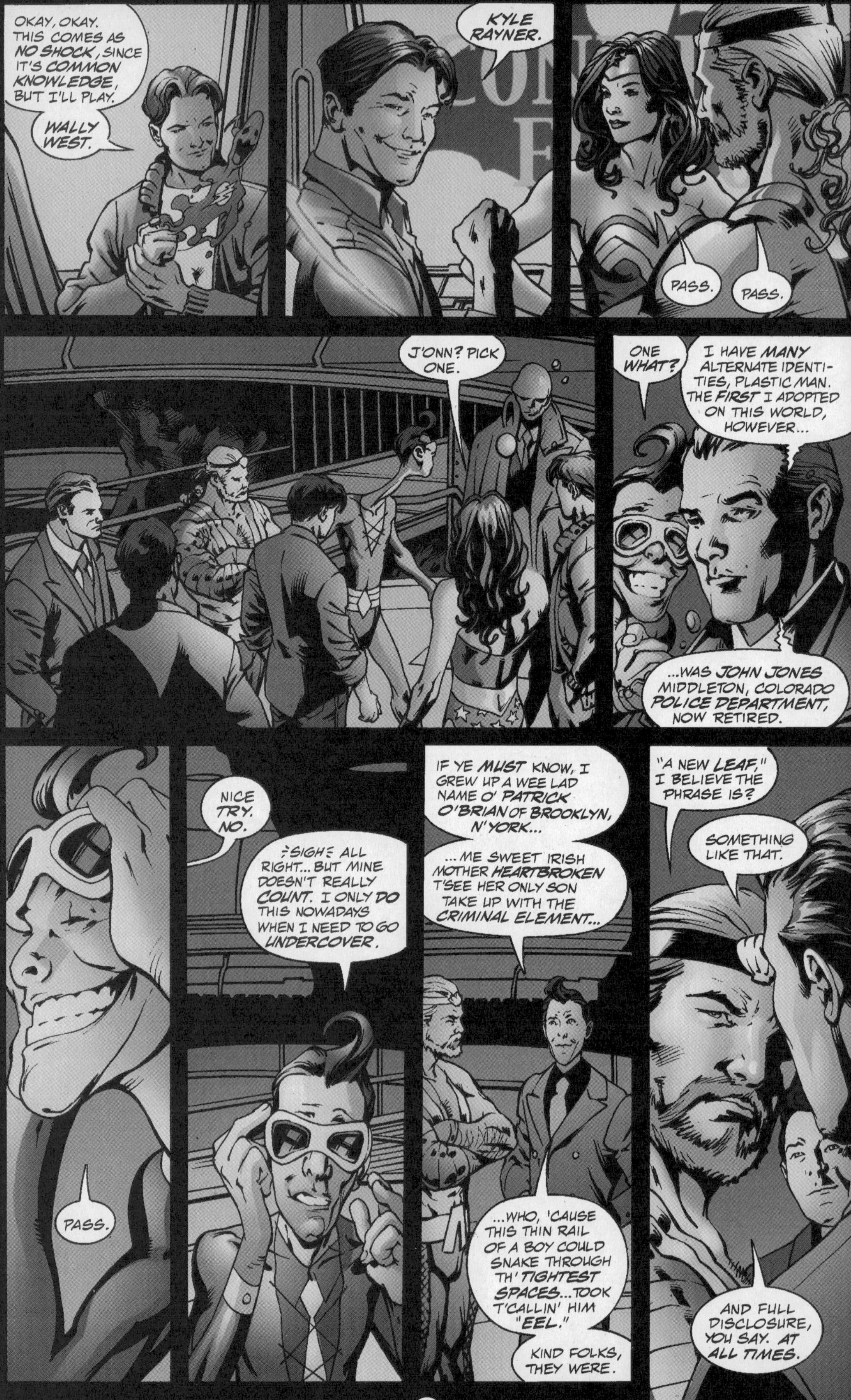
OKAY, OKAY. THIS COMES AS NO SHOCK, SINCE IT'S COMMON KNOWLEDGE, BUT I'LL PLAY.
WALLY WEST.
KYLE RAYNER.
PASS.
PASS.
J'ONN? PICK ONE.
ONE WHAT?
I HAVE MANY ALTERNATE IDENTITIES, PLASTIC MAN. THE FIRST I ADOPTED ON THIS WORLD, HOWEVER...
...WAS JOHN JONES MIDDLETON, COLORADO POLICE DEPARTMENT, NOW RETIRED.
PASS.
NICE TRY. NO.
SIGH ALL RIGHT... BUT MINE DOESN'T REALLY COUNT. I ONLY DO THIS NOWADAYS WHEN I NEED TO GO UNDERCOVER.
IF YE MUST KNOW, I GREW UP A WEE LAD NAME O' PATRICK O'BRIAN OF BROOKLYN, N'YORK...
... ME SWEET IRISH MOTHER HEARTBROKEN T'SEE HER ONLY SON TAKE UP WITH THE CRIMINAL ELEMENT...
...WHO, 'CAUSE THIS THIN RAIL OF A BOY COULD SNAKE THROUGH TH' TIGHTEST SPACES... TOOK T'CALLIN' HIM "EEL."
KIND FOLKS, THEY WERE.
"A NEW LEAF," I BELIEVE THE PHRASE IS?
SOMETHING LIKE THAT.
AND FULL DISCLOSURE, YOU SAY. AT ALL TIMES.

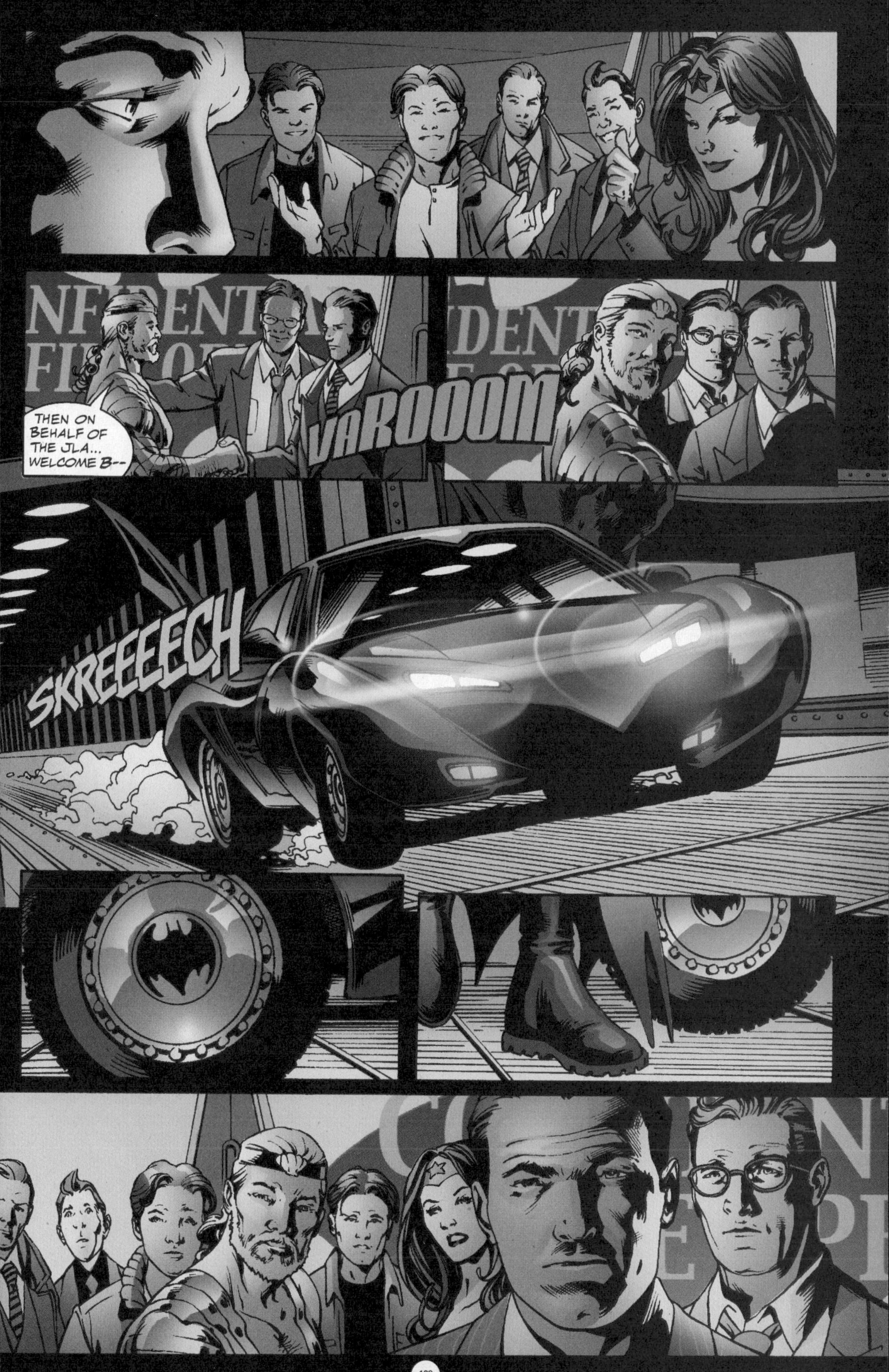
THEN ON BEHALF OF THE JLA... WELCOME B--
VAROOOM
SKREEEEECH

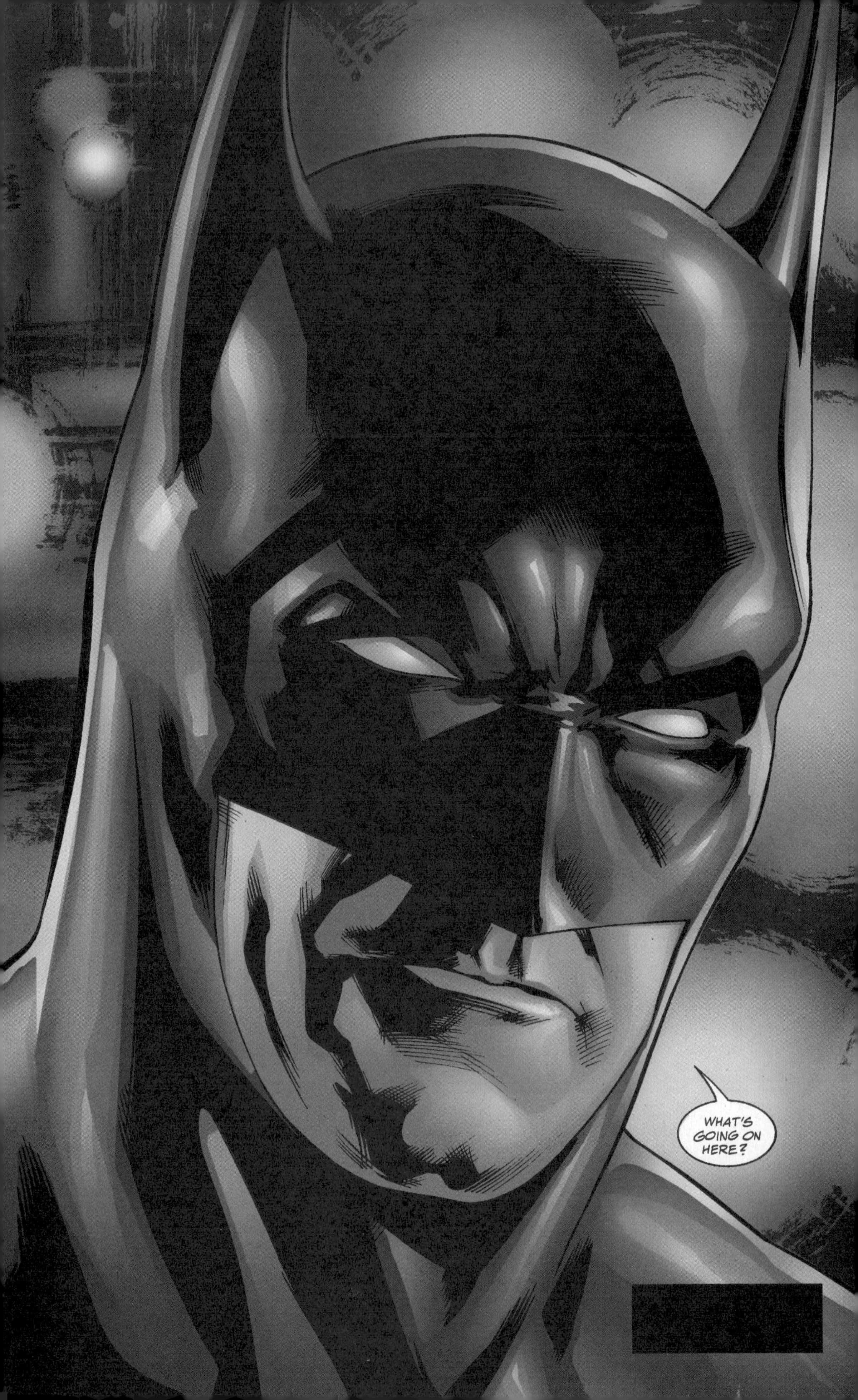
WHAT'S GOING ON HERE?
[redacted]

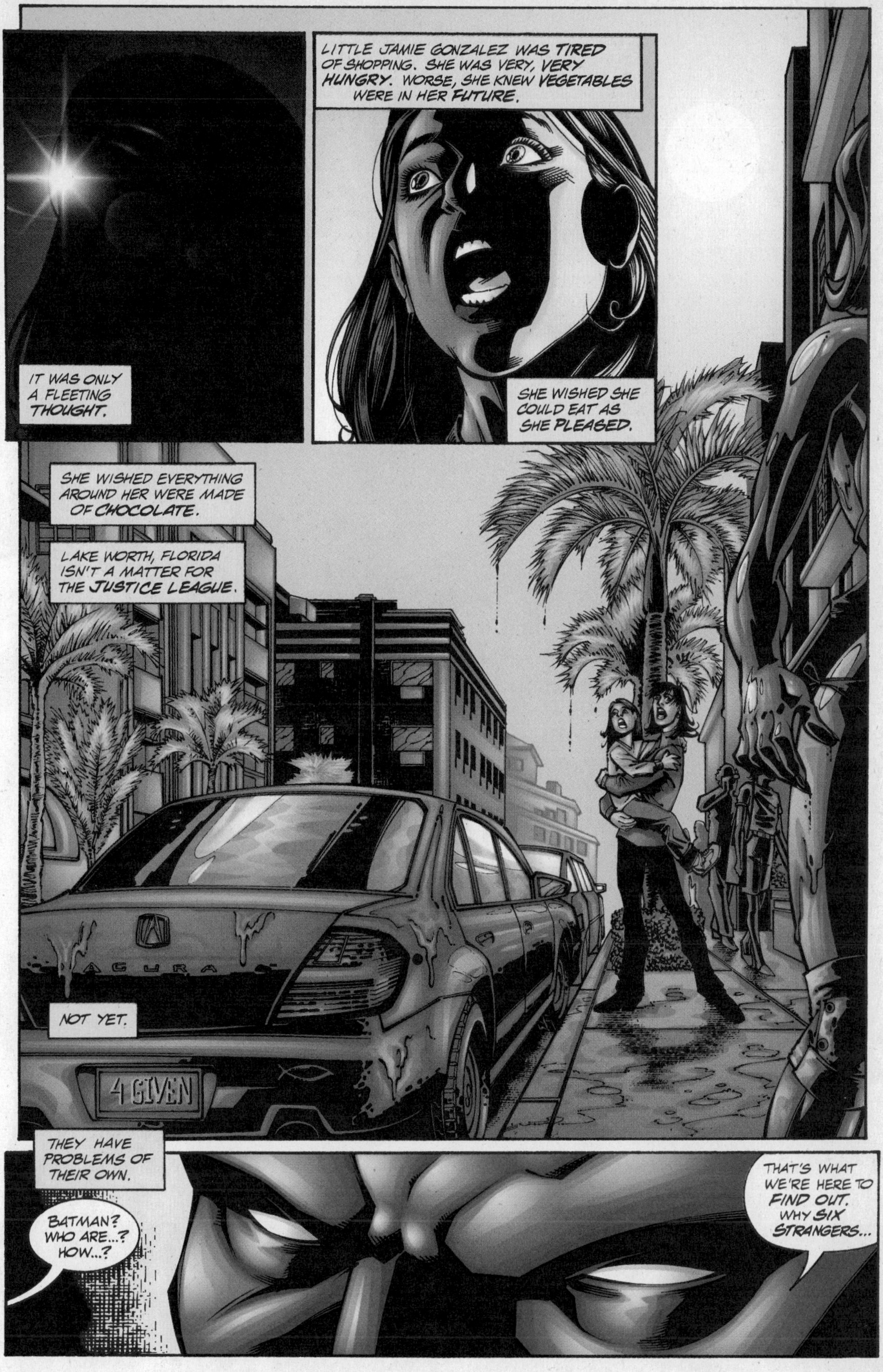
LITTLE JAMIE GONZALEZ WAS TIRED OF SHOPPING. SHE WAS VERY, VERY HUNGRY. WORSE, SHE KNEW VEGETABLES WERE IN HER FUTURE.
IT WAS ONLY A FLEETING THOUGHT.
SHE WISHED SHE COULD EAT AS SHE PLEASED.
SHE WISHED EVERYTHING AROUND HER WERE MADE OF CHOCOLATE.
LAKE WORTH, FLORIDA ISN'T A MATTER FOR THE JUSTICE LEAGUE.
NOT YET.
ACURA
4 GIVEN
THEY HAVE PROBLEMS OF THEIR OWN.
BATMAN? WHO ARE...? HOW...?
THAT'S WHAT WE'RE HERE TO FIND OUT. WHY SIX STRANGERS...

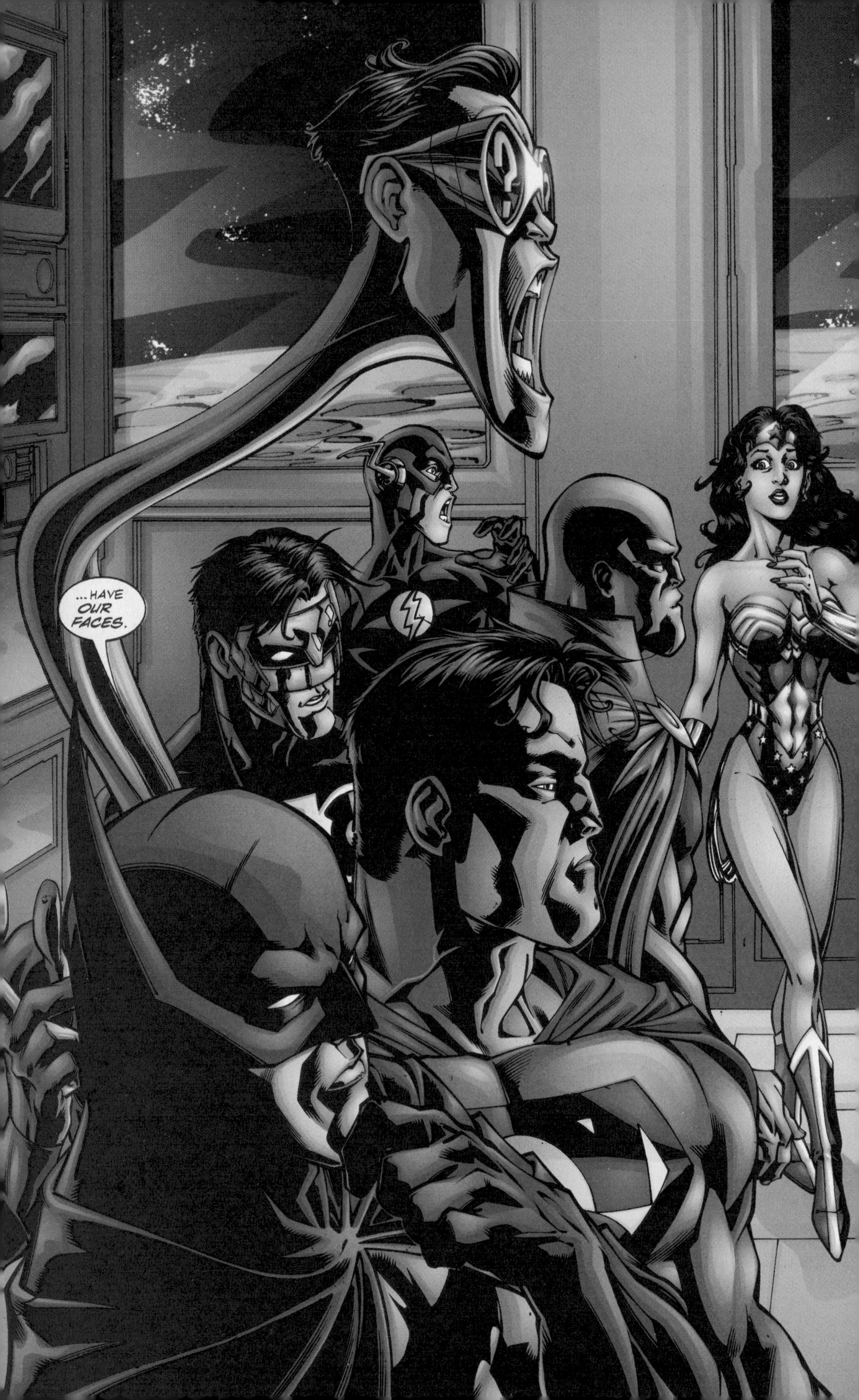
...HAVE OUR FACES.

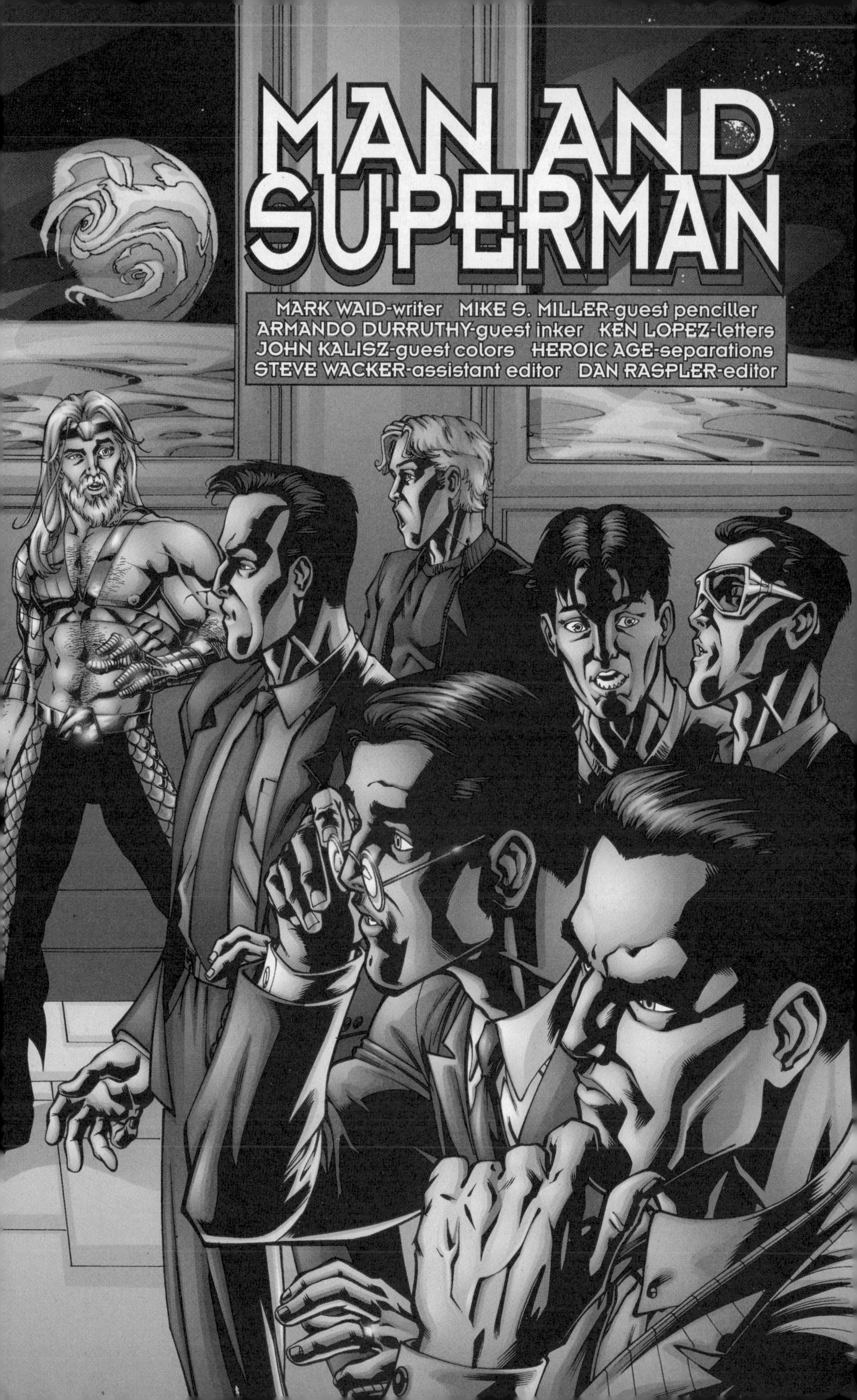
MAN AND SUPERMAN
MARK WAID-writer MIKE S. MILLER-guest penciller
ARMANDO DURRUTHY-guest inker KEN LOPEZ-letters
JOHN KALISZ-guest colors HEROIC AGE-separations
STEVE WACKER-assistant editor DAN RASPLER-editor

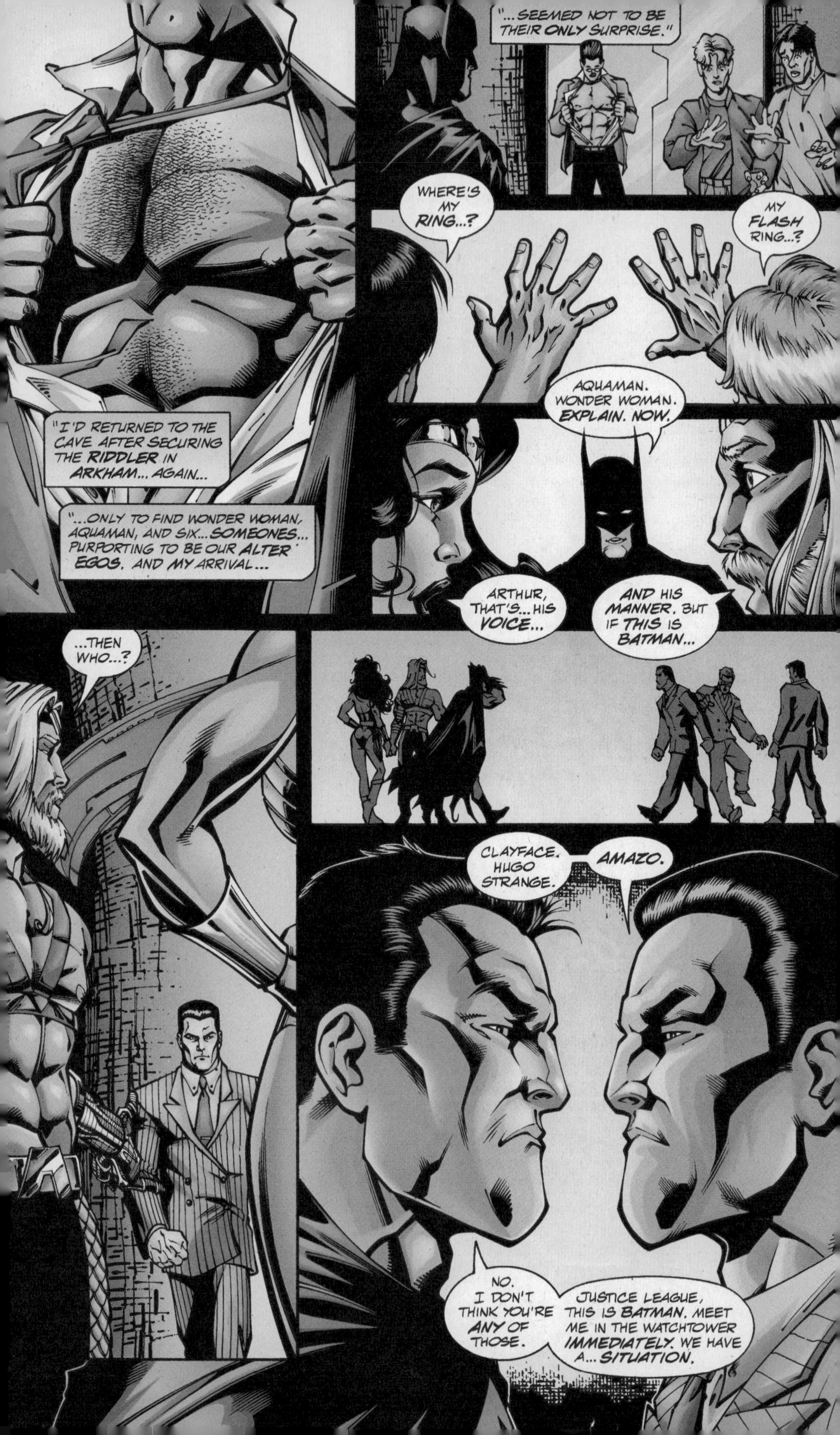
"I'D RETURNED TO THE CAVE AFTER SECURING THE RIDDLER IN ARKHAM... AGAIN...
"...ONLY TO FIND WONDER WOMAN, AQUAMAN, AND SIX... SOMEONES... PURPORTING TO BE OUR ALTER EGOS. AND MY ARRIVAL...
"...SEEMED NOT TO BE THEIR ONLY SURPRISE."
WHERE'S MY RING...?
MY FLASH RING...?
AQUAMAN. WONDER WOMAN. EXPLAIN. NOW.
ARTHUR, THAT'S... HIS VOICE...
AND HIS MANNER. BUT IF THIS IS BATMAN...
...THEN WHO...?
CLAYFACE. HUGO STRANGE.
AMAZO.
NO. I DON'T THINK YOU'RE ANY OF THOSE.
JUSTICE LEAGUE, THIS IS BATMAN. MEET ME IN THE WATCHTOWER IMMEDIATELY. WE HAVE A... SITUATION.

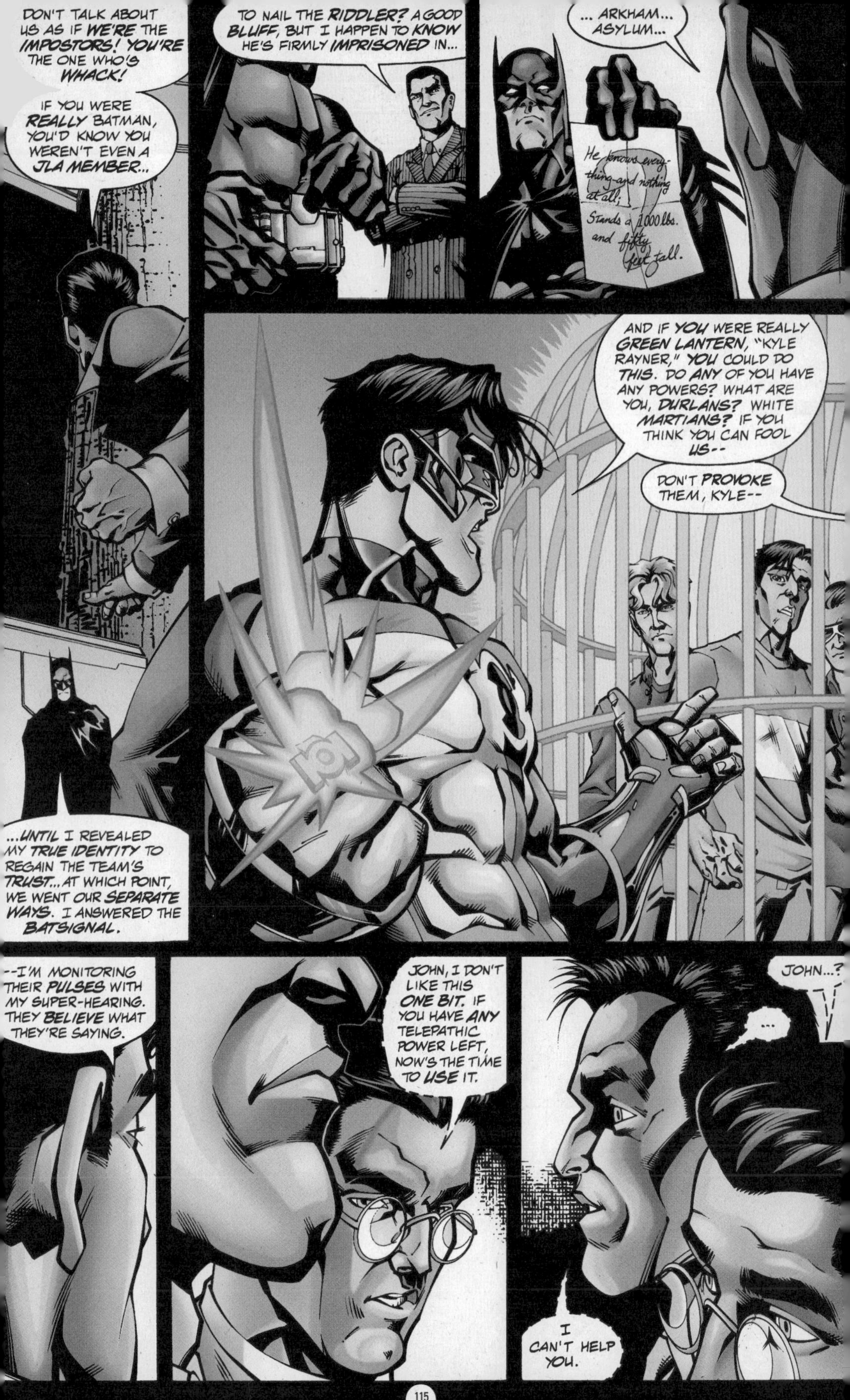

DON'T TALK ABOUT US AS IF WE'RE THE IMPOSTORS! YOU'RE THE ONE WHO'S WHACK!
IF YOU WERE REALLY BATMAN, YOU'D KNOW YOU WEREN'T EVEN A JLA MEMBER...
TO NAIL THE RIDDLER? A GOOD BLUFF, BUT I HAPPEN TO KNOW HE'S FIRMLY IMPRISONED IN...
... ARKHAM... ASYLUM...
He knows everything and nothing at all; Stands a 1,000 lbs. and fifty feet tall.
...UNTIL I REVEALED MY TRUE IDENTITY TO REGAIN THE TEAM'S TRUST... AT WHICH POINT, WE WENT OUR SEPARATE WAYS. I ANSWERED THE BATSIGNAL.
AND IF YOU WERE REALLY GREEN LANTERN, "KYLE RAYNER," YOU COULD DO THIS. DO ANY OF YOU HAVE ANY POWERS? WHAT ARE YOU, DURLANS? WHITE MARTIANS? IF YOU THINK YOU CAN FOOL US--
DON'T PROVOKE THEM, KYLE--
--I'M MONITORING THEIR PULSES WITH MY SUPER-HEARING. THEY BELIEVE WHAT THEY'RE SAYING.
JOHN, I DON'T LIKE THIS ONE BIT. IF YOU HAVE ANY TELEPATHIC POWER LEFT, NOW'S THE TIME TO USE IT.
JOHN...?
...
I CAN'T HELP YOU.

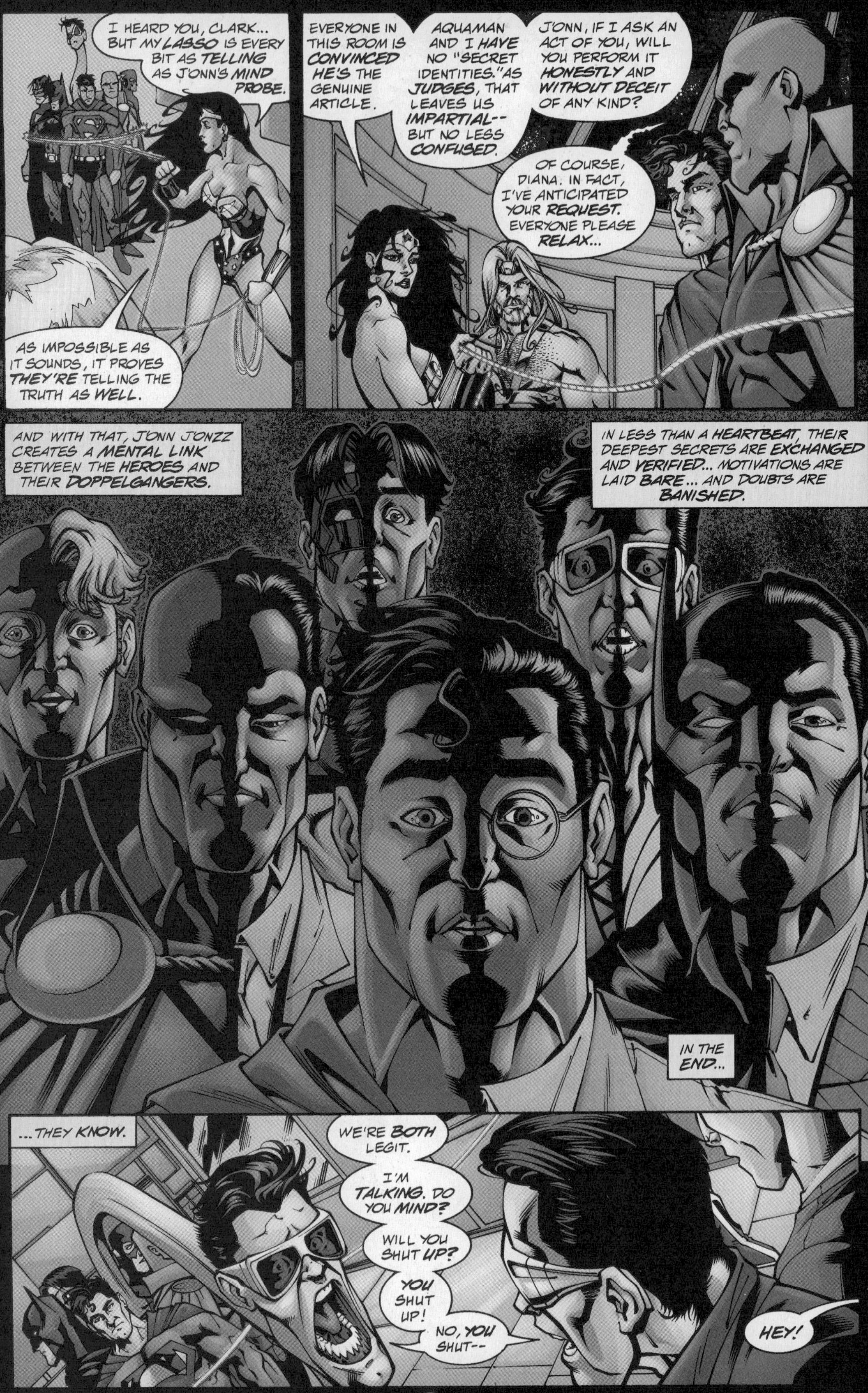
I HEARD YOU, CLARK... BUT MY LASSO IS EVERY BIT AS TELLING AS J'ONN'S MIND PROBE.
AS IMPOSSIBLE AS IT SOUNDS, IT PROVES THEY'RE TELLING THE TRUTH AS WELL.
EVERYONE IN THIS ROOM IS CONVINCED HE'S THE GENUINE ARTICLE.
AQUAMAN AND I HAVE NO "SECRET IDENTITIES." AS JUDGES, THAT LEAVES US IMPARTIAL-- BUT NO LESS CONFUSED.
J'ONN, IF I ASK AN ACT OF YOU, WILL YOU PERFORM IT HONESTLY AND WITHOUT DECEIT OF ANY KIND?
OF COURSE, DIANA. IN FACT, I'VE ANTICIPATED YOUR REQUEST. EVERYONE PLEASE RELAX...
AND WITH THAT, J'ONN J'ONZZ CREATES A MENTAL LINK BETWEEN THE HEROES AND THEIR DOPPELGANGERS.
IN LESS THAN A HEARTBEAT, THEIR DEEPEST SECRETS ARE EXCHANGED AND VERIFIED... MOTIVATIONS ARE LAID BARE... AND DOUBTS ARE BANISHED.
IN THE END...
...THEY KNOW.
WE'RE BOTH LEGIT.
I'M TALKING. DO YOU MIND?
WILL YOU SHUT UP?
YOU SHUT UP!
NO, YOU SHUT--
HEY!

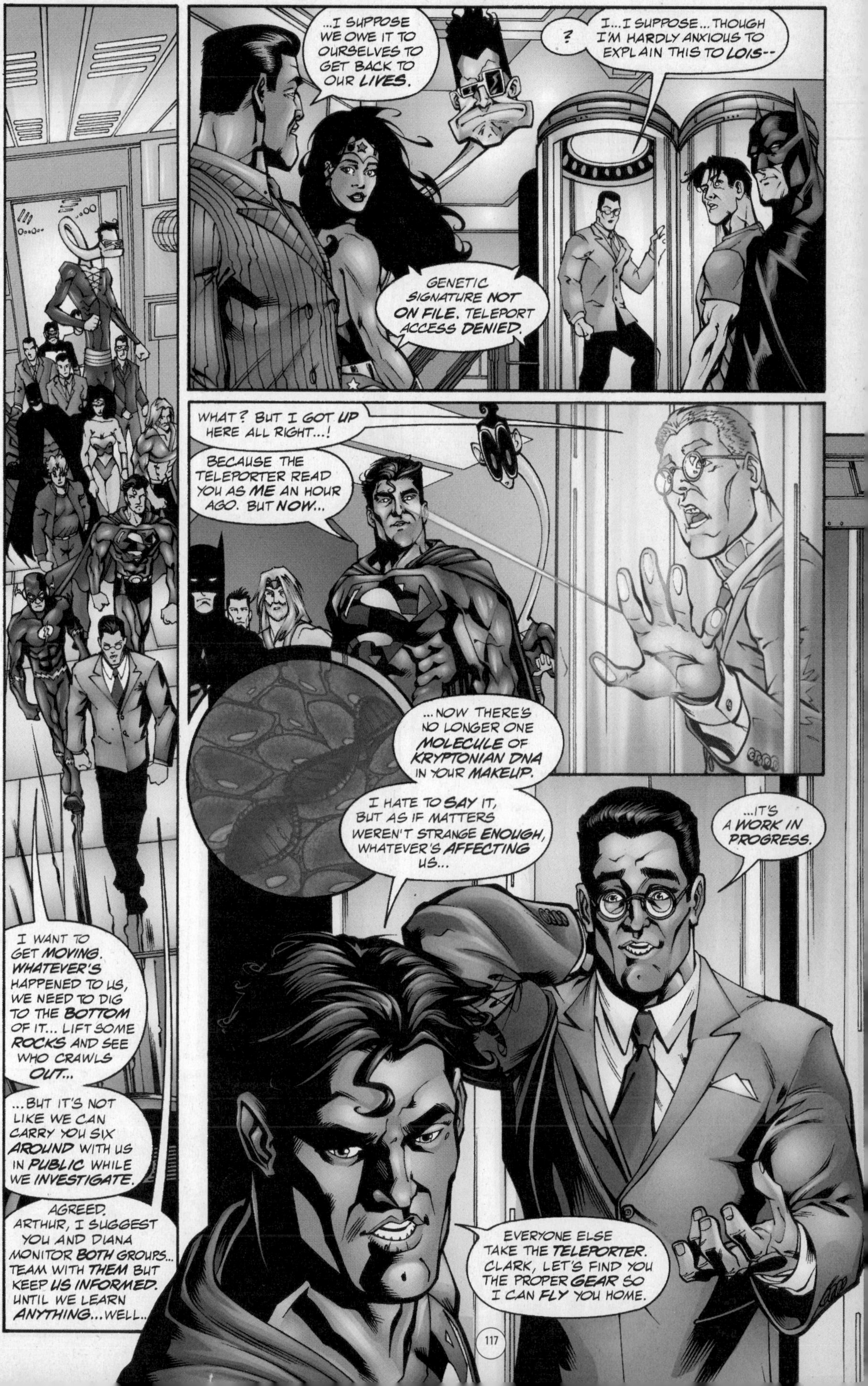

...I SUPPOSE WE OWE IT TO OURSELVES TO GET BACK TO OUR LIVES.
?
I...I SUPPOSE...THOUGH I'M HARDLY ANXIOUS TO EXPLAIN THIS TO LOIS--
GENETIC SIGNATURE NOT ON FILE. TELEPORT ACCESS DENIED.
WHAT? BUT I GOT UP HERE ALL RIGHT...!
BECAUSE THE TELEPORTER READ YOU AS ME AN HOUR AGO. BUT NOW...
...NOW THERE'S NO LONGER ONE MOLECULE OF KRYPTONIAN DNA IN YOUR MAKEUP.
I HATE TO SAY IT, BUT AS IF MATTERS WEREN'T STRANGE ENOUGH, WHATEVER'S AFFECTING US...
...IT'S A WORK IN PROGRESS.
I WANT TO GET MOVING. WHATEVER'S HAPPENED TO US, WE NEED TO DIG TO THE BOTTOM OF IT... LIFT SOME ROCKS AND SEE WHO CRAWLS OUT...
...BUT IT'S NOT LIKE WE CAN CARRY YOU SIX AROUND WITH US IN PUBLIC WHILE WE INVESTIGATE.
AGREED. ARTHUR, I SUGGEST YOU AND DIANA MONITOR BOTH GROUPS... TEAM WITH THEM BUT KEEP US INFORMED. UNTIL WE LEARN ANYTHING...WELL...
EVERYONE ELSE TAKE THE TELEPORTER. CLARK, LET'S FIND YOU THE PROPER GEAR SO I CAN FLY YOU HOME.

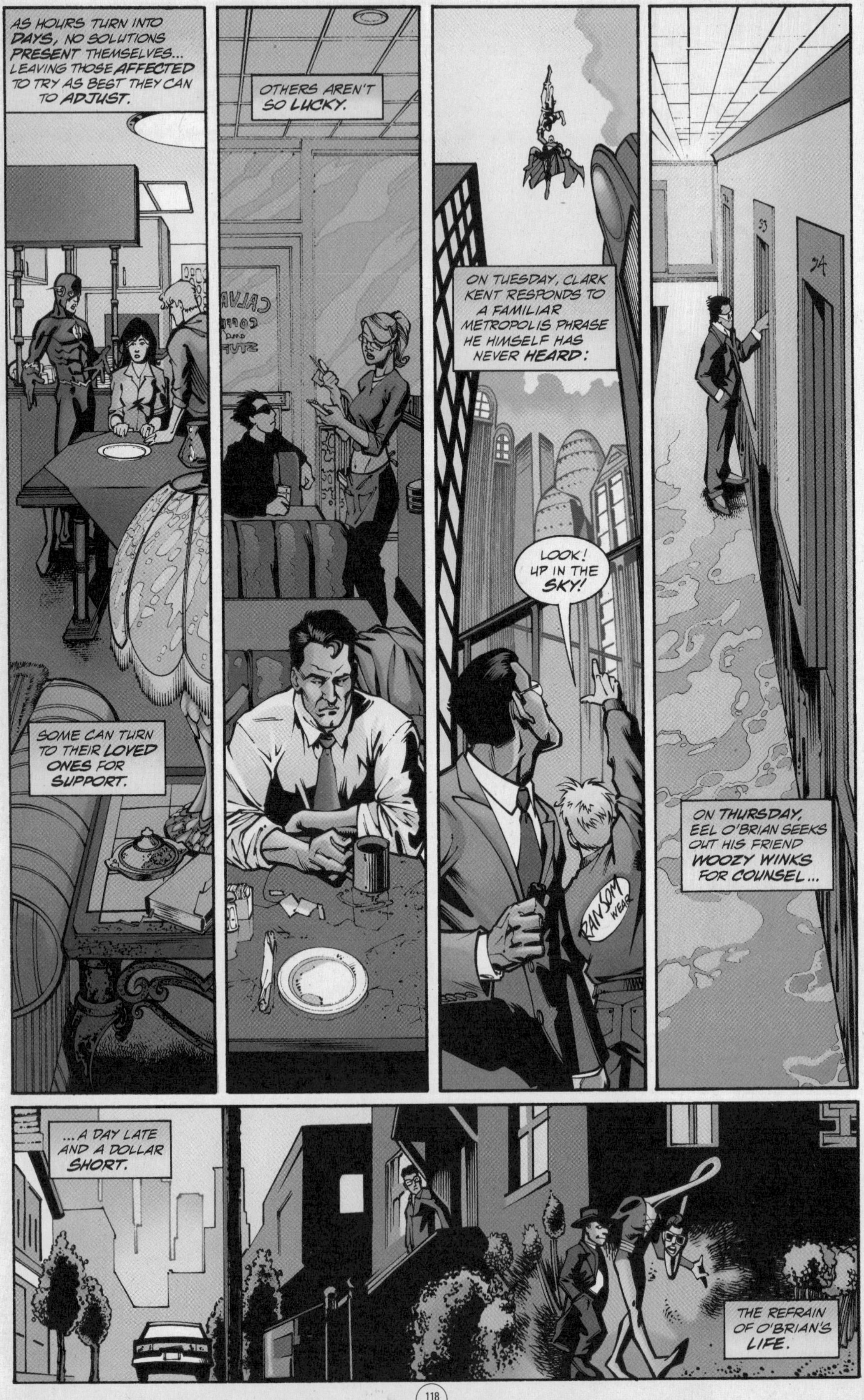
AS HOURS TURN INTO DAYS, NO SOLUTIONS PRESENT THEMSELVES... LEAVING THOSE AFFECTED TO TRY AS BEST THEY CAN TO ADJUST.
SOME CAN TURN TO THEIR LOVED ONES FOR SUPPORT.
OTHERS AREN'T SO LUCKY.
CALVA COFFEE AND STUFF
ON TUESDAY, CLARK KENT RESPONDS TO A FAMILIAR METROPOLIS PHRASE HE HIMSELF HAS NEVER HEARD:
LOOK! UP IN THE SKY!
RANSOM WEAR
ON THURSDAY, EEL O'BRIAN SEEKS OUT HIS FRIEND WOOZY WINKS FOR COUNSEL...
...A DAY LATE AND A DOLLAR SHORT.
THE REFRAIN OF O'BRIAN'S LIFE.

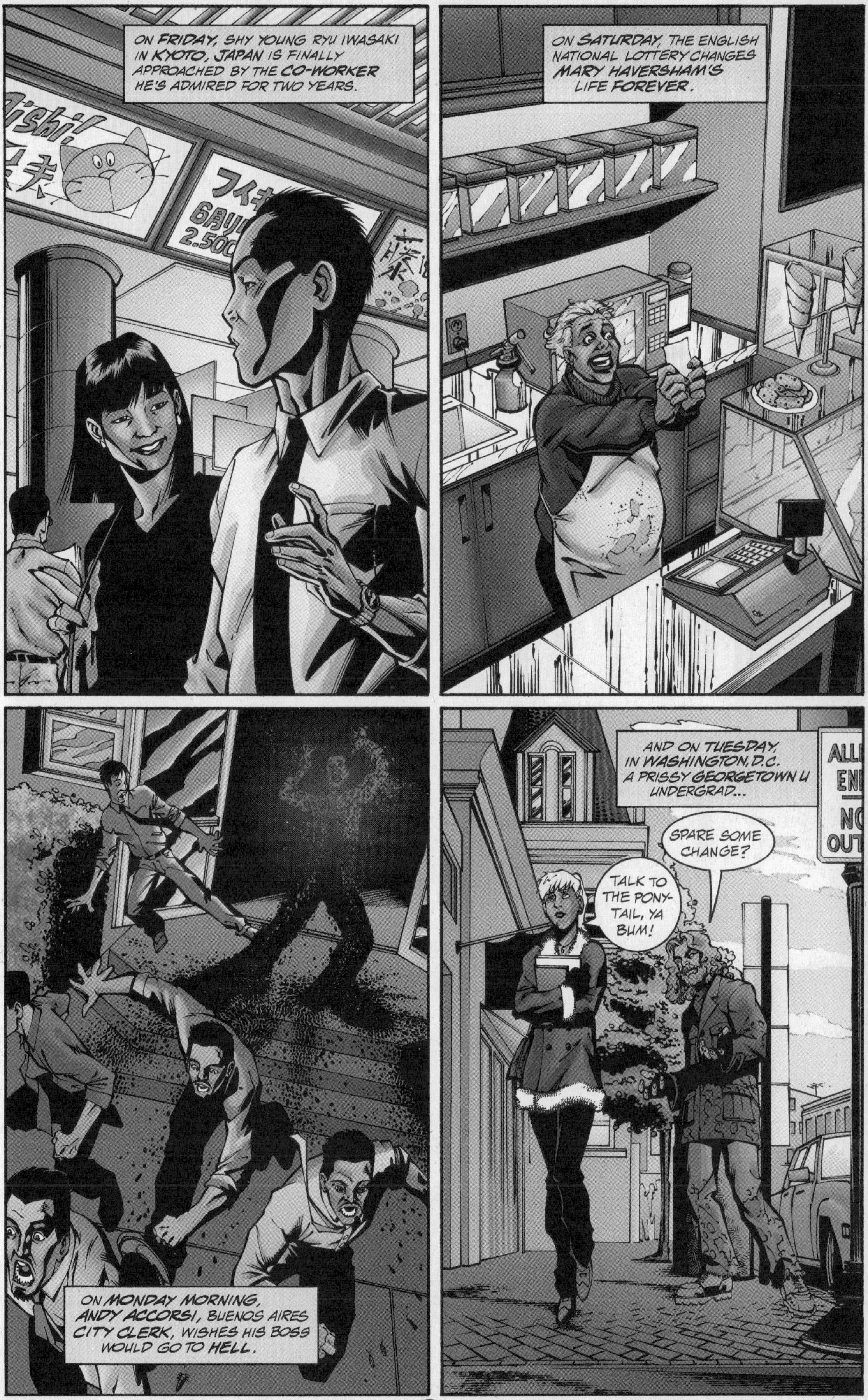
ON FRIDAY, SHY YOUNG RYU IWASAKI IN KYOTO, JAPAN IS FINALLY APPROACHED BY THE CO-WORKER HE'S ADMIRED FOR TWO YEARS.
ON SATURDAY, THE ENGLISH NATIONAL LOTTERY CHANGES MARY HAVERSHAM'S LIFE FOREVER.
ON MONDAY MORNING, ANDY ACCORSI, BUENOS AIRES CITY CLERK, WISHES HIS BOSS WOULD GO TO HELL.
AND ON TUESDAY, IN WASHINGTON, D.C. A PRISSY GEORGETOWN U UNDERGRAD...
SPARE SOME CHANGE?
TALK TO THE PONY-TAIL, YA BUM!

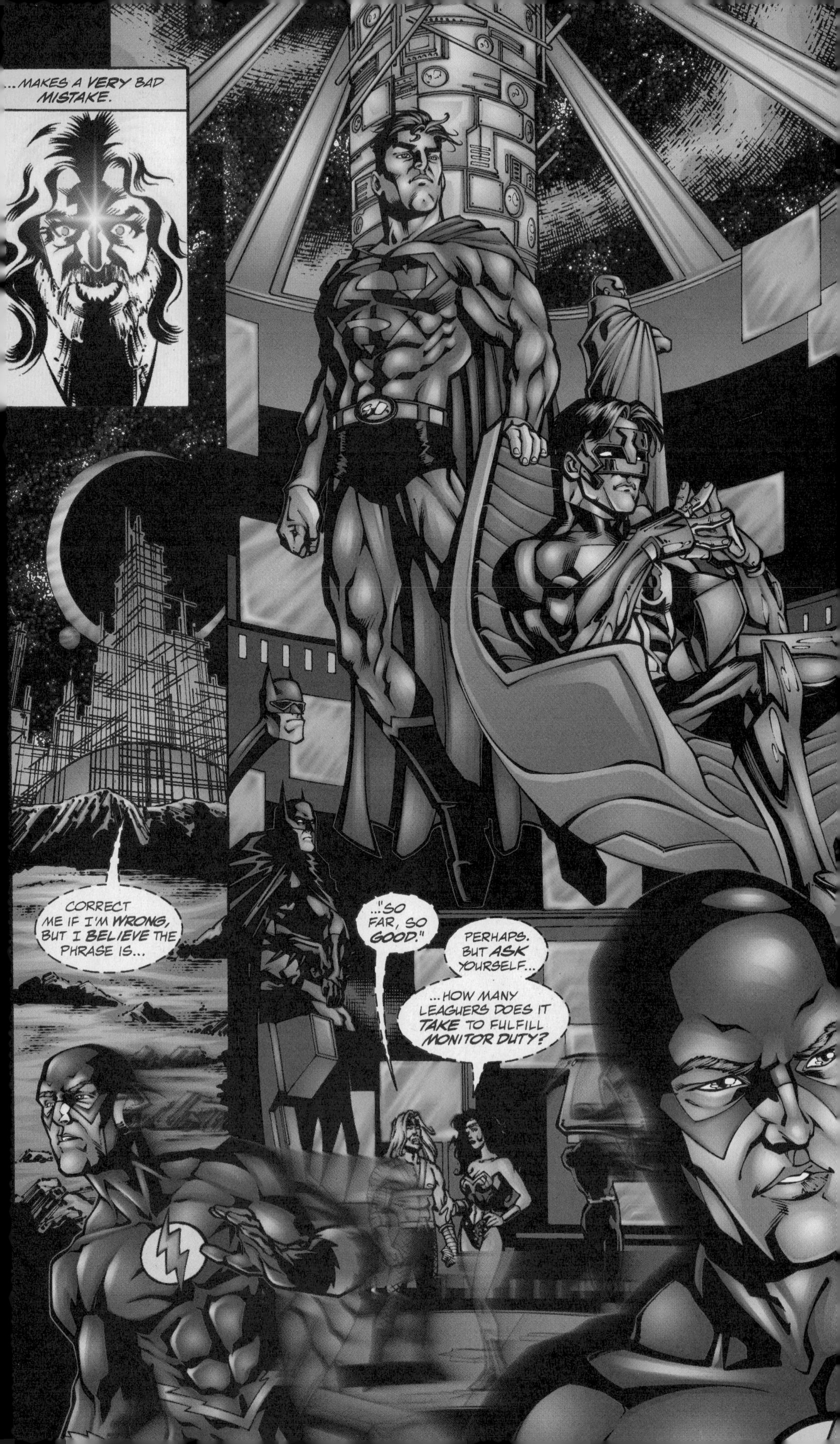
...MAKES A VERY BAD MISTAKE.
CORRECT ME IF I'M WRONG, BUT I BELIEVE THE PHRASE IS...
..."SO FAR, SO GOOD."
PERHAPS. BUT ASK YOURSELF...
...HOW MANY LEAGUERS DOES IT TAKE TO FULFILL MONITOR DUTY?

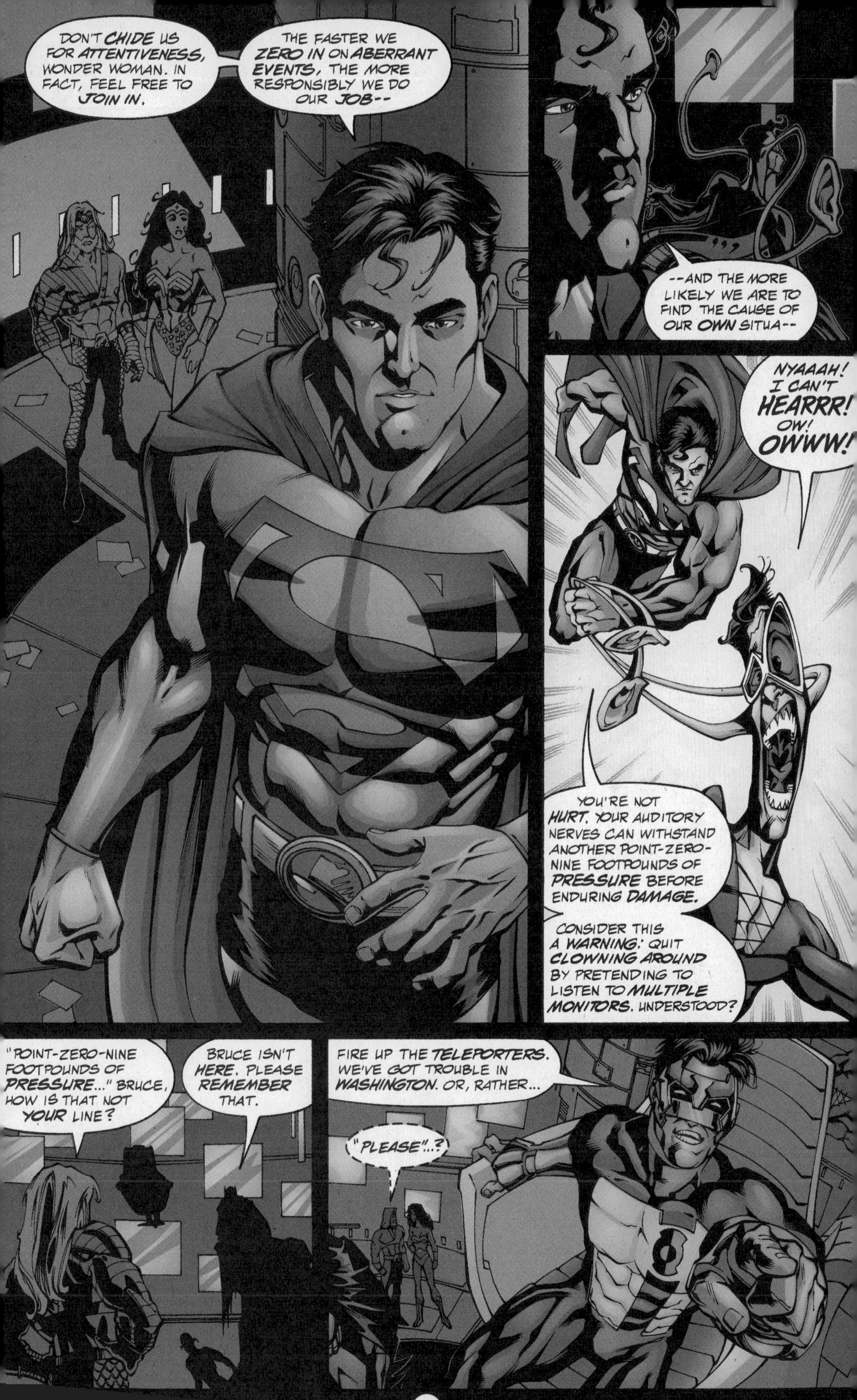

DON'T CHIDE US FOR ATTENTIVENESS, WONDER WOMAN. IN FACT, FEEL FREE TO JOIN IN.
THE FASTER WE ZERO IN ON ABERRANT EVENTS, THE MORE RESPONSIBLY WE DO OUR JOB--
--AND THE MORE LIKELY WE ARE TO FIND THE CAUSE OF OUR OWN SITUA--
NYAAAH! I CAN'T HEARRR! OW! OWWW!
YOU'RE NOT HURT. YOUR AUDITORY NERVES CAN WITHSTAND ANOTHER POINT-ZERO-NINE FOOTPOUNDS OF PRESSURE BEFORE ENDURING DAMAGE.
CONSIDER THIS A WARNING: QUIT CLOWNING AROUND BY PRETENDING TO LISTEN TO MULTIPLE MONITORS. UNDERSTOOD?
"POINT-ZERO-NINE FOOTPOUNDS OF PRESSURE..." BRUCE, HOW IS THAT NOT YOUR LINE?
BRUCE ISN'T HERE. PLEASE REMEMBER THAT.
FIRE UP THE TELEPORTERS. WE'VE GOT TROUBLE IN WASHINGTON. OR, RATHER...
"PLEASE"..?

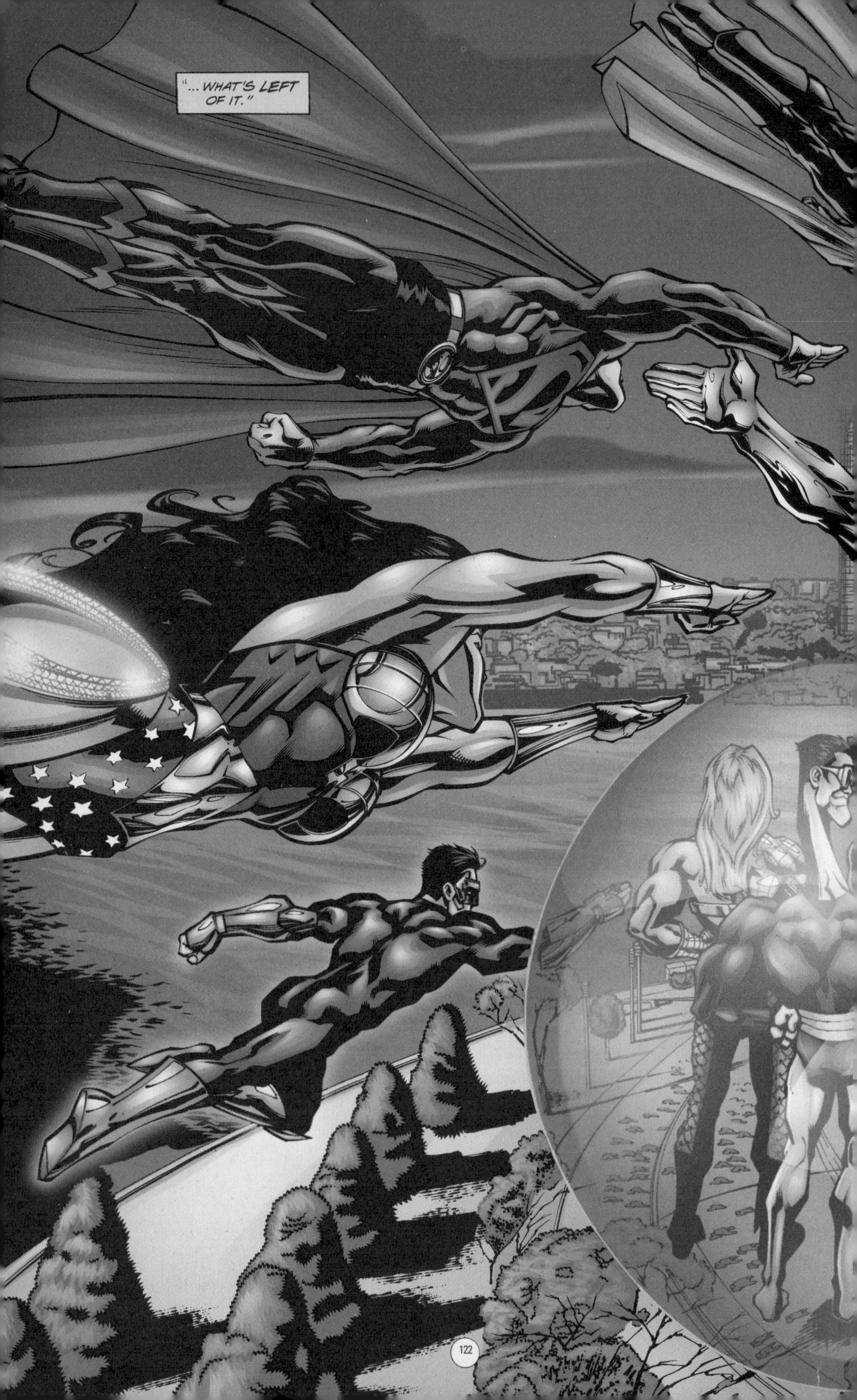
"...WHAT'S LEFT
OF IT."

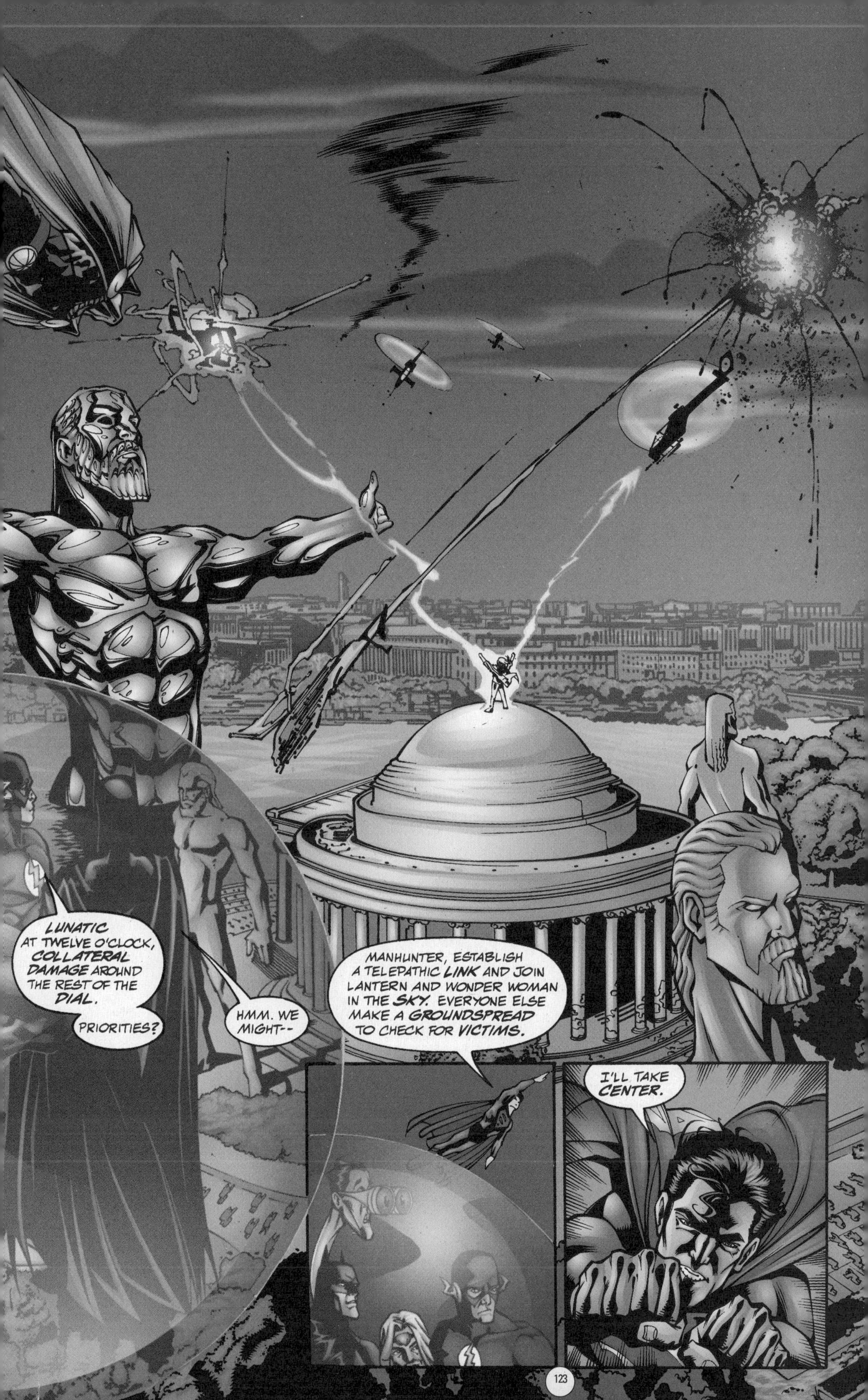
LUNATIC AT TWELVE O'CLOCK, COLLATERAL DAMAGE AROUND THE REST OF THE DIAL.
PRIORITIES?
HMM. WE MIGHT--
MANHUNTER, ESTABLISH A TELEPATHIC LINK AND JOIN LANTERN AND WONDER WOMAN IN THE SKY. EVERYONE ELSE MAKE A GROUNDSPREAD TO CHECK FOR VICTIMS.
I'LL TAKE CENTER.

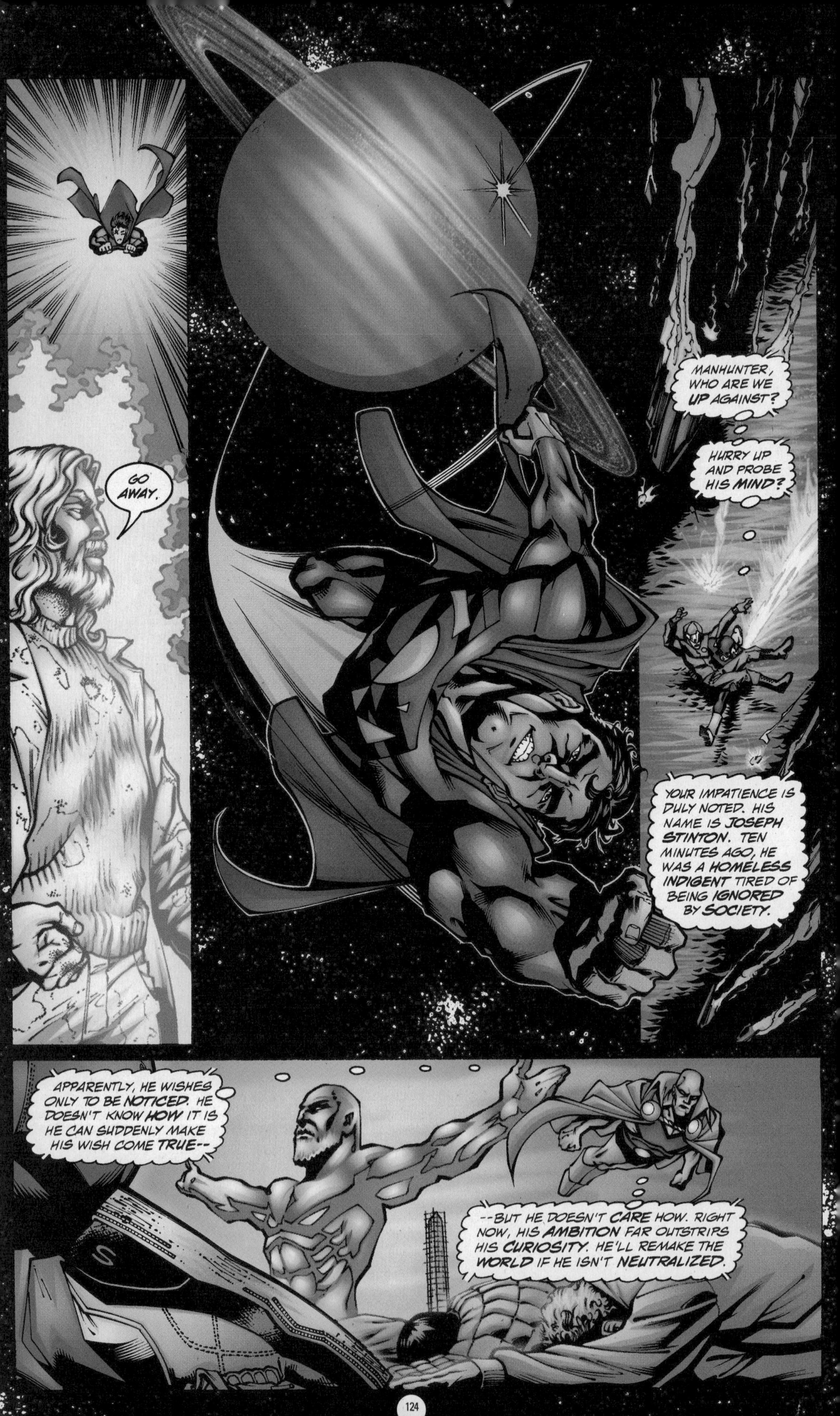
GO AWAY.
MANHUNTER, WHO ARE WE UP AGAINST?
HURRY UP AND PROBE HIS MIND?
YOUR IMPATIENCE IS DULY NOTED. HIS NAME IS JOSEPH STINTON. TEN MINUTES AGO, HE WAS A HOMELESS INDIGENT TIRED OF BEING IGNORED BY SOCIETY.
APPARENTLY, HE WISHES ONLY TO BE NOTICED. HE DOESN'T KNOW HOW IT IS HE CAN SUDDENLY MAKE HIS WISH COME TRUE--
--BUT HE DOESN'T CARE HOW. RIGHT NOW, HIS AMBITION FAR OUTSTRIPS HIS CURIOSITY. HE'LL REMAKE THE WORLD IF HE ISN'T NEUTRALIZED.

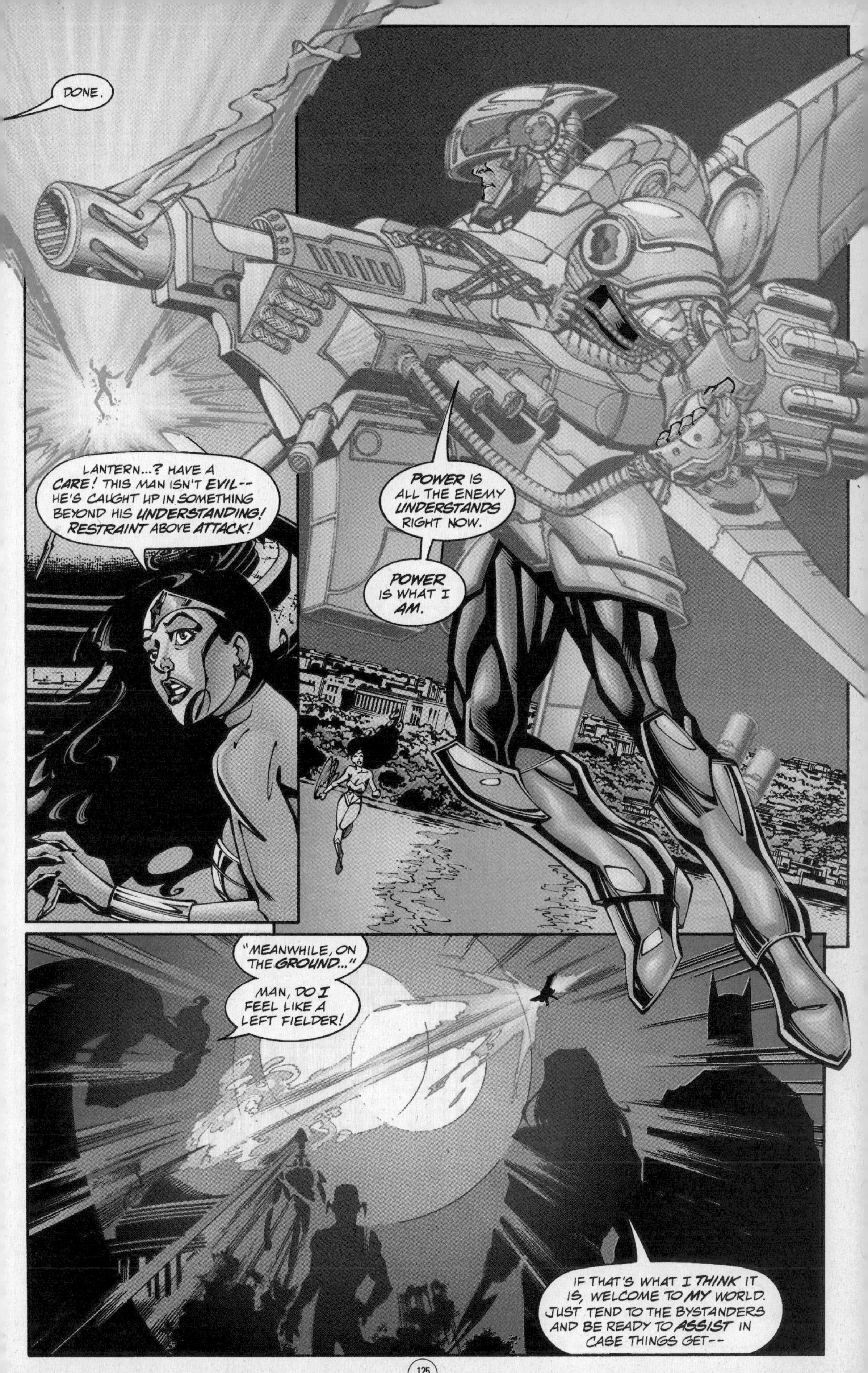
DONE.
LANTERN...? HAVE A CARE! THIS MAN ISN'T EVIL-- HE'S CAUGHT UP IN SOMETHING BEYOND HIS UNDERSTANDING! RESTRAINT ABOVE ATTACK!
POWER IS ALL THE ENEMY UNDERSTANDS RIGHT NOW.
POWER IS WHAT I AM.
"MEANWHILE, ON THE GROUND..."
MAN, DO I FEEL LIKE A LEFT FIELDER!
IF THAT'S WHAT I THINK IT IS, WELCOME TO MY WORLD. JUST TEND TO THE BYSTANDERS AND BE READY TO ASSIST IN CASE THINGS GET--

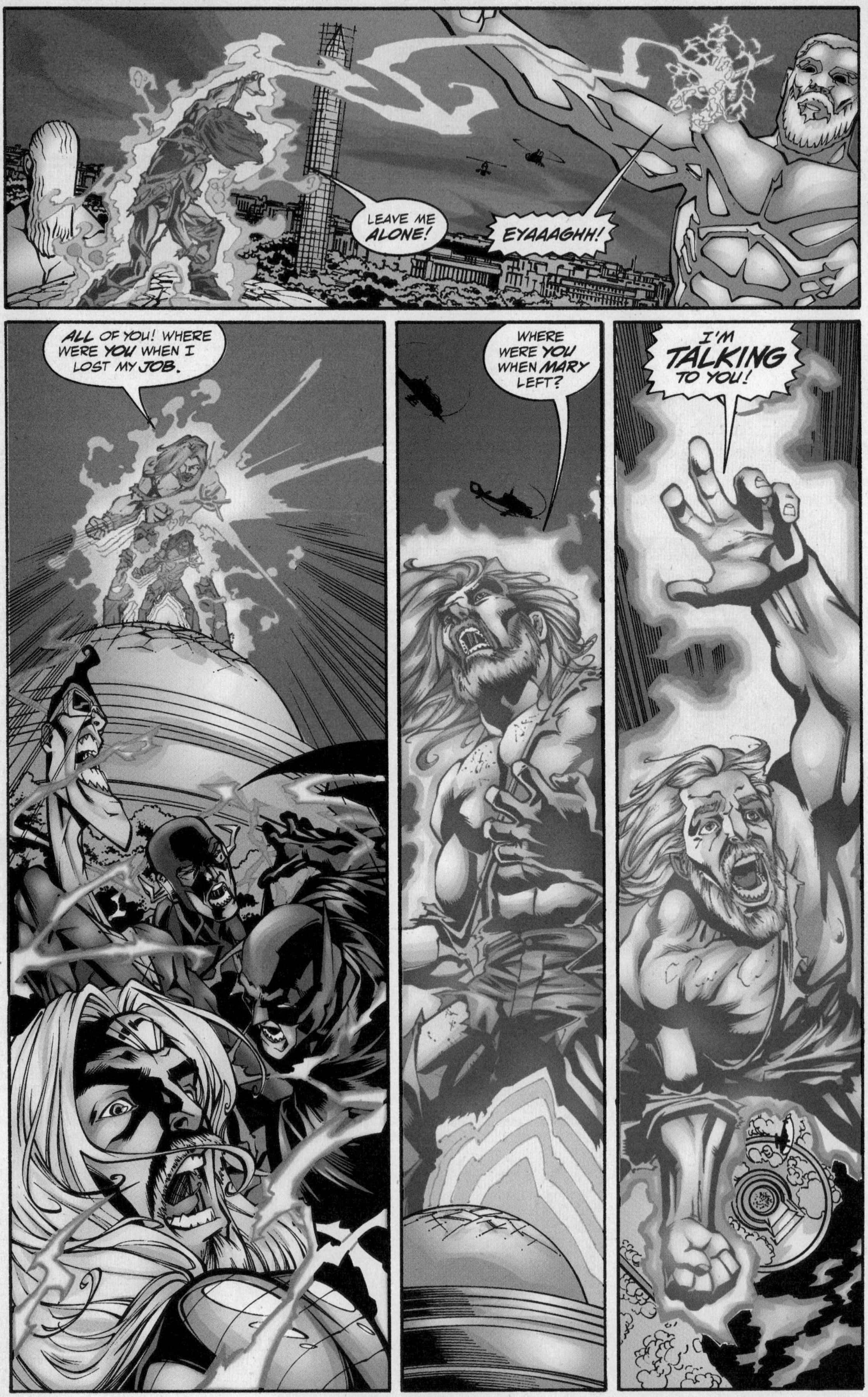
LEAVE ME ALONE!
EYAAAGHH!
ALL OF YOU! WHERE WERE YOU WHEN I LOST MY JOB.
WHERE WERE YOU WHEN MARY LEFT?
I'M TALKING TO YOU!

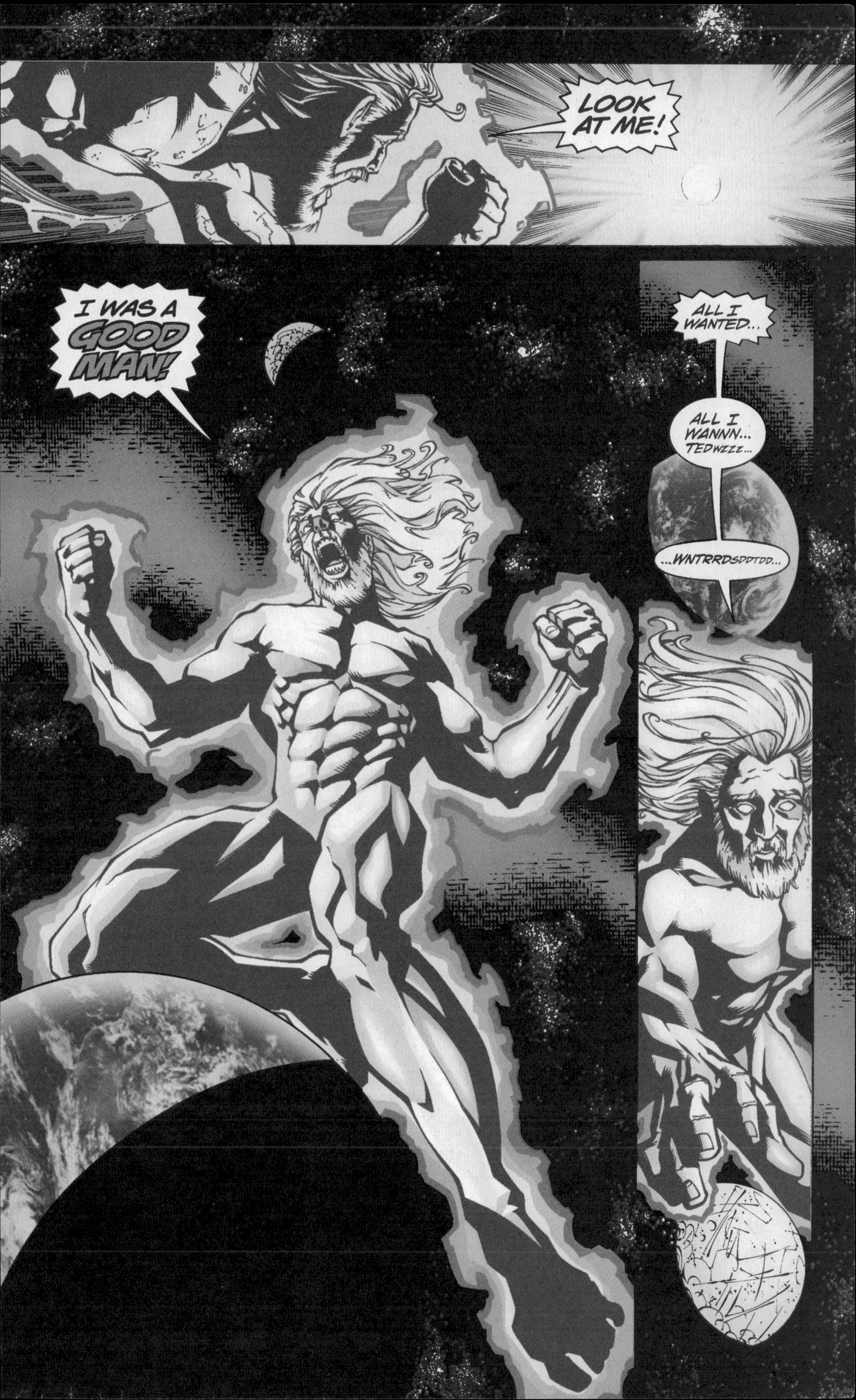
LOOK AT ME!
I WAS A GOOD MAN!
ALL I WANTED...
ALL I WANNN... TEDWZZZ...
...WNTRRDSDDTDD...

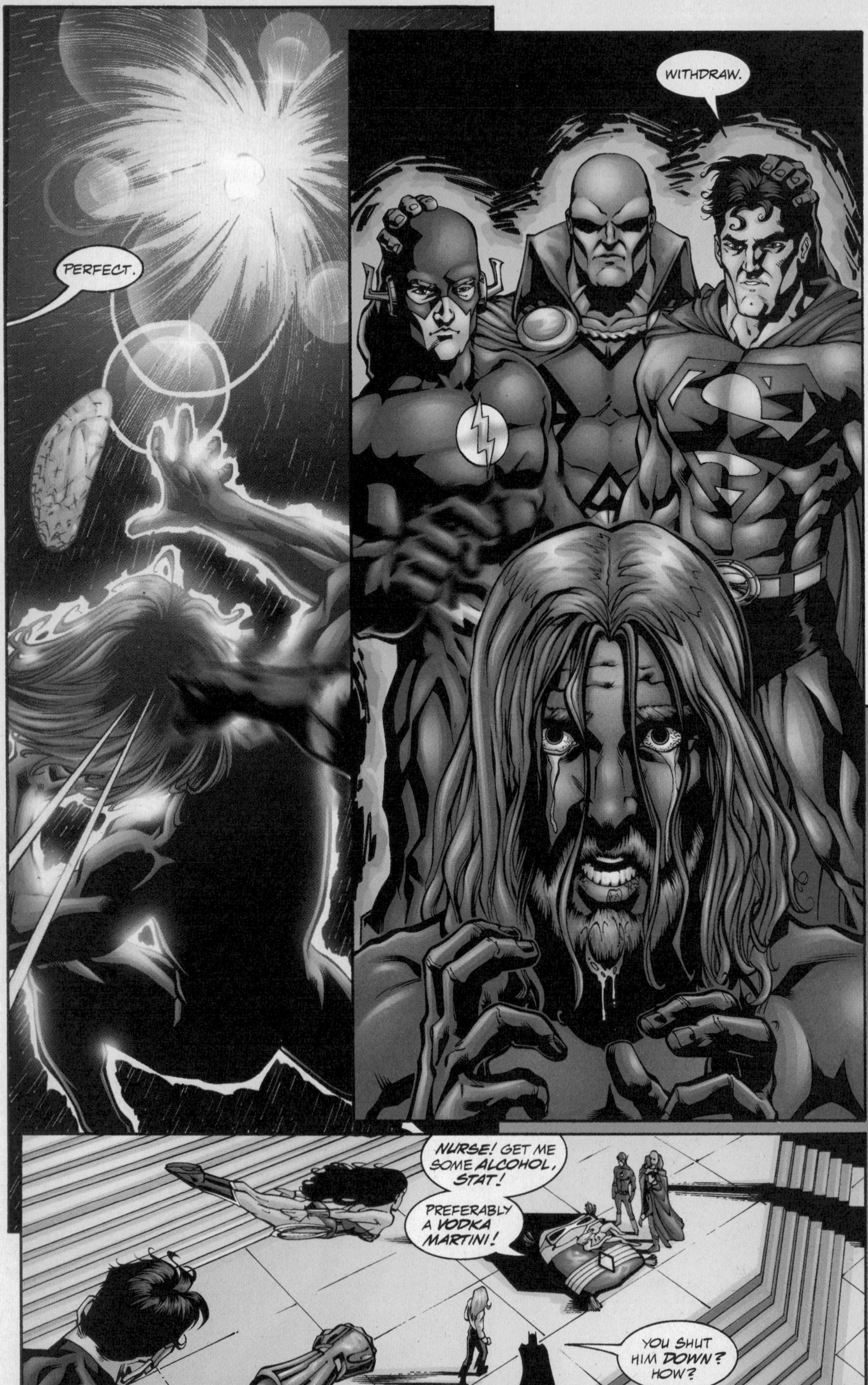
PERFECT.
WITHDRAW.
NURSE! GET ME SOME ALCOHOL, STAT!
PREFERABLY A VODKA MARTINI!
YOU SHUT HIM DOWN? HOW?

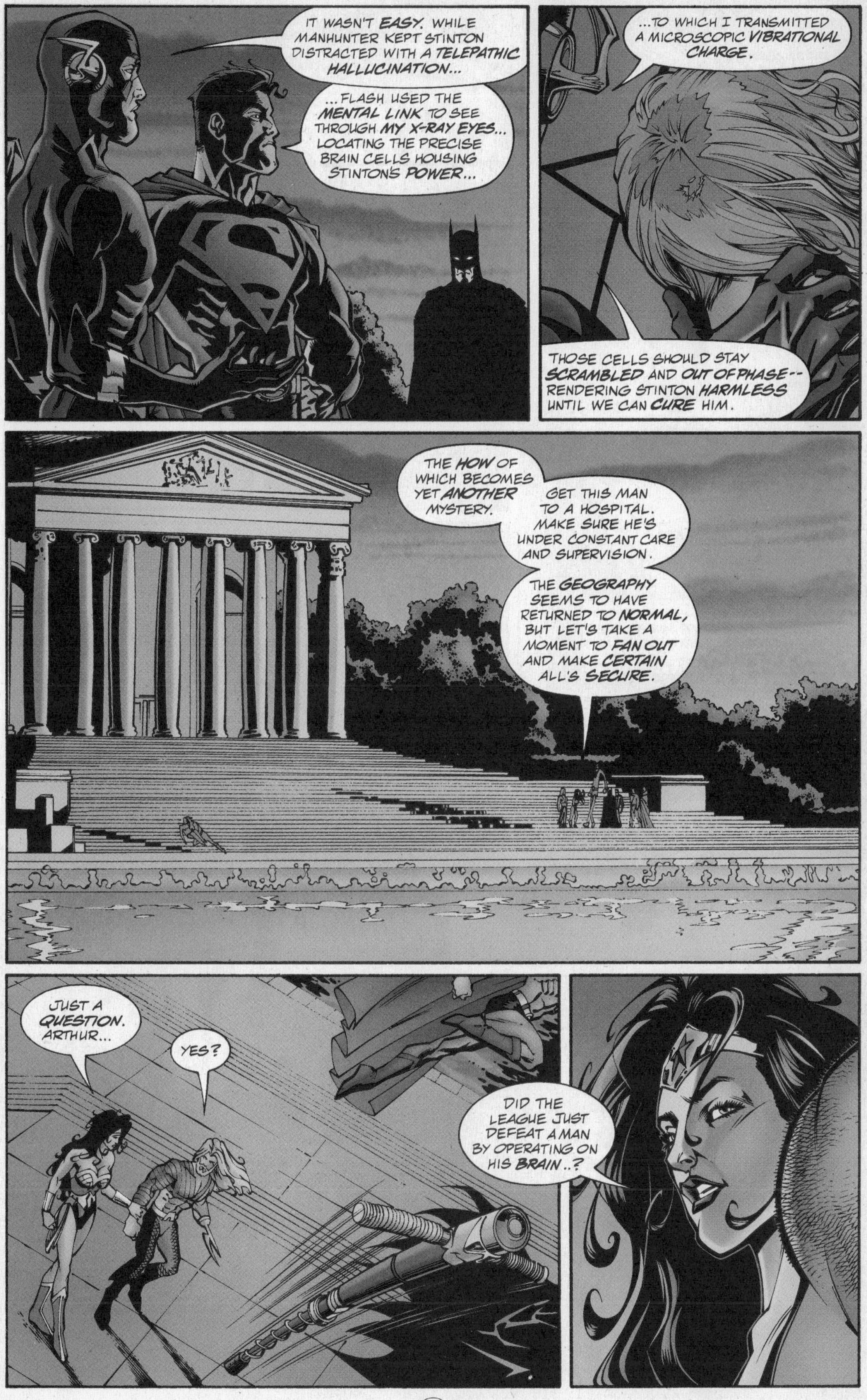
IT WASN'T EASY. WHILE MANHUNTER KEPT STINTON DISTRACTED WITH A TELEPATHIC HALLUCINATION...
...FLASH USED THE MENTAL LINK TO SEE THROUGH MY X-RAY EYES... LOCATING THE PRECISE BRAIN CELLS HOUSING STINTON'S POWER...
...TO WHICH I TRANSMITTED A MICROSCOPIC VIBRATIONAL CHARGE.
THOSE CELLS SHOULD STAY SCRAMBLED AND OUT OF PHASE-- RENDERING STINTON HARMLESS UNTIL WE CAN CURE HIM.
THE HOW OF WHICH BECOMES YET ANOTHER MYSTERY.
GET THIS MAN TO A HOSPITAL. MAKE SURE HE'S UNDER CONSTANT CARE AND SUPERVISION.
THE GEOGRAPHY SEEMS TO HAVE RETURNED TO NORMAL, BUT LET'S TAKE A MOMENT TO FAN OUT AND MAKE CERTAIN ALL'S SECURE.
JUST A QUESTION. ARTHUR...
YES?
DID THE LEAGUE JUST DEFEAT A MAN BY OPERATING ON HIS BRAIN..?

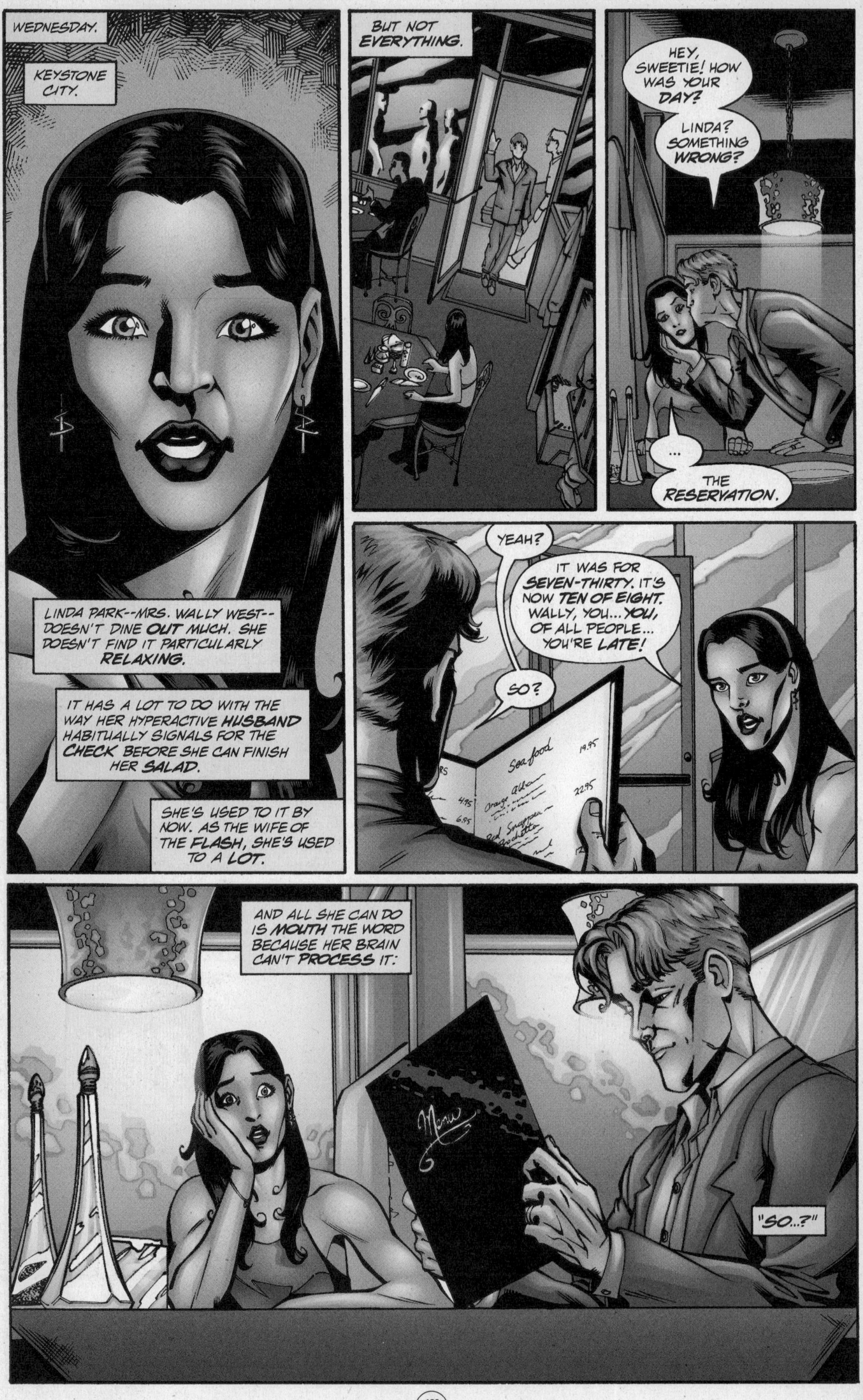

WEDNESDAY.
KEYSTONE CITY.
LINDA PARK--MRS. WALLY WEST--DOESN'T DINE OUT MUCH. SHE DOESN'T FIND IT PARTICULARLY RELAXING.
IT HAS A LOT TO DO WITH THE WAY HER HYPERACTIVE HUSBAND HABITUALLY SIGNALS FOR THE CHECK BEFORE SHE CAN FINISH HER SALAD.
SHE'S USED TO IT BY NOW. AS THE WIFE OF THE FLASH, SHE'S USED TO A LOT.
BUT NOT EVERYTHING.
HEY, SWEETIE! HOW WAS YOUR DAY?
LINDA? SOMETHING WRONG?
...
THE RESERVATION.
YEAH?
IT WAS FOR SEVEN-THIRTY. IT'S NOW TEN OF EIGHT. WALLY, YOU... YOU, OF ALL PEOPLE... YOU'RE LATE!
SO?
AND ALL SHE CAN DO IS MOUTH THE WORD BECAUSE HER BRAIN CAN'T PROCESS IT:
"SO...?"

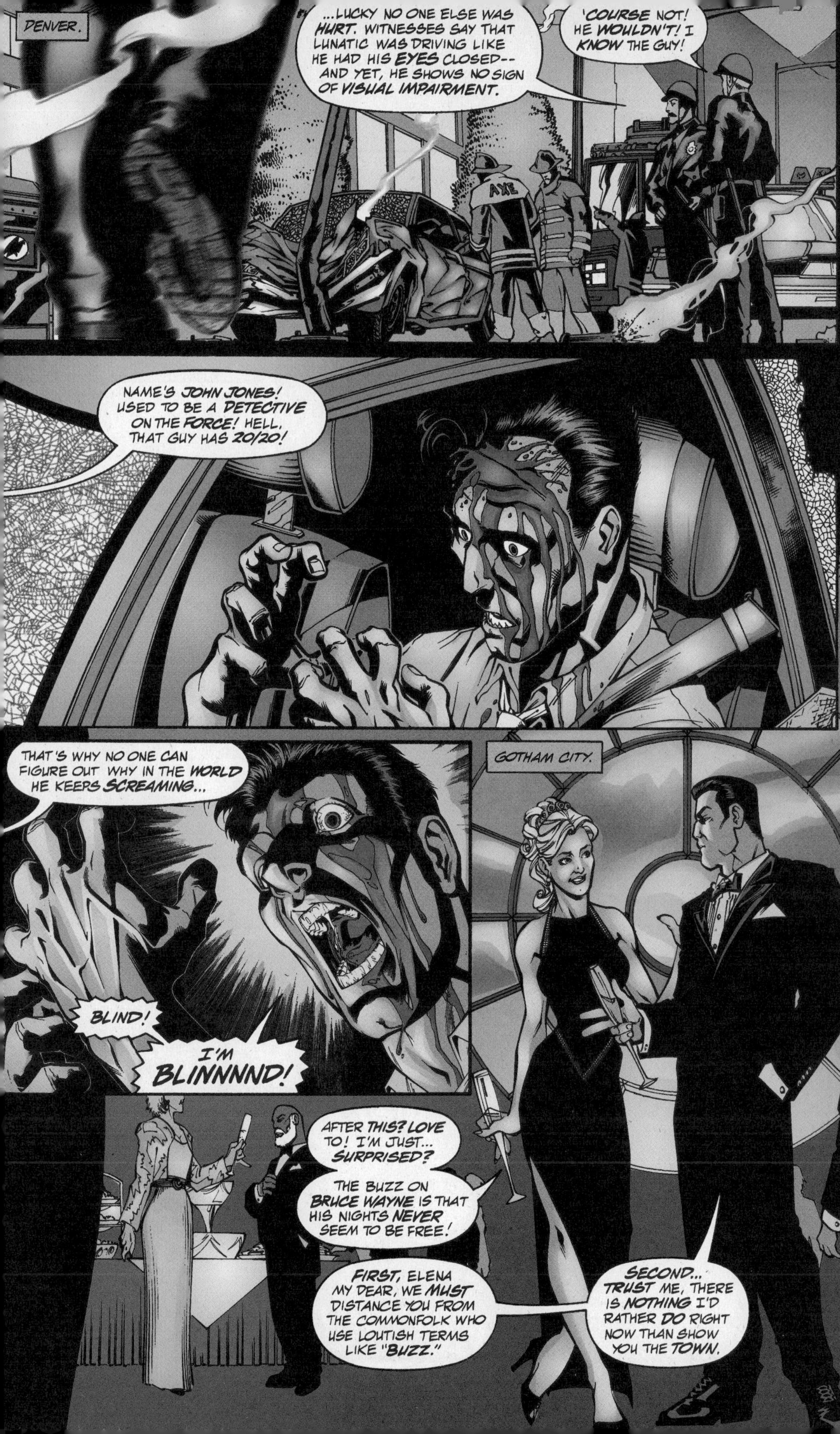
DENVER.
...LUCKY NO ONE ELSE WAS HURT. WITNESSES SAY THAT LUNATIC WAS DRIVING LIKE HE HAD HIS EYES CLOSED-- AND YET, HE SHOWS NO SIGN OF VISUAL IMPAIRMENT.
'COURSE NOT! HE WOULDN'T! I KNOW THE GUY!
AXE
NAME'S JOHN JONES! USED TO BE A DETECTIVE ON THE FORCE! HELL, THAT GUY HAS 20/20!
THAT'S WHY NO ONE CAN FIGURE OUT WHY IN THE WORLD HE KEEPS SCREAMING...
BLIND!
I'M BLINNNND!
GOTHAM CITY.
AFTER THIS? LOVE TO! I'M JUST... SURPRISED?
THE BUZZ ON BRUCE WAYNE IS THAT HIS NIGHTS NEVER SEEM TO BE FREE!
FIRST, ELENA MY DEAR, WE MUST DISTANCE YOU FROM THE COMMONFOLK WHO USE LOUTISH TERMS LIKE "BUZZ."
SECOND... TRUST ME, THERE IS NOTHING I'D RATHER DO RIGHT NOW THAN SHOW YOU THE TOWN.

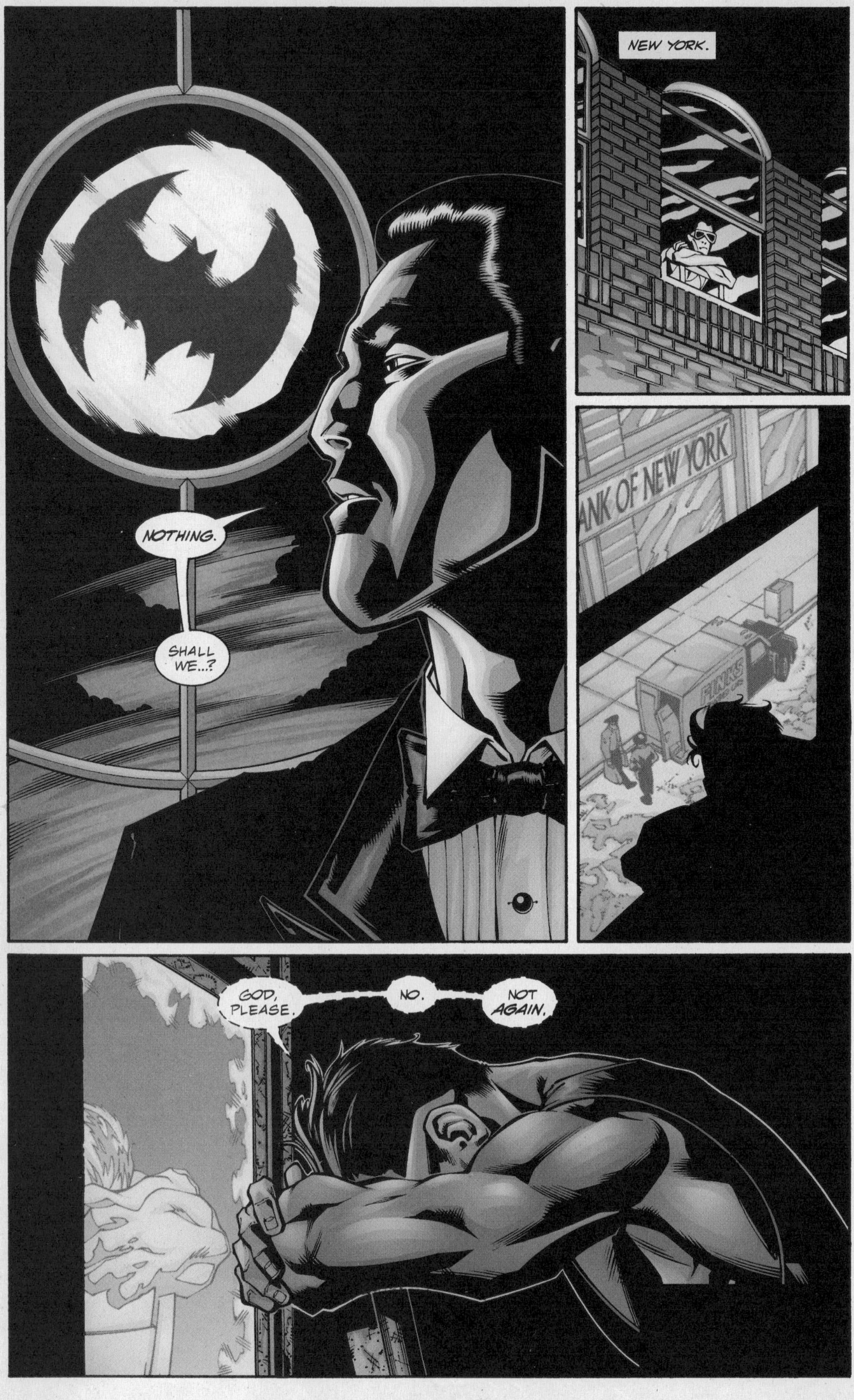
NOTHING.
SHALL WE...?
NEW YORK.
BANK OF NEW YORK
GOD, PLEASE.
NO.
NOT AGAIN.

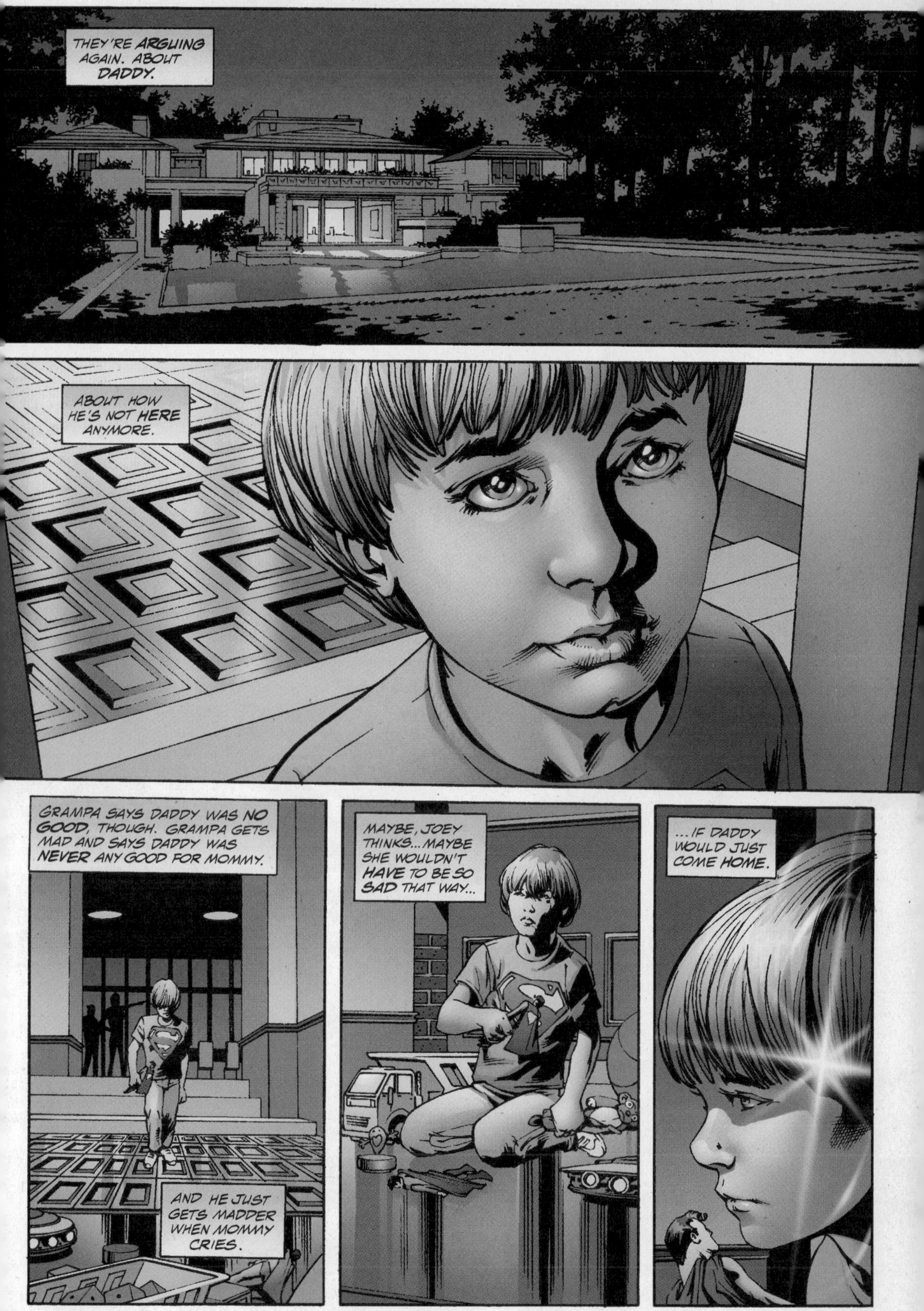
THEY'RE ARGUING AGAIN. ABOUT DADDY.
ABOUT HOW HE'S NOT HERE ANYMORE.
GRAMPA SAYS DADDY WAS NO GOOD, THOUGH. GRAMPA GETS MAD AND SAYS DADDY WAS NEVER ANY GOOD FOR MOMMY.
AND HE JUST GETS MADDER WHEN MOMMY CRIES.
MAYBE, JOEY THINKS... MAYBE SHE WOULDN'T HAVE TO BE SO SAD THAT WAY...
...IF DADDY WOULD JUST COME HOME.

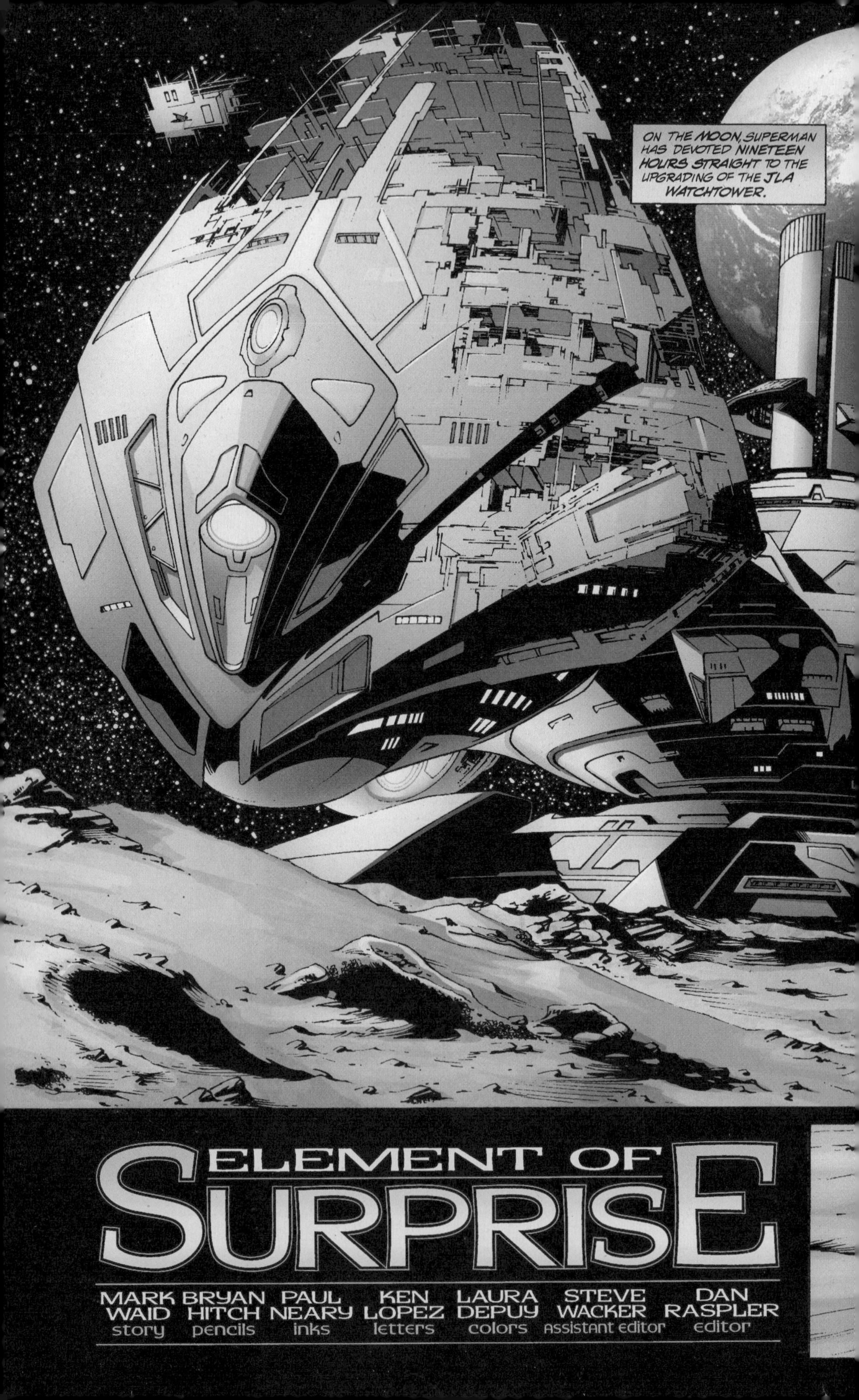
ON THE MOON, SUPERMAN HAS DEVOTED NINETEEN HOURS STRAIGHT TO THE UPGRADING OF THE JLA WATCHTOWER.
ELEMENT OF SURPRISE
MARK WAID story
BRYAN HITCH pencils
PAUL NEARY inks
KEN LOPEZ letters
LAURA DEPUY colors
STEVE WACKER assistant editor
DAN RASPLER editor

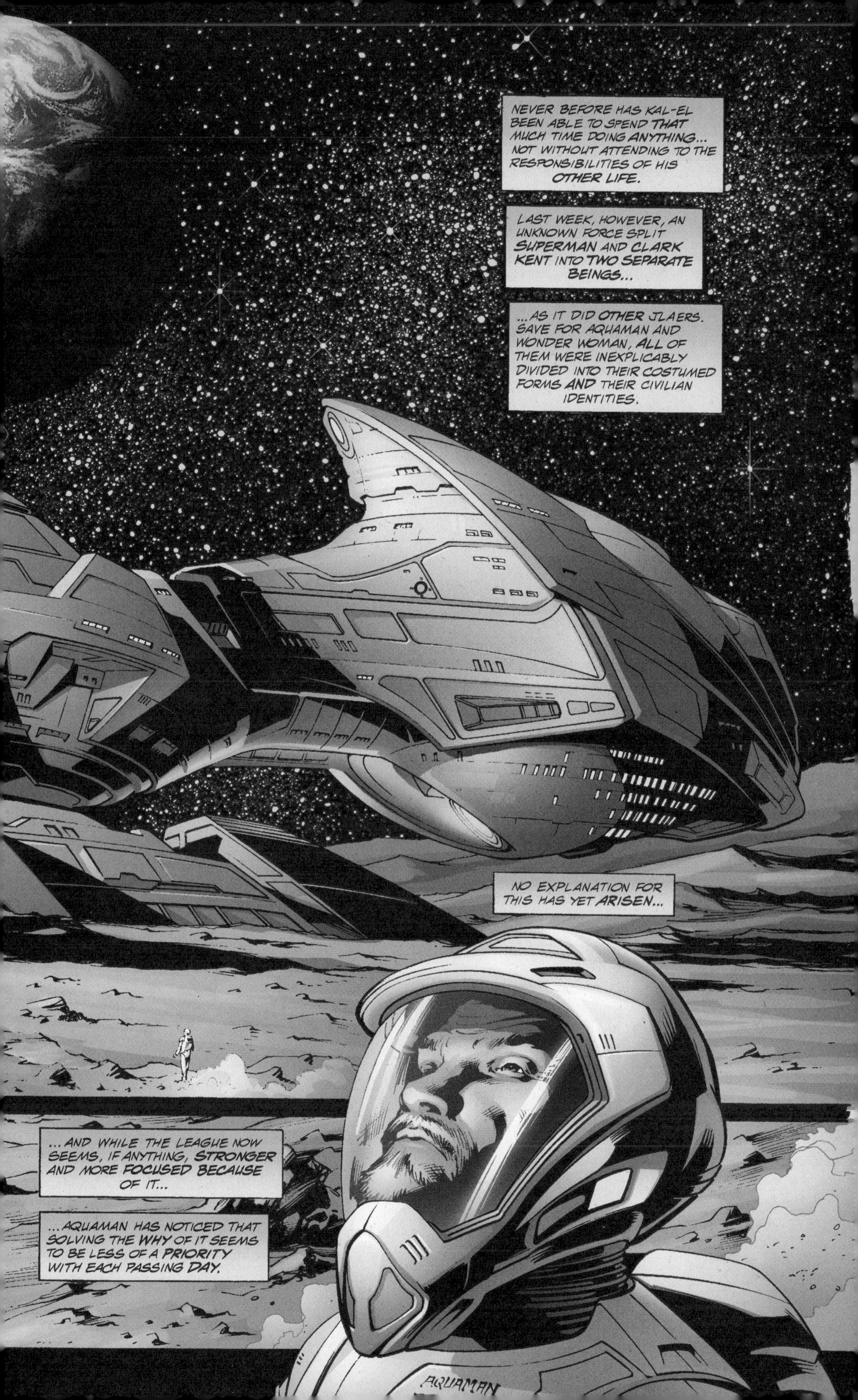
NEVER BEFORE HAS KAL-EL BEEN ABLE TO SPEND THAT MUCH TIME DOING ANYTHING... NOT WITHOUT ATTENDING TO THE RESPONSIBILITIES OF HIS OTHER LIFE.
LAST WEEK, HOWEVER, AN UNKNOWN FORCE SPLIT SUPERMAN AND CLARK KENT INTO TWO SEPARATE BEINGS...
...AS IT DID OTHER JLAERS. SAVE FOR AQUAMAN AND WONDER WOMAN, ALL OF THEM WERE INEXPLICABLY DIVIDED INTO THEIR COSTUMED FORMS AND THEIR CIVILIAN IDENTITIES.
NO EXPLANATION FOR THIS HAS YET ARISEN...
...AND WHILE THE LEAGUE NOW SEEMS, IF ANYTHING, STRONGER AND MORE FOCUSED BECAUSE OF IT...
...AQUAMAN HAS NOTICED THAT SOLVING THE WHY OF IT SEEMS TO BE LESS OF A PRIORITY WITH EACH PASSING DAY.
AQUAMAN

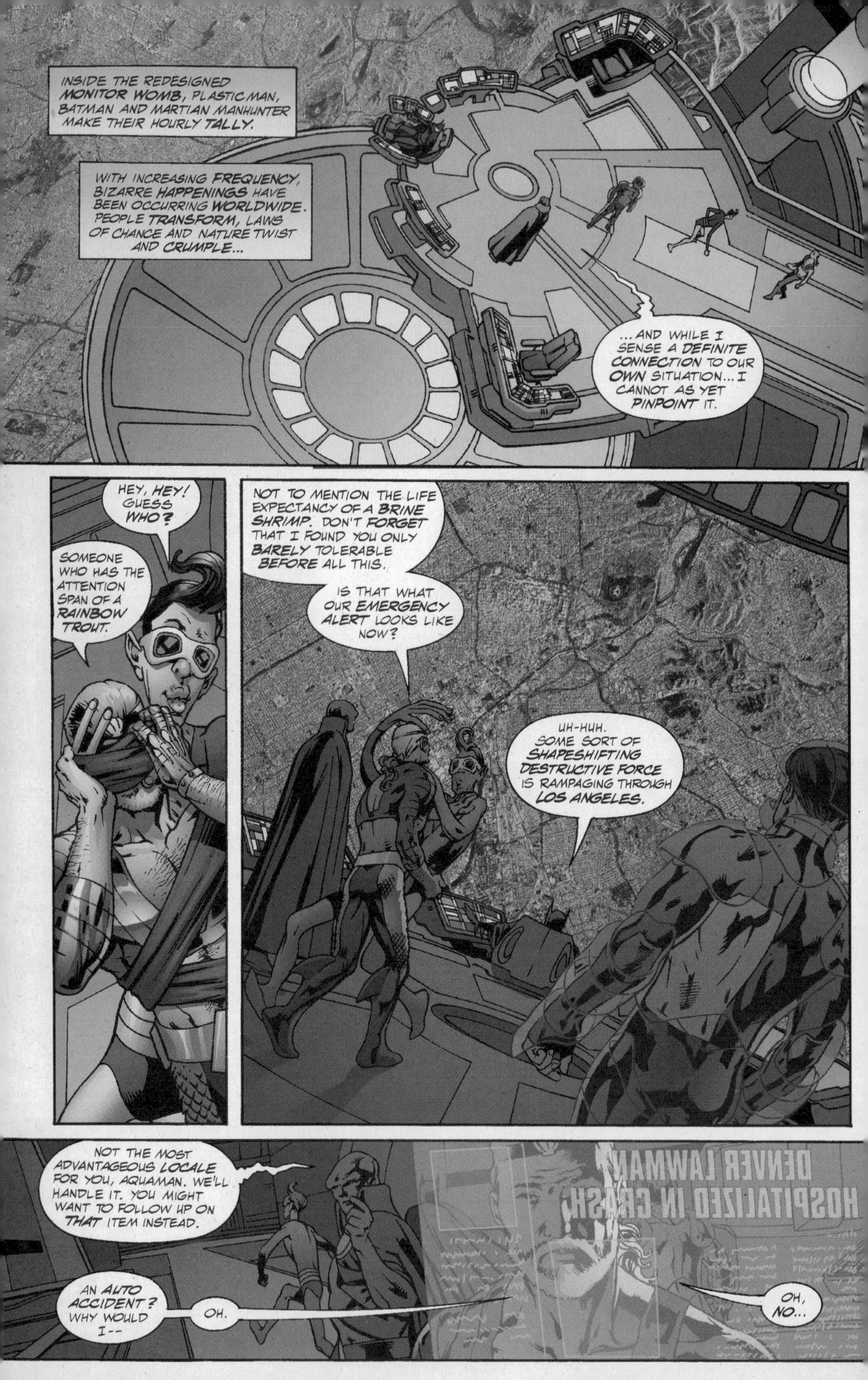
INSIDE THE REDESIGNED MONITOR WOMB, PLASTIC MAN, BATMAN AND MARTIAN MANHUNTER MAKE THEIR HOURLY TALLY.
WITH INCREASING FREQUENCY, BIZARRE HAPPENINGS HAVE BEEN OCCURRING WORLDWIDE. PEOPLE TRANSFORM, LAWS OF CHANCE AND NATURE TWIST AND CRUMPLE...
...AND WHILE I SENSE A DEFINITE CONNECTION TO OUR OWN SITUATION... I CANNOT AS YET PINPOINT IT.
HEY, HEY! GUESS WHO?
SOMEONE WHO HAS THE ATTENTION SPAN OF A RAINBOW TROUT.
NOT TO MENTION THE LIFE EXPECTANCY OF A BRINE SHRIMP. DON'T FORGET THAT I FOUND YOU ONLY BARELY TOLERABLE BEFORE ALL THIS.
IS THAT WHAT OUR EMERGENCY ALERT LOOKS LIKE NOW?
UH-HUH. SOME SORT OF SHAPESHIFTING DESTRUCTIVE FORCE IS RAMPAGING THROUGH LOS ANGELES.
NOT THE MOST ADVANTAGEOUS LOCALE FOR YOU, AQUAMAN. WE'LL HANDLE IT. YOU MIGHT WANT TO FOLLOW UP ON THAT ITEM INSTEAD.
DENVER LAWMAN HOSPITALIZED IN CRASH
AN AUTO ACCIDENT? WHY WOULD I--
OH.
OH, NO...

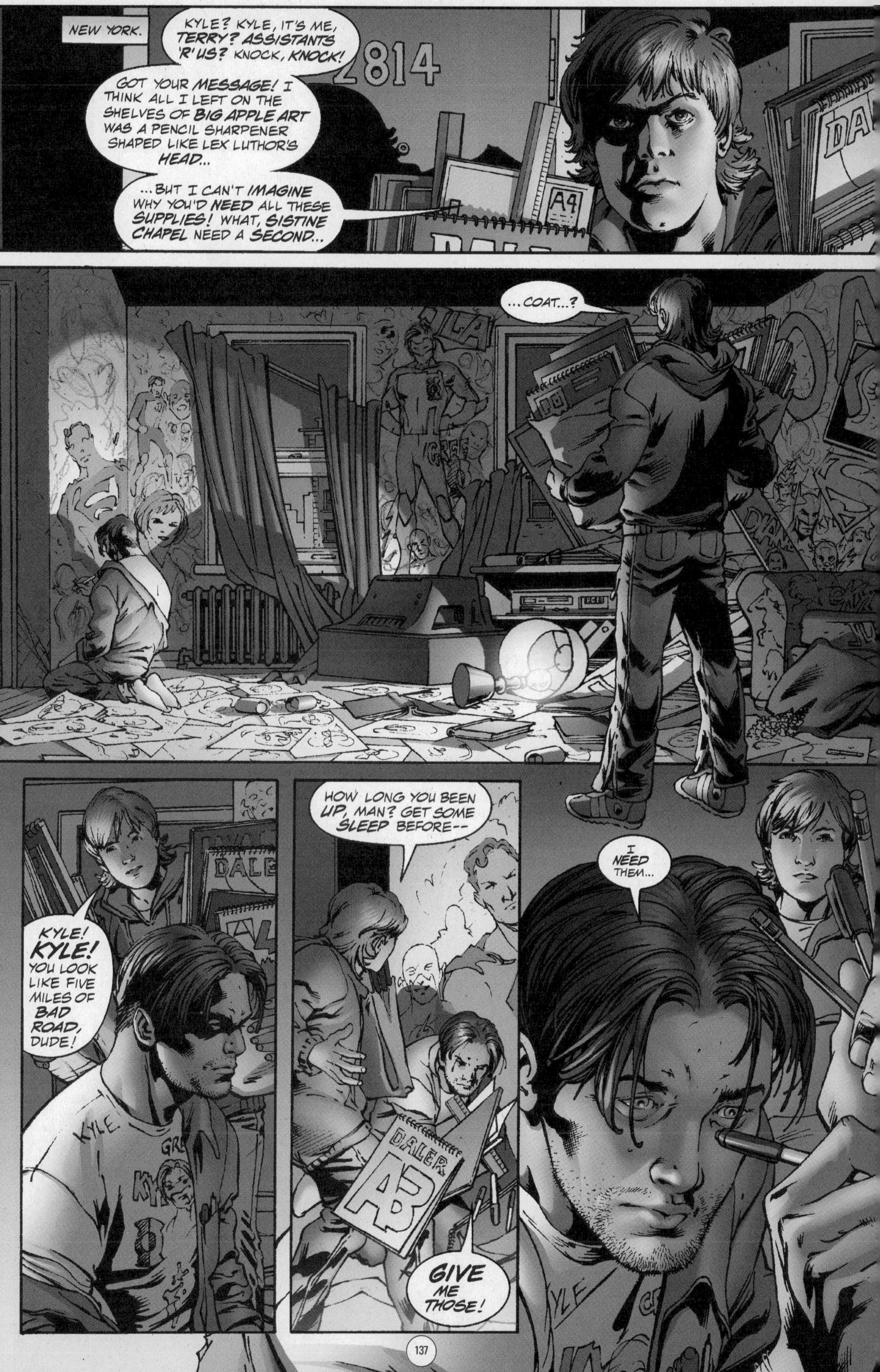
NEW YORK.
KYLE? KYLE, IT'S ME, TERRY? ASSISTANTS 'R' US? KNOCK, KNOCK!
GOT YOUR MESSAGE! I THINK ALL I LEFT ON THE SHELVES OF BIG APPLE ART WAS A PENCIL SHARPENER SHAPED LIKE LEX LUTHOR'S HEAD...
...BUT I CAN'T IMAGINE WHY YOU'D NEED ALL THESE SUPPLIES! WHAT, SISTINE CHAPEL NEED A SECOND...
...COAT...?
KYLE! KYLE! YOU LOOK LIKE FIVE MILES OF BAD ROAD, DUDE!
HOW LONG YOU BEEN UP, MAN? GET SOME SLEEP BEFORE--
GIVE ME THOSE!
I NEED THEM...

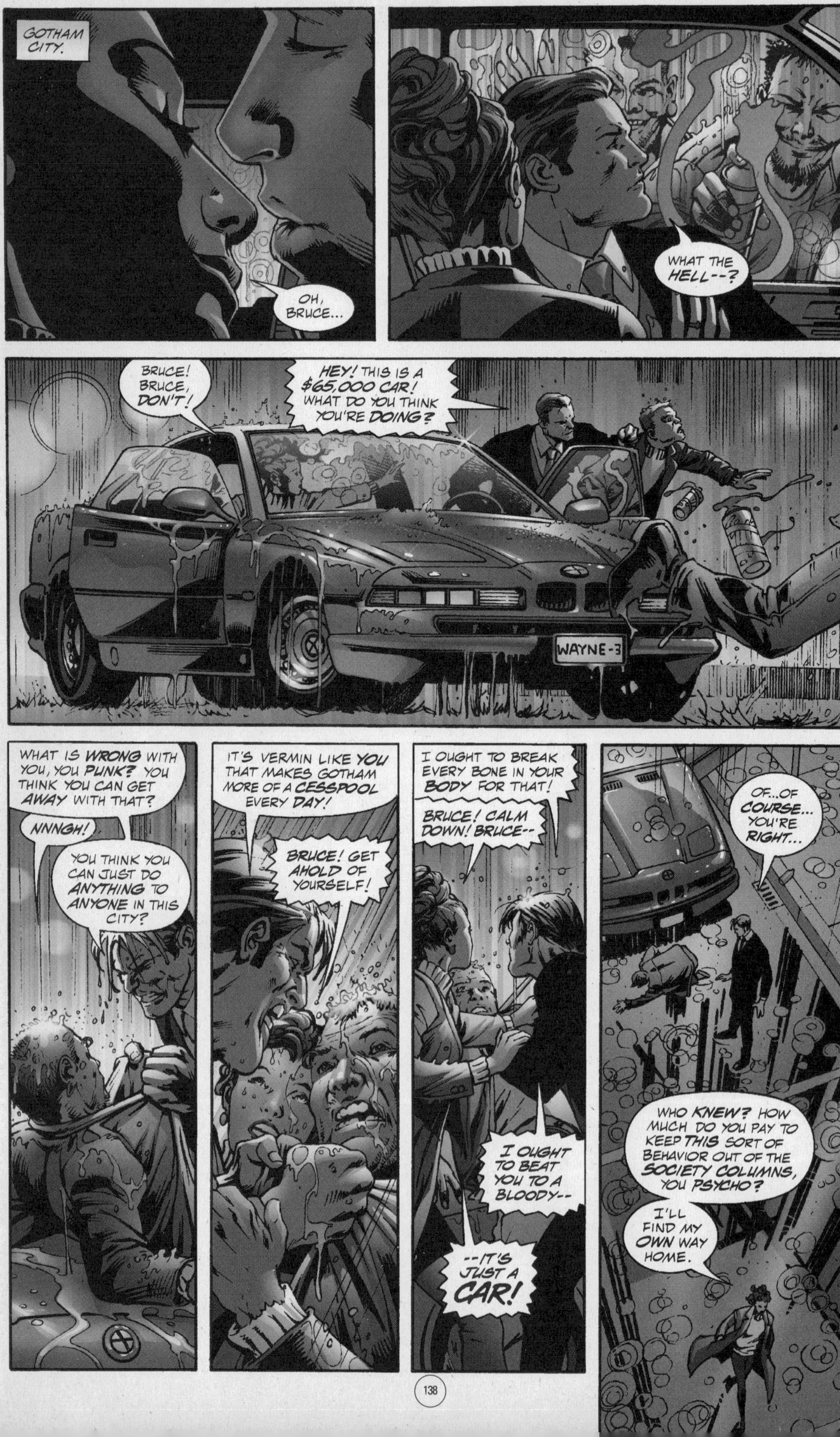
GOTHAM CITY.
OH, BRUCE...
WHAT THE HELL--?
BRUCE! BRUCE, DON'T!
HEY! THIS IS A $65,000 CAR! WHAT DO YOU THINK YOU'RE DOING?
WAYNE-3
WHAT IS WRONG WITH YOU, YOU PUNK? YOU THINK YOU CAN GET AWAY WITH THAT?
NNNGH!
YOU THINK YOU CAN JUST DO ANYTHING TO ANYONE IN THIS CITY?
IT'S VERMIN LIKE YOU THAT MAKES GOTHAM MORE OF A CESSPOOL EVERY DAY!
BRUCE! GET AHOLD OF YOURSELF!
I OUGHT TO BREAK EVERY BONE IN YOUR BODY FOR THAT!
BRUCE! CALM DOWN! BRUCE--
I OUGHT TO BEAT YOU TO A BLOODY--
--IT'S JUST A CAR!
OF...OF COURSE... YOU'RE RIGHT...
WHO KNEW? HOW MUCH DO YOU PAY TO KEEP THIS SORT OF BEHAVIOR OUT OF THE SOCIETY COLUMNS, YOU PSYCHO?
I'LL FIND MY OWN WAY HOME.

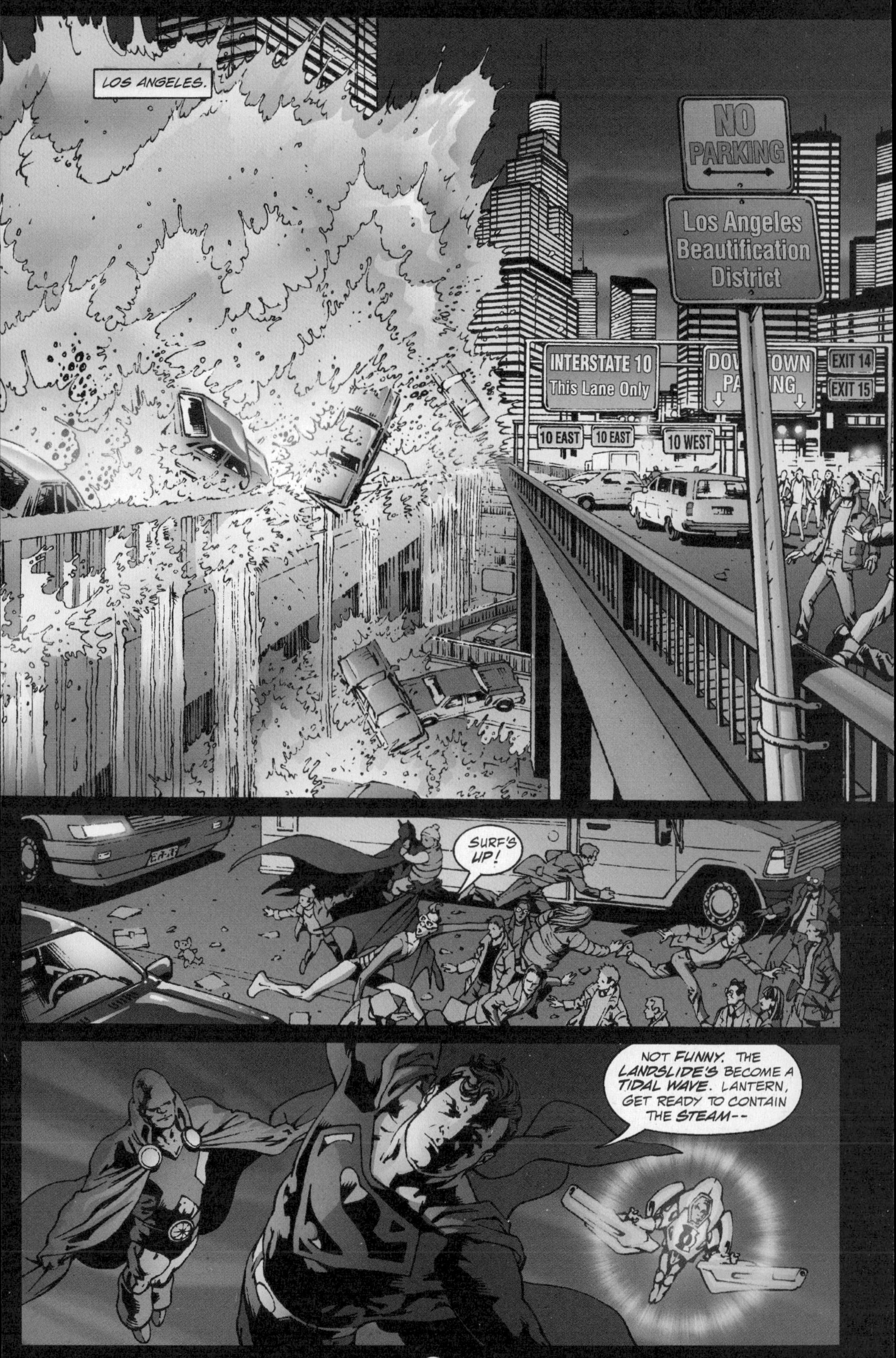
LOS ANGELES.
NO PARKING
Los Angeles Beautification District
INTERSTATE 10 This Lane Only
EXIT 14
EXIT 15
10 EAST
10 EAST
10 WEST
SURF'S UP!
NOT FUNNY. THE LANDSLIDE'S BECOME A TIDAL WAVE. LANTERN, GET READY TO CONTAIN THE STEAM--

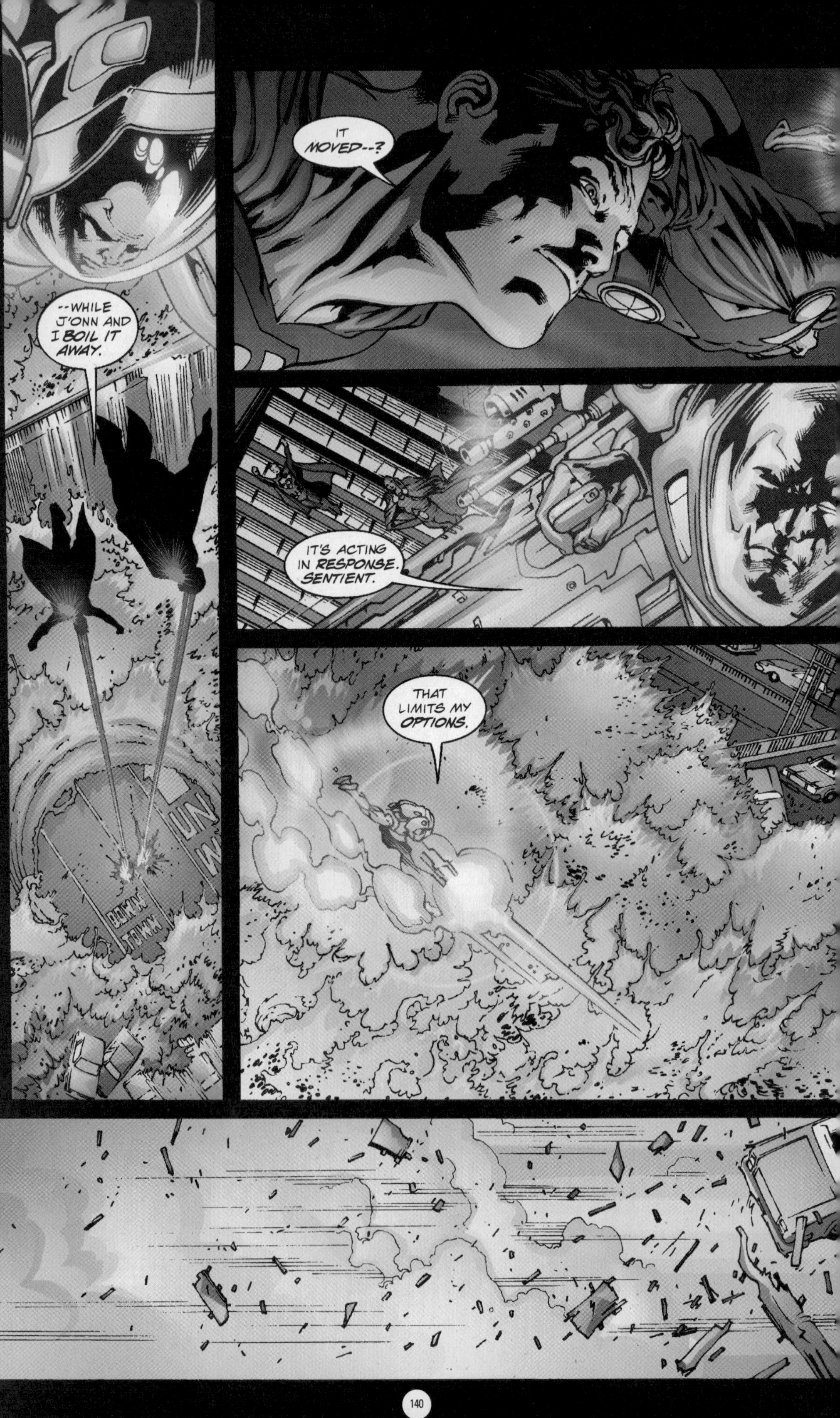
--WHILE J'ONN AND I BOIL IT AWAY.
IT MOVED--?
IT'S ACTING IN RESPONSE. SENTIENT.
THAT LIMITS MY OPTIONS.

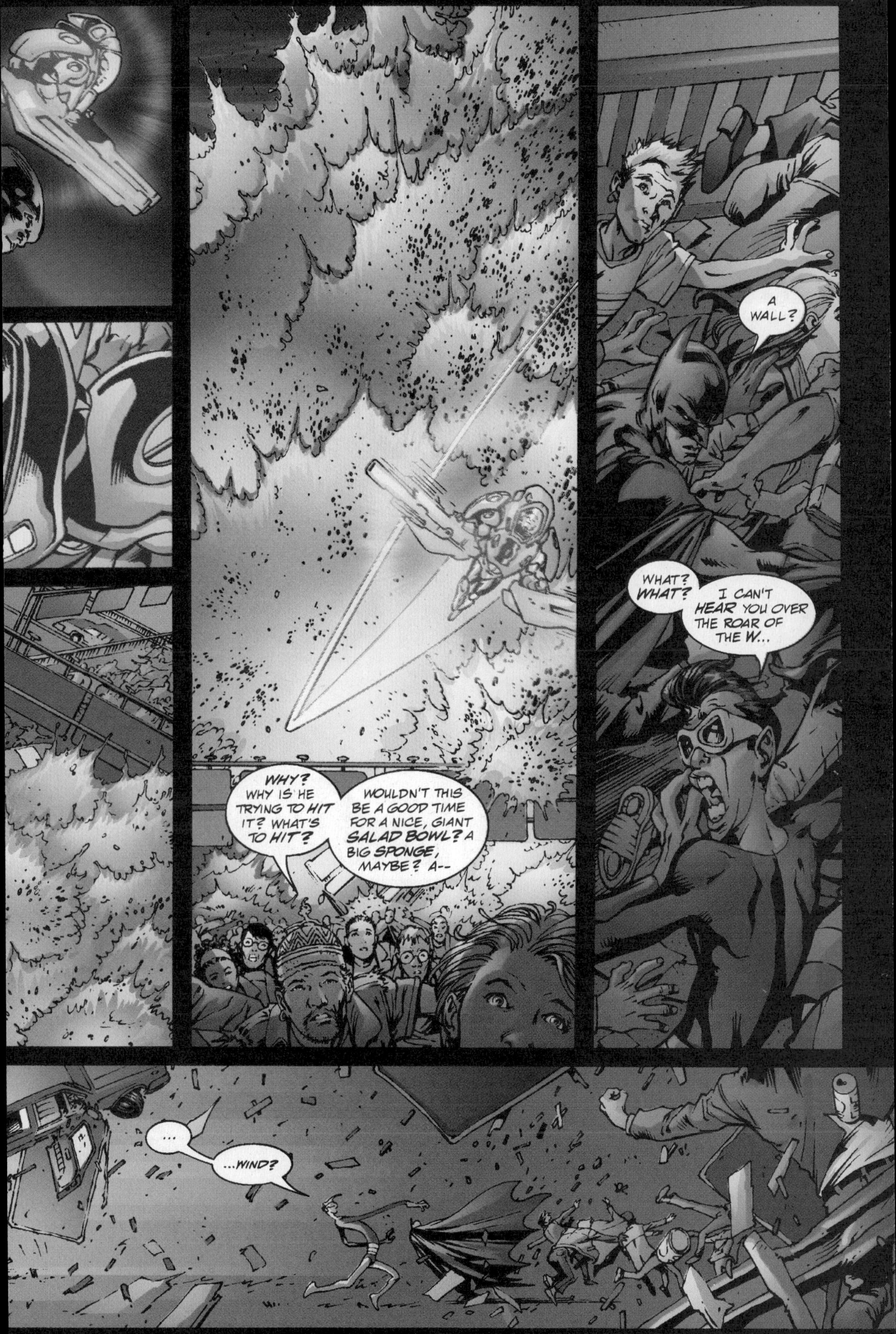
A WALL?
WHY? WHY IS HE TRYING TO HIT IT? WHAT'S TO HIT?
WOULDN'T THIS BE A GOOD TIME FOR A NICE, GIANT SALAD BOWL? A BIG SPONGE, MAYBE? A--
WHAT? WHAT?
I CAN'T HEAR YOU OVER THE ROAR OF THE W...
...
...WIND?

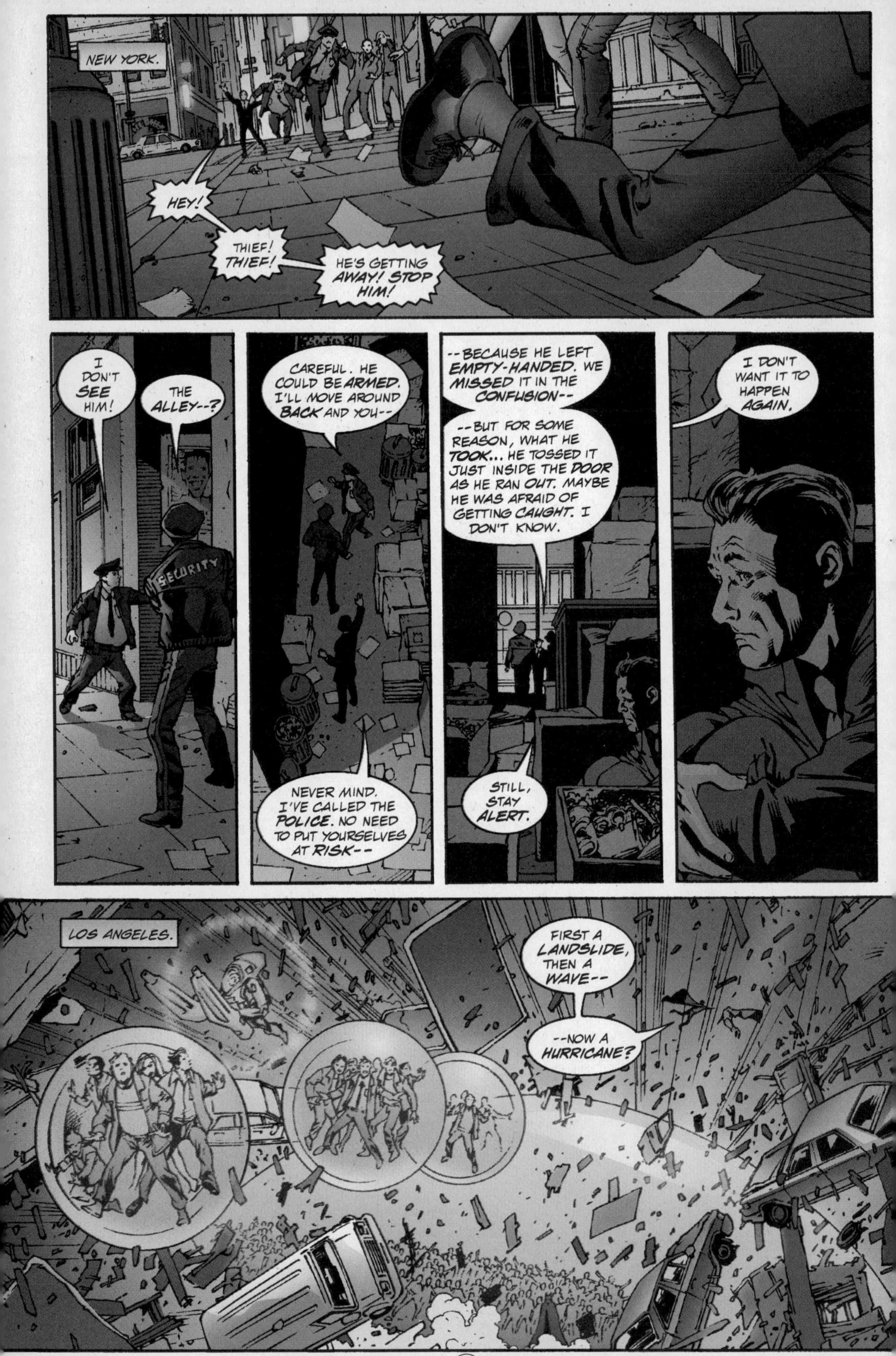

NEW YORK.
HEY!
THIEF! THIEF!
HE'S GETTING AWAY! STOP HIM!
I DON'T SEE HIM!
THE ALLEY--?
CAREFUL. HE COULD BE ARMED. I'LL MOVE AROUND BACK AND YOU--
NEVER MIND. I'VE CALLED THE POLICE. NO NEED TO PUT YOURSELVES AT RISK--
--BECAUSE HE LEFT EMPTY-HANDED. WE MISSED IT IN THE CONFUSION--
--BUT FOR SOME REASON, WHAT HE TOOK... HE TOSSED IT JUST INSIDE THE DOOR AS HE RAN OUT. MAYBE HE WAS AFRAID OF GETTING CAUGHT. I DON'T KNOW.
STILL, STAY ALERT.
I DON'T WANT IT TO HAPPEN AGAIN.
LOS ANGELES.
FIRST A LANDSLIDE, THEN A WAVE--
--NOW A HURRICANE?

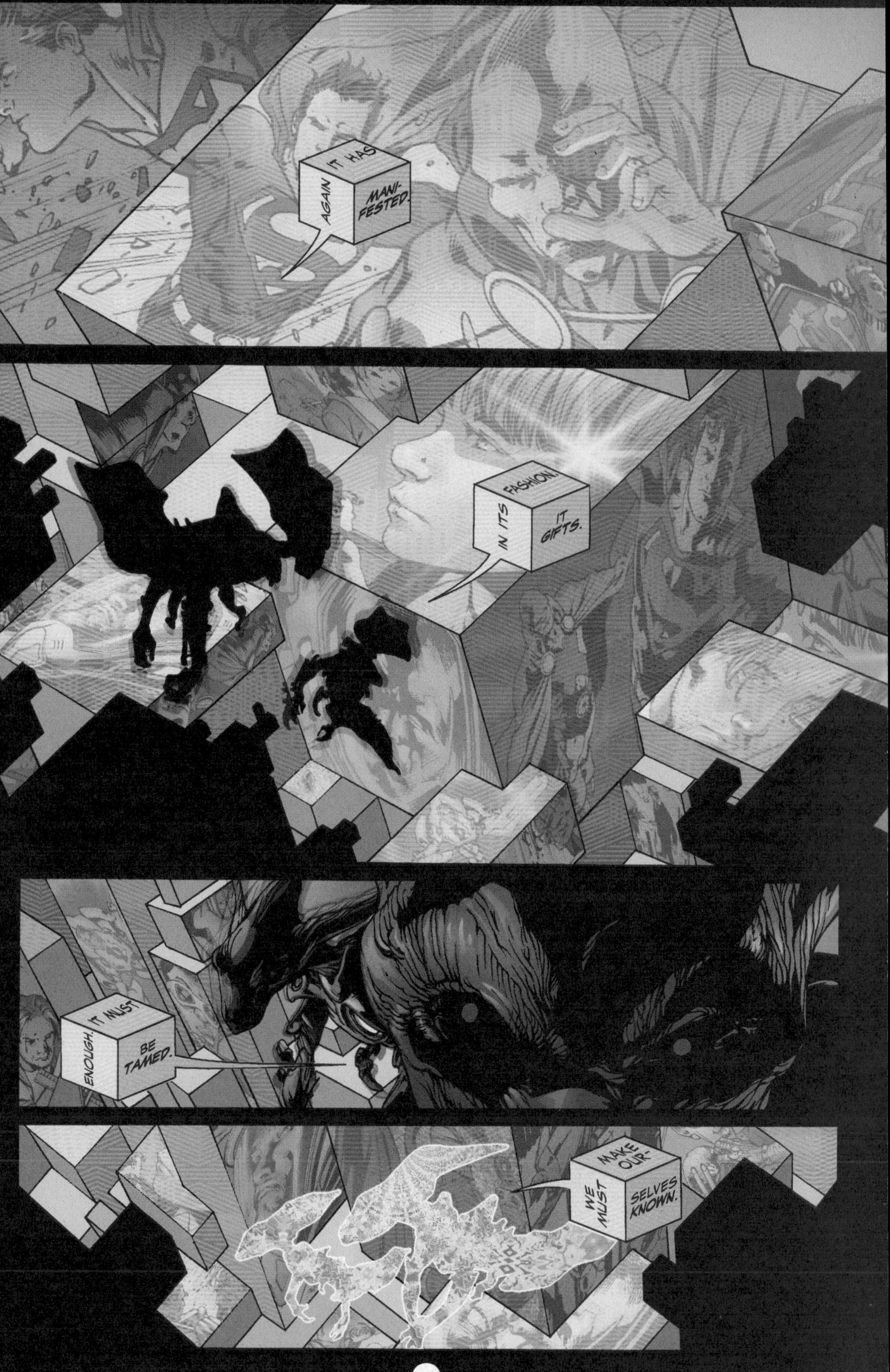
IT HAS AGAIN MANI-FESTED.
IN ITS FASHION, IT GIFTS.
IT MUST BE ENOUGH. TAMED.
WE MUST MAKE OUR-SELVES KNOWN.

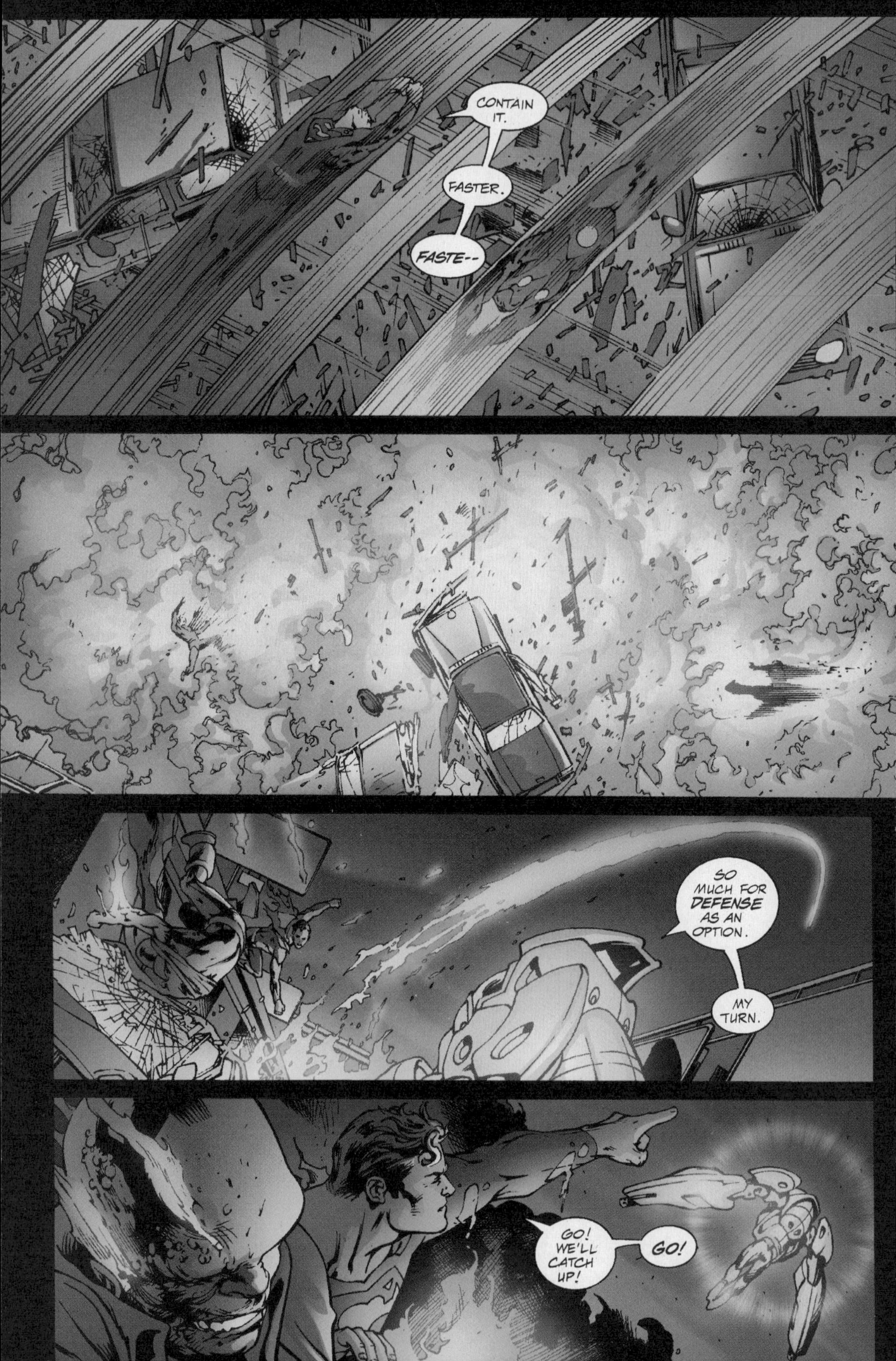
CONTAIN IT.
FASTER.
FASTE--
SO MUCH FOR DEFENSE AS AN OPTION.
MY TURN.
GO! WE'LL CATCH UP!
GO!

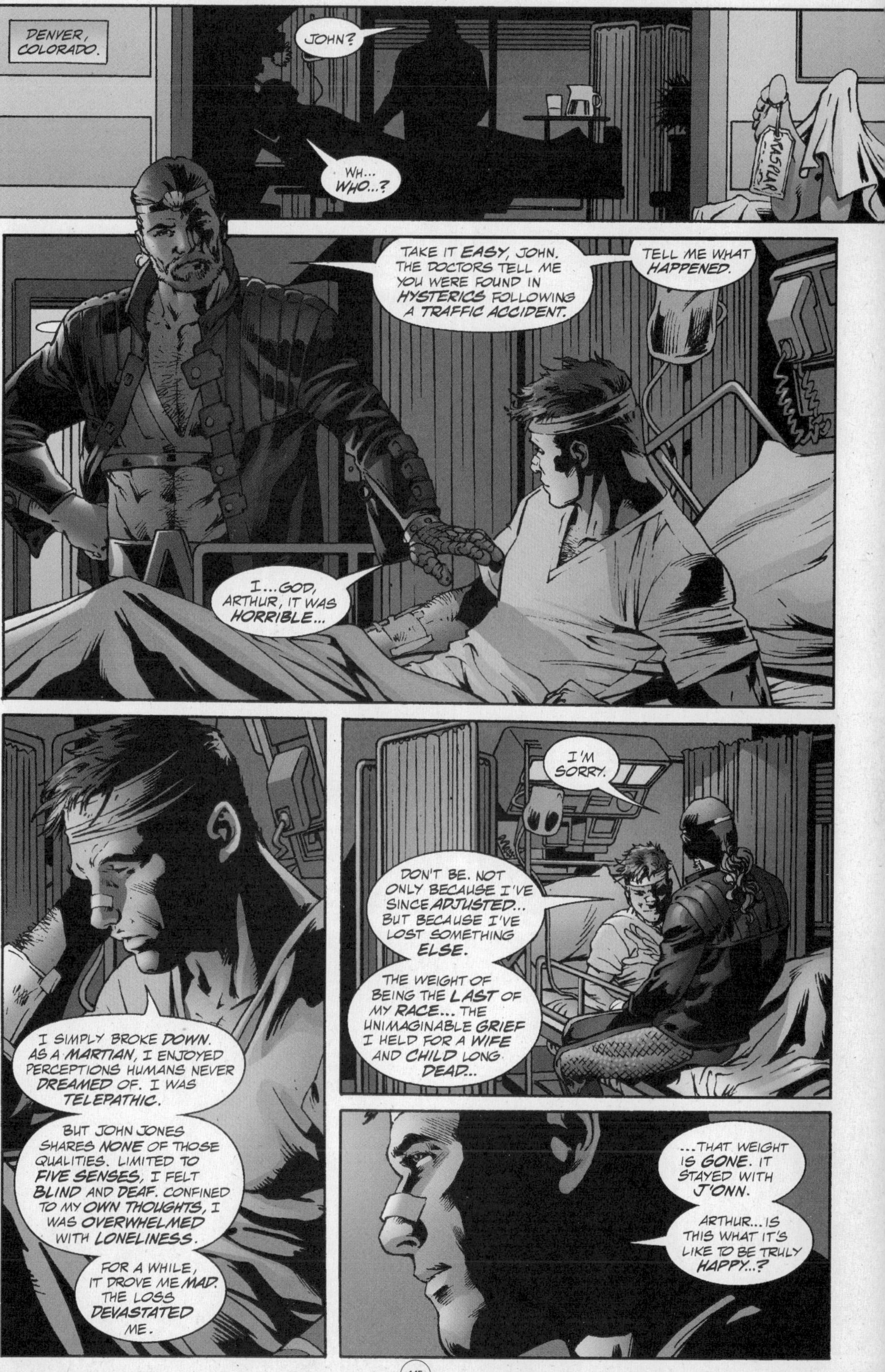
DENVER, COLORADO.
JOHN?
WH... WHO...?
TAKE IT EASY, JOHN. THE DOCTORS TELL ME YOU WERE FOUND IN HYSTERICS FOLLOWING A TRAFFIC ACCIDENT.
TELL ME WHAT HAPPENED.
I...GOD, ARTHUR, IT WAS HORRIBLE...
I SIMPLY BROKE DOWN. AS A MARTIAN, I ENJOYED PERCEPTIONS HUMANS NEVER DREAMED OF. I WAS TELEPATHIC.
BUT JOHN JONES SHARES NONE OF THOSE QUALITIES. LIMITED TO FIVE SENSES, I FELT BLIND AND DEAF. CONFINED TO MY OWN THOUGHTS, I WAS OVERWHELMED WITH LONELINESS.
FOR A WHILE, IT DROVE ME MAD. THE LOSS DEVASTATED ME.
I'M SORRY.
DON'T BE. NOT ONLY BECAUSE I'VE SINCE ADJUSTED... BUT BECAUSE I'VE LOST SOMETHING ELSE.
THE WEIGHT OF BEING THE LAST OF MY RACE... THE UNIMAGINABLE GRIEF I HELD FOR A WIFE AND CHILD LONG DEAD...
...THAT WEIGHT IS GONE. IT STAYED WITH J'ONN.
ARTHUR... IS THIS WHAT IT'S LIKE TO BE TRULY HAPPY...?

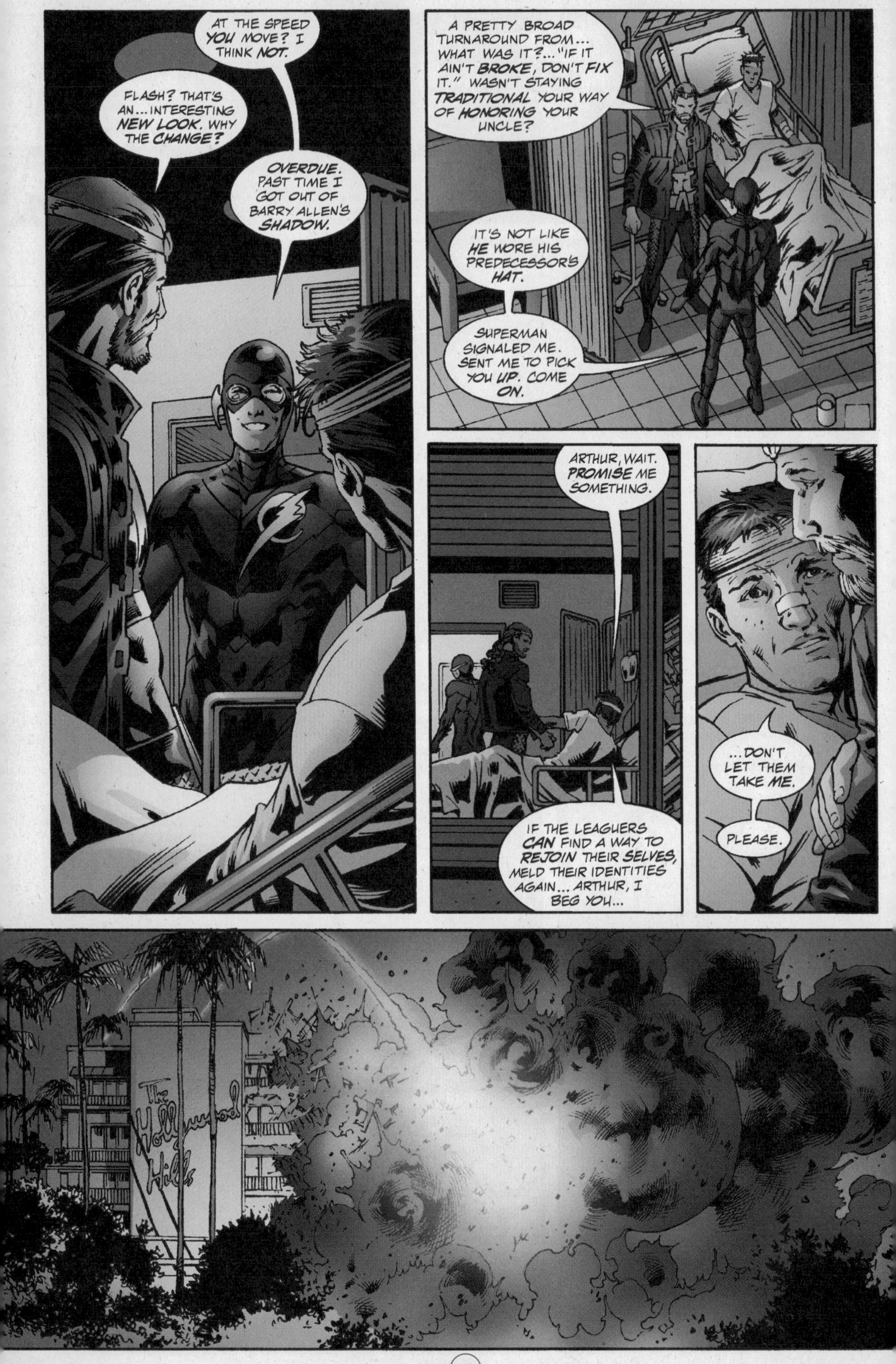
FLASH? THAT'S AN... INTERESTING NEW LOOK. WHY THE CHANGE?
AT THE SPEED YOU MOVE? I THINK NOT.
OVERDUE. PAST TIME I GOT OUT OF BARRY ALLEN'S SHADOW.
A PRETTY BROAD TURNAROUND FROM... WHAT WAS IT?... "IF IT AIN'T BROKE, DON'T FIX IT." WASN'T STAYING TRADITIONAL YOUR WAY OF HONORING YOUR UNCLE?
IT'S NOT LIKE HE WORE HIS PREDECESSOR'S HAT.
SUPERMAN SIGNALED ME. SENT ME TO PICK YOU UP. COME ON.
ARTHUR, WAIT. PROMISE ME SOMETHING.
IF THE LEAGUERS CAN FIND A WAY TO REJOIN THEIR SELVES, MELD THEIR IDENTITIES AGAIN... ARTHUR, I BEG YOU...
...DON'T LET THEM TAKE ME.
PLEASE.
The Hollywood Hills

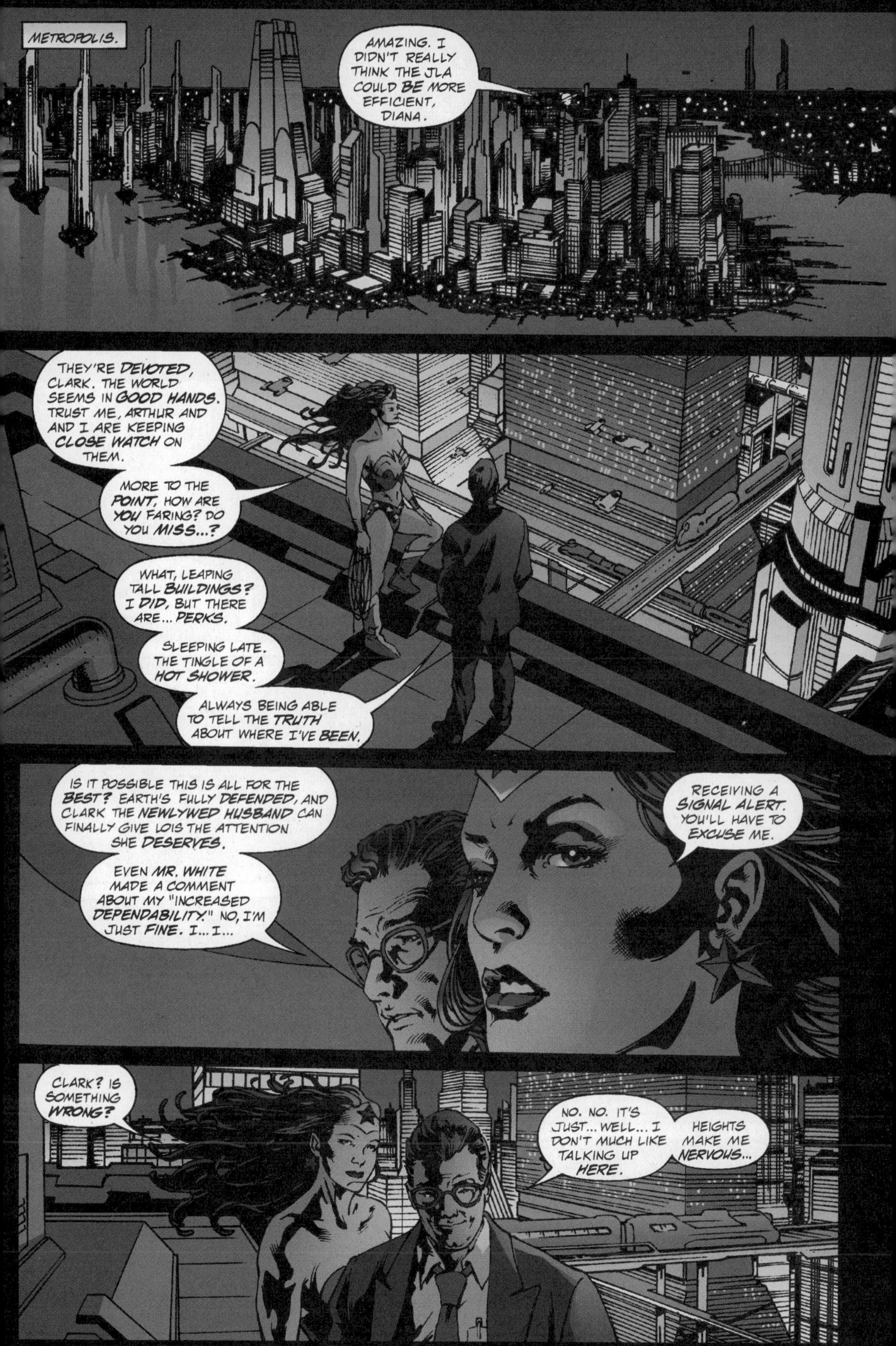
METROPOLIS.
AMAZING. I DIDN'T REALLY THINK THE JLA COULD BE MORE EFFICIENT, DIANA.
THEY'RE DEVOTED, CLARK. THE WORLD SEEMS IN GOOD HANDS. TRUST ME, ARTHUR AND AND I ARE KEEPING CLOSE WATCH ON THEM.
MORE TO THE POINT, HOW ARE YOU FARING? DO YOU MISS...?
WHAT, LEAPING TALL BUILDINGS? I DID, BUT THERE ARE... PERKS.
SLEEPING LATE. THE TINGLE OF A HOT SHOWER.
ALWAYS BEING ABLE TO TELL THE TRUTH ABOUT WHERE I'VE BEEN.
IS IT POSSIBLE THIS IS ALL FOR THE BEST? EARTH'S FULLY DEFENDED, AND CLARK THE NEWLYWED HUSBAND CAN FINALLY GIVE LOIS THE ATTENTION SHE DESERVES.
EVEN MR. WHITE MADE A COMMENT ABOUT MY "INCREASED DEPENDABILITY." NO, I'M JUST FINE. I... I...
RECEIVING A SIGNAL ALERT. YOU'LL HAVE TO EXCUSE ME.
CLARK? IS SOMETHING WRONG?
NO. NO. IT'S JUST... WELL... I DON'T MUCH LIKE TALKING UP HERE.
HEIGHTS MAKE ME NERVOUS...

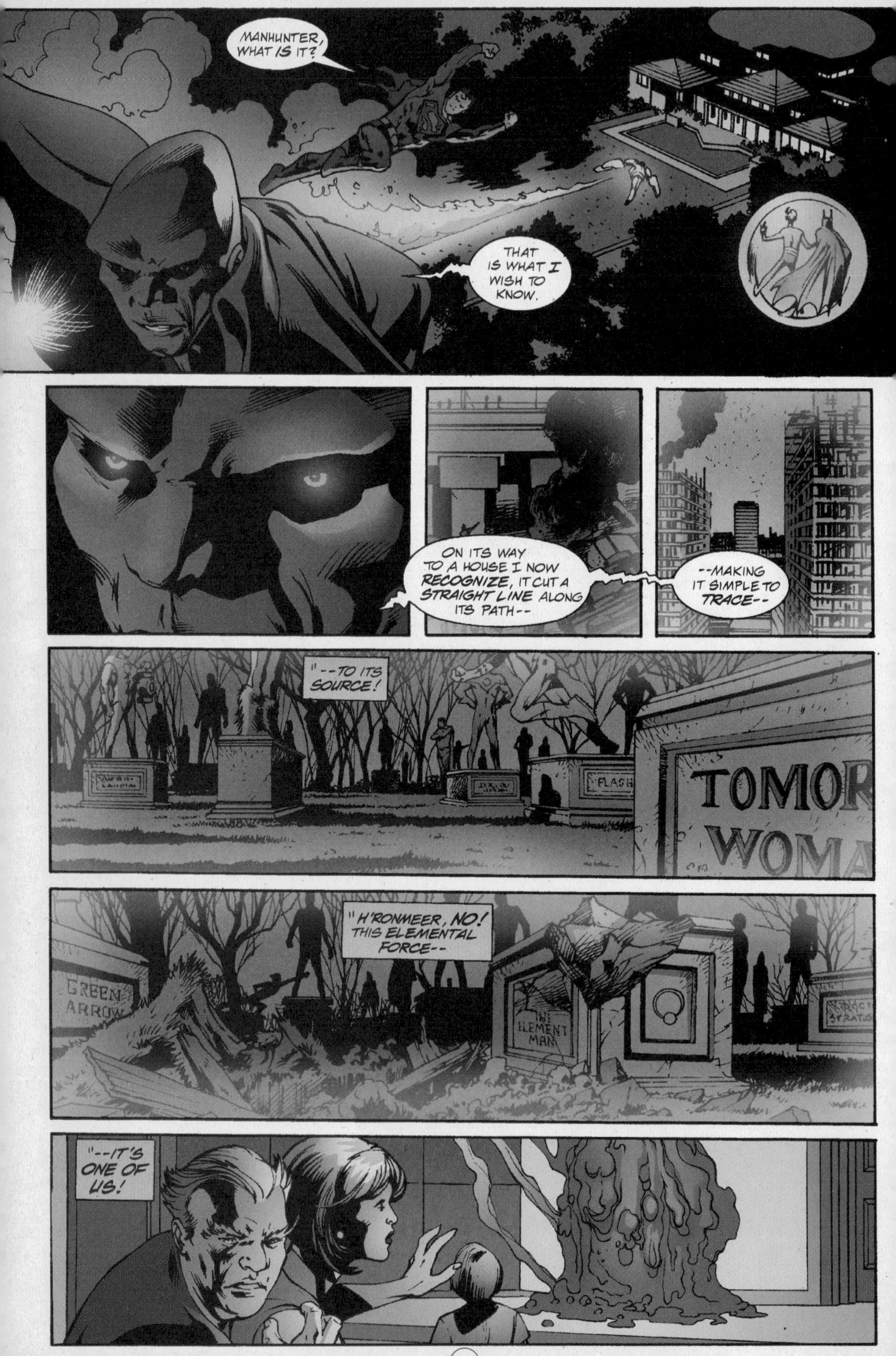
MANHUNTER, WHAT IS IT?
THAT IS WHAT I WISH TO KNOW.
ON ITS WAY TO A HOUSE I NOW RECOGNIZE, IT CUT A STRAIGHT LINE ALONG ITS PATH--
--MAKING IT SIMPLE TO TRACE--
"--TO ITS SOURCE!
FLASH
TOMOR
WOMA
"H'RONMEER, NO! THIS ELEMENTAL FORCE--
GREEN ARROW
THE ELEMENT MAN
"--IT'S ONE OF US!

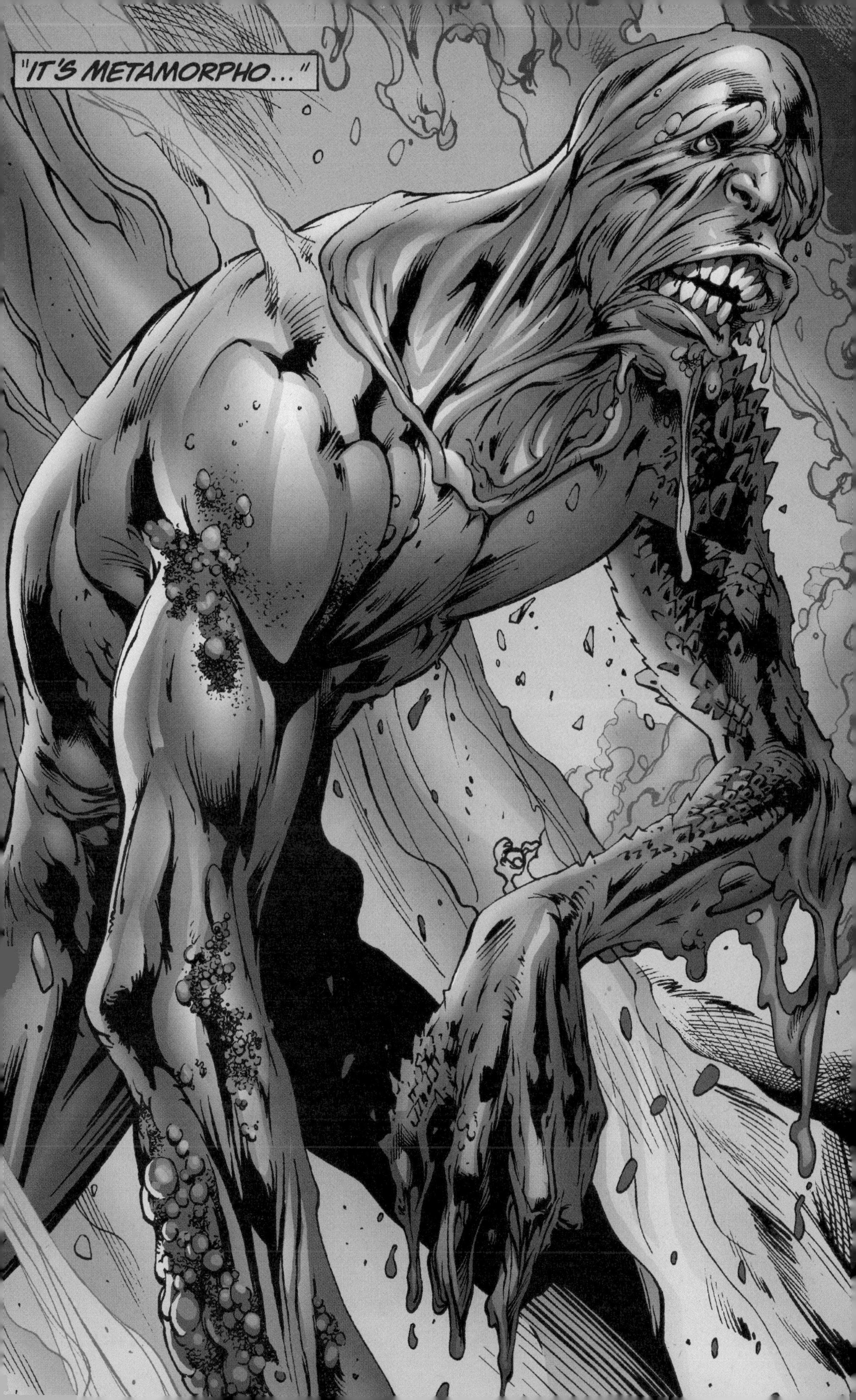
"IT'S METAMORPHO..."

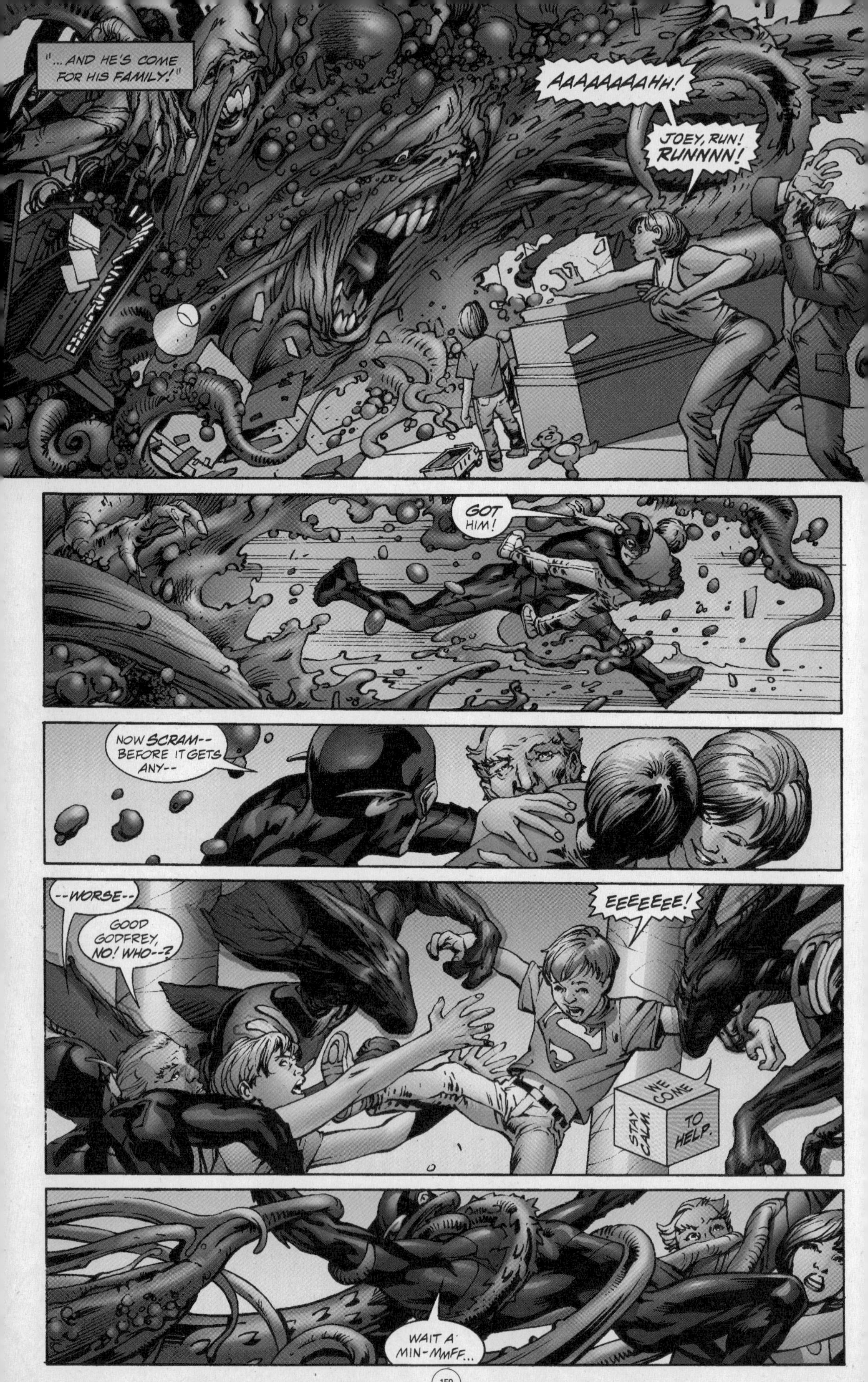
"...AND HE'S COME FOR HIS FAMILY!"
AAAAAAAAHH!
JOEY, RUN! RUNNNN!
GOT HIM!
NOW SCRAM-- BEFORE IT GETS ANY--
--WORSE--
GOOD GODFREY, NO! WHO--?
EEEEEEE!
WE COME TO HELP. STAY CALM.
WAIT A MIN-MMFF...

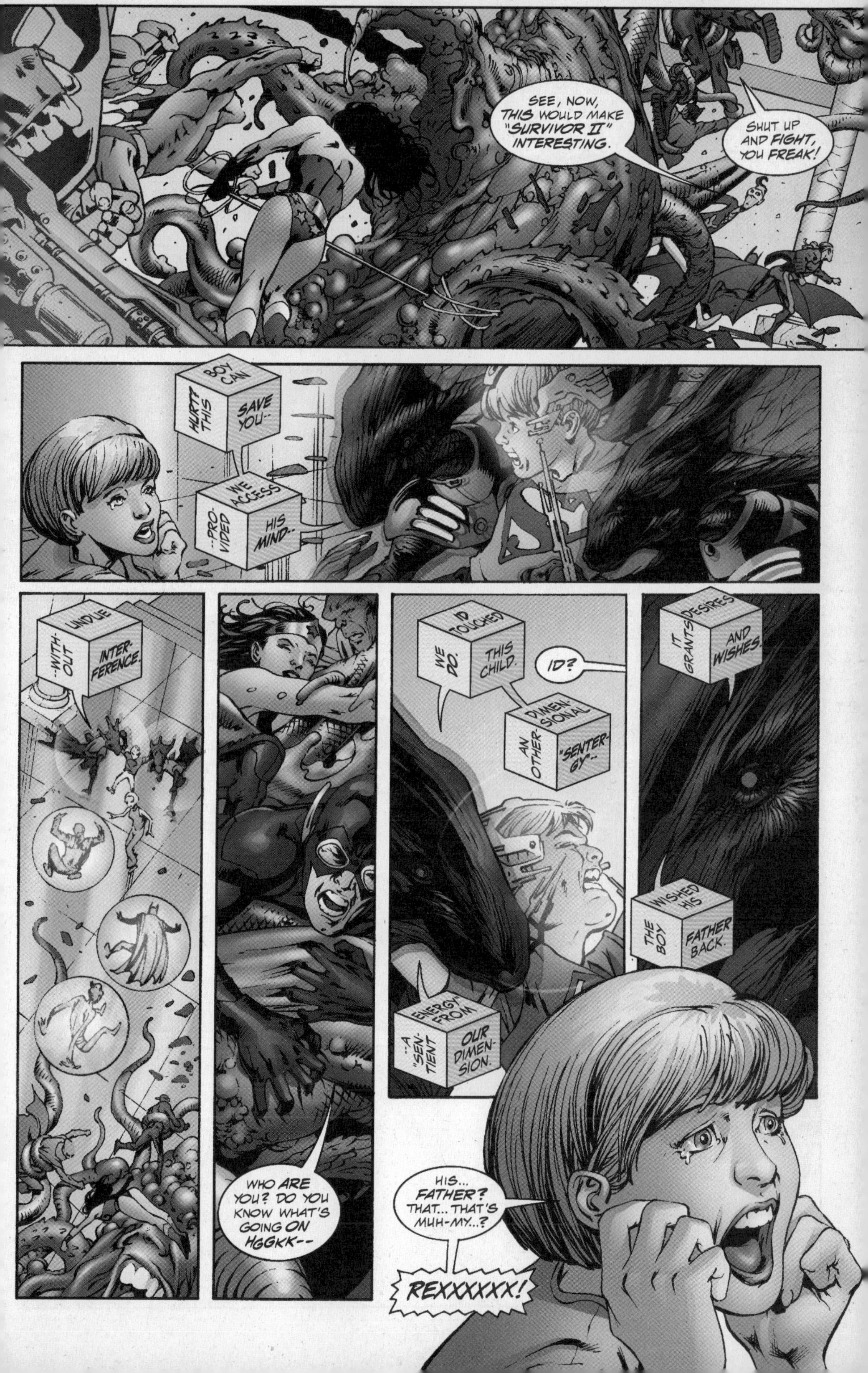
SEE, NOW, THIS WOULD MAKE "SURVIVOR II" INTERESTING.
SHUT UP AND FIGHT, YOU FREAK!
HURT? THIS BOY CAN SAVE YOU--
--PROVIDED WE ACCESS HIS MIND--
--WITHOUT UNDUE INTERFERENCE.
WE DO. ID TOUCHED THIS CHILD.
ID?
AN OTHER-DIMENSIONAL "SENTERGY"--
--A "SENTIENT ENERGY" FROM OUR DIMENSION.
IT GRANTS DESIRES AND WISHES.
THE BOY WISHED HIS FATHER BACK.
WHO ARE YOU? DO YOU KNOW WHAT'S GOING ON HGGKK--
HIS... FATHER? THAT... THAT'S MUH-MY...?
REXXXXXX!

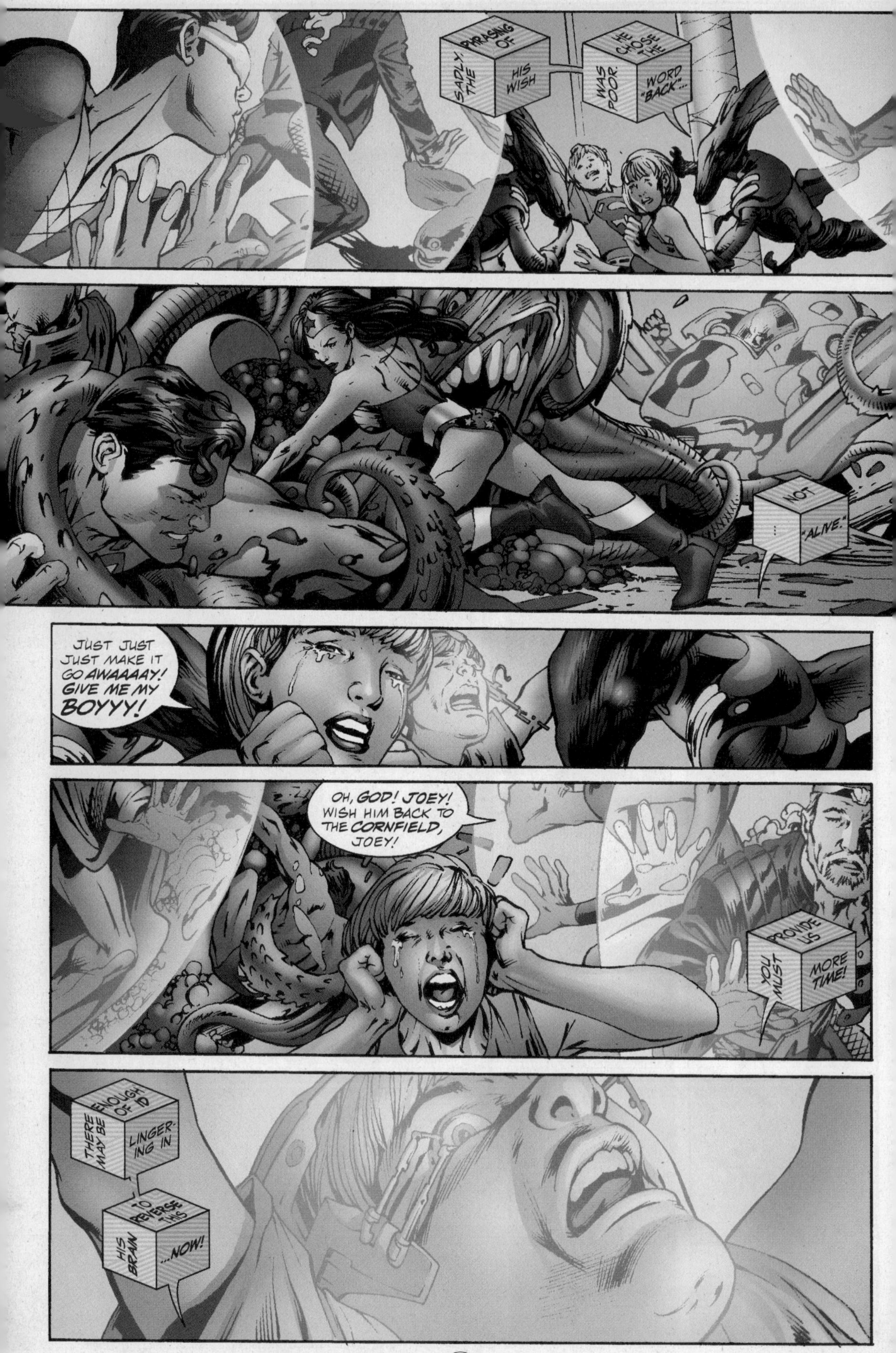
SADLY, THE PHRASING OF HIS WISH
WAS POOR. HE CHOSE THE WORD "BACK"...
...NOT "ALIVE."
JUST JUST JUST MAKE IT GO AWAAAAY! GIVE ME MY BOYYY!
OH, GOD! JOEY! WISH HIM BACK TO THE CORNFIELD, JOEY!
YOU MUST PROVIDE US MORE TIME!
THERE MAY BE ENOUGH OF ID LINGER-ING IN
HIS BRAIN TO REVERSE THIS ...NOW!

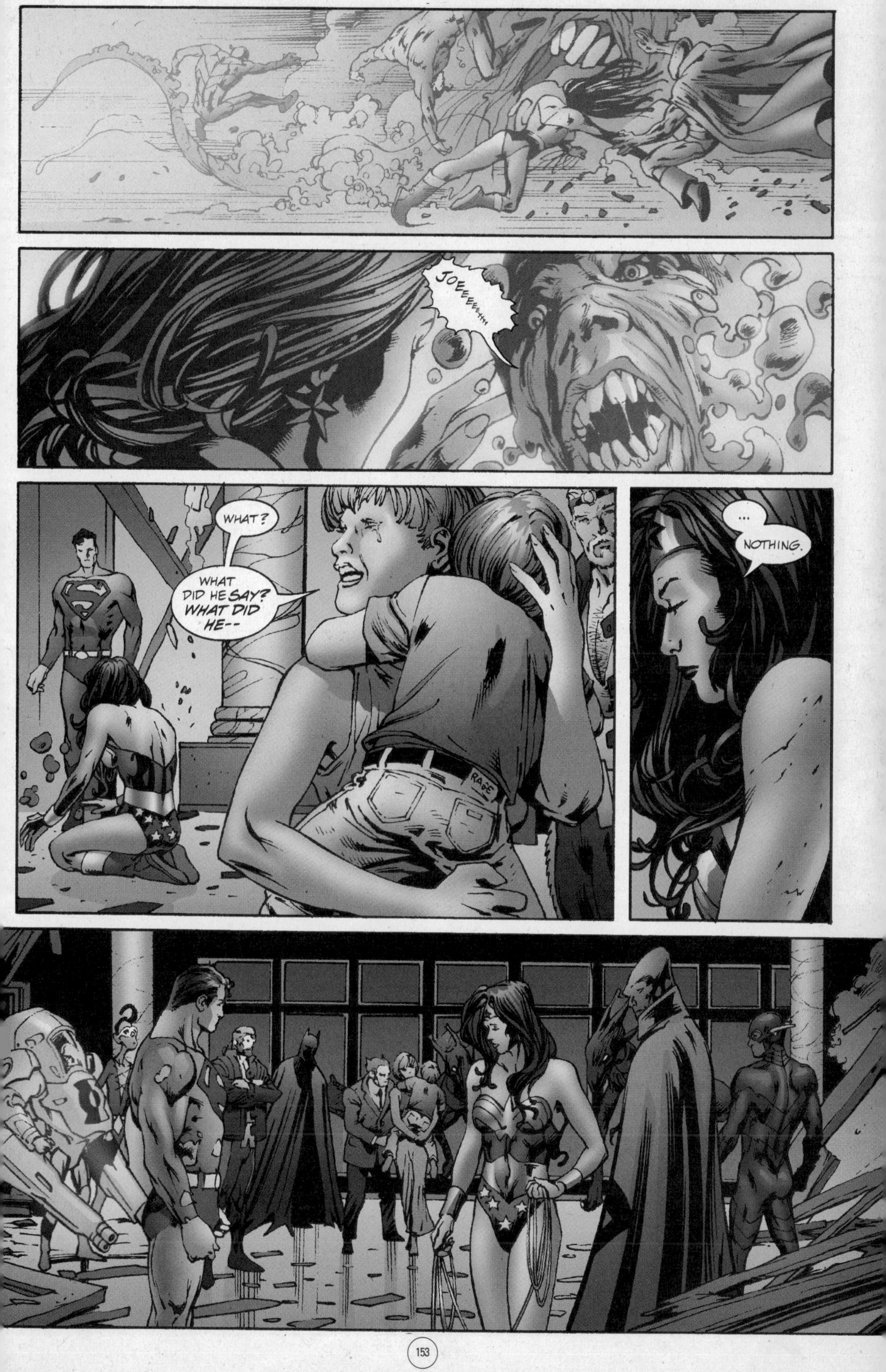
JOEEEEEHHH
WHAT?
WHAT DID HE SAY? WHAT DID HE--
...
NOTHING.
RAGE

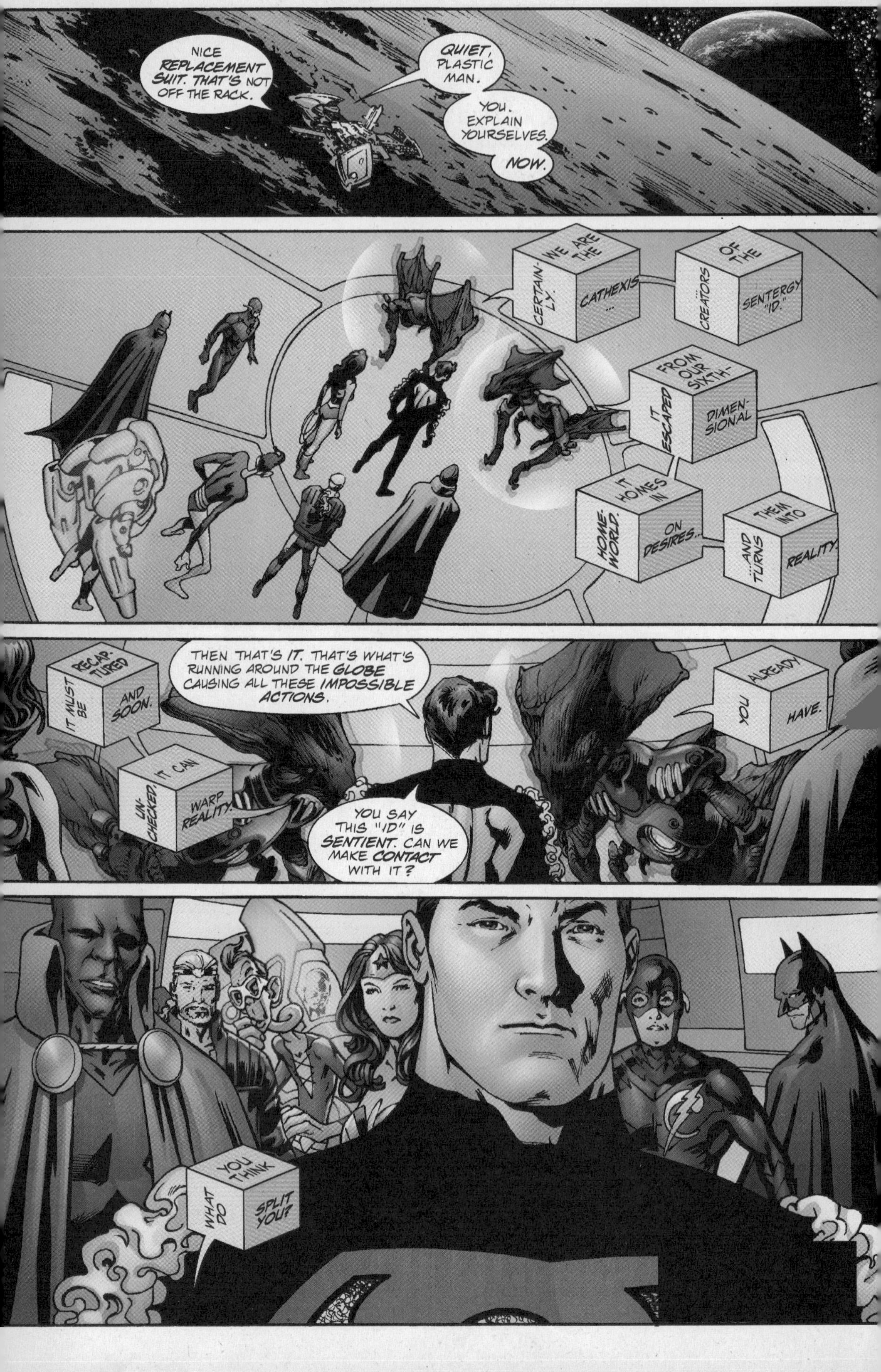
NICE REPLACEMENT SUIT. THAT'S NOT OFF THE RACK.
QUIET, PLASTIC MAN.
YOU. EXPLAIN YOURSELVES.
NOW.
CERTAIN-LY. WE ARE THE CATHEXIS...
...CREATORS OF THE SENTERGY "ID."
IT ESCAPED FROM OUR SIXTH-DIMENSIONAL
HOME-WORLD. IT HOMES IN ON DESIRES...
...AND TURNS THEM INTO REALITY.
IT MUST BE RECAP-TURED AND SOON.
THEN THAT'S IT. THAT'S WHAT'S RUNNING AROUND THE GLOBE CAUSING ALL THESE IMPOSSIBLE ACTIONS.
YOU ALREADY HAVE.
UN-CHECKED, IT CAN WARP REALITY.
YOU SAY THIS "ID" IS SENTIENT. CAN WE MAKE CONTACT WITH IT?
WHAT DO YOU THINK SPLIT YOU?

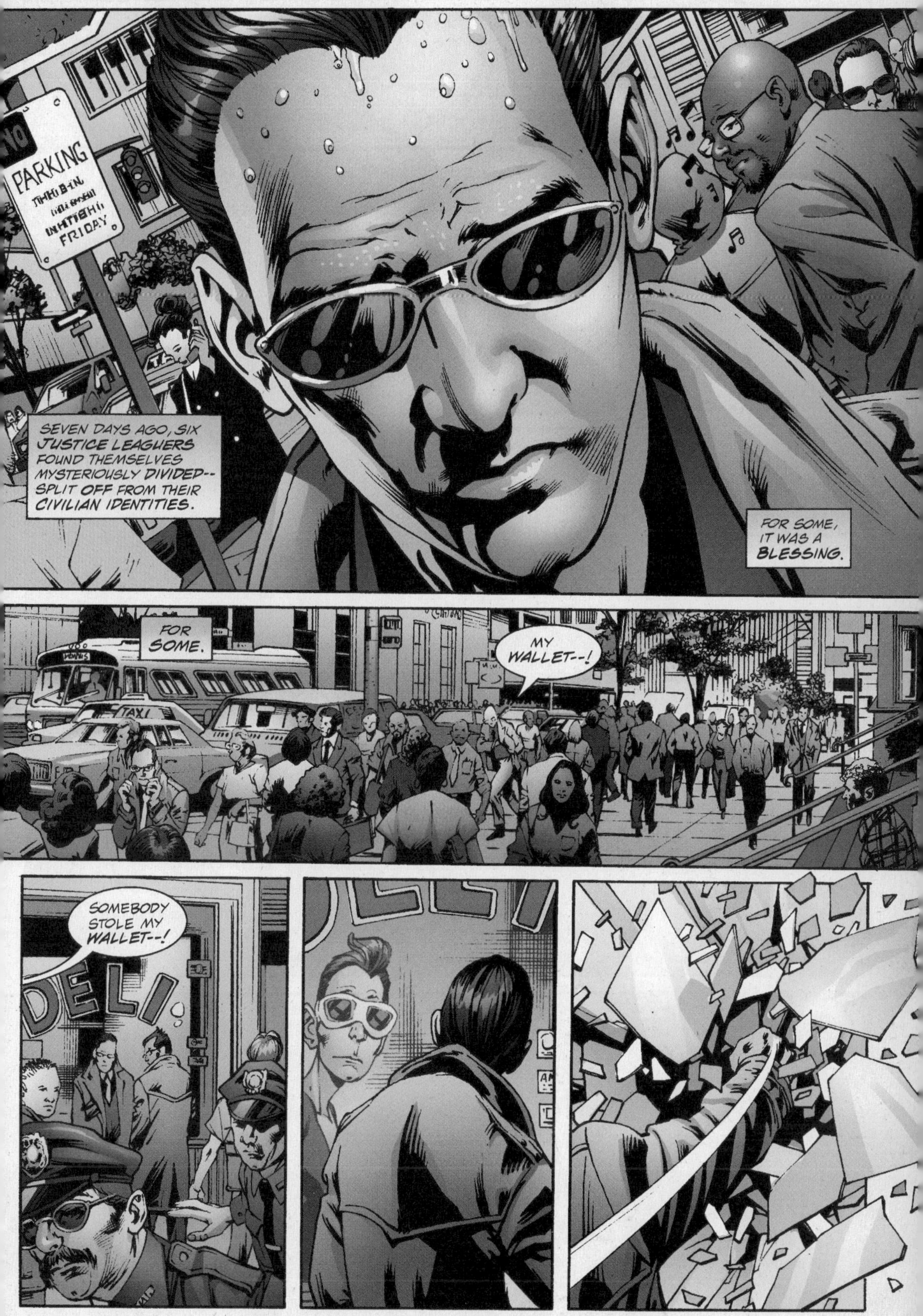
PARKING
FRIDAY
SEVEN DAYS AGO, SIX JUSTICE LEAGUERS FOUND THEMSELVES MYSTERIOUSLY DIVIDED-- SPLIT OFF FROM THEIR CIVILIAN IDENTITIES.
FOR SOME, IT WAS A BLESSING.
FOR SOME.
TAXI
MY WALLET--!
SOMEBODY STOLE MY WALLET--!
DELI

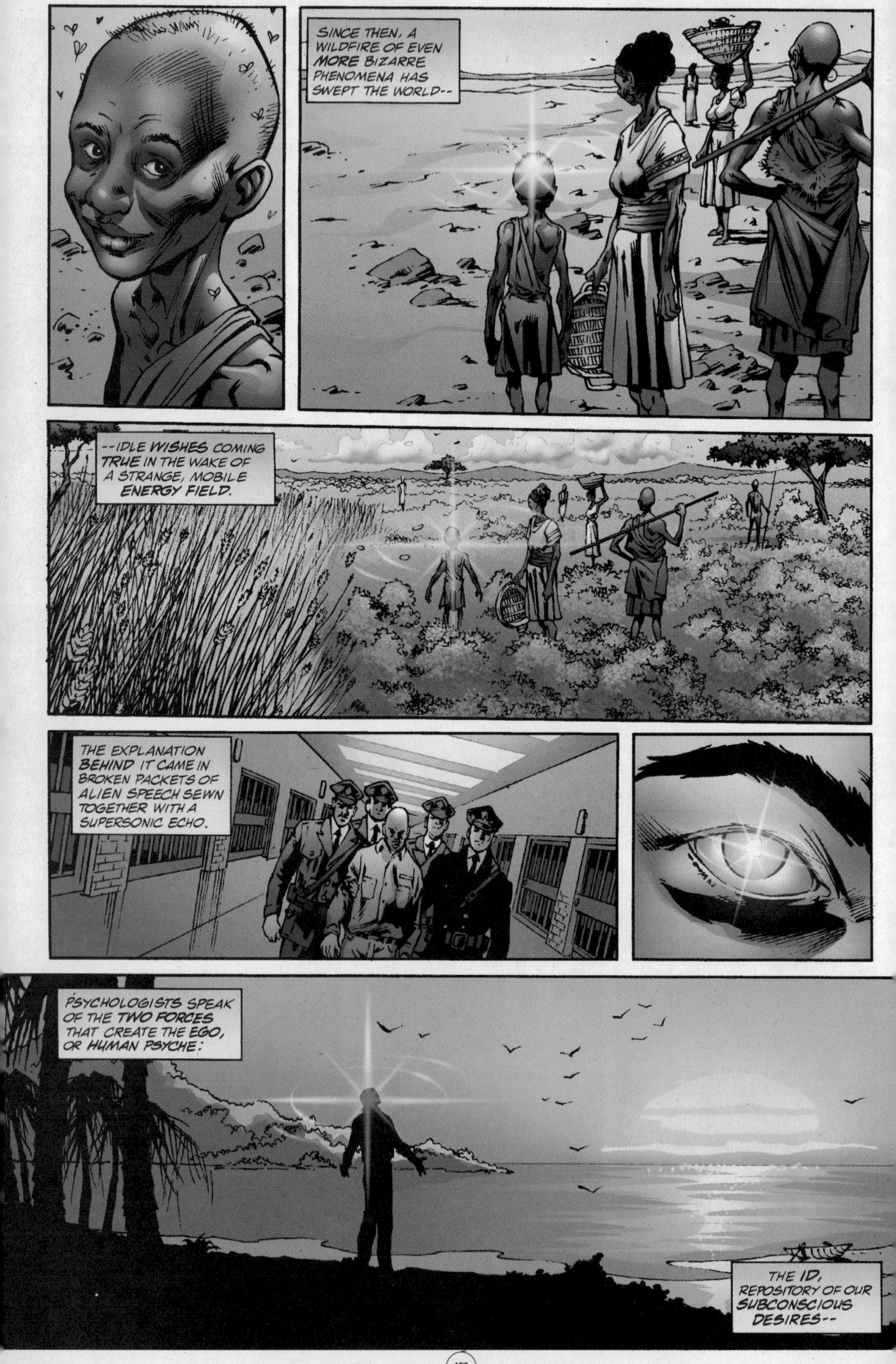
SINCE THEN, A WILDFIRE OF EVEN MORE BIZARRE PHENOMENA HAS SWEPT THE WORLD--
--IDLE WISHES COMING TRUE IN THE WAKE OF A STRANGE, MOBILE ENERGY FIELD.
THE EXPLANATION BEHIND IT CAME IN BROKEN PACKETS OF ALIEN SPEECH SEWN TOGETHER WITH A SUPERSONIC ECHO.
PSYCHOLOGISTS SPEAK OF THE TWO FORCES THAT CREATE THE EGO, OR HUMAN PSYCHE:
THE ID, REPOSITORY OF OUR SUBCONSCIOUS DESIRES--

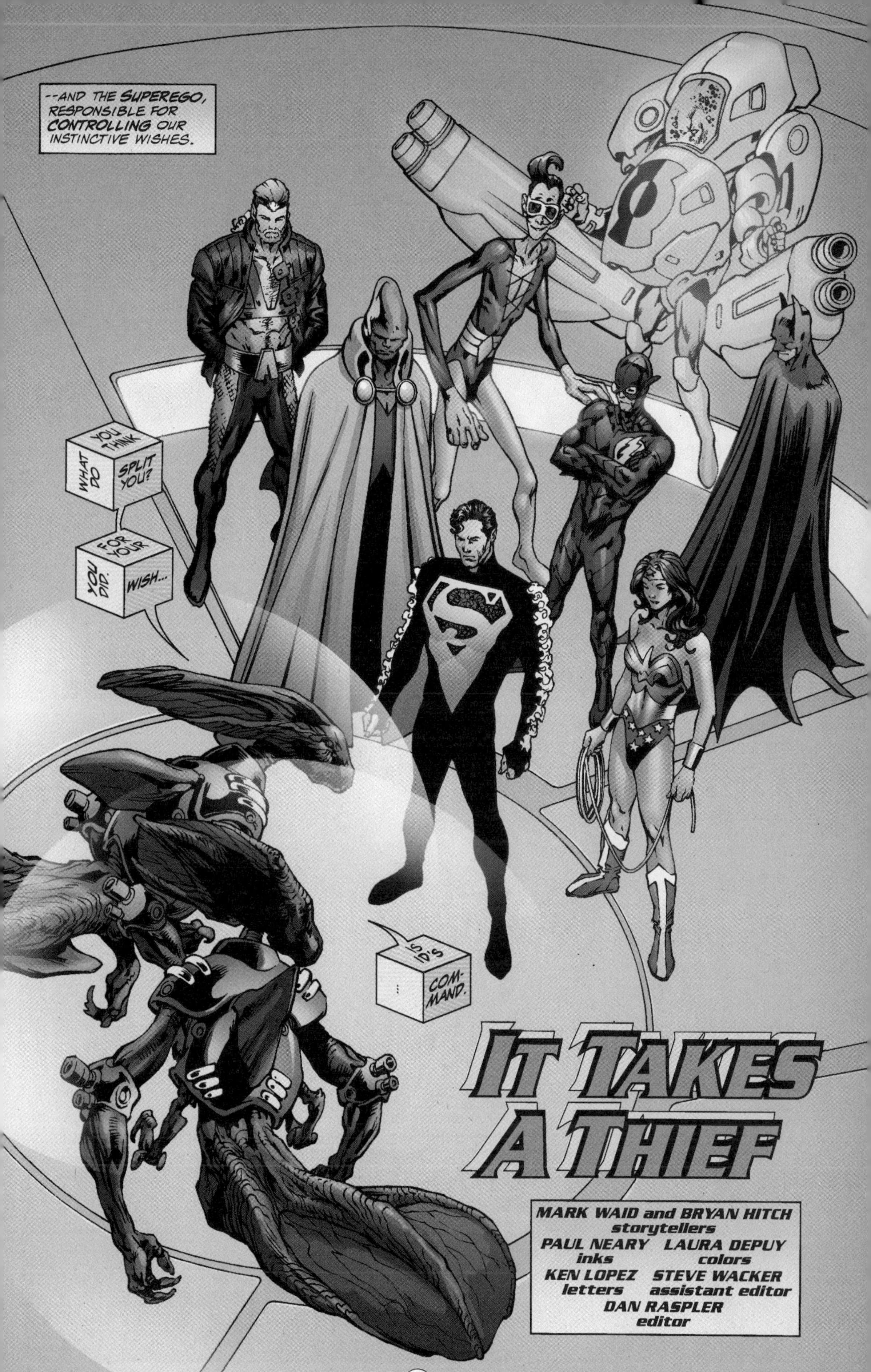
--AND THE SUPEREGO, RESPONSIBLE FOR CONTROLLING OUR INSTINCTIVE WISHES.
WHAT DO YOU THINK SPLIT YOU?
YOU DID. FOR YOUR WISH...
...IS D'S COMMAND.
IT TAKES A THIEF
MARK WAID and BRYAN HITCH storytellers
PAUL NEARY inks
LAURA DEPUY colors
KEN LOPEZ letters
STEVE WACKER assistant editor
DAN RASPLER editor

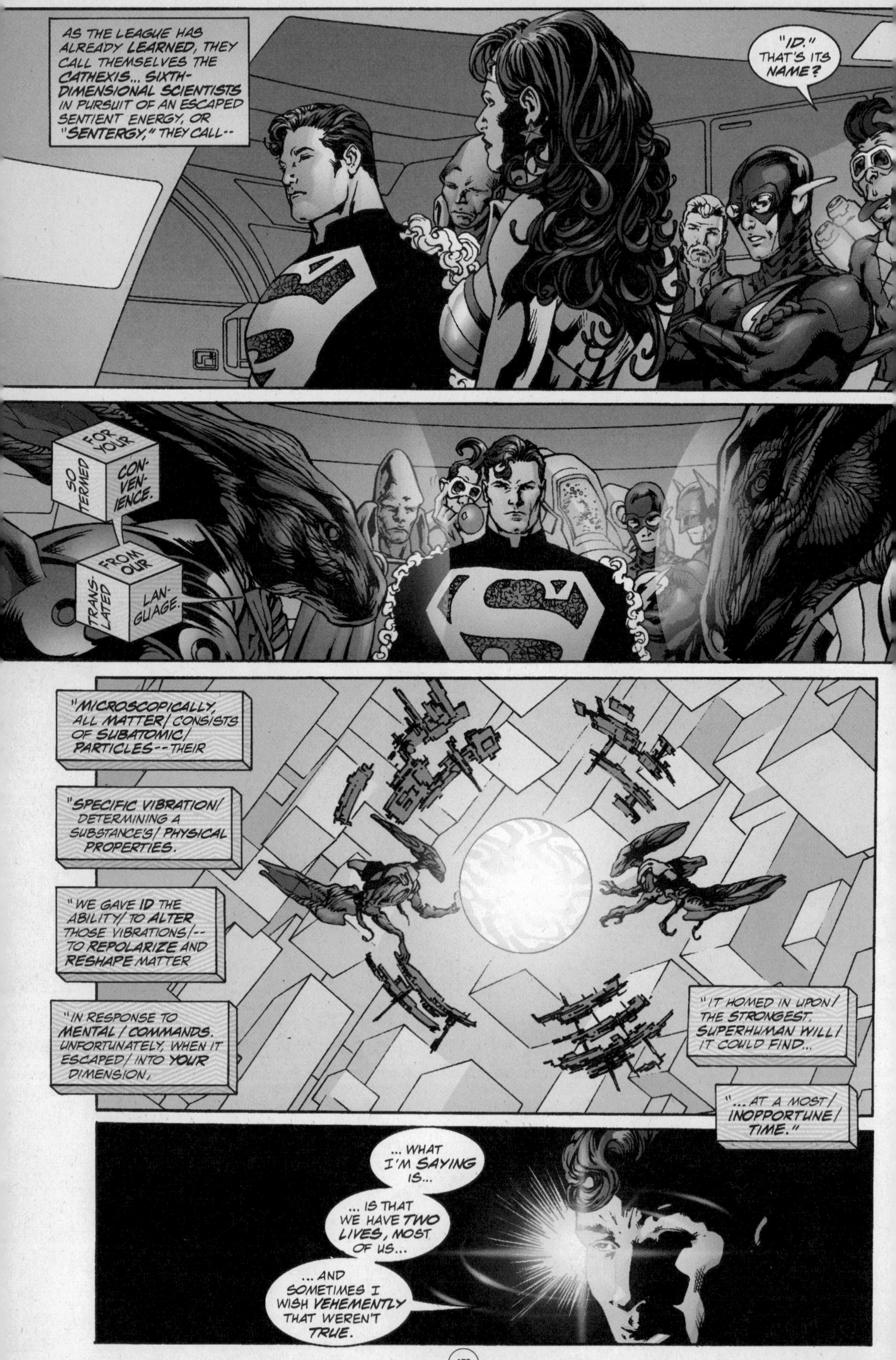

AS THE LEAGUE HAS ALREADY LEARNED, THEY CALL THEMSELVES THE CATHEXIS... SIXTH-DIMENSIONAL SCIENTISTS IN PURSUIT OF AN ESCAPED SENTIENT ENERGY, OR "SENTERGY," THEY CALL--
"ID." THAT'S ITS NAME?
SO TERMED FOR YOUR CONVENIENCE.
TRANSLATED FROM OUR LANGUAGE.
"MICROSCOPICALLY, ALL MATTER/ CONSISTS OF SUBATOMIC/ PARTICLES--THEIR
"SPECIFIC VIBRATION/ DETERMINING A SUBSTANCE'S/ PHYSICAL PROPERTIES.
"WE GAVE ID THE ABILITY/ TO ALTER THOSE VIBRATIONS/-- TO REPOLARIZE AND RESHAPE MATTER
"IN RESPONSE TO MENTAL / COMMANDS. UNFORTUNATELY, WHEN IT ESCAPED/ INTO YOUR DIMENSION,
"IT HOMED IN UPON/ THE STRONGEST SUPERHUMAN WILL/ IT COULD FIND...
"...AT A MOST/ INOPPORTUNE/ TIME."
...WHAT I'M SAYING IS...
...IS THAT WE HAVE TWO LIVES, MOST OF US...
...AND SOMETIMES I WISH VEHEMENTLY THAT WEREN'T TRUE.

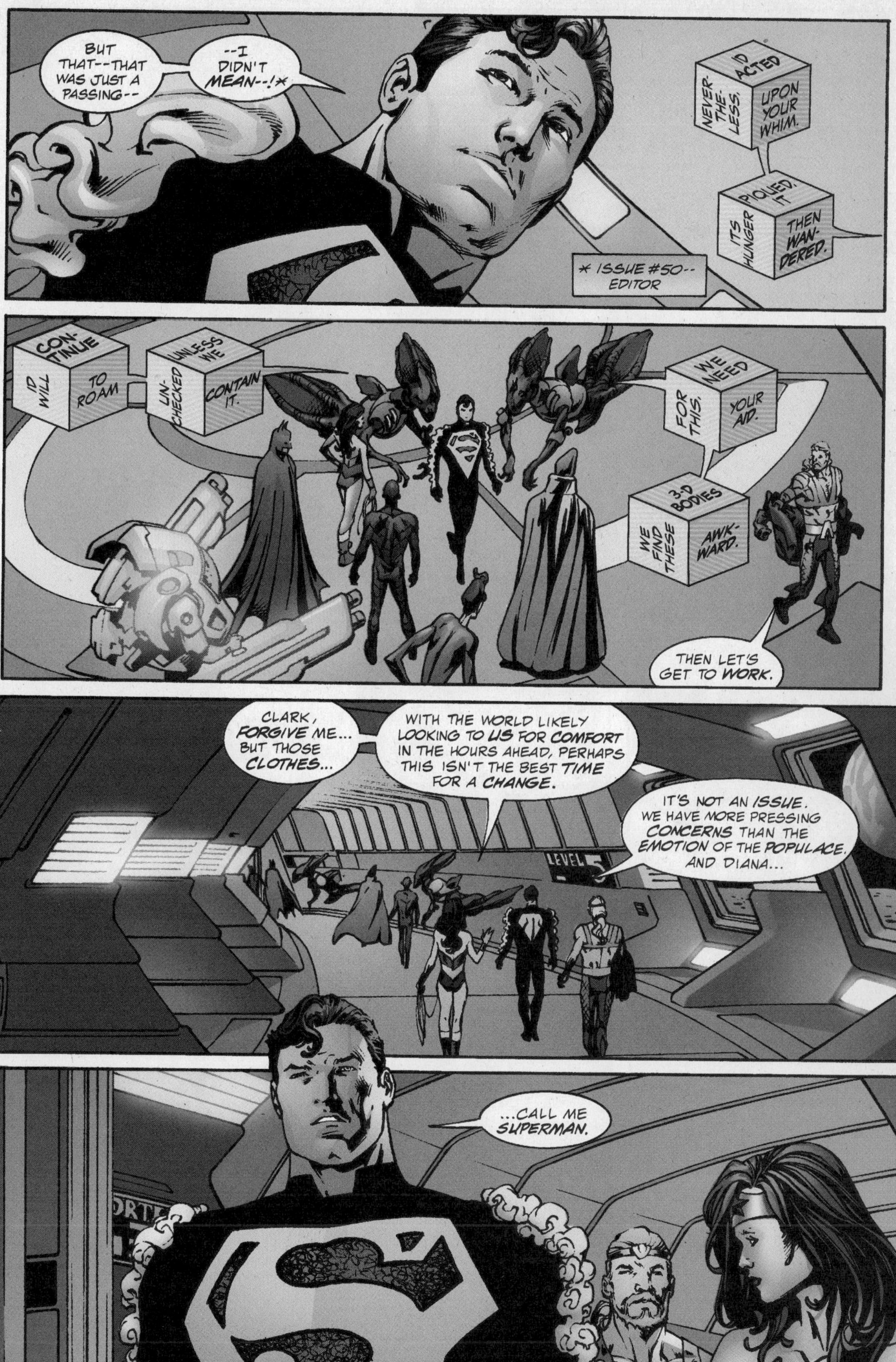

BUT THAT--THAT WAS JUST A PASSING--
--I DIDN'T MEAN--!*
NEVERTHELESS, ID ACTED UPON YOUR WHIM.
ITS HUNGER PIQUED, IT THEN WANDERED.
* ISSUE #50--EDITOR
ID WILL CONTINUE TO ROAM
UNCHECKED UNLESS WE CONTAIN IT.
FOR THIS, WE NEED YOUR AID.
WE FIND THESE 3-D BODIES AWKWARD.
THEN LET'S GET TO WORK.
CLARK, FORGIVE ME... BUT THOSE CLOTHES...
WITH THE WORLD LIKELY LOOKING TO US FOR COMFORT IN THE HOURS AHEAD, PERHAPS THIS ISN'T THE BEST TIME FOR A CHANGE.
LEVEL 5
IT'S NOT AN ISSUE. WE HAVE MORE PRESSING CONCERNS THAN THE EMOTION OF THE POPULACE. AND DIANA...
...CALL ME SUPERMAN.

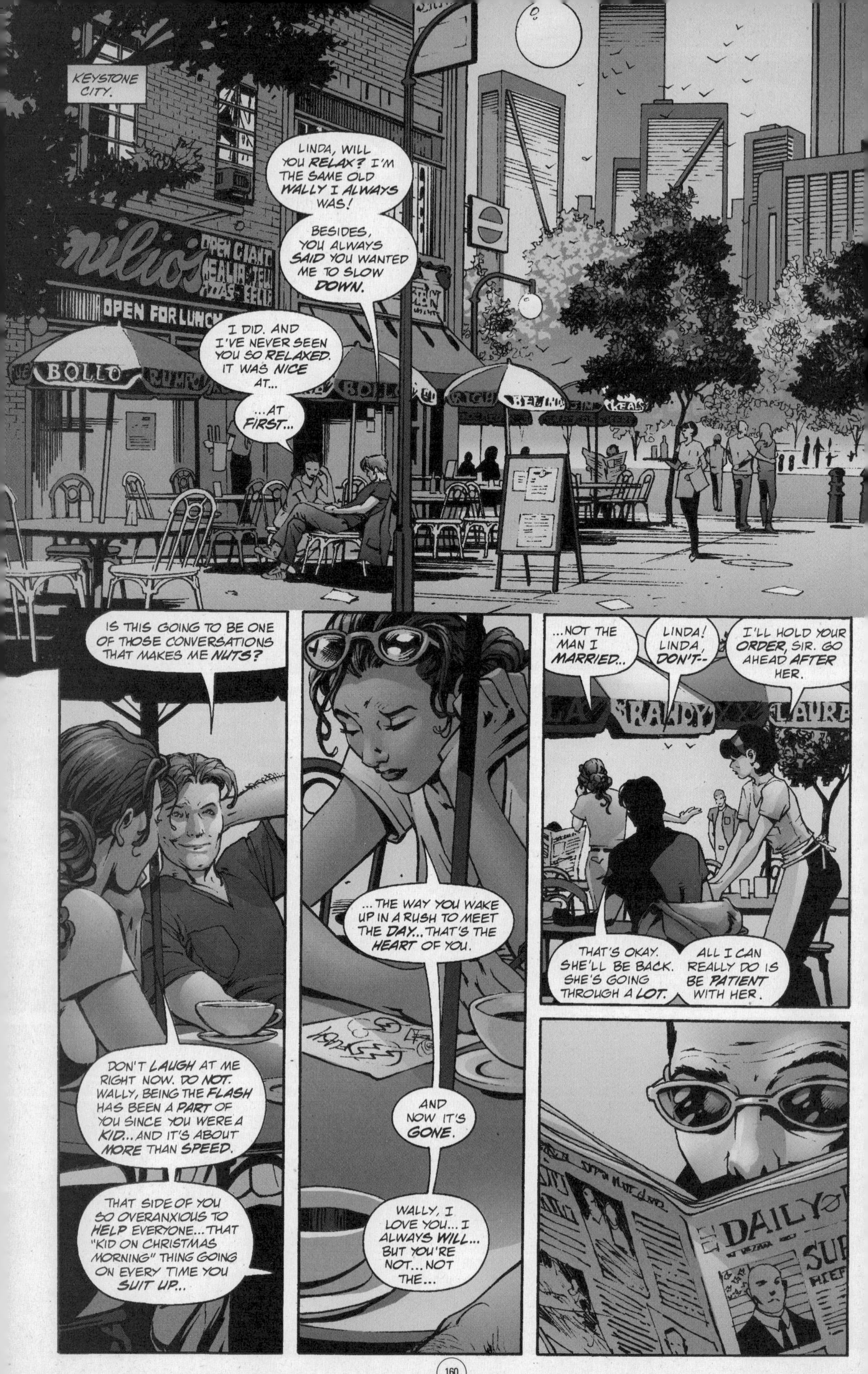
KEYSTONE CITY.
LINDA, WILL YOU RELAX? I'M THE SAME OLD WALLY I ALWAYS WAS!
BESIDES, YOU ALWAYS SAID YOU WANTED ME TO SLOW DOWN.
I DID. AND I'VE NEVER SEEN YOU SO RELAXED. IT WAS NICE AT...
...AT FIRST...
OPEN FOR LUNCH
BOLLO
IS THIS GOING TO BE ONE OF THOSE CONVERSATIONS THAT MAKES ME NUTS?
DON'T LAUGH AT ME RIGHT NOW. DO NOT. WALLY, BEING THE FLASH HAS BEEN A PART OF YOU SINCE YOU WERE A KID... AND IT'S ABOUT MORE THAN SPEED.
THAT SIDE OF YOU SO OVERANXIOUS TO HELP EVERYONE... THAT "KID ON CHRISTMAS MORNING" THING GOING ON EVERY TIME YOU SUIT UP...
...THE WAY YOU WAKE UP IN A RUSH TO MEET THE DAY... THAT'S THE HEART OF YOU.
AND NOW IT'S GONE.
WALLY, I LOVE YOU... I ALWAYS WILL... BUT YOU'RE NOT... NOT THE...
...NOT THE MAN I MARRIED...
LINDA! LINDA, DON'T--
I'LL HOLD YOUR ORDER, SIR. GO AHEAD AFTER HER.
THAT'S OKAY. SHE'LL BE BACK. SHE'S GOING THROUGH A LOT.
ALL I CAN REALLY DO IS BE PATIENT WITH HER.
DAILY

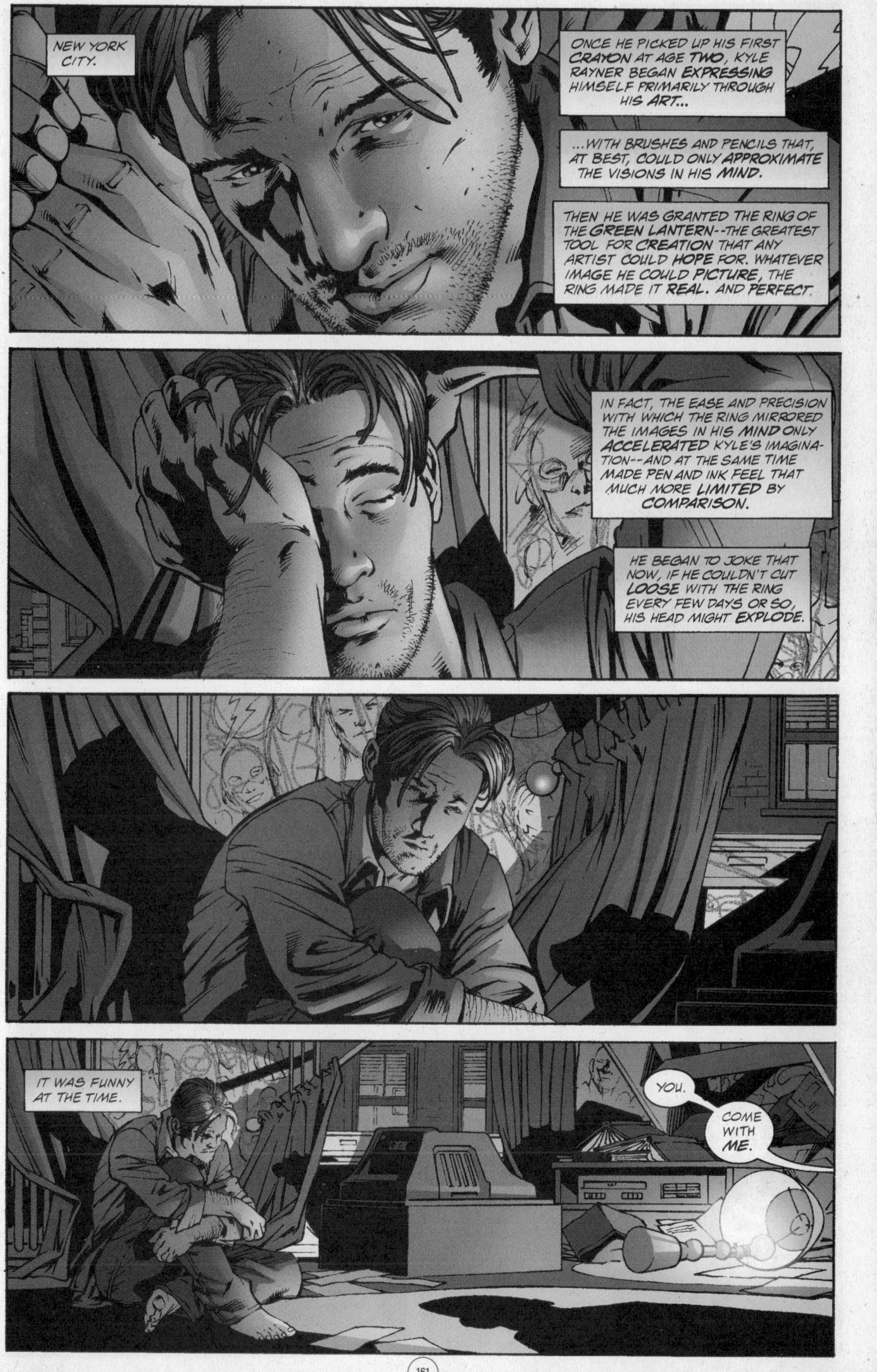
NEW YORK CITY.
ONCE HE PICKED UP HIS FIRST CRAYON AT AGE TWO, KYLE RAYNER BEGAN EXPRESSING HIMSELF PRIMARILY THROUGH HIS ART...
...WITH BRUSHES AND PENCILS THAT, AT BEST, COULD ONLY APPROXIMATE THE VISIONS IN HIS MIND.
THEN HE WAS GRANTED THE RING OF THE GREEN LANTERN--THE GREATEST TOOL FOR CREATION THAT ANY ARTIST COULD HOPE FOR. WHATEVER IMAGE HE COULD PICTURE, THE RING MADE IT REAL. AND PERFECT.
IN FACT, THE EASE AND PRECISION WITH WHICH THE RING MIRRORED THE IMAGES IN HIS MIND ONLY ACCELERATED KYLE'S IMAGINATION--AND AT THE SAME TIME MADE PEN AND INK FEEL THAT MUCH MORE LIMITED BY COMPARISON.
HE BEGAN TO JOKE THAT NOW, IF HE COULDN'T CUT LOOSE WITH THE RING EVERY FEW DAYS OR SO, HIS HEAD MIGHT EXPLODE.
IT WAS FUNNY AT THE TIME.
YOU.
COME WITH ME.

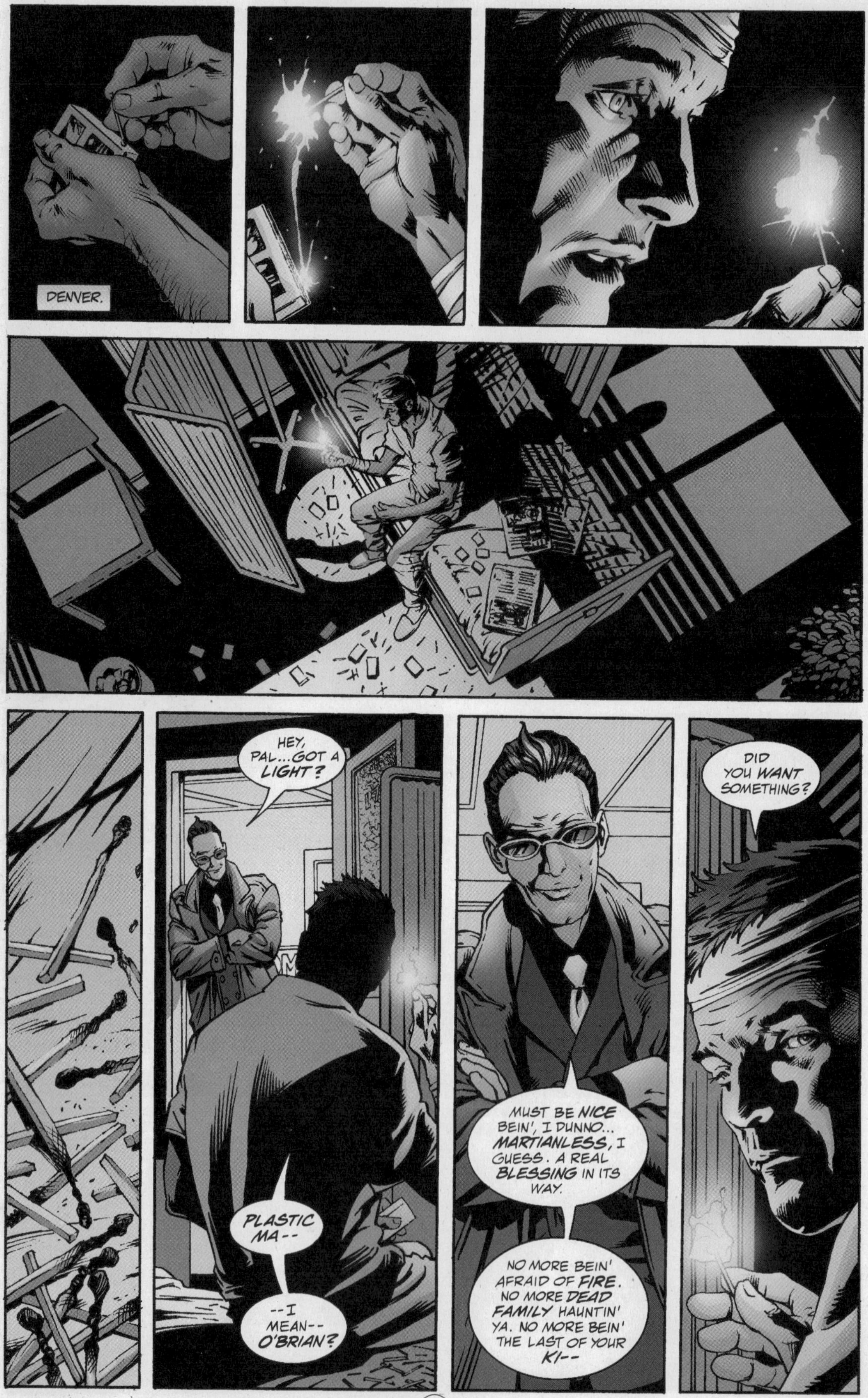
DENVER.
HEY, PAL...GOT A LIGHT?
PLASTIC MA--
--I MEAN-- O'BRIAN?
MUST BE NICE BEIN', I DUNNO... MARTIANLESS, I GUESS. A REAL BLESSING IN ITS WAY.
NO MORE BEIN' AFRAID OF FIRE. NO MORE DEAD FAMILY HAUNTIN' YA. NO MORE BEIN' THE LAST OF YOUR KI--
DID YOU WANT SOMETHING?

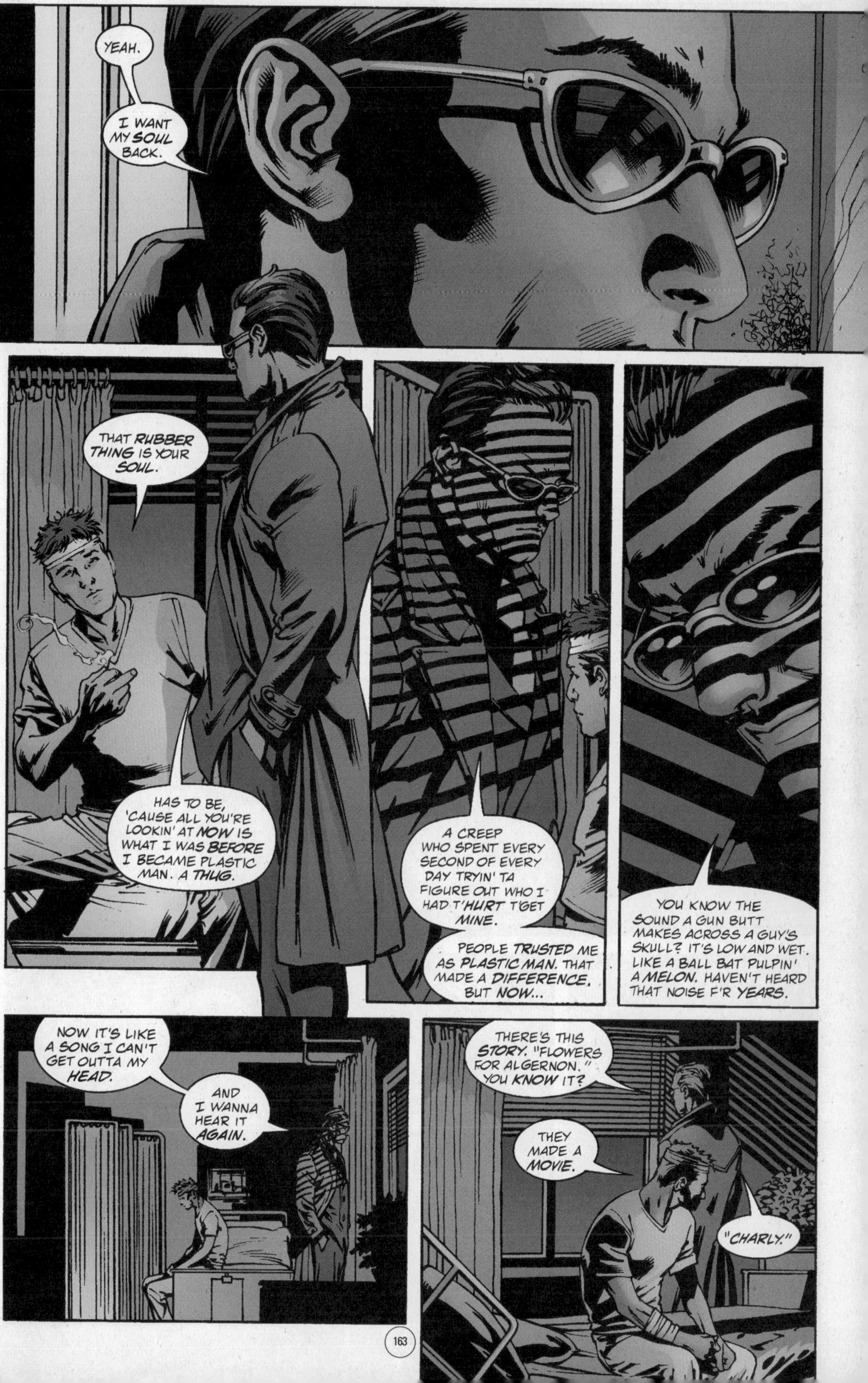

YEAH.
I WANT MY SOUL BACK.
THAT RUBBER THING IS YOUR SOUL.
HAS TO BE, 'CAUSE ALL YOU'RE LOOKIN' AT NOW IS WHAT I WAS BEFORE I BECAME PLASTIC MAN. A THUG.
A CREEP WHO SPENT EVERY SECOND OF EVERY DAY TRYIN' TA FIGURE OUT WHO I HAD T'HURT T'GET MINE.
PEOPLE TRUSTED ME AS PLASTIC MAN. THAT MADE A DIFFERENCE. BUT NOW...
YOU KNOW THE SOUND A GUN BUTT MAKES ACROSS A GUY'S SKULL? IT'S LOW AND WET. LIKE A BALL BAT PULPIN' A MELON. HAVEN'T HEARD THAT NOISE F'R YEARS.
NOW IT'S LIKE A SONG I CAN'T GET OUTTA MY HEAD.
AND I WANNA HEAR IT AGAIN.
THERE'S THIS STORY. "FLOWERS FOR ALGERNON." YOU KNOW IT?
THEY MADE A MOVIE.
"CHARLY."

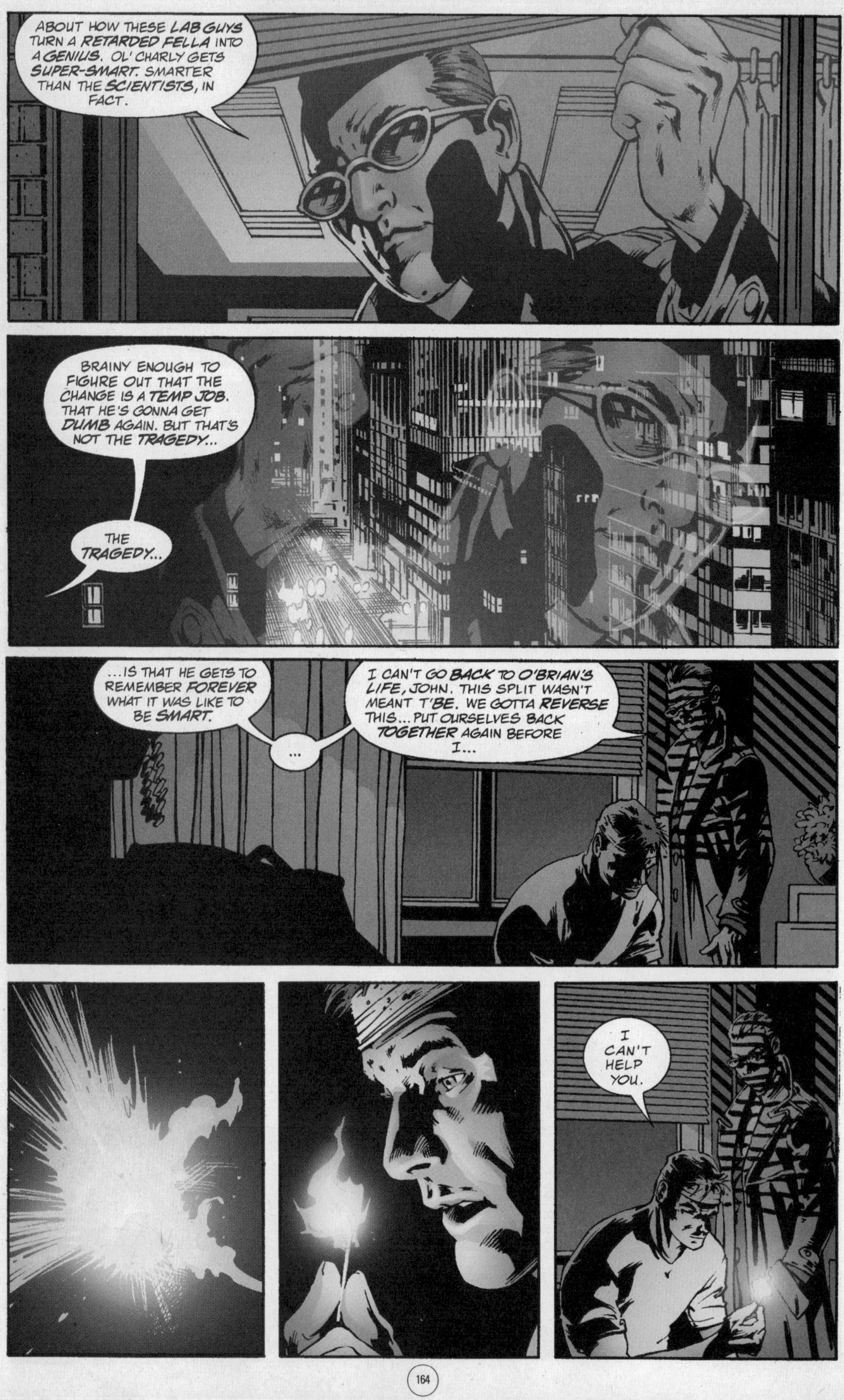
ABOUT HOW THESE LAB GUYS TURN A RETARDED FELLA INTO A GENIUS. OL' CHARLY GETS SUPER-SMART. SMARTER THAN THE SCIENTISTS, IN FACT.
BRAINY ENOUGH TO FIGURE OUT THAT THE CHANGE IS A TEMP JOB. THAT HE'S GONNA GET DUMB AGAIN. BUT THAT'S NOT THE TRAGEDY...
THE TRAGEDY...
...IS THAT HE GETS TO REMEMBER FOREVER WHAT IT WAS LIKE TO BE SMART.
...
I CAN'T GO BACK TO O'BRIAN'S LIFE, JOHN. THIS SPLIT WASN'T MEANT T'BE. WE GOTTA REVERSE THIS... PUT OURSELVES BACK TOGETHER AGAIN BEFORE I...
I CAN'T HELP YOU.

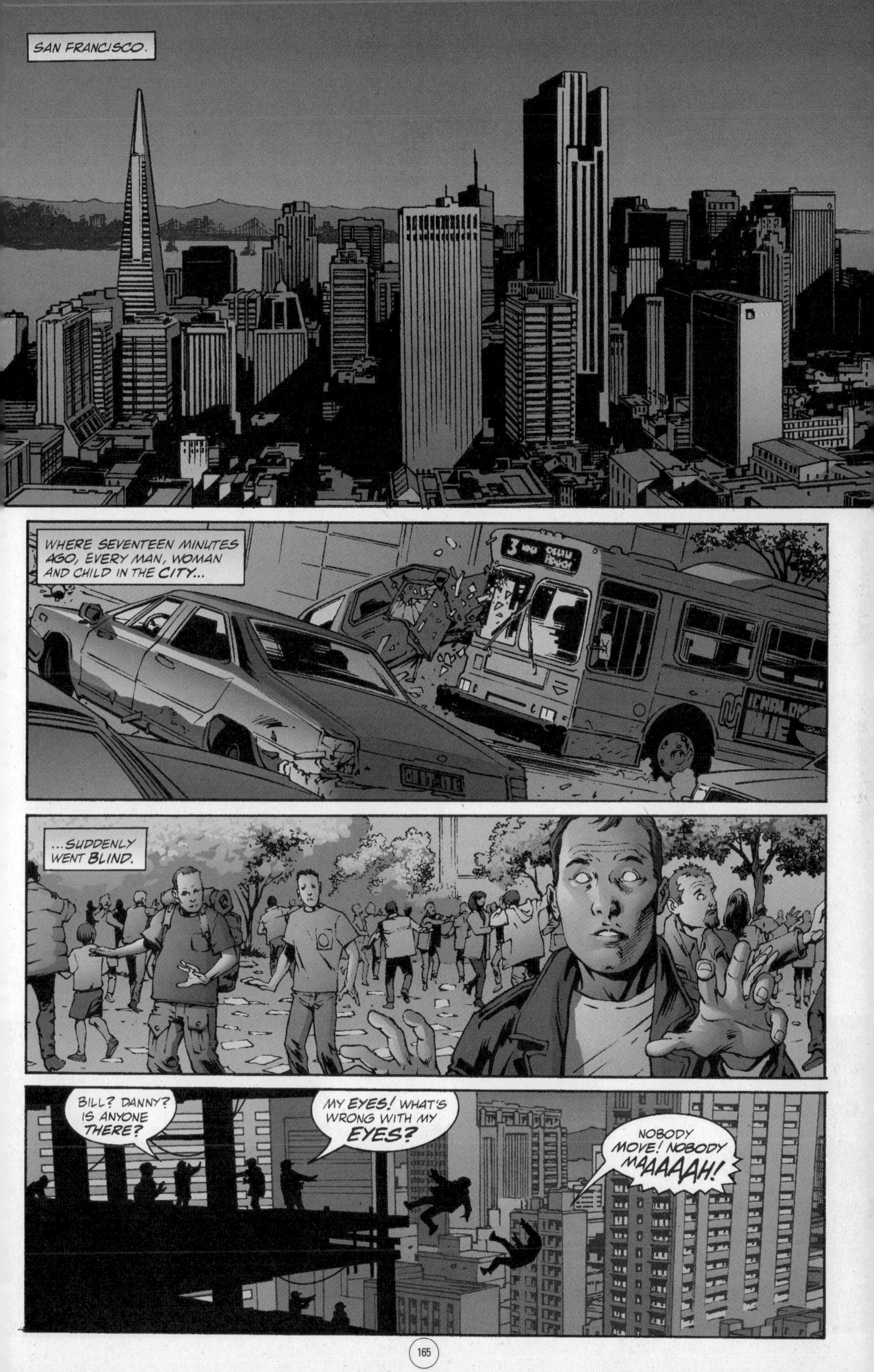
SAN FRANCISCO.
WHERE SEVENTEEN MINUTES AGO, EVERY MAN, WOMAN AND CHILD IN THE CITY...
...SUDDENLY WENT BLIND.
BILL? DANNY? IS ANYONE THERE?
MY EYES! WHAT'S WRONG WITH MY EYES?
NOBODY MOVE! NOBODY MAAAAAH!

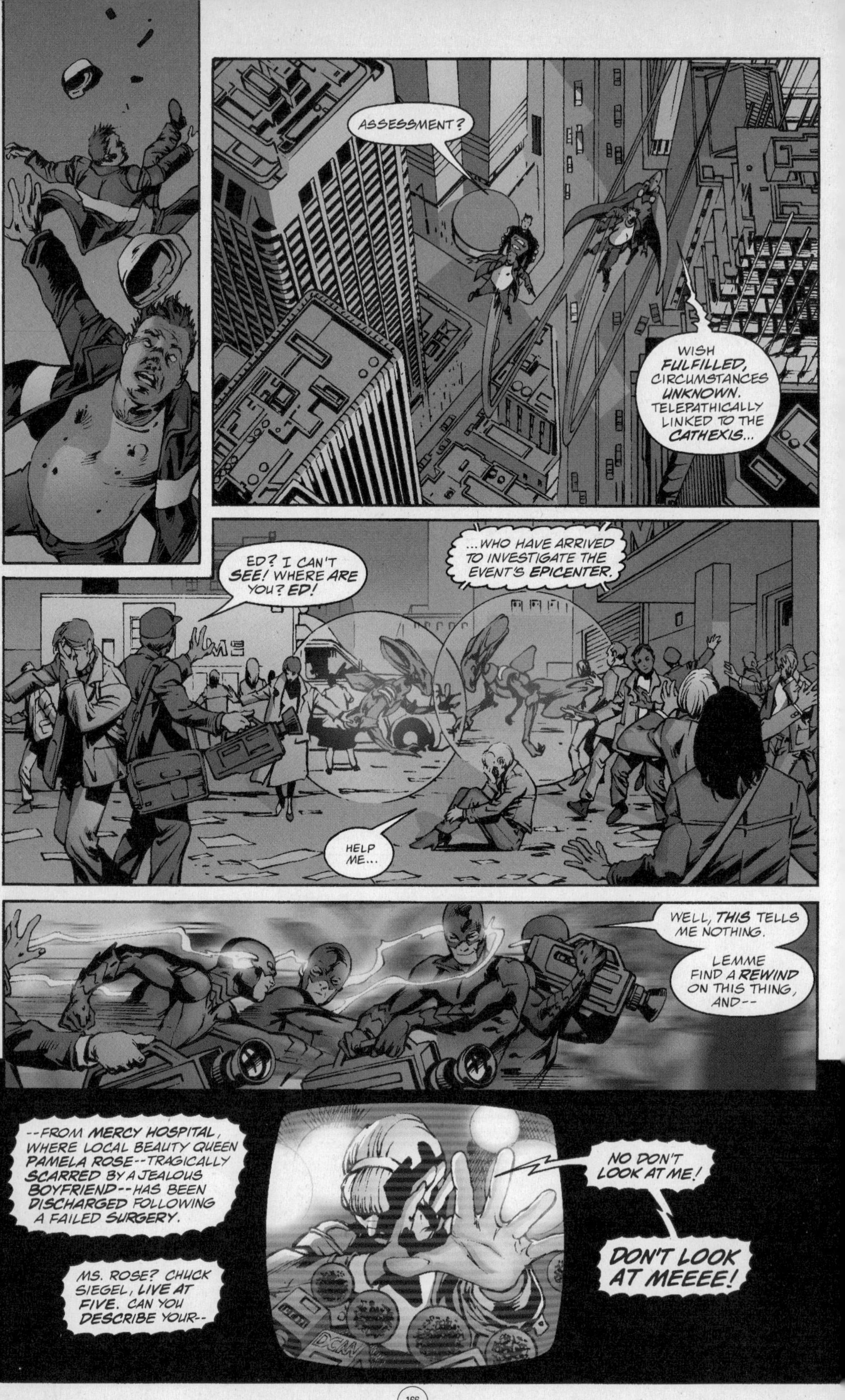

ASSESSMENT?
WISH FULFILLED, CIRCUMSTANCES UNKNOWN. TELEPATHICALLY LINKED TO THE CATHEXIS...
ED? I CAN'T SEE! WHERE ARE YOU? ED!
...WHO HAVE ARRIVED TO INVESTIGATE THE EVENT'S EPICENTER.
HELP ME...
WELL, THIS TELLS ME NOTHING.
LEMME FIND A REWIND ON THIS THING, AND--
--FROM MERCY HOSPITAL, WHERE LOCAL BEAUTY QUEEN PAMELA ROSE--TRAGICALLY SCARRED BY A JEALOUS BOYFRIEND--HAS BEEN DISCHARGED FOLLOWING A FAILED SURGERY.
MS. ROSE? CHUCK SIEGEL, LIVE AT FIVE. CAN YOU DESCRIBE YOUR--
NO DON'T LOOK AT ME!
DON'T LOOK AT MEEEE!

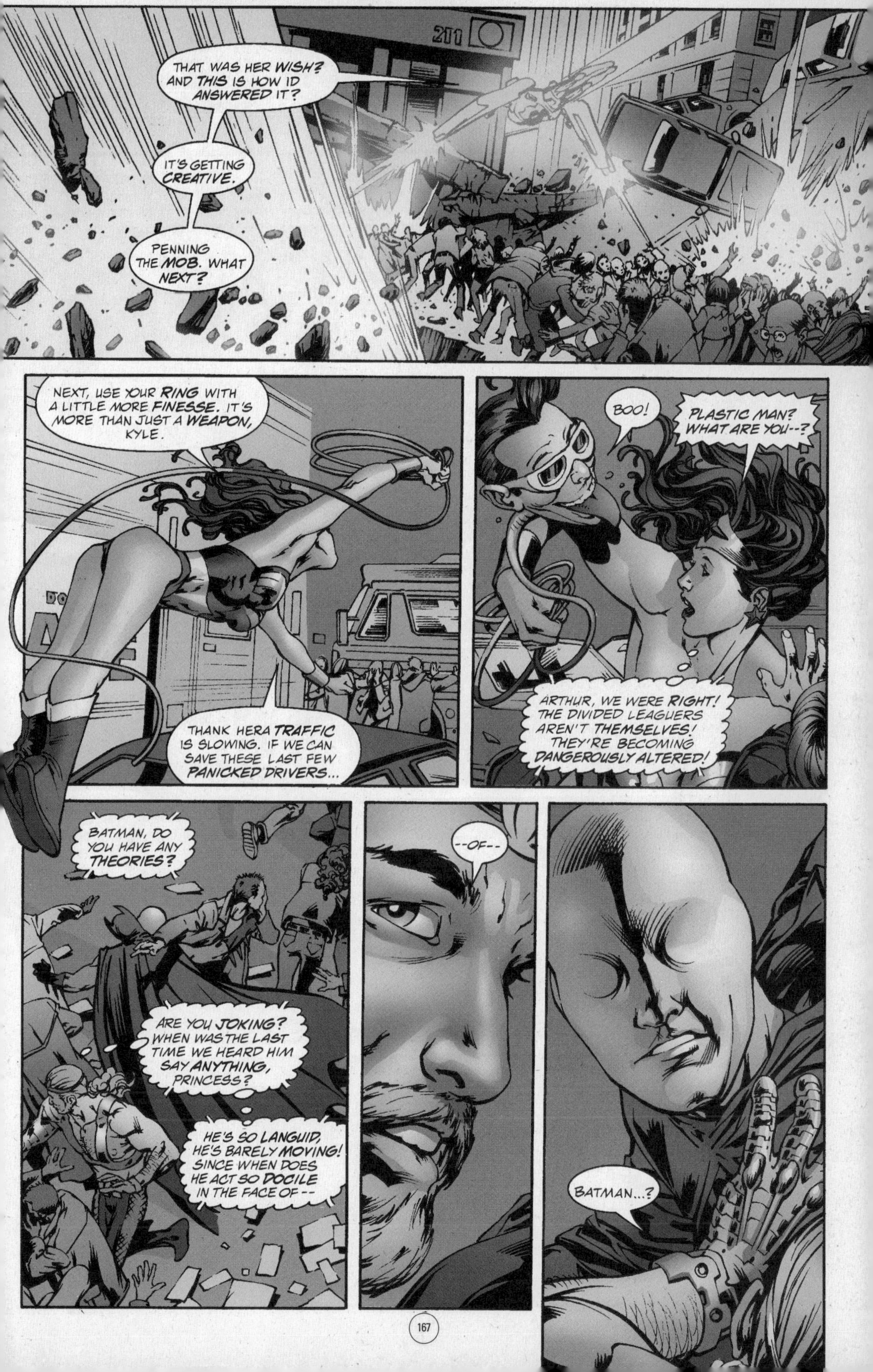
211
THAT WAS HER WISH? AND THIS IS HOW ID ANSWERED IT?
IT'S GETTING CREATIVE.
PENNING THE MOB. WHAT NEXT?
NEXT, USE YOUR RING WITH A LITTLE MORE FINESSE. IT'S MORE THAN JUST A WEAPON, KYLE.
THANK HERA TRAFFIC IS SLOWING. IF WE CAN SAVE THESE LAST FEW PANICKED DRIVERS...
BOO!
PLASTIC MAN? WHAT ARE YOU--?
ARTHUR, WE WERE RIGHT! THE DIVIDED LEAGUERS AREN'T THEMSELVES! THEY'RE BECOMING DANGEROUSLY ALTERED!
BATMAN, DO YOU HAVE ANY THEORIES?
ARE YOU JOKING? WHEN WAS THE LAST TIME WE HEARD HIM SAY ANYTHING, PRINCESS?
HE'S SO LANGUID, HE'S BARELY MOVING! SINCE WHEN DOES HE ACT SO DOCILE IN THE FACE OF --
--OF--
BATMAN...?

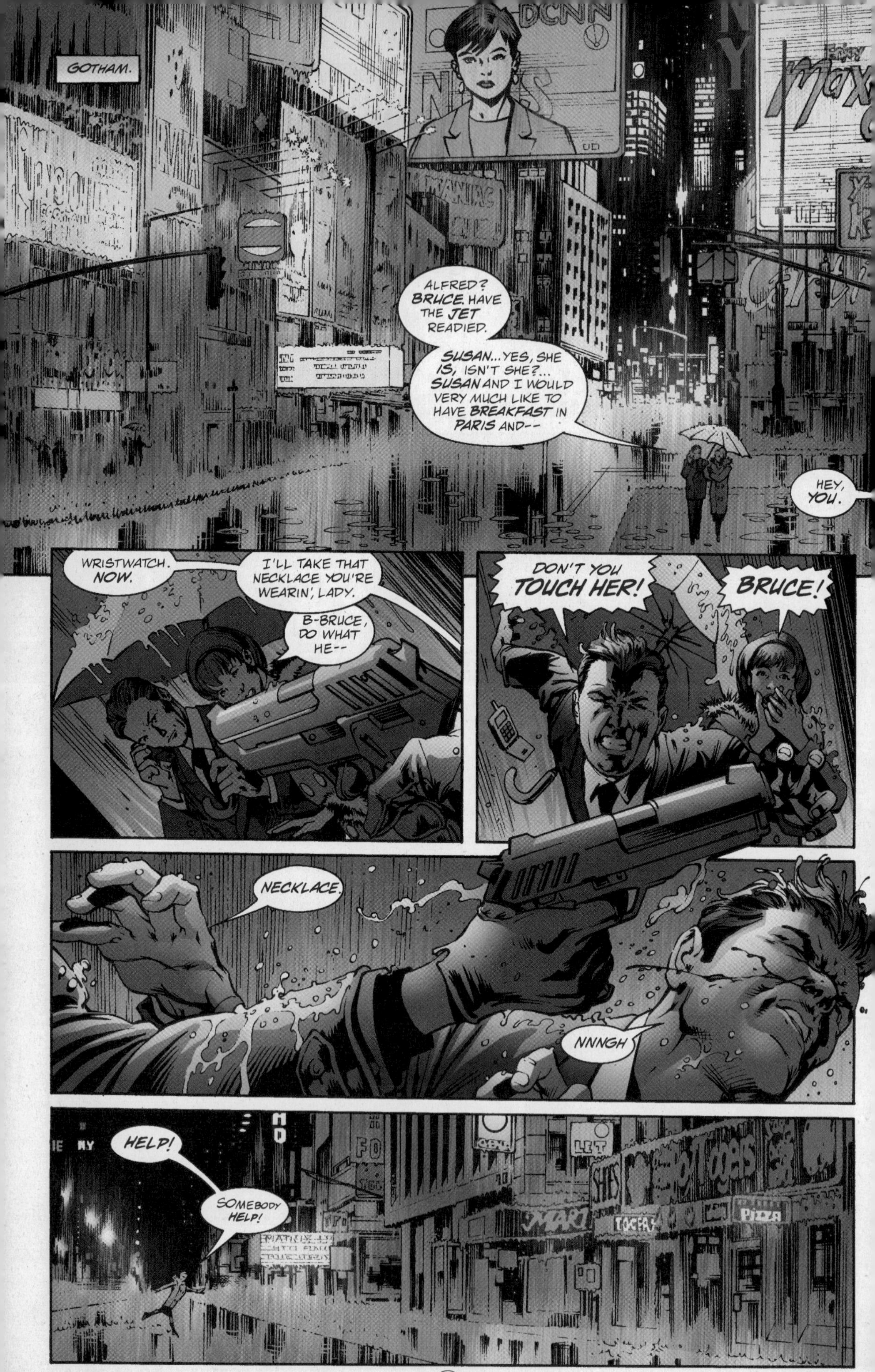
GOTHAM.
ALFRED? BRUCE. HAVE THE JET READIED.
SUSAN...YES, SHE IS, ISN'T SHE?... SUSAN AND I WOULD VERY MUCH LIKE TO HAVE BREAKFAST IN PARIS AND--
HEY, YOU.
WRISTWATCH. NOW.
I'LL TAKE THAT NECKLACE YOU'RE WEARIN', LADY.
B-BRUCE, DO WHAT HE--
DON'T YOU TOUCH HER!
BRUCE!
NECKLACE.
NNNGH
HELP!
SOMEBODY HELP!

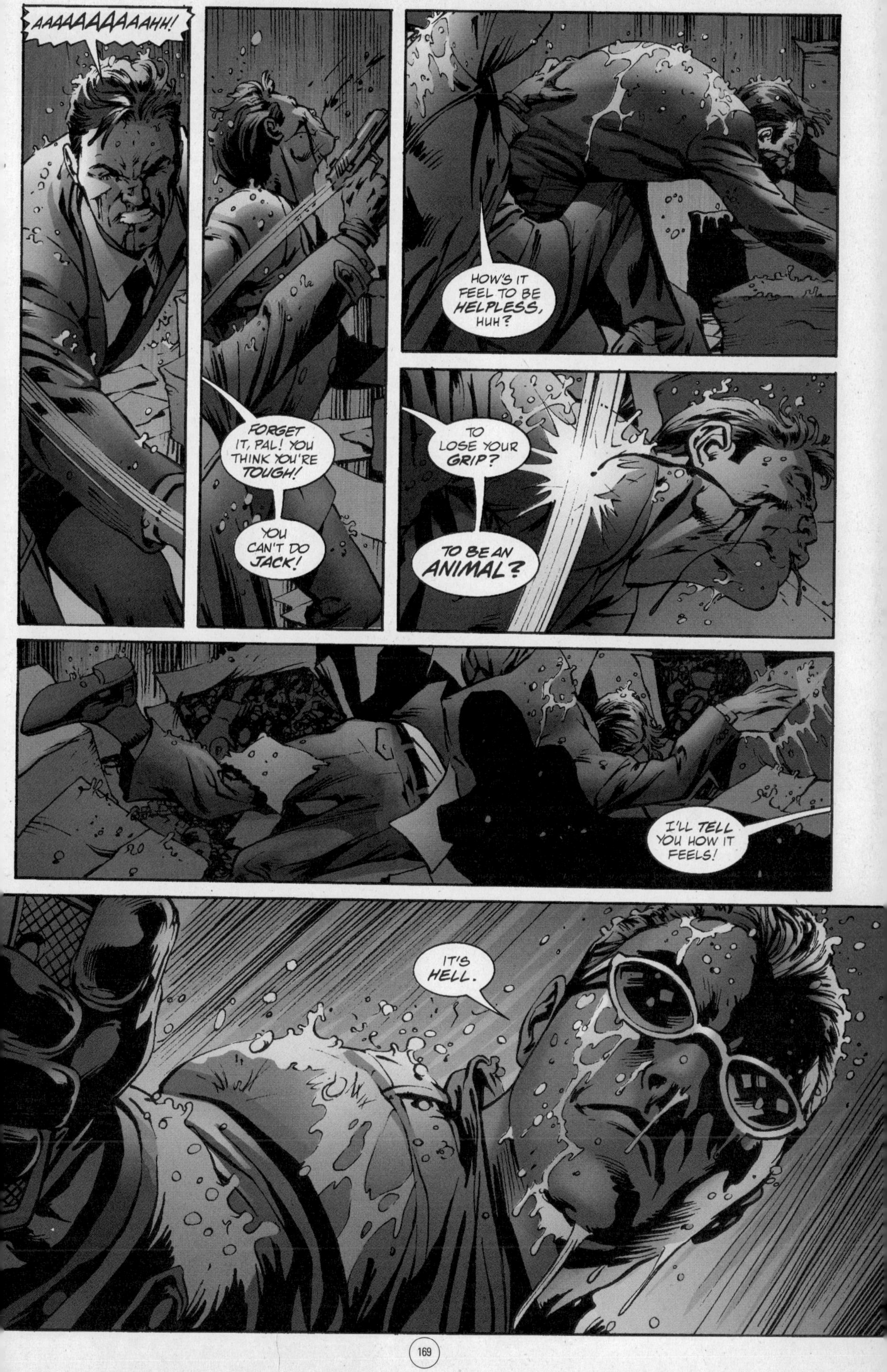
AAAAAAAAAAHH!
FORGET IT, PAL! YOU THINK YOU'RE TOUGH!
YOU CAN'T DO JACK!
HOW'S IT FEEL TO BE HELPLESS, HUH?
TO LOSE YOUR GRIP?
TO BE AN ANIMAL?
I'LL TELL YOU HOW IT FEELS!
IT'S HELL.

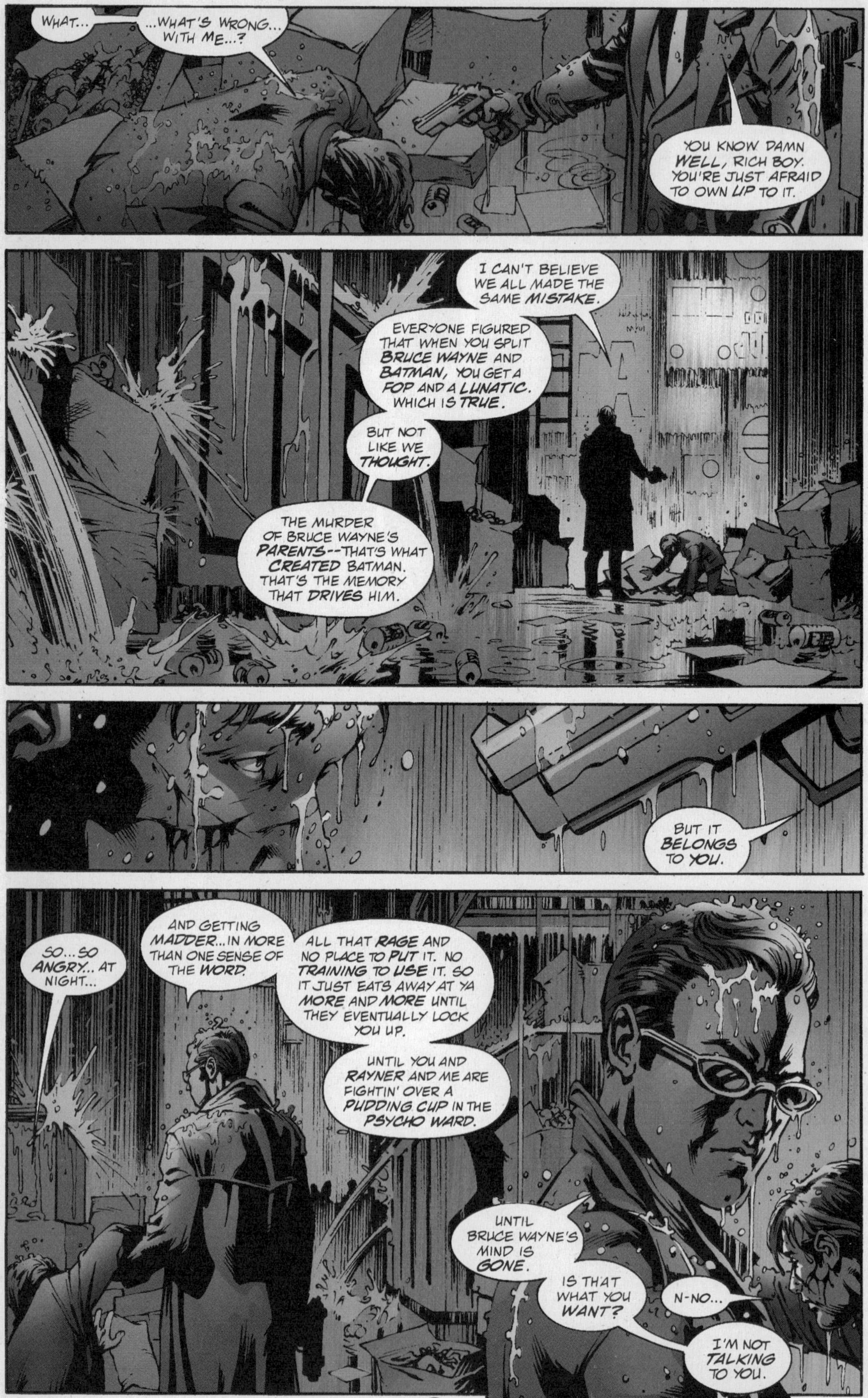

WHAT...
...WHAT'S WRONG... WITH ME...?
YOU KNOW DAMN WELL, RICH BOY. YOU'RE JUST AFRAID TO OWN UP TO IT.
I CAN'T BELIEVE WE ALL MADE THE SAME MISTAKE.
EVERYONE FIGURED THAT WHEN YOU SPLIT BRUCE WAYNE AND BATMAN, YOU GET A FOP AND A LUNATIC. WHICH IS TRUE.
BUT NOT LIKE WE THOUGHT.
THE MURDER OF BRUCE WAYNE'S PARENTS--THAT'S WHAT CREATED BATMAN. THAT'S THE MEMORY THAT DRIVES HIM.
BUT IT BELONGS TO YOU.
SO...SO ANGRY... AT NIGHT...
AND GETTING MADDER...IN MORE THAN ONE SENSE OF THE WORD.
ALL THAT RAGE AND NO PLACE TO PUT IT. NO TRAINING TO USE IT. SO IT JUST EATS AWAY AT YA MORE AND MORE UNTIL THEY EVENTUALLY LOCK YOU UP.
UNTIL YOU AND RAYNER AND ME ARE FIGHTIN' OVER A PUDDING CUP IN THE PSYCHO WARD.
UNTIL BRUCE WAYNE'S MIND IS GONE.
IS THAT WHAT YOU WANT?
N-NO...
I'M NOT TALKING TO YOU.

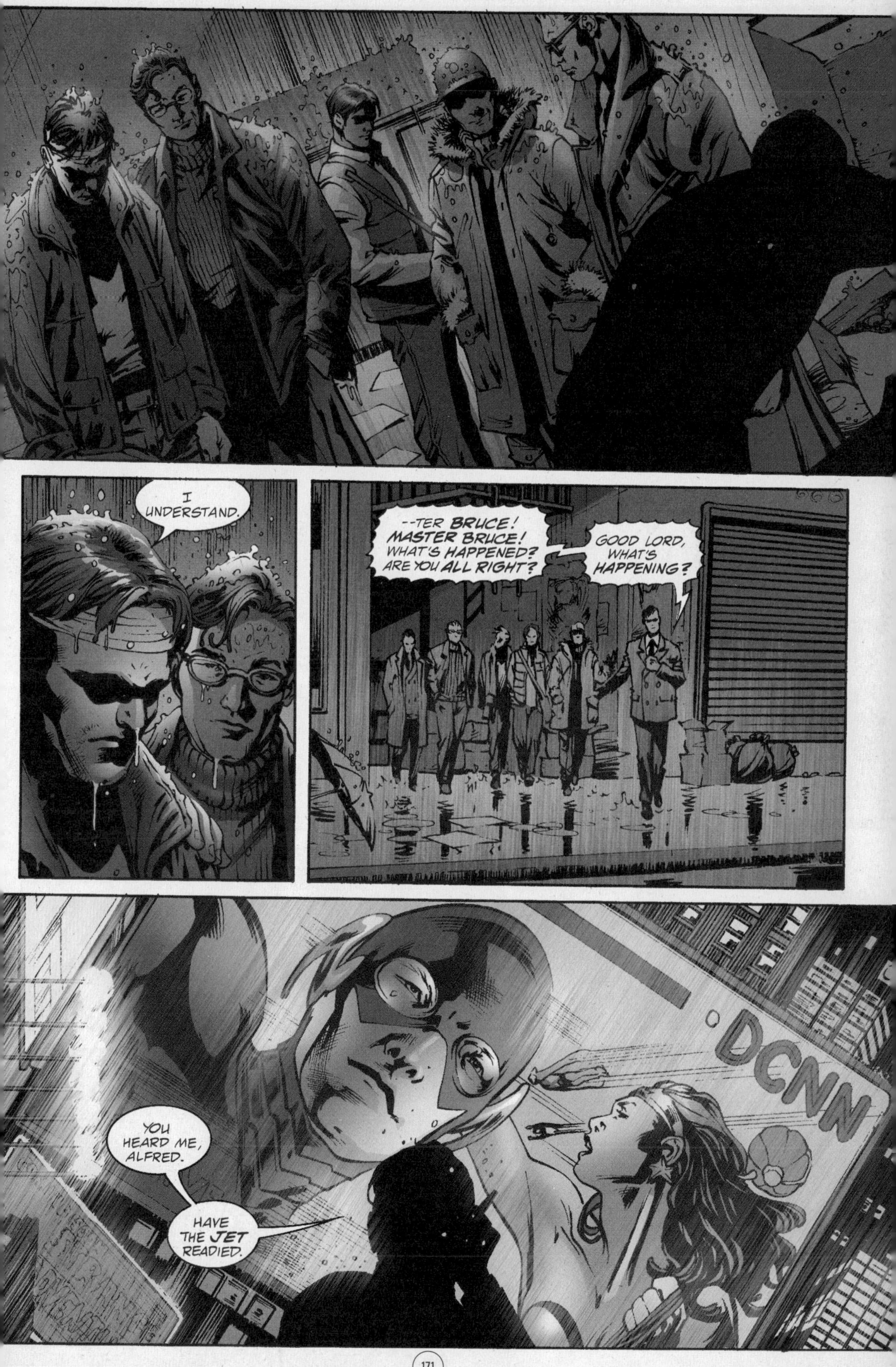
I UNDERSTAND.
--TER BRUCE! MASTER BRUCE! WHAT'S HAPPENED? ARE YOU ALL RIGHT?
GOOD LORD, WHAT'S HAPPENING?
DCNN
YOU HEARD ME, ALFRED.
HAVE THE JET READIED.

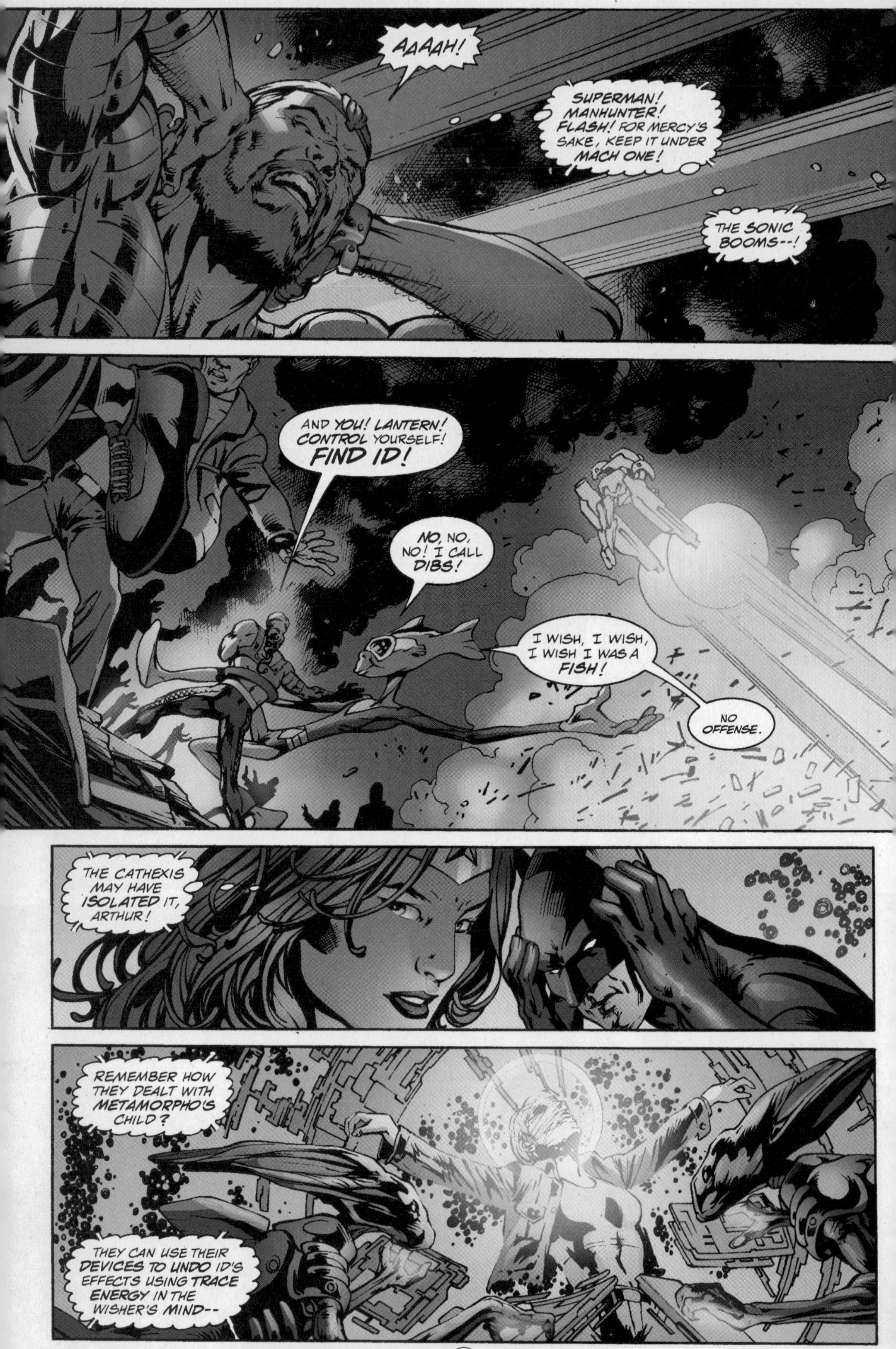
AAAAH!
SUPERMAN! MANHUNTER! FLASH! FOR MERCY'S SAKE, KEEP IT UNDER MACH ONE!
THE SONIC BOOMS--!
AND YOU! LANTERN! CONTROL YOURSELF! FIND ID!
NO, NO, NO! I CALL DIBS!
I WISH, I WISH, I WISH I WAS A FISH!
NO OFFENSE.
THE CATHEXIS MAY HAVE ISOLATED IT, ARTHUR!
REMEMBER HOW THEY DEALT WITH METAMORPHO'S CHILD?
THEY CAN USE THEIR DEVICES TO UNDO ID'S EFFECTS USING TRACE ENERGY IN THE WISHER'S MIND--

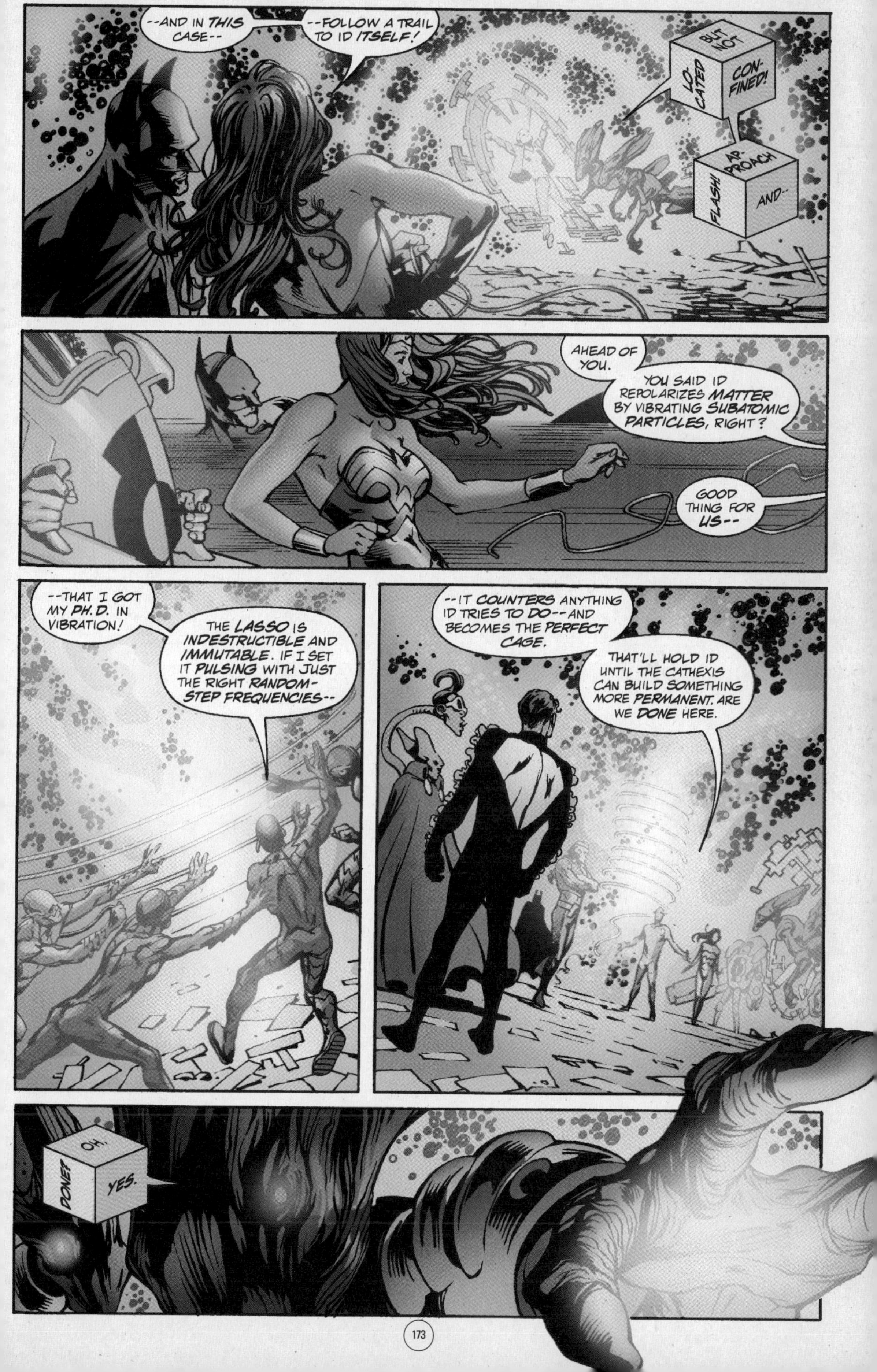
--AND IN THIS CASE--
--FOLLOW A TRAIL TO ID ITSELF!
LO-CATED BUT NOT CON-FINED!
FLASH! AP-PROACH AND--
AHEAD OF YOU.
YOU SAID ID REPOLARIZES MATTER BY VIBRATING SUBATOMIC PARTICLES, RIGHT?
GOOD THING FOR US--
--THAT I GOT MY PH.D. IN VIBRATION!
THE LASSO IS INDESTRUCTIBLE AND IMMUTABLE. IF I SET IT PULSING WITH JUST THE RIGHT RANDOM-STEP FREQUENCIES--
--IT COUNTERS ANYTHING ID TRIES TO DO--AND BECOMES THE PERFECT CAGE.
THAT'LL HOLD ID UNTIL THE CATHEXIS CAN BUILD SOMETHING MORE PERMANENT. ARE WE DONE HERE.
DONE? OH, YES.

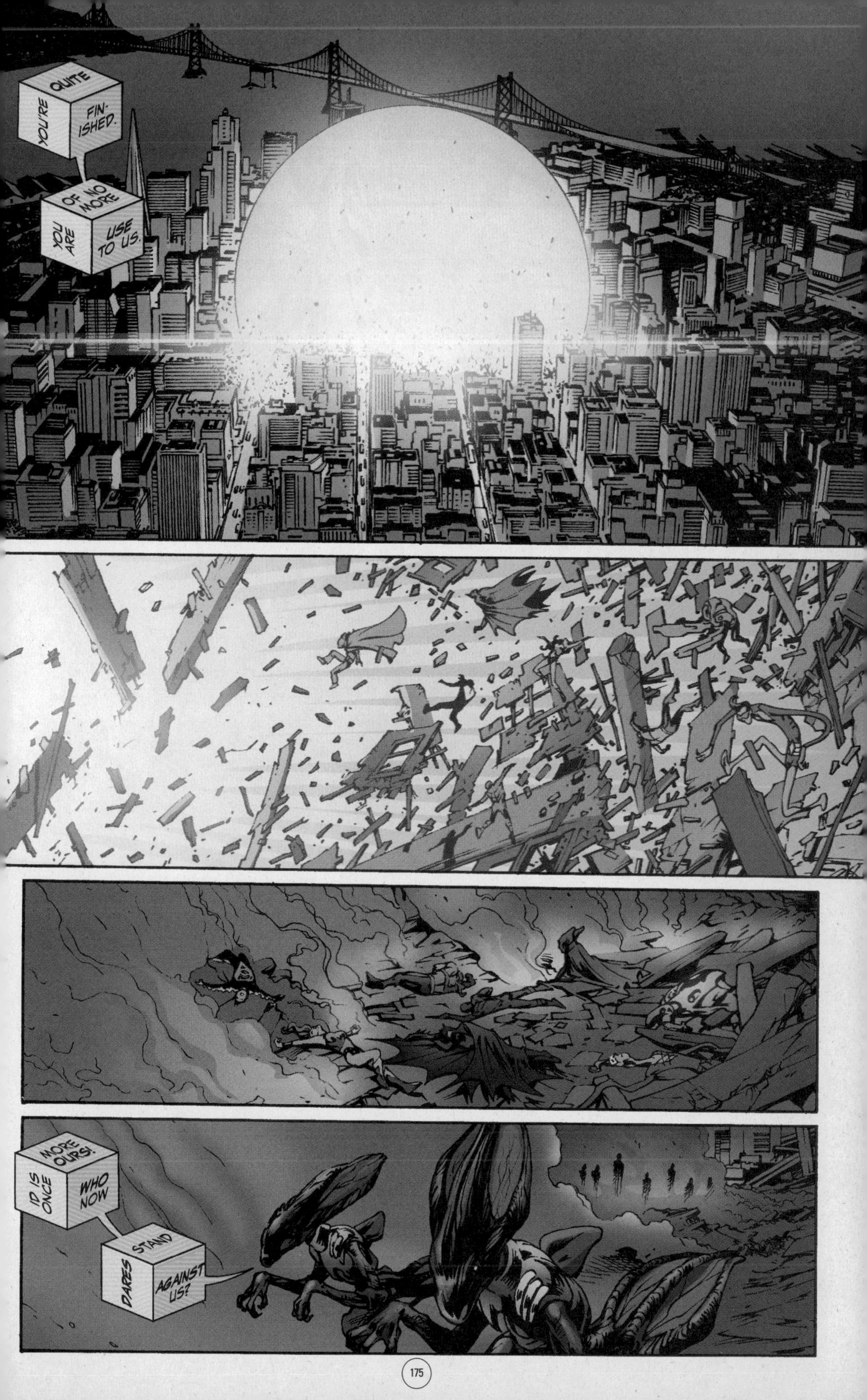
YOU'RE QUITE FIN-ISHED.
YOU ARE OF NO MORE USE TO US.
ID IS ONCE MORE OURS! WHO NOW
DARES STAND AGAINST US?

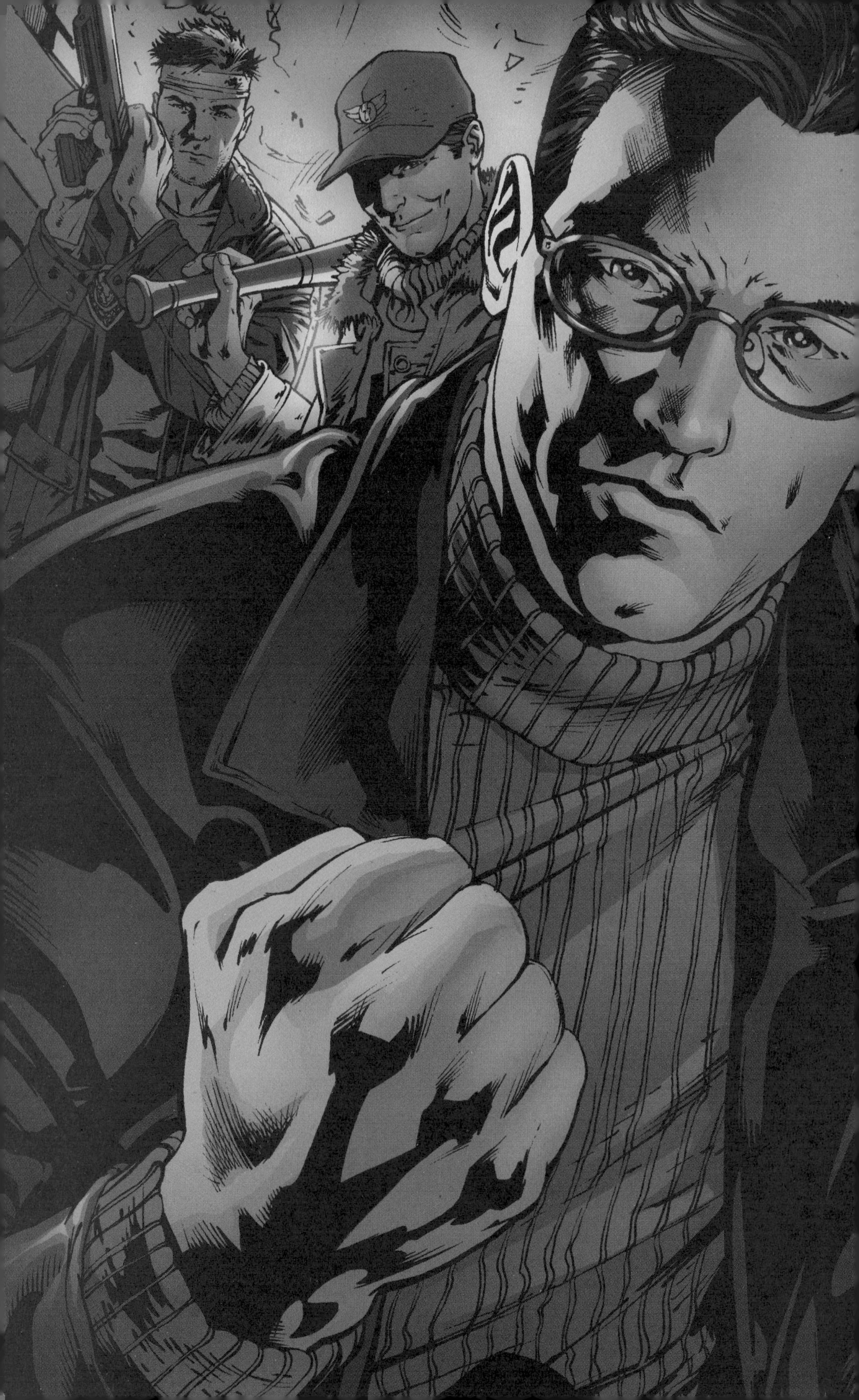

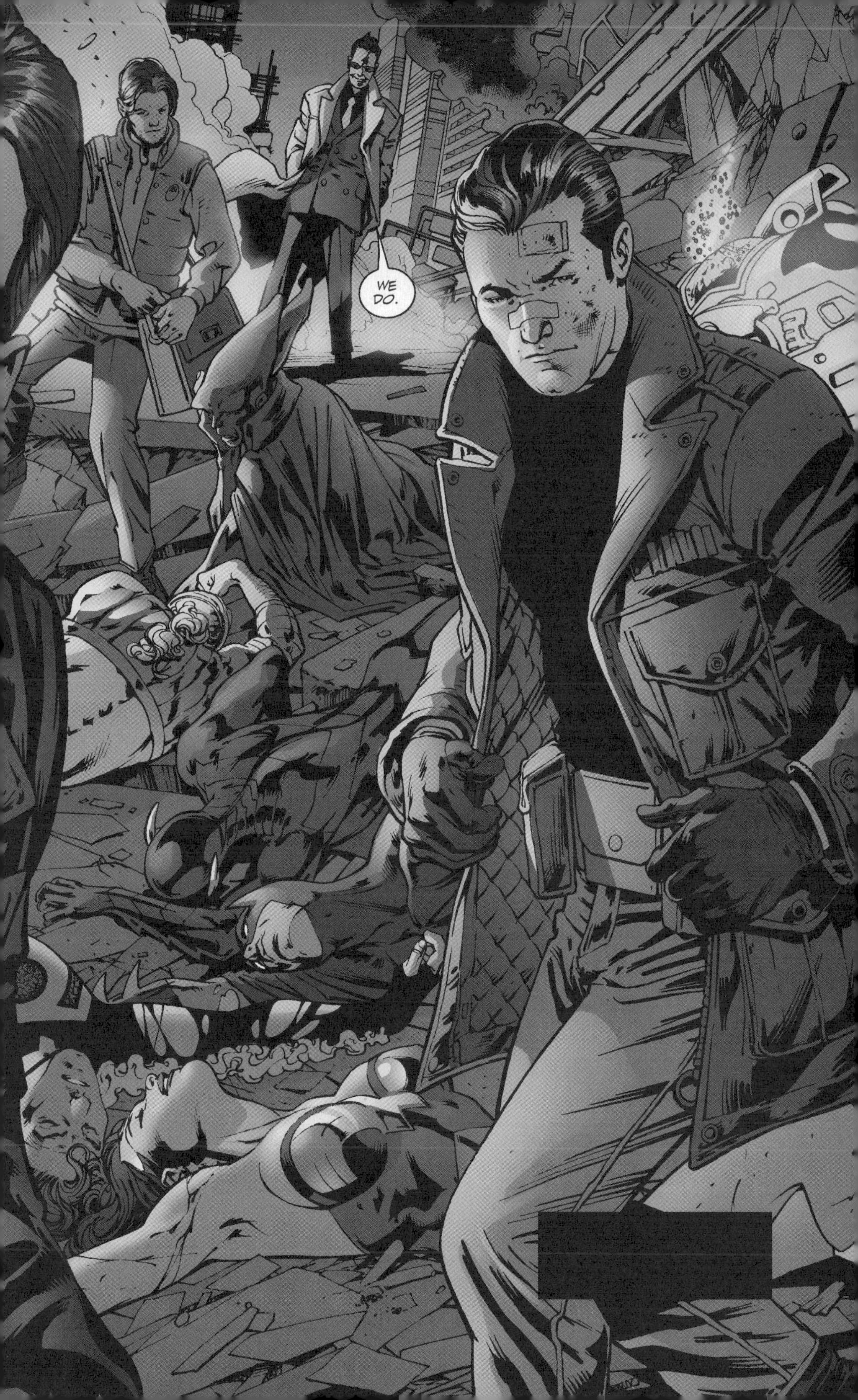
WE DO.
[redacted]

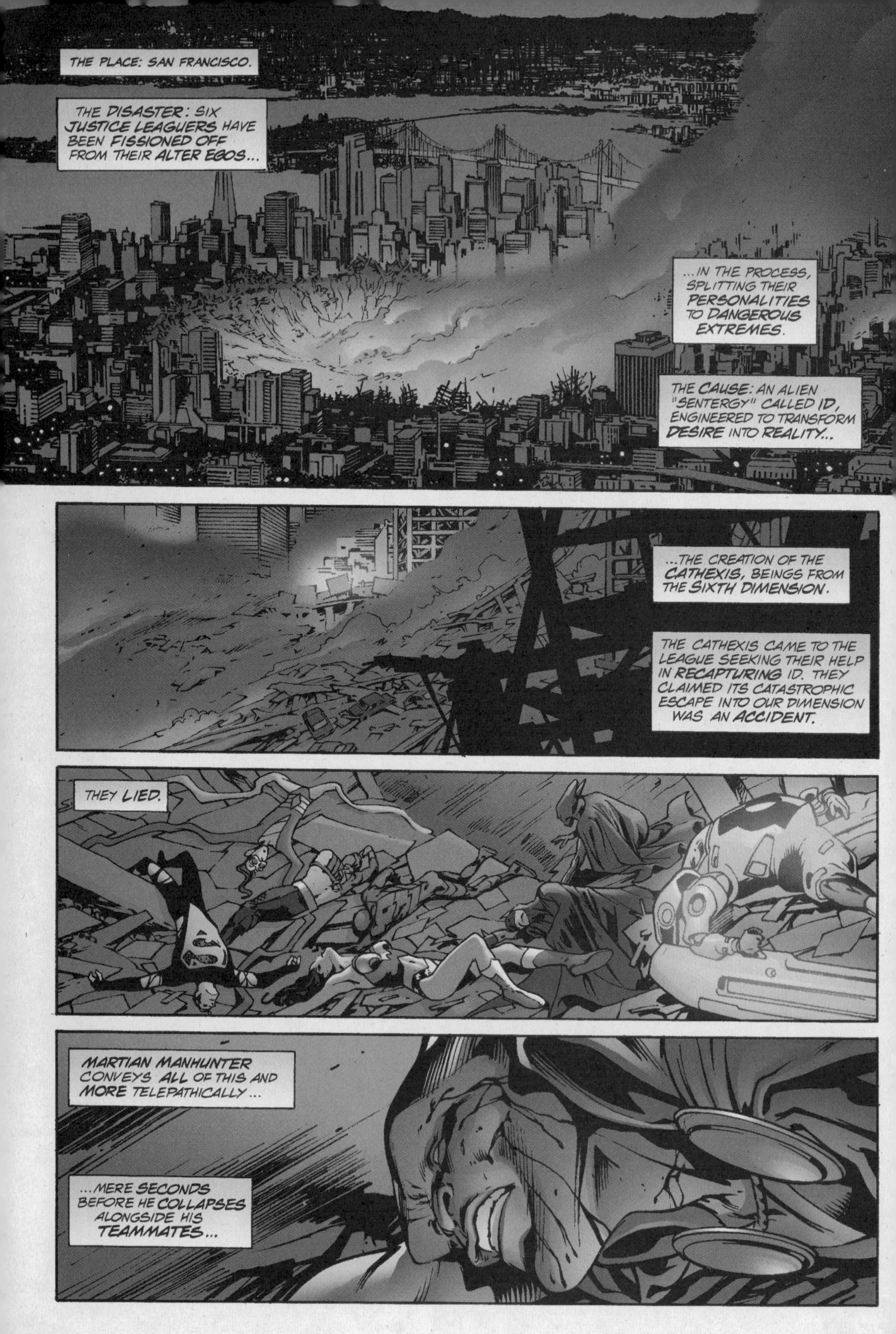
THE PLACE: SAN FRANCISCO.
THE DISASTER: SIX JUSTICE LEAGUERS HAVE BEEN FISSIONED OFF FROM THEIR ALTER EGOS...
...IN THE PROCESS, SPLITTING THEIR PERSONALITIES TO DANGEROUS EXTREMES.
THE CAUSE: AN ALIEN "SENTERGY" CALLED ID, ENGINEERED TO TRANSFORM DESIRE INTO REALITY...
...THE CREATION OF THE CATHEXIS, BEINGS FROM THE SIXTH DIMENSION.
THE CATHEXIS CAME TO THE LEAGUE SEEKING THEIR HELP IN RECAPTURING ID. THEY CLAIMED ITS CATASTROPHIC ESCAPE INTO OUR DIMENSION WAS AN ACCIDENT.
THEY LIED.
MARTIAN MANHUNTER CONVEYS ALL OF THIS AND MORE TELEPATHICALLY...
...MERE SECONDS BEFORE HE COLLAPSES ALONGSIDE HIS TEAMMATES...

...LEAVING THE FATE OF THE EARTH IN THE HANDS OF SIX MORTAL MEN AND KNOWING BEYOND ALL CERTAINTY...

...THAT THEY HAVEN'T A CHANCE.

UNITED WE FALL

MARK WAID and BRYAN HITCH
storytellers

| PAUL NEARY | LAURA DEPUY | KEN LOPEZ | STEVE WACKER | DAN RASPLER |
| inks | colors | letters | assistant ed. | editor |

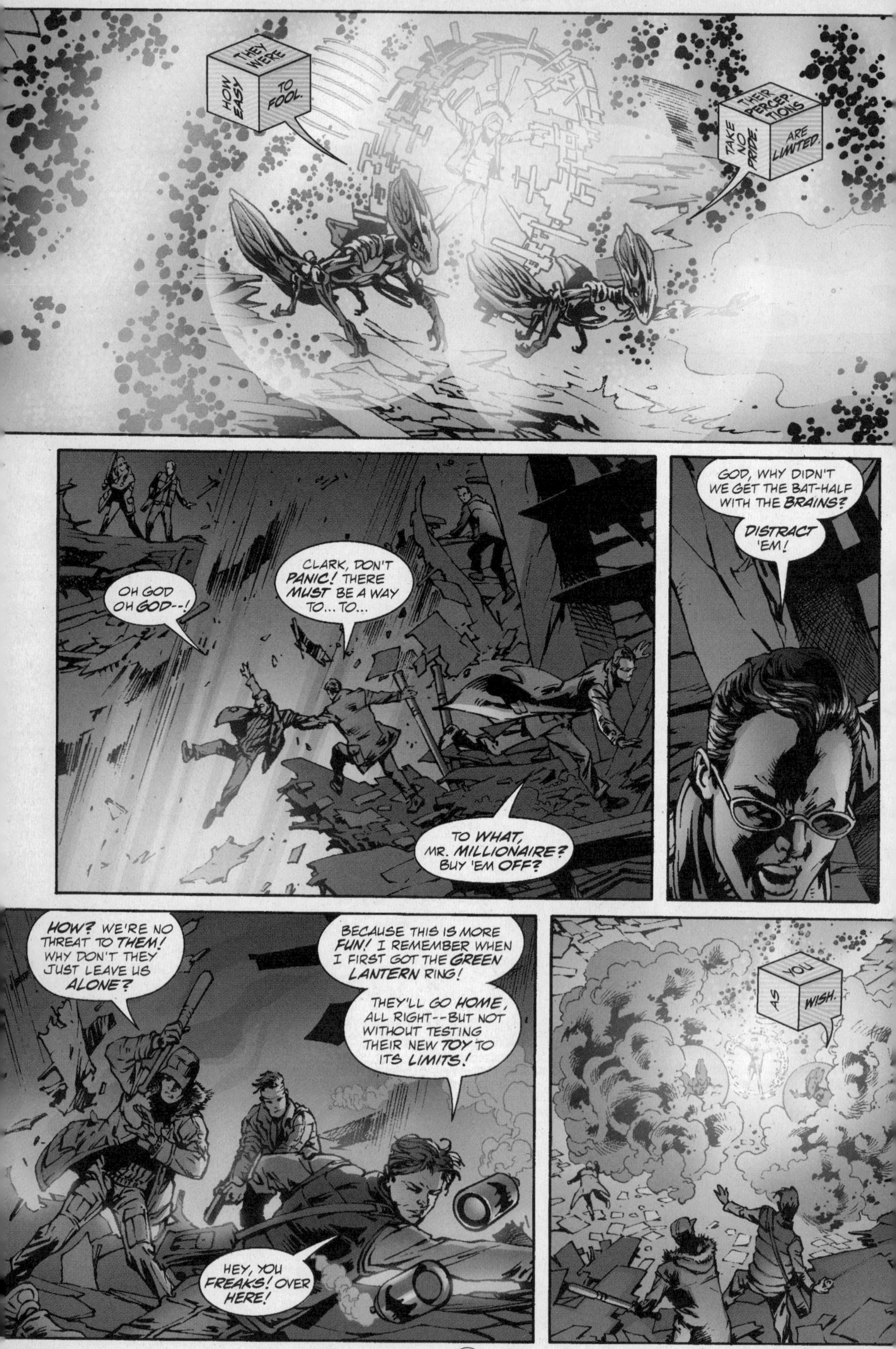
HOW EASY THEY WERE TO FOOL.
TAKE NO PRIDE. THEIR PERCEPTIONS ARE LIMITED.
OH GOD OH GOD--!
CLARK, DON'T PANIC! THERE MUST BE A WAY TO... TO...
TO WHAT, MR. MILLIONAIRE? BUY 'EM OFF?
GOD, WHY DIDN'T WE GET THE BAT-HALF WITH THE BRAINS?
DISTRACT 'EM!
HOW? WE'RE NO THREAT TO THEM! WHY DON'T THEY JUST LEAVE US ALONE?
BECAUSE THIS IS MORE FUN! I REMEMBER WHEN I FIRST GOT THE GREEN LANTERN RING!
THEY'LL GO HOME, ALL RIGHT--BUT NOT WITHOUT TESTING THEIR NEW TOY TO ITS LIMITS!
HEY, YOU FREAKS! OVER HERE!
AS YOU WISH.

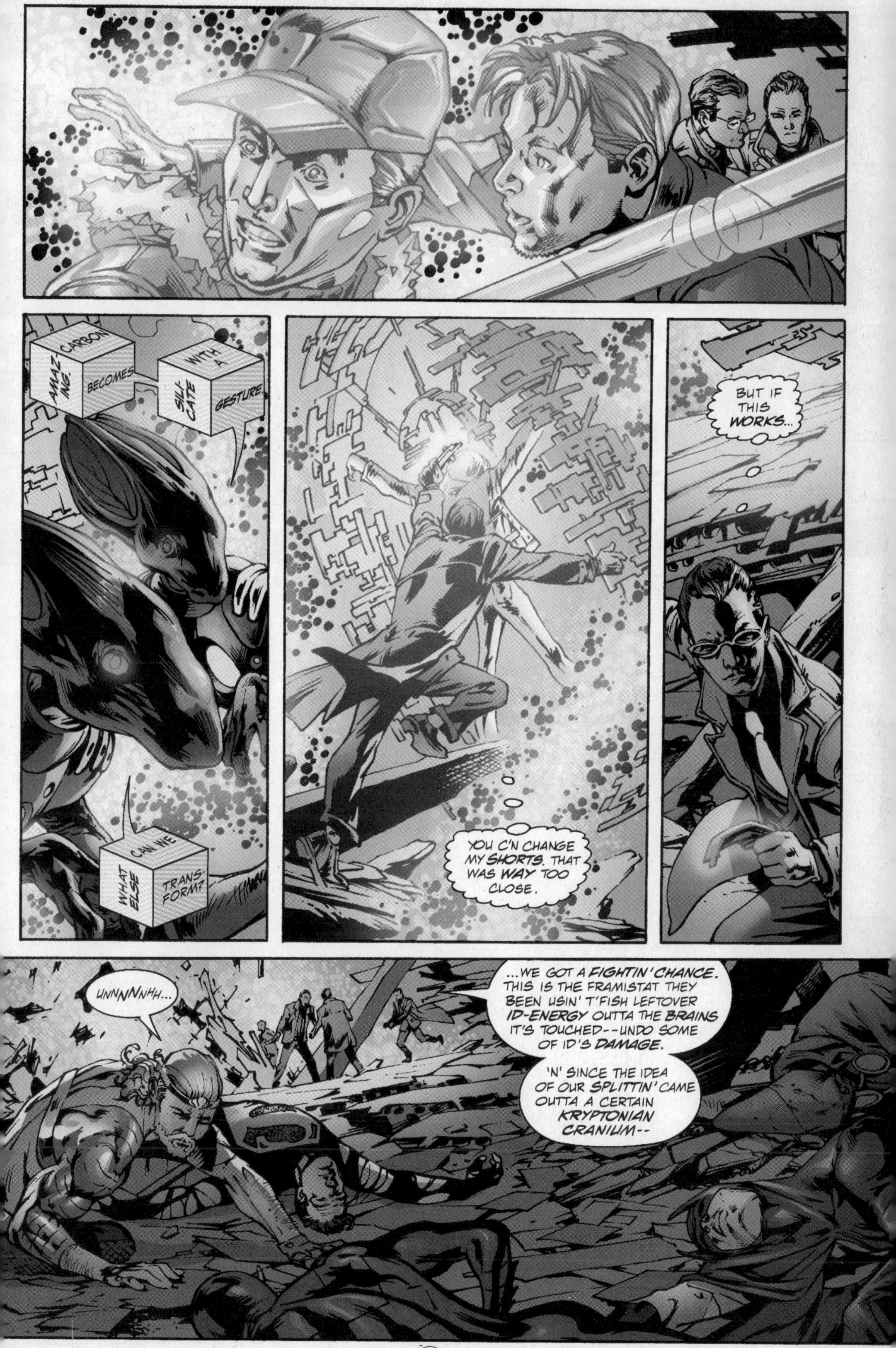
AMAZING. CARBON BECOMES
SILICATE WITH A GESTURE.
WHAT ELSE CAN WE TRANSFORM?
YOU C'N CHANGE MY SHORTS. THAT WAS WAY TOO CLOSE.
BUT IF THIS WORKS...
UNNNNNHH...
...WE GOT A FIGHTIN' CHANCE. THIS IS THE FRAMISTAT THEY BEEN USIN' T'FISH LEFTOVER ID-ENERGY OUTTA THE BRAINS IT'S TOUCHED--UNDO SOME OF ID'S DAMAGE.
'N' SINCE THE IDEA OF OUR SPLITTIN' CAME OUTTA A CERTAIN KRYPTONIAN CRANIUM--

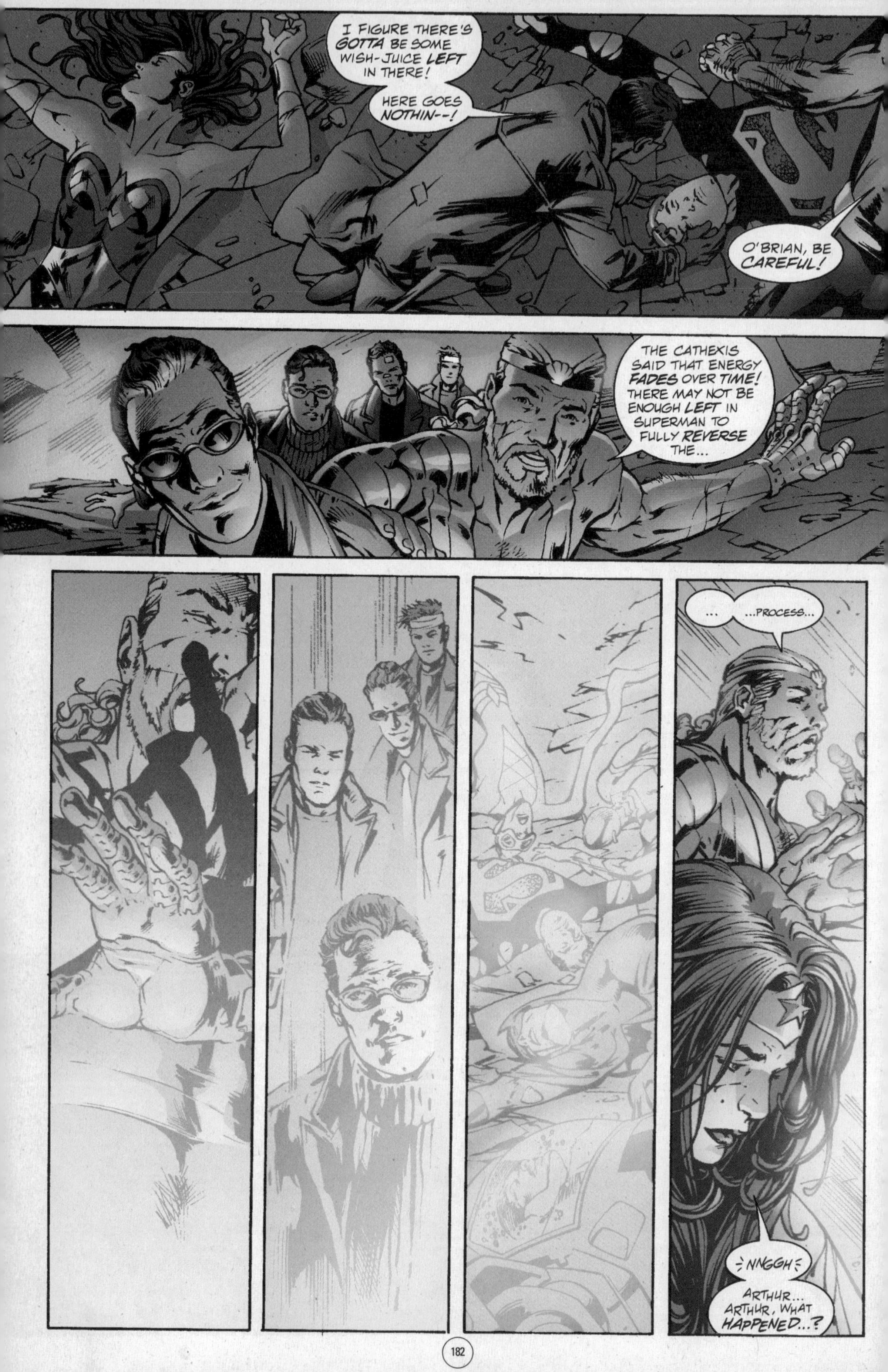
I FIGURE THERE'S GOTTA BE SOME WISH-JUICE LEFT IN THERE!
HERE GOES NOTHIN--!
O'BRIAN, BE CAREFUL!
THE CATHEXIS SAID THAT ENERGY FADES OVER TIME! THERE MAY NOT BE ENOUGH LEFT IN SUPERMAN TO FULLY REVERSE THE...
...
...PROCESS...
NNGGH
ARTHUR... ARTHUR, WHAT HAPPENED...?

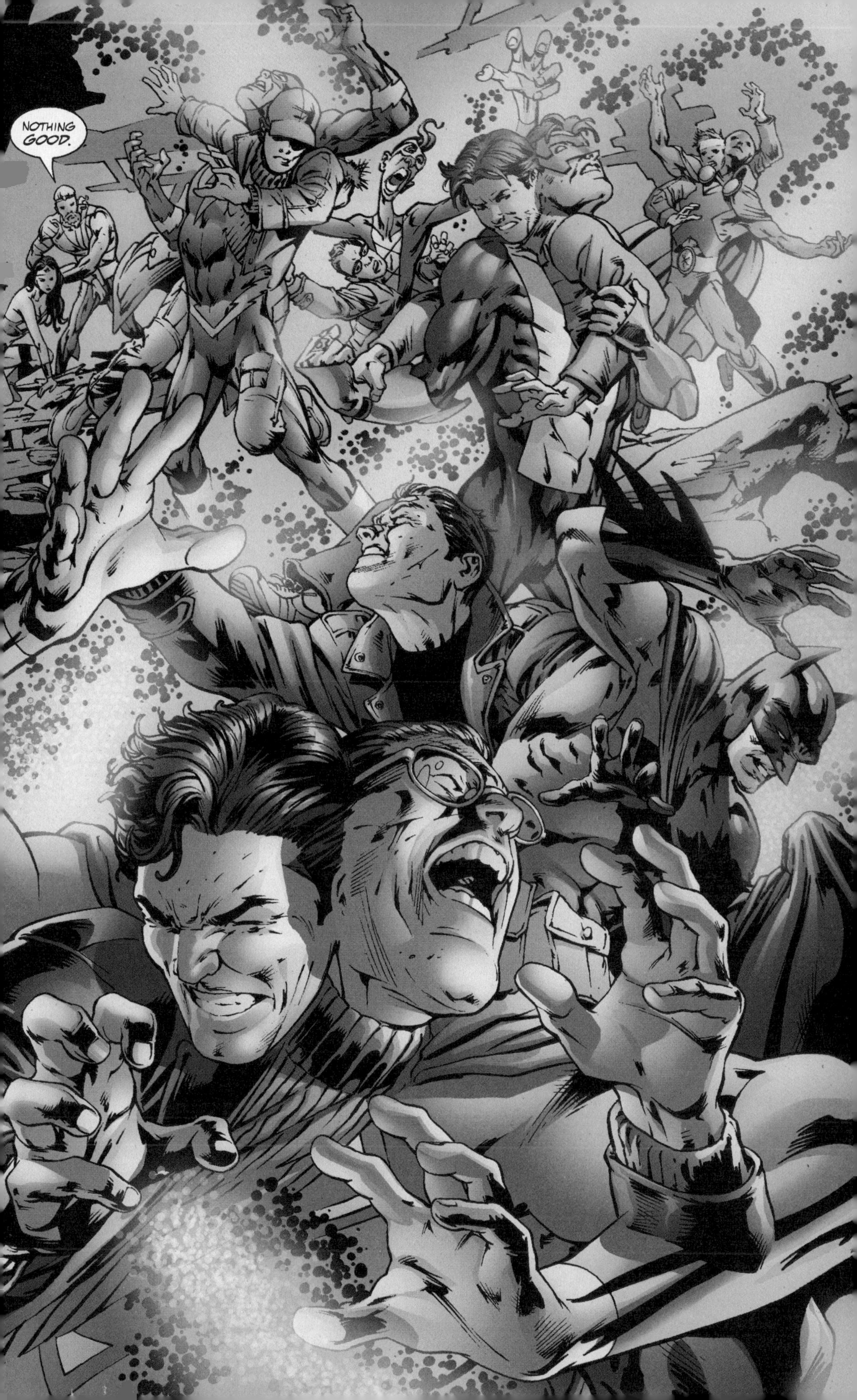
NOTHING GOOD.

GIVE ME FLESH AND THE RING! BLOOD HOLDING THE RING! ME BACK

DON'T ⧖⫽⊹⟐⫽. UNDERSTAND KRYPTONESE ⟐⧖ ⊠⟐⟐⊳ SCARED ⫽⫽⊠⧖⊳⊠ I'M SCARED ⟐⫽⫽⊠∞⊠!

HERA, THEY'RE AT WAR—WITH THEMSELVES—!

GOTTAMOVE SICK OF RUNNING! SICK OF BLOWING THROUGH GETTINGAWAY LIFE NEVER STANDING FROM HERE! STILL!

NOOOO... ARTHUR, I DON'T WANT THIS... I CAN'T SHOULDER J'ONN'S DEMONS ANYMORE! I—

JOHN, LISTEN TO ME! WE DON'T HAVE TIME FOR DEBATE! FOR THE MOMENT, WE'RE BENEATH THE CATHEXIS'S NOTICE—

"—BUT THAT WON'T LAST!"

NOPLEASE NOPLEASE NOPLEASE

LIFE FORMS: SO THREE.

FASCINATING

AND YET SO COMPLEX.

DIMENSIONAL

BENEATH THEIR SURFACE!

WHAT LIES

LET US SEE.

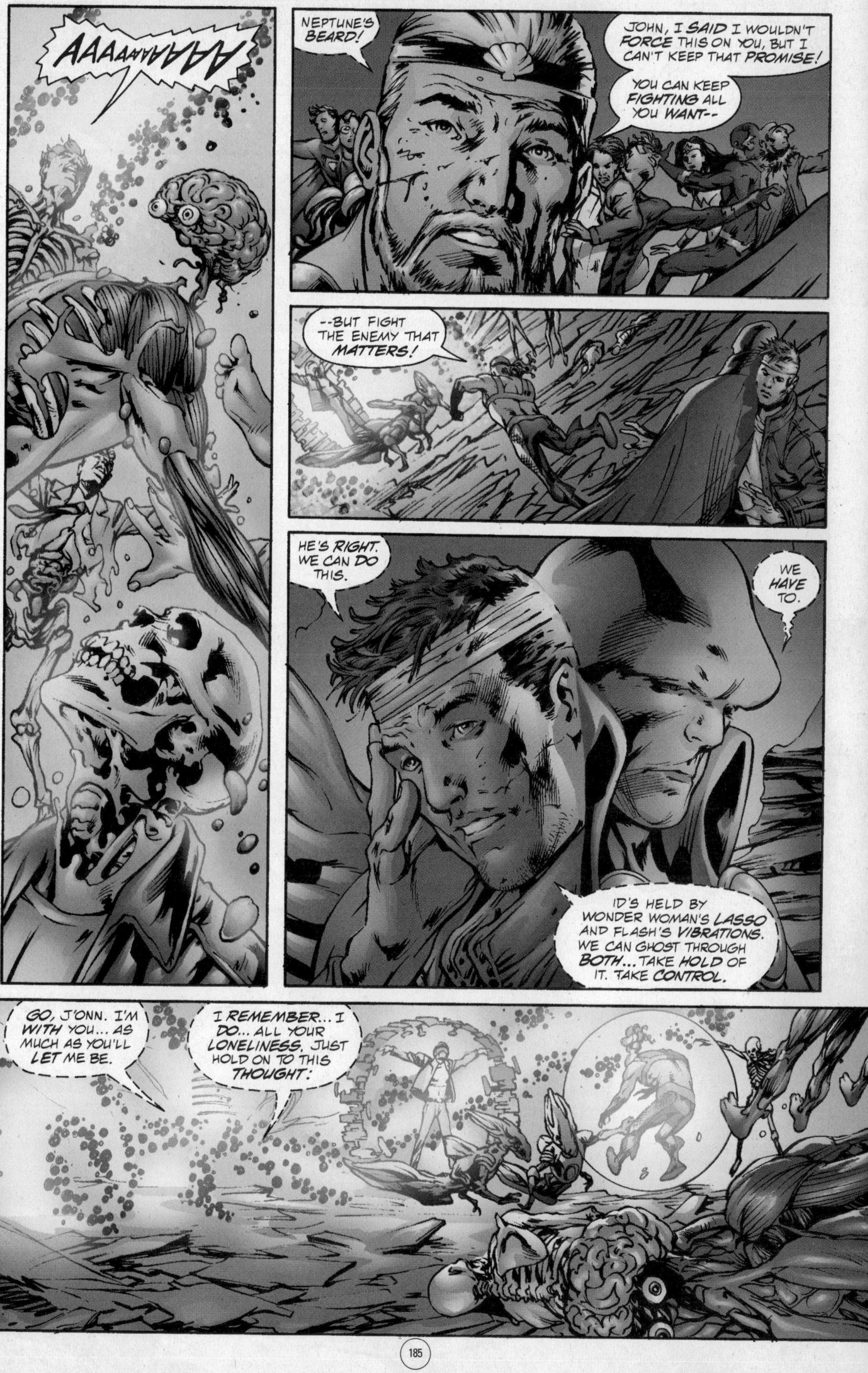
AAAAAAAAAAA
NEPTUNE'S BEARD!
JOHN, I SAID I WOULDN'T FORCE THIS ON YOU, BUT I CAN'T KEEP THAT PROMISE!
YOU CAN KEEP FIGHTING ALL YOU WANT--
--BUT FIGHT THE ENEMY THAT MATTERS!
HE'S RIGHT. WE CAN DO THIS.
WE HAVE TO.
ID'S HELD BY WONDER WOMAN'S LASSO AND FLASH'S VIBRATIONS. WE CAN GHOST THROUGH BOTH... TAKE HOLD OF IT. TAKE CONTROL.
GO, J'ONN. I'M WITH YOU... AS MUCH AS YOU'LL LET ME BE.
I REMEMBER... I DO... ALL YOUR LONELINESS. JUST HOLD ON TO THIS THOUGHT:

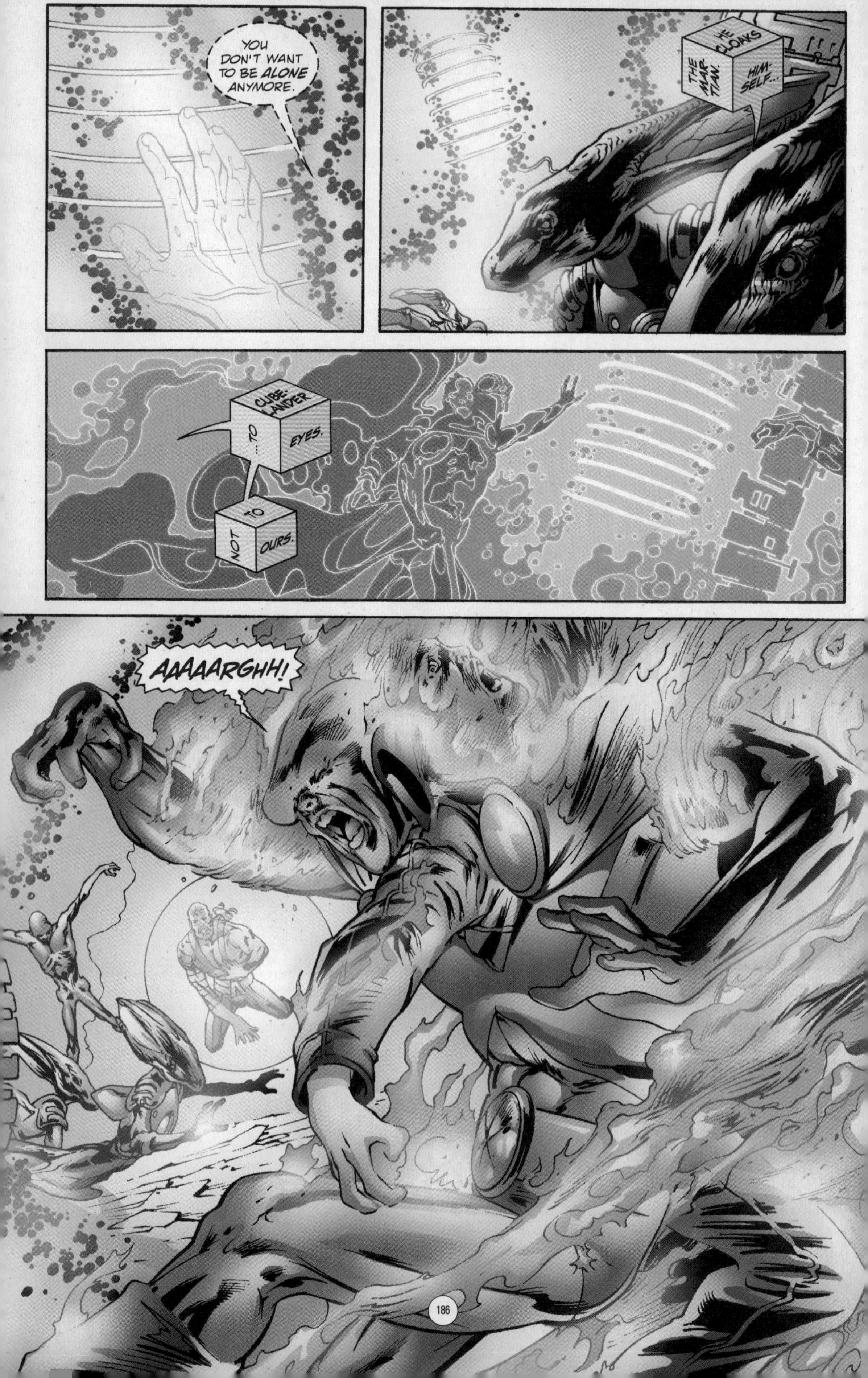
YOU DON'T WANT TO BE ALONE ANYMORE.
THE MAR-TIAN. HE CLOAKS HIM-SELF...
...TO CUBE-LANDER EYES.
NOT TO OURS.
AAAAARGHH!

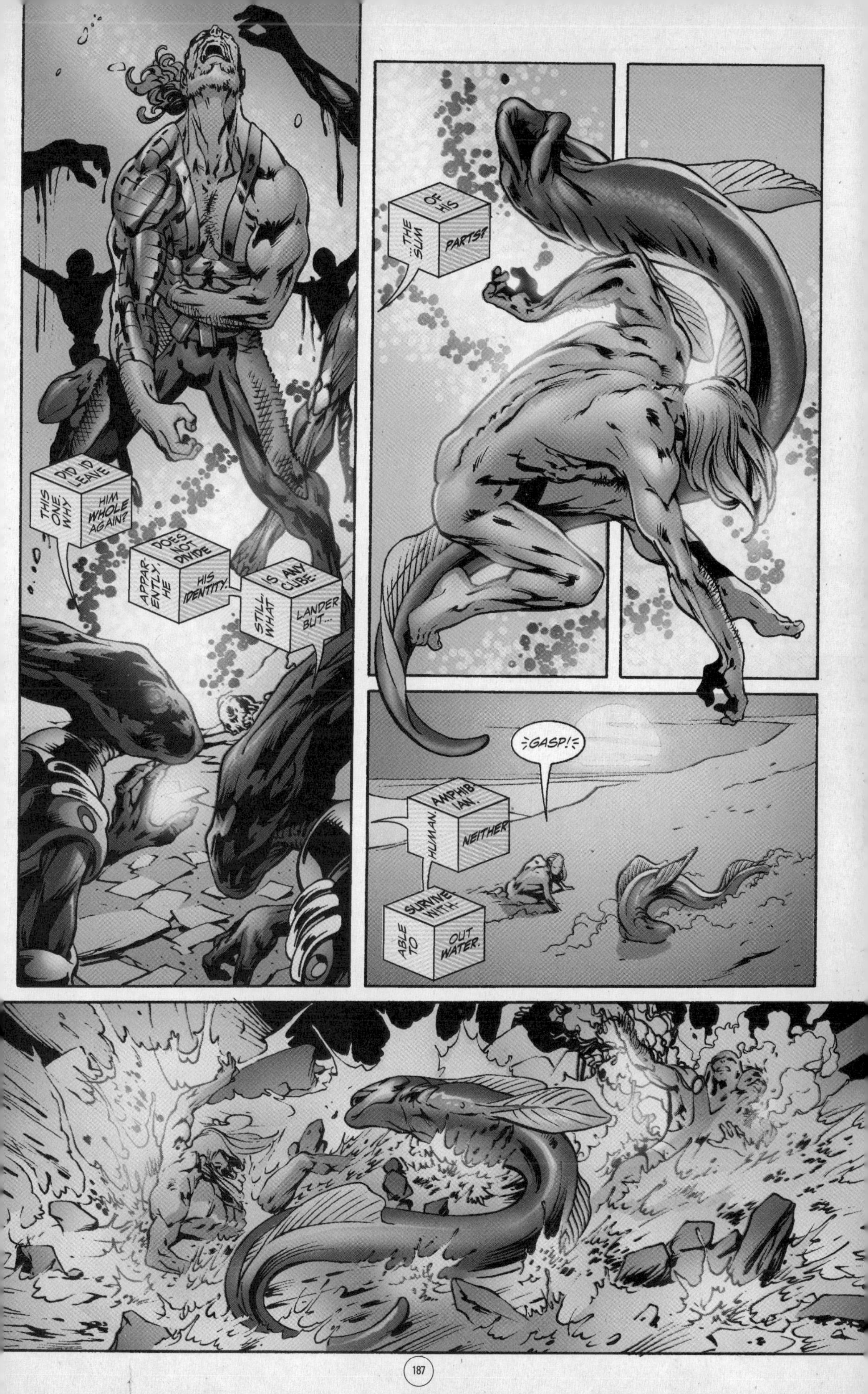
THIS ONE. WHY DID ID LEAVE HIM WHOLE AGAIN?
APPARENTLY, HE DOES NOT DIVIDE HIS IDENTITY.
STILL, WHAT IS ANY CUBE: LANDER BUT...
...THE SUM OF HIS PARTS?
GASP!
HUMAN. AMPHIBIAN. NEITHER
ABLE TO SURVIVE WITHOUT WATER.

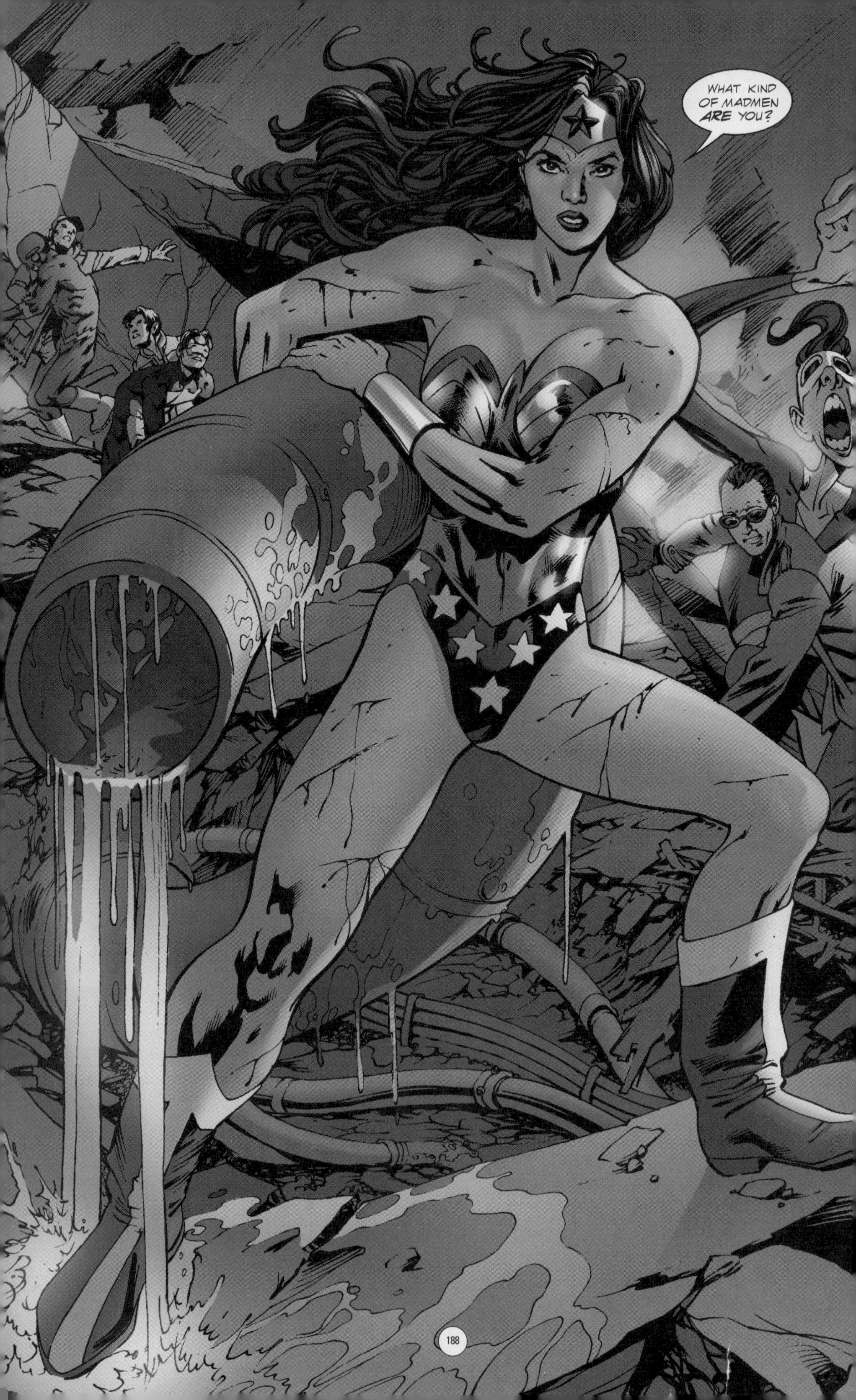
WHAT KIND OF MADMEN ARE YOU?

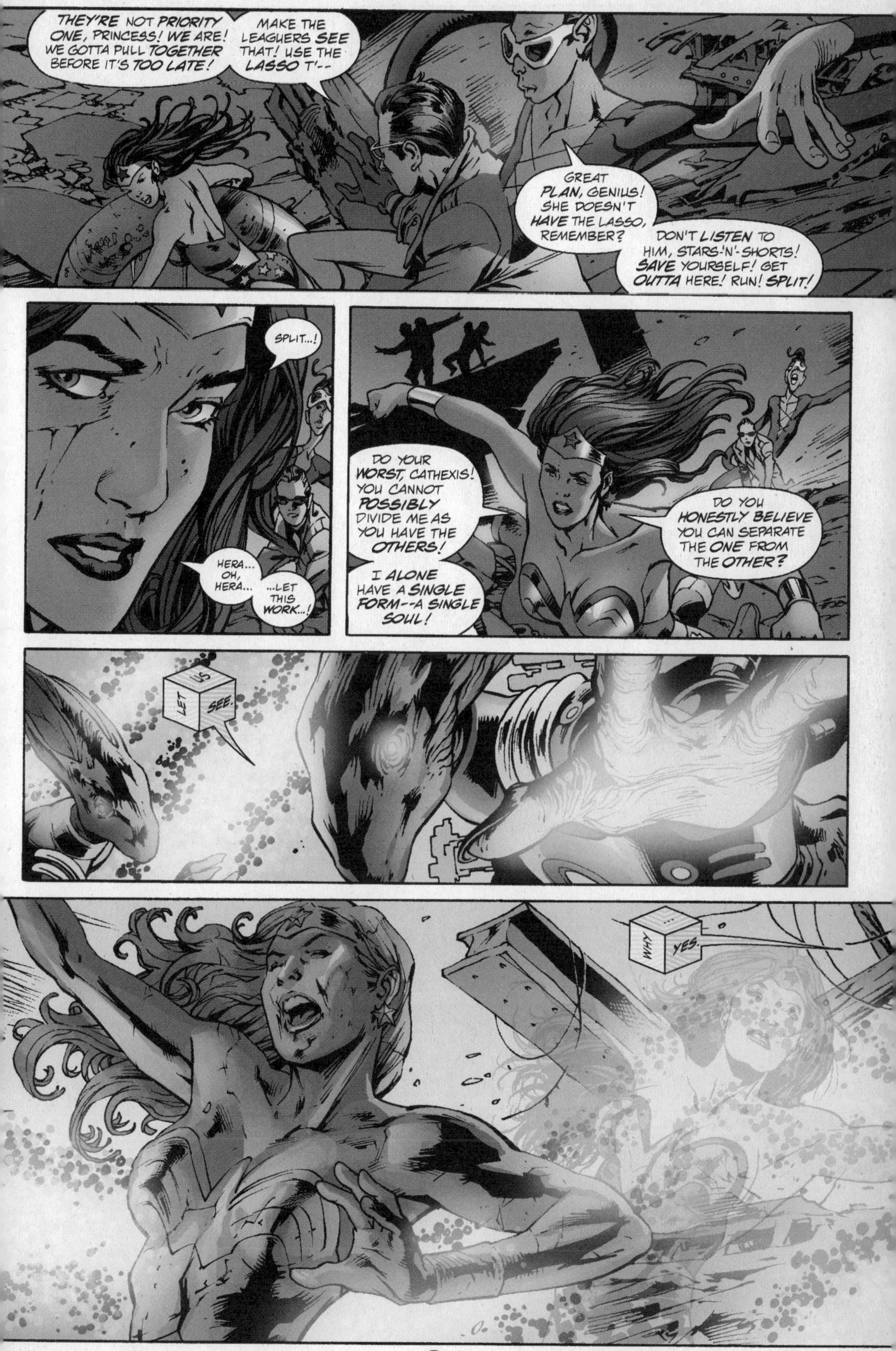
THEY'RE NOT PRIORITY ONE, PRINCESS! WE ARE! WE GOTTA PULL TOGETHER BEFORE IT'S TOO LATE!
MAKE THE LEAGUERS SEE THAT! USE THE LASSO T'--
GREAT PLAN, GENIUS! SHE DOESN'T HAVE THE LASSO, REMEMBER?
DON'T LISTEN TO HIM, STARS-'N'-SHORTS! SAVE YOURSELF! GET OUTTA HERE! RUN! SPLIT!
SPLIT...!
HERA... OH, HERA...
...LET THIS WORK...!
DO YOUR WORST, CATHEXIS! YOU CANNOT POSSIBLY DIVIDE ME AS YOU HAVE THE OTHERS!
I ALONE HAVE A SINGLE FORM--A SINGLE SOUL!
DO YOU HONESTLY BELIEVE YOU CAN SEPARATE THE ONE FROM THE OTHER?
LET US SEE.
WHY ... YES.

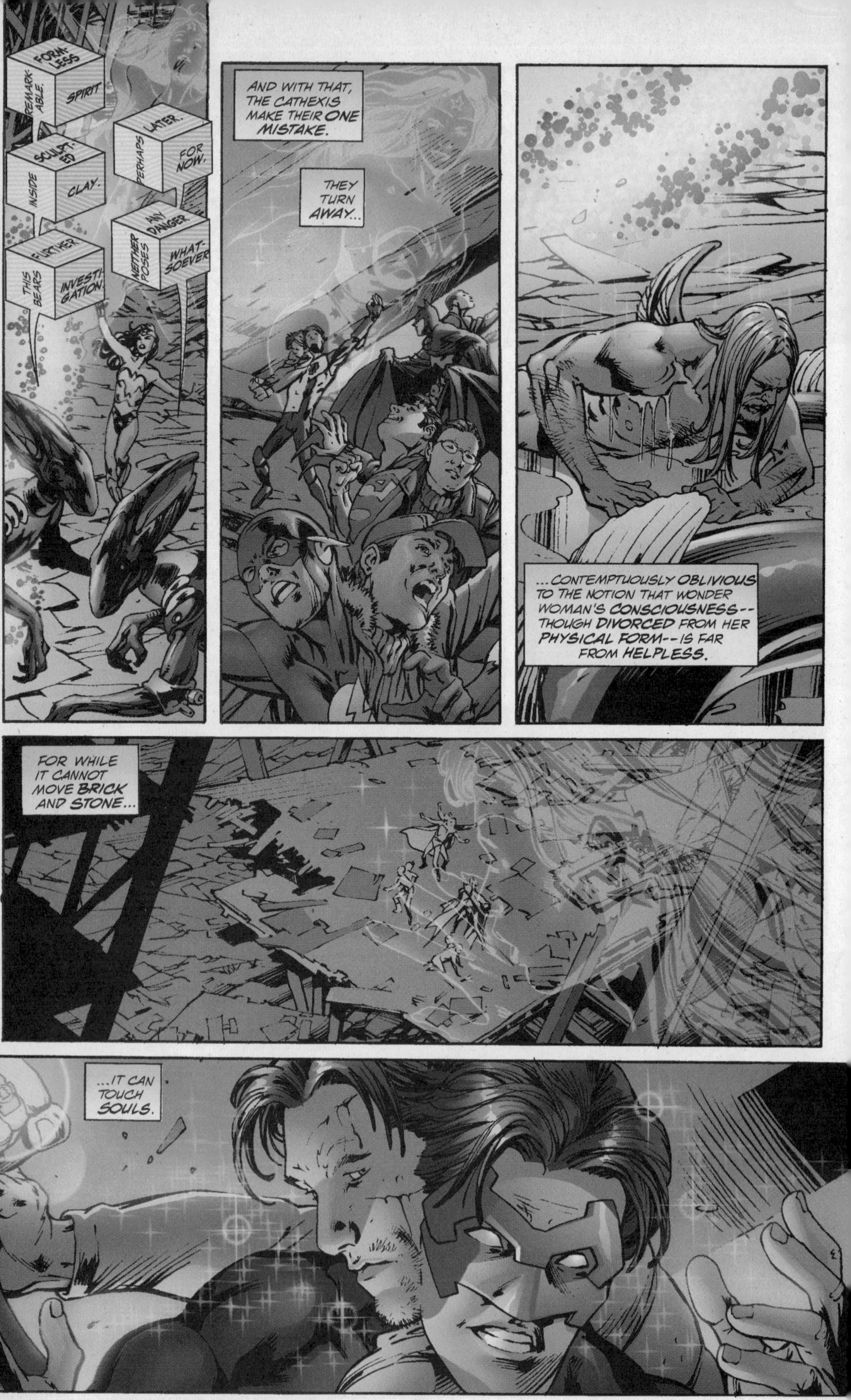

REMARK-ABLE. FORM-LESS SPIRIT
SCULPT-ED INSIDE CLAY.
PERHAPS LATER. FOR NOW,
THIS BEARS FURTHER INVESTI-GATION.
NEITHER POSES ANY DANGER WHAT-SOEVER
AND WITH THAT, THE CATHEXIS MAKE THEIR ONE MISTAKE.
THEY TURN AWAY...
...CONTEMPTUOUSLY OBLIVIOUS TO THE NOTION THAT WONDER WOMAN'S CONSCIOUSNESS--THOUGH DIVORCED FROM HER PHYSICAL FORM--IS FAR FROM HELPLESS.
FOR WHILE IT CANNOT MOVE BRICK AND STONE...
...IT CAN TOUCH SOULS.

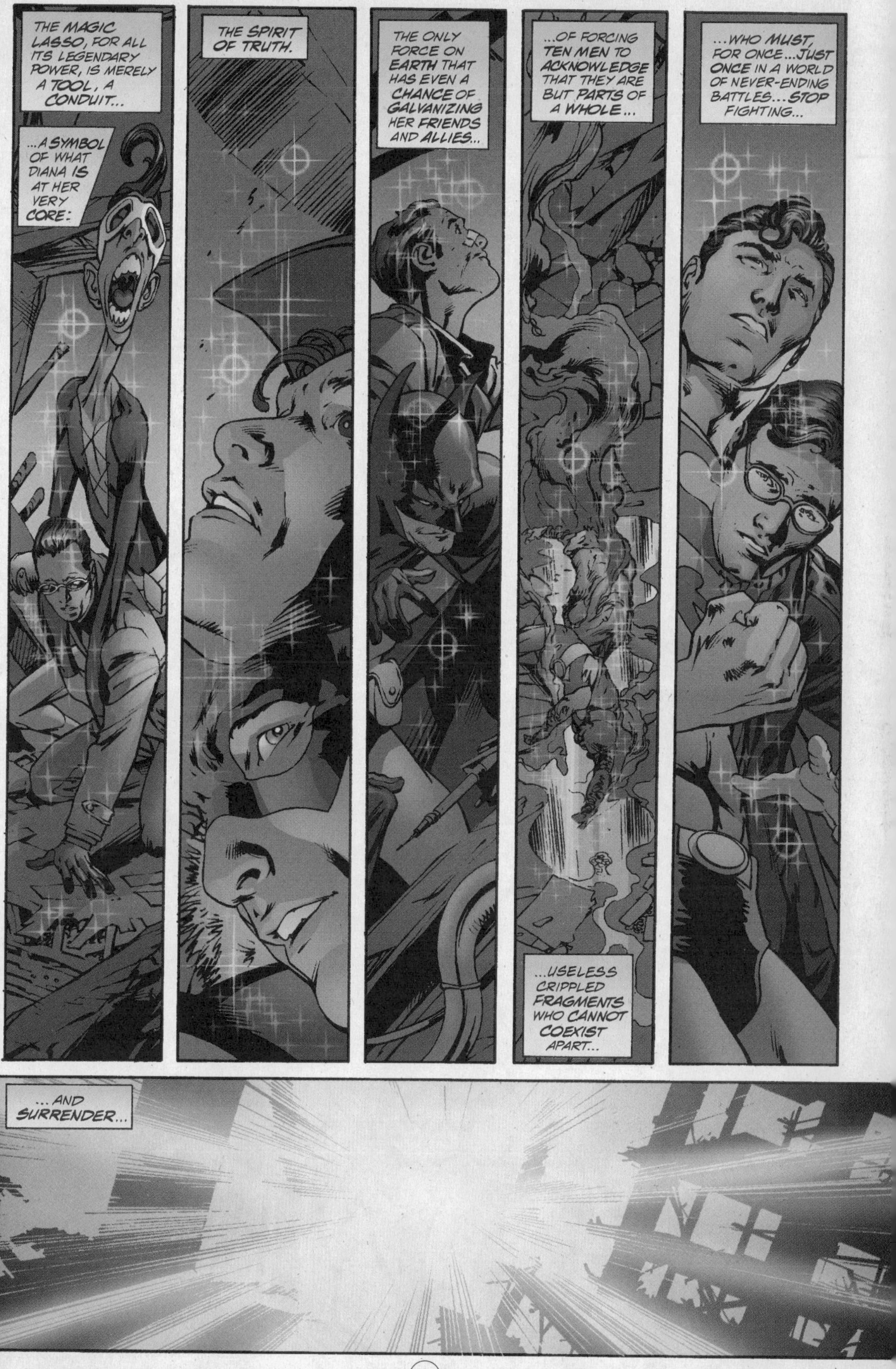
THE MAGIC LASSO, FOR ALL ITS LEGENDARY POWER, IS MERELY A TOOL, A CONDUIT...
...A SYMBOL OF WHAT DIANA IS AT HER VERY CORE:
THE SPIRIT OF TRUTH.
THE ONLY FORCE ON EARTH THAT HAS EVEN A CHANCE OF GALVANIZING HER FRIENDS AND ALLIES...
...OF FORCING TEN MEN TO ACKNOWLEDGE THAT THEY ARE BUT PARTS OF A WHOLE...
...USELESS CRIPPLED FRAGMENTS WHO CANNOT COEXIST APART...
...WHO MUST, FOR ONCE...JUST ONCE IN A WORLD OF NEVER-ENDING BATTLES...STOP FIGHTING...
...AND SURRENDER...

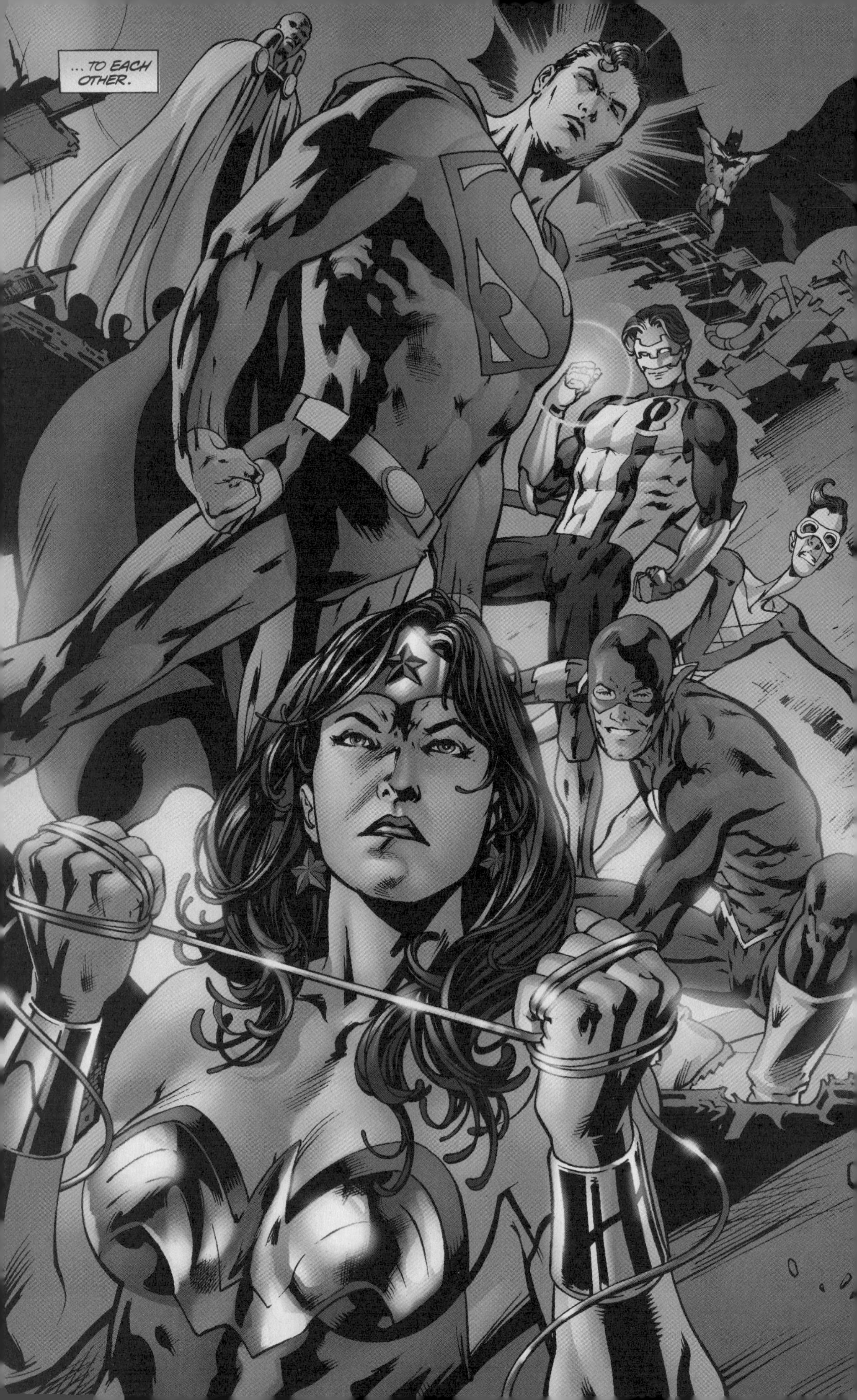
...TO EACH OTHER.

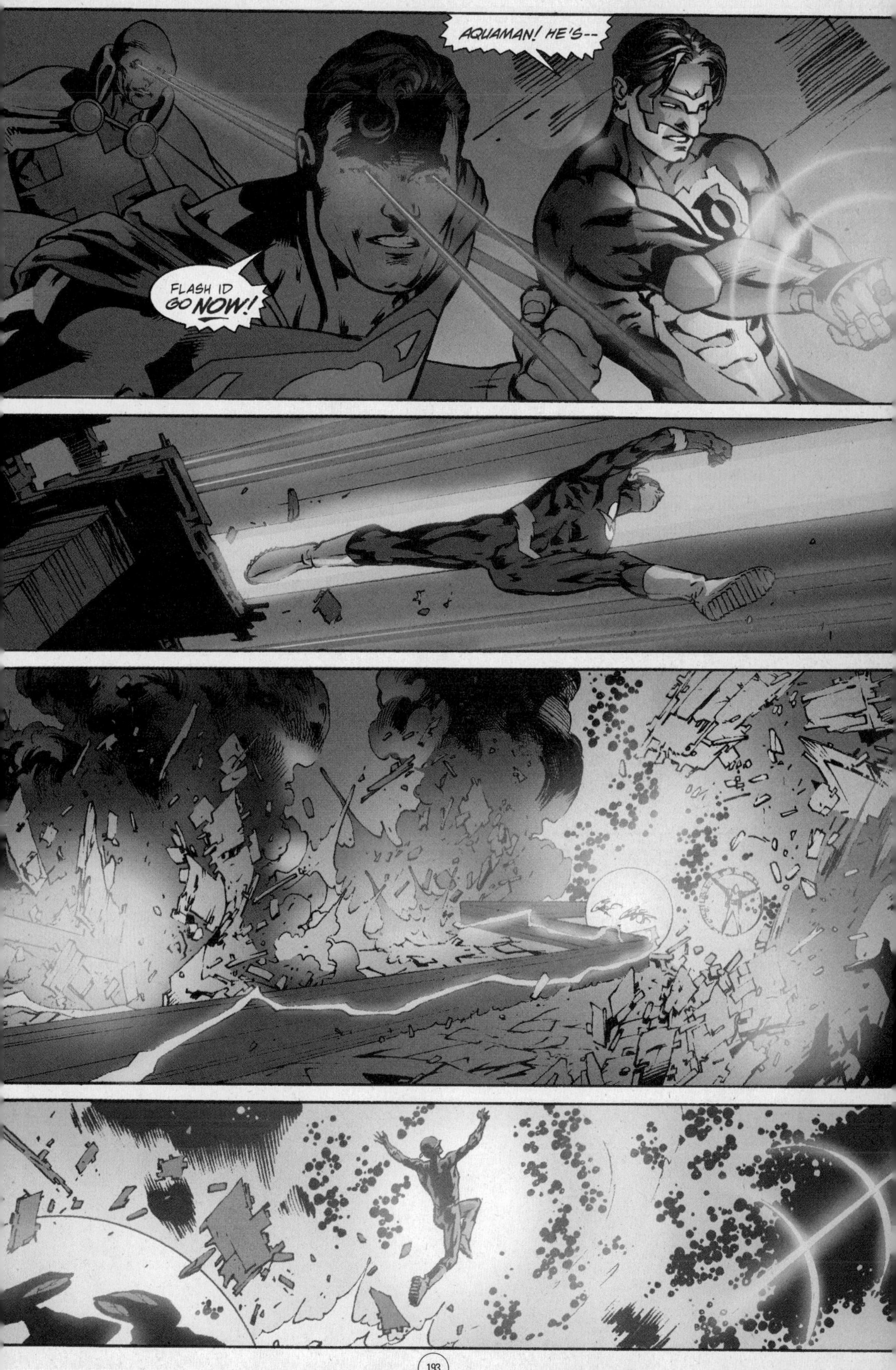
AQUAMAN! HE'S--
FLASH ID GO NOW!

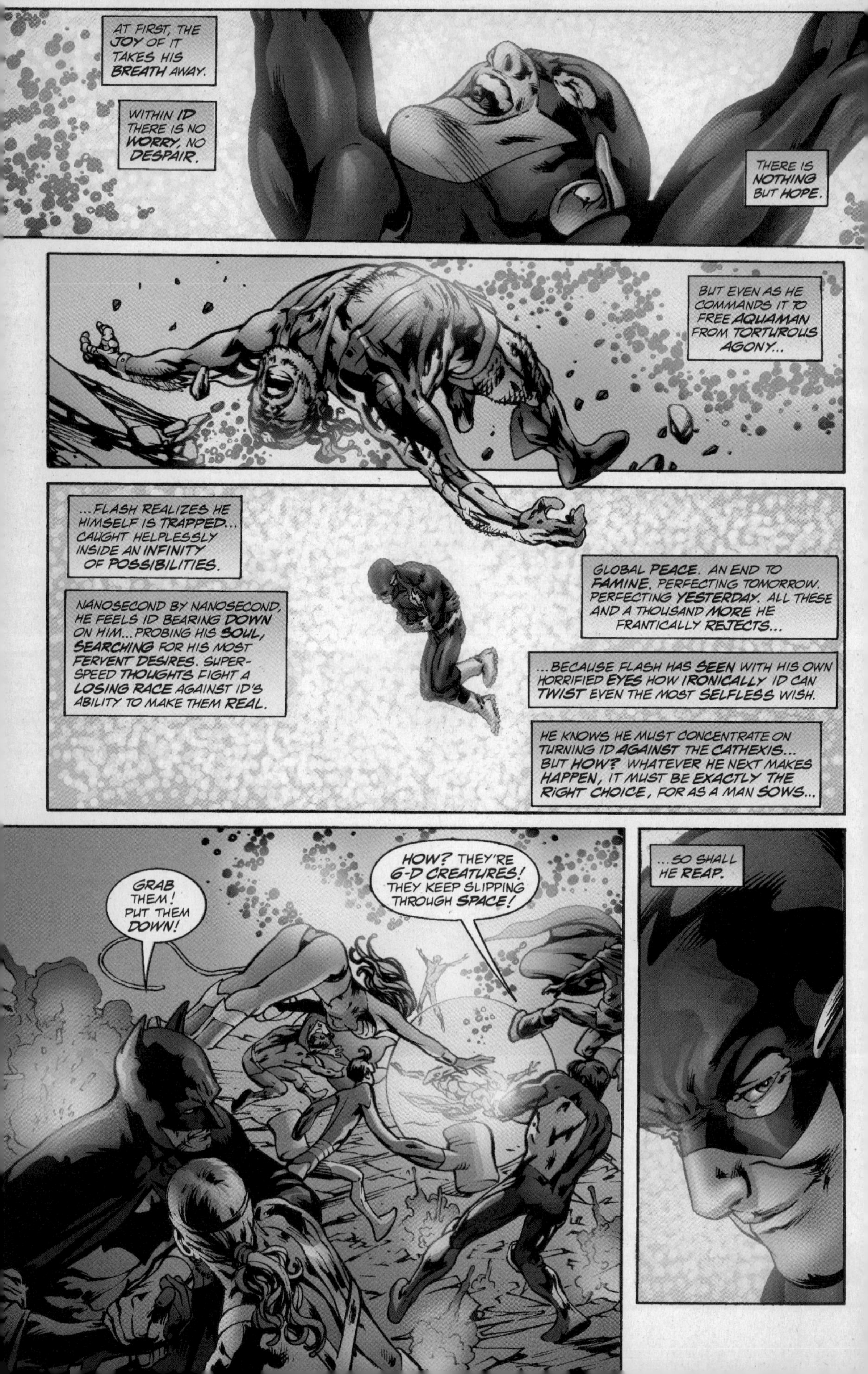
AT FIRST, THE JOY OF IT TAKES HIS BREATH AWAY.
WITHIN ID THERE IS NO WORRY, NO DESPAIR.
THERE IS NOTHING BUT HOPE.
BUT EVEN AS HE COMMANDS IT TO FREE AQUAMAN FROM TORTUROUS AGONY...
...FLASH REALIZES HE HIMSELF IS TRAPPED... CAUGHT HELPLESSLY INSIDE AN INFINITY OF POSSIBILITIES.
NANOSECOND BY NANOSECOND, HE FEELS ID BEARING DOWN ON HIM...PROBING HIS SOUL, SEARCHING FOR HIS MOST FERVENT DESIRES. SUPER-SPEED THOUGHTS FIGHT A LOSING RACE AGAINST ID'S ABILITY TO MAKE THEM REAL.
GLOBAL PEACE. AN END TO FAMINE. PERFECTING TOMORROW. PERFECTING YESTERDAY. ALL THESE AND A THOUSAND MORE HE FRANTICALLY REJECTS...
...BECAUSE FLASH HAS SEEN WITH HIS OWN HORRIFIED EYES HOW IRONICALLY ID CAN TWIST EVEN THE MOST SELFLESS WISH.
HE KNOWS HE MUST CONCENTRATE ON TURNING ID AGAINST THE CATHEXIS... BUT HOW? WHATEVER HE NEXT MAKES HAPPEN, IT MUST BE EXACTLY THE RIGHT CHOICE, FOR AS A MAN SOWS...
GRAB THEM! PUT THEM DOWN!
HOW? THEY'RE 6-D CREATURES! THEY KEEP SLIPPING THROUGH SPACE!
...SO SHALL HE REAP.

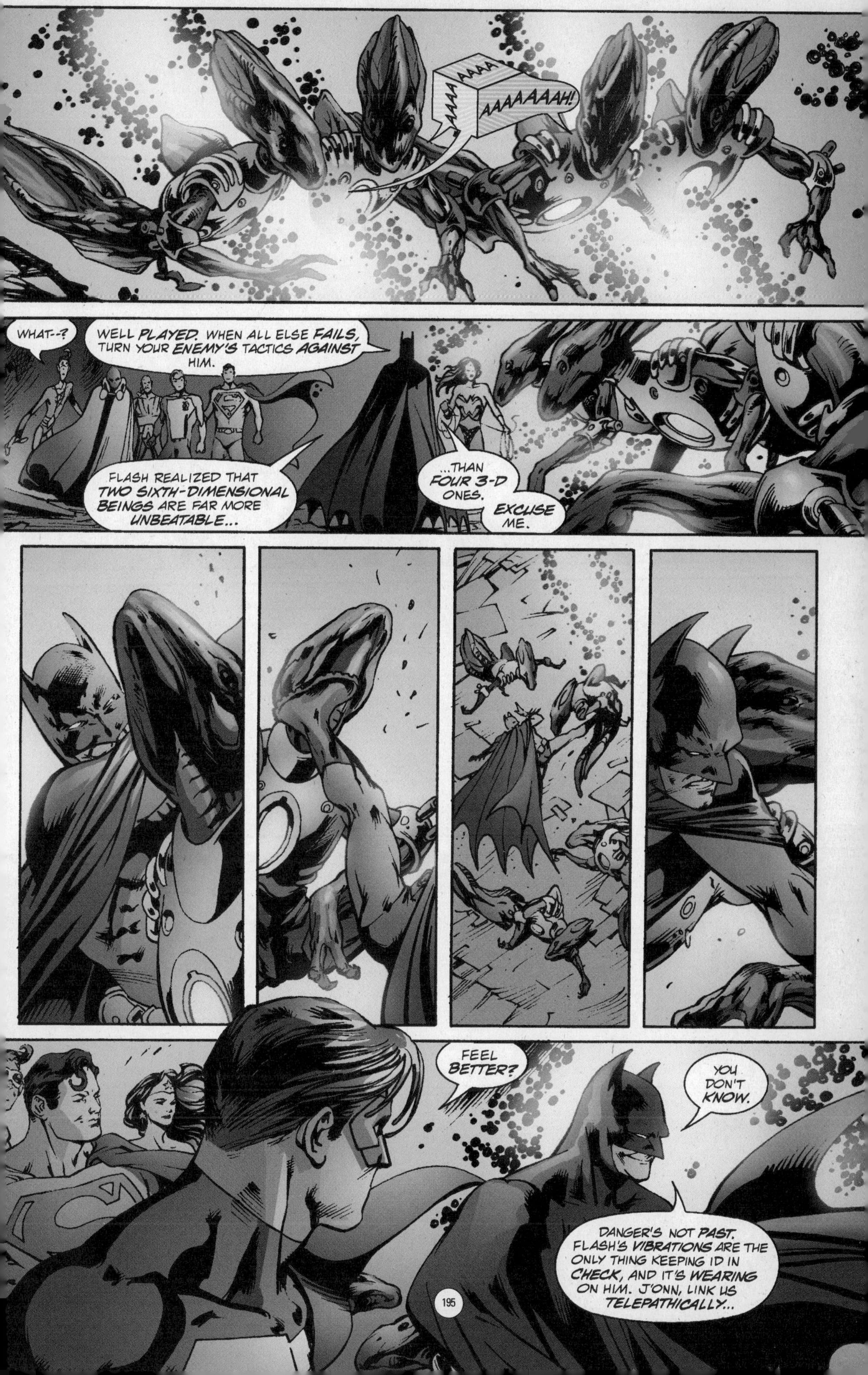
AAAAAAAA AAAAAAAH!
WHAT--?
WELL PLAYED. WHEN ALL ELSE FAILS, TURN YOUR ENEMY'S TACTICS AGAINST HIM.
FLASH REALIZED THAT TWO SIXTH-DIMENSIONAL BEINGS ARE FAR MORE UNBEATABLE...
...THAN FOUR 3-D ONES.
EXCUSE ME.
FEEL BETTER?
YOU DON'T KNOW.
DANGER'S NOT PAST. FLASH'S VIBRATIONS ARE THE ONLY THING KEEPING ID IN CHECK, AND IT'S WEARING ON HIM. J'ONN, LINK US TELEPATHICALLY...

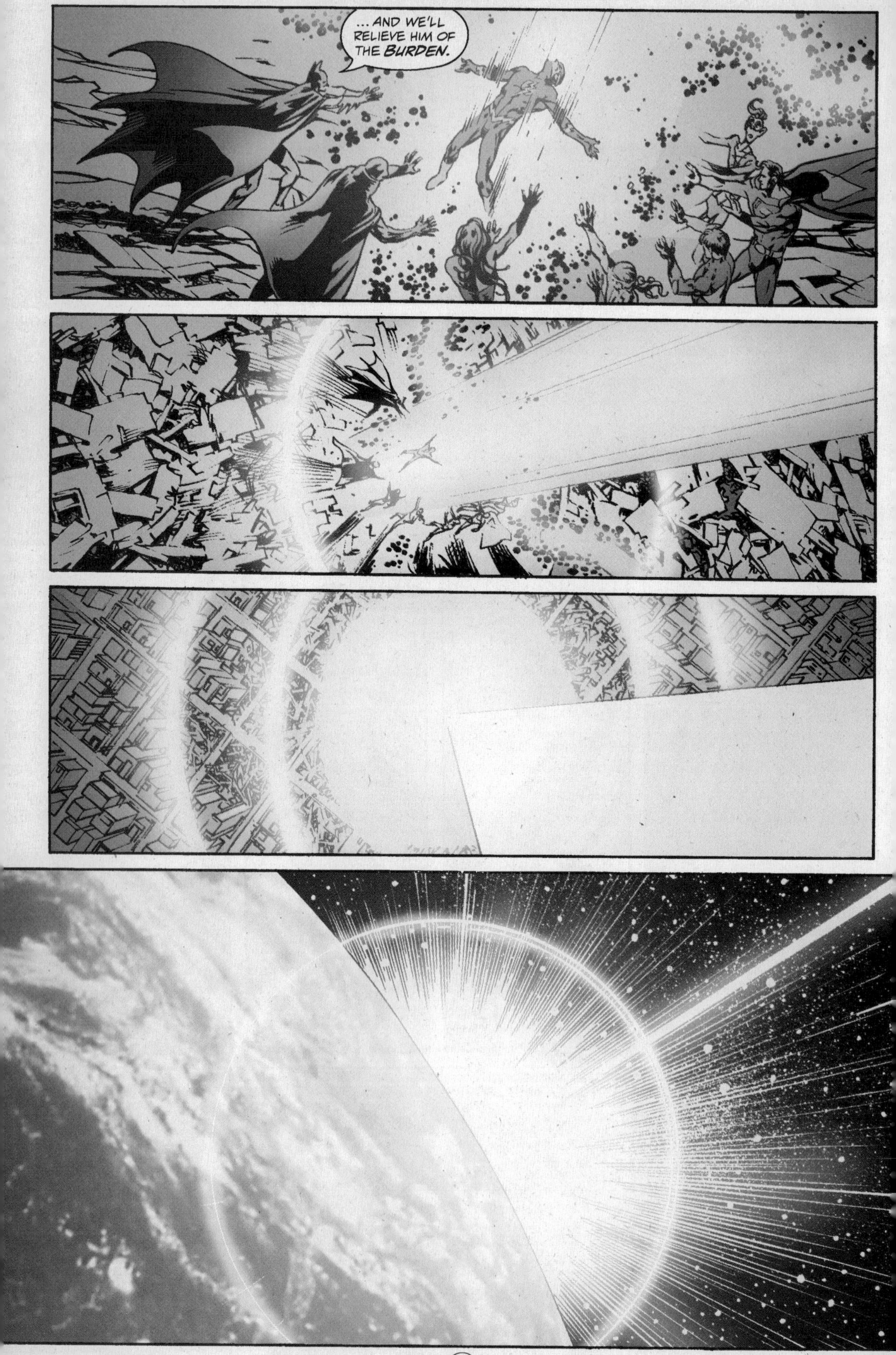
... AND WE'LL RELIEVE HIM OF THE *BURDEN*.

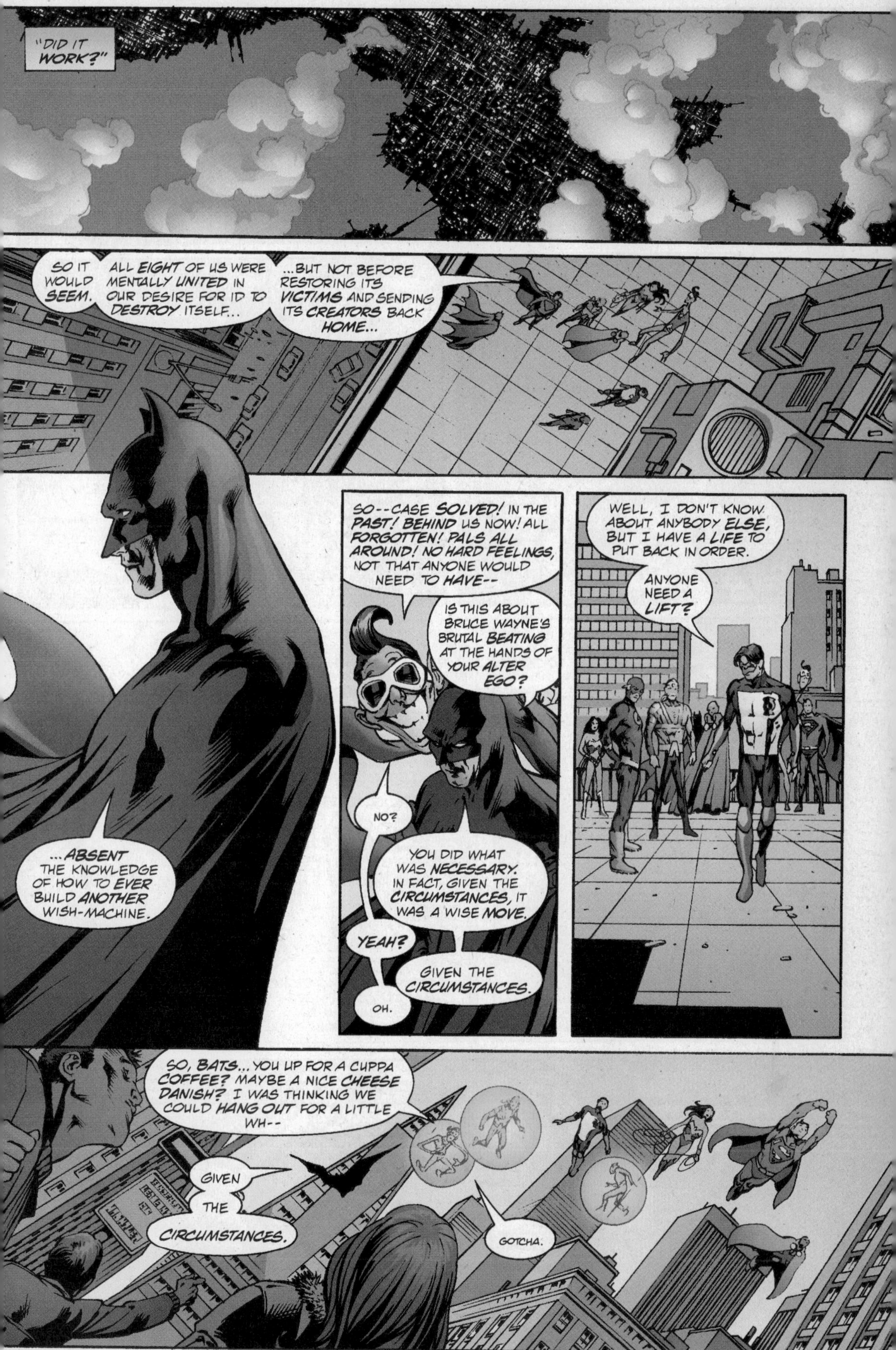
"DID IT WORK?"
SO IT WOULD SEEM.
ALL EIGHT OF US WERE MENTALLY UNITED IN OUR DESIRE FOR ID TO DESTROY ITSELF...
...BUT NOT BEFORE RESTORING ITS VICTIMS AND SENDING ITS CREATORS BACK HOME...
...ABSENT THE KNOWLEDGE OF HOW TO EVER BUILD ANOTHER WISH-MACHINE.
SO--CASE SOLVED! IN THE PAST! BEHIND US NOW! ALL FORGOTTEN! PALS ALL AROUND! NO HARD FEELINGS, NOT THAT ANYONE WOULD NEED TO HAVE--
IS THIS ABOUT BRUCE WAYNE'S BRUTAL BEATING AT THE HANDS OF YOUR ALTER EGO?
NO?
YOU DID WHAT WAS NECESSARY. IN FACT, GIVEN THE CIRCUMSTANCES, IT WAS A WISE MOVE.
YEAH?
GIVEN THE CIRCUMSTANCES.
OH.
WELL, I DON'T KNOW ABOUT ANYBODY ELSE, BUT I HAVE A LIFE TO PUT BACK IN ORDER.
ANYONE NEED A LIFT?
SO, BATS... YOU UP FOR A CUPPA COFFEE? MAYBE A NICE CHEESE DANISH? I WAS THINKING WE COULD HANG OUT FOR A LITTLE WH--
GIVEN THE CIRCUMSTANCES.
GOTCHA.

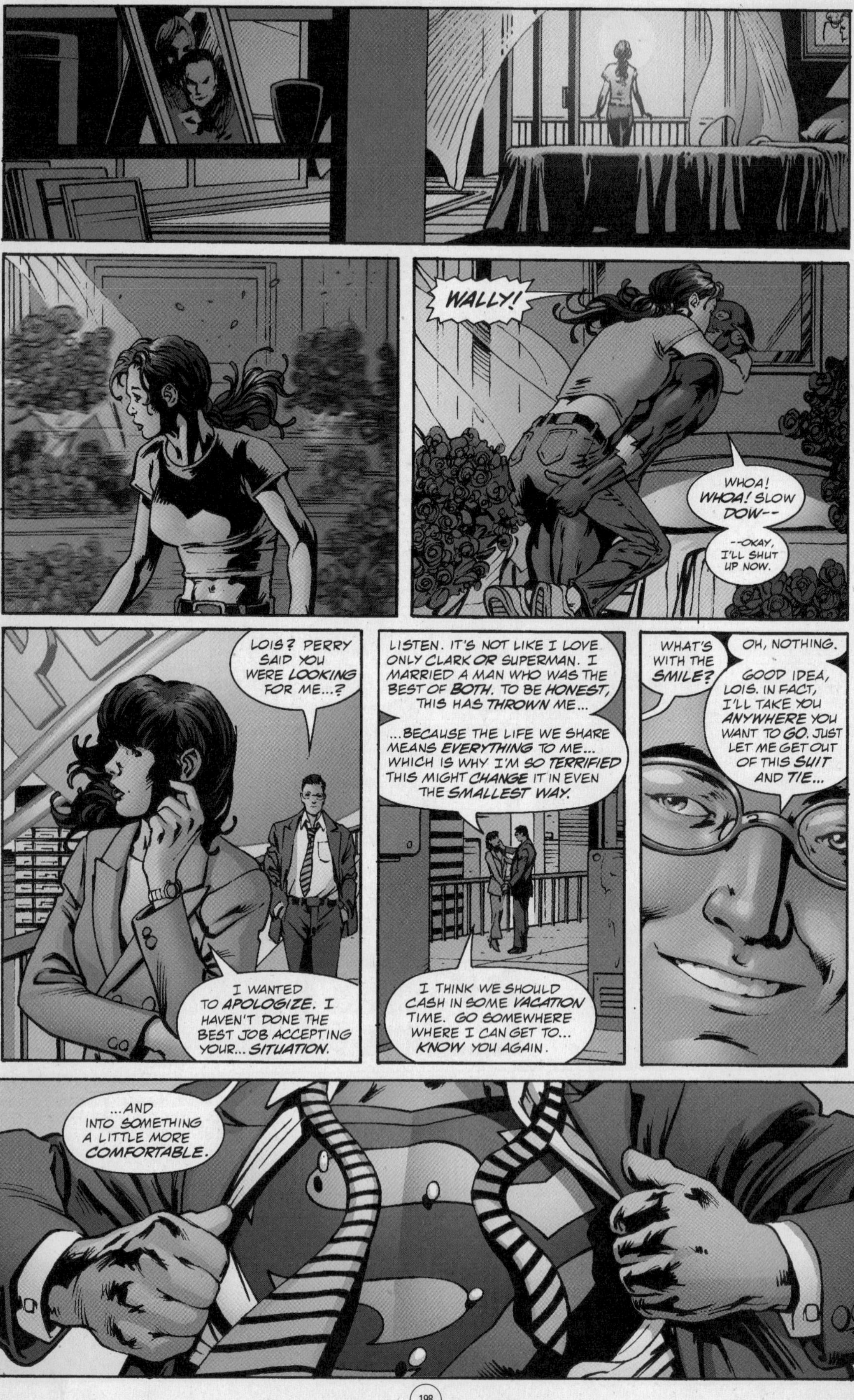
WALLY!
WHOA! WHOA! SLOW DOW--
--OKAY, I'LL SHUT UP NOW.
LOIS? PERRY SAID YOU WERE LOOKING FOR ME...?
I WANTED TO APOLOGIZE. I HAVEN'T DONE THE BEST JOB ACCEPTING YOUR... SITUATION.
LISTEN. IT'S NOT LIKE I LOVE ONLY CLARK OR SUPERMAN. I MARRIED A MAN WHO WAS THE BEST OF BOTH. TO BE HONEST, THIS HAS THROWN ME...
...BECAUSE THE LIFE WE SHARE MEANS EVERYTHING TO ME... WHICH IS WHY I'M SO TERRIFIED THIS MIGHT CHANGE IT IN EVEN THE SMALLEST WAY.
I THINK WE SHOULD CASH IN SOME VACATION TIME. GO SOMEWHERE WHERE I CAN GET TO... KNOW YOU AGAIN.
WHAT'S WITH THE SMILE?
OH, NOTHING.
GOOD IDEA, LOIS. IN FACT, I'LL TAKE YOU ANYWHERE YOU WANT TO GO. JUST LET ME GET OUT OF THIS SUIT AND TIE...
...AND INTO SOMETHING A LITTLE MORE COMFORTABLE.

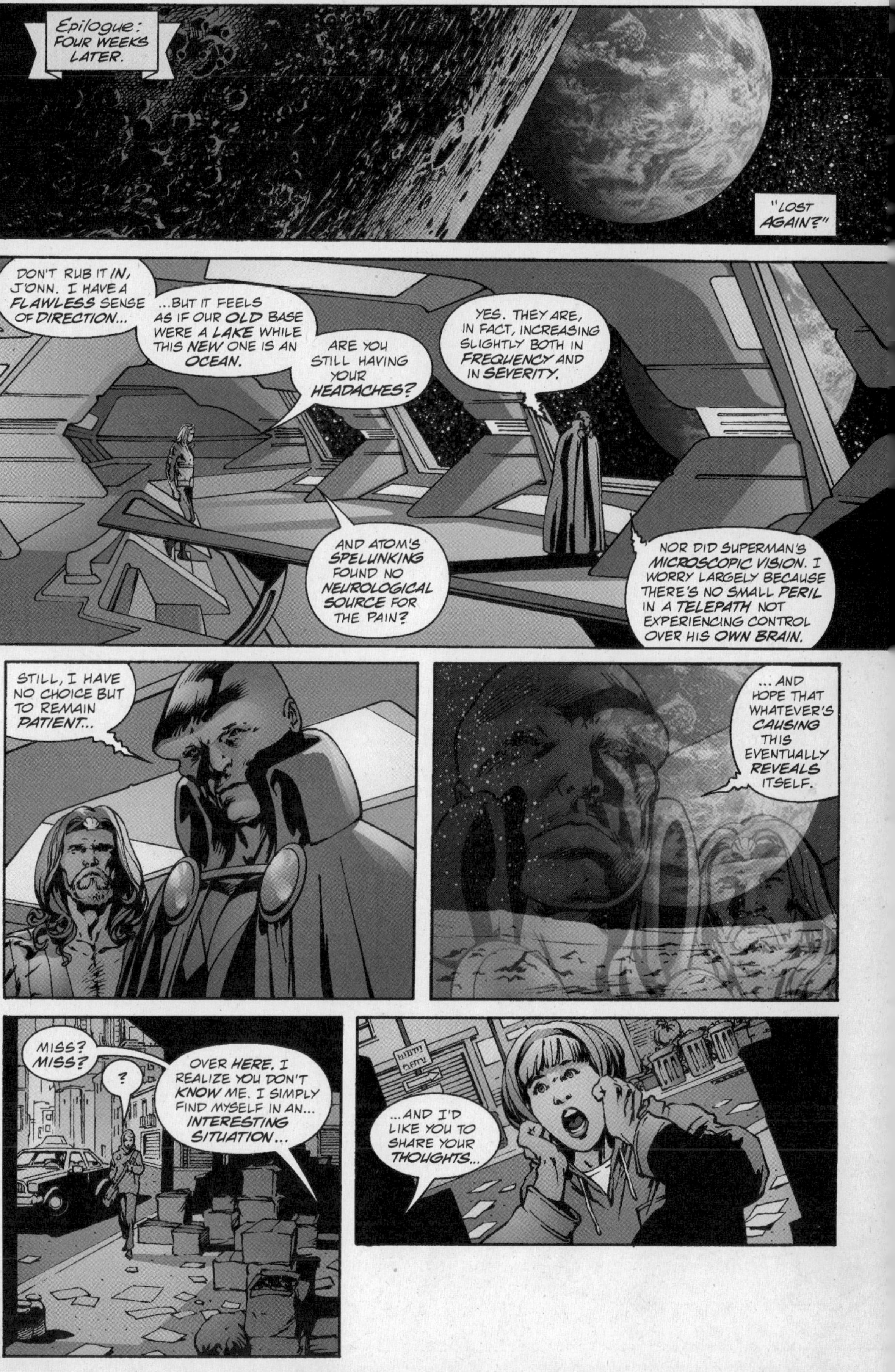
Epilogue: FOUR WEEKS LATER.
"LOST AGAIN?"
DON'T RUB IT IN, J'ONN. I HAVE A FLAWLESS SENSE OF DIRECTION...
...BUT IT FEELS AS IF OUR OLD BASE WERE A LAKE WHILE THIS NEW ONE IS AN OCEAN.
ARE YOU STILL HAVING YOUR HEADACHES?
YES. THEY ARE, IN FACT, INCREASING SLIGHTLY BOTH IN FREQUENCY AND IN SEVERITY.
AND ATOM'S SPELUNKING FOUND NO NEUROLOGICAL SOURCE FOR THE PAIN?
NOR DID SUPERMAN'S MICROSCOPIC VISION. I WORRY LARGELY BECAUSE THERE'S NO SMALL PERIL IN A TELEPATH NOT EXPERIENCING CONTROL OVER HIS OWN BRAIN.
STILL, I HAVE NO CHOICE BUT TO REMAIN PATIENT...
... AND HOPE THAT WHATEVER'S CAUSING THIS EVENTUALLY REVEALS ITSELF.
MISS? MISS?
?
OVER HERE. I REALIZE YOU DON'T KNOW ME. I SIMPLY FIND MYSELF IN AN... INTERESTING SITUATION...
...AND I'D LIKE YOU TO SHARE YOUR THOUGHTS...

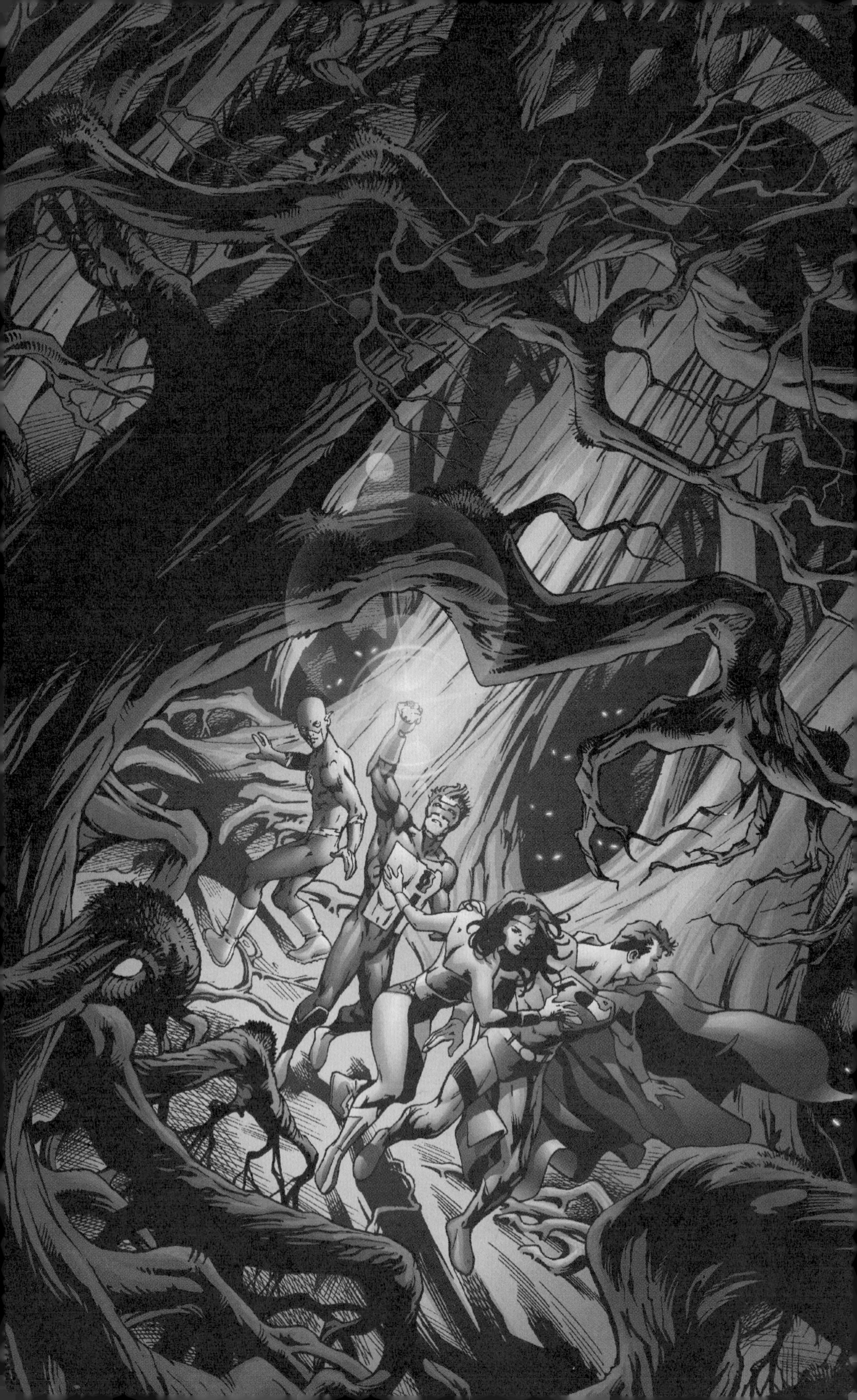

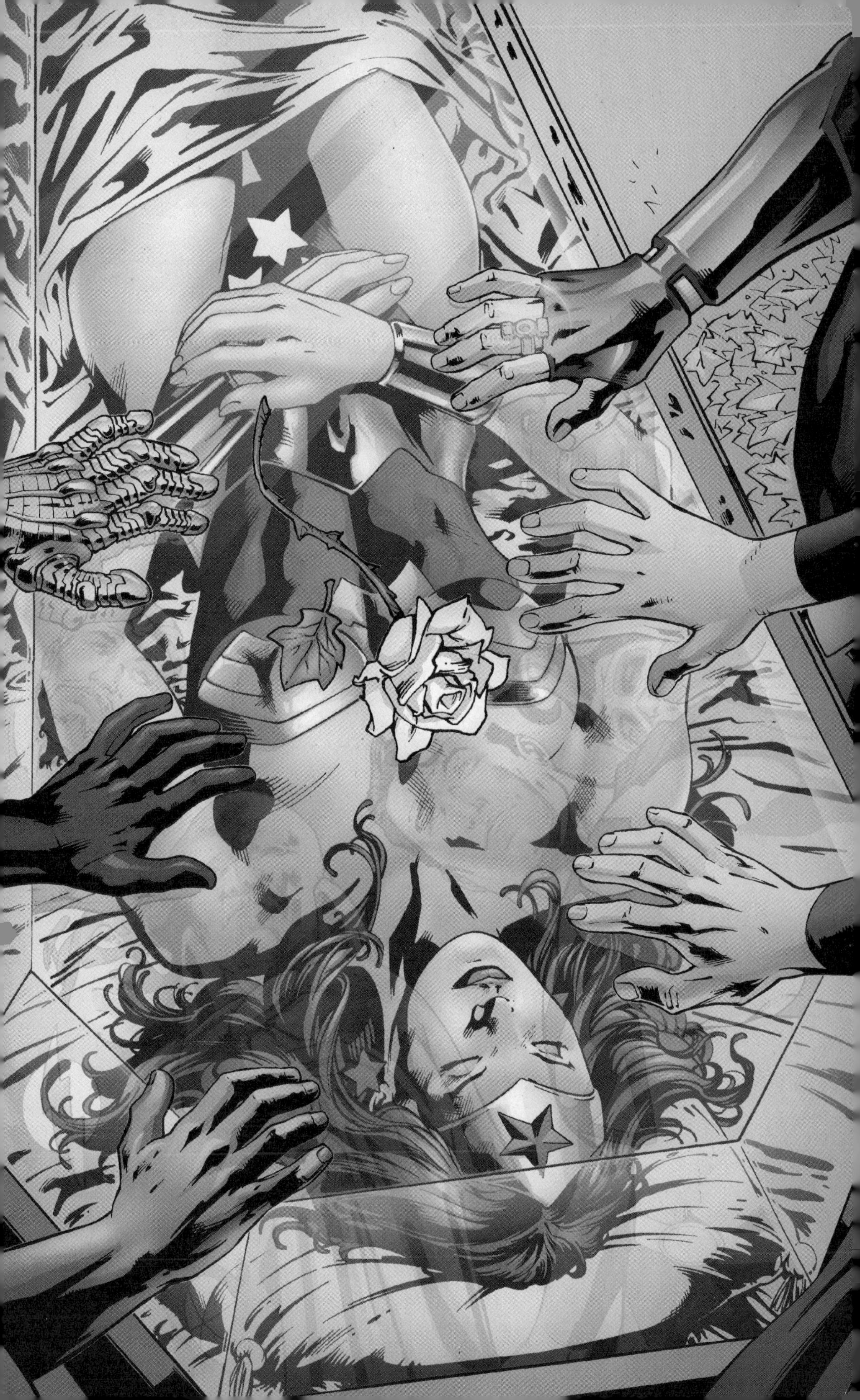

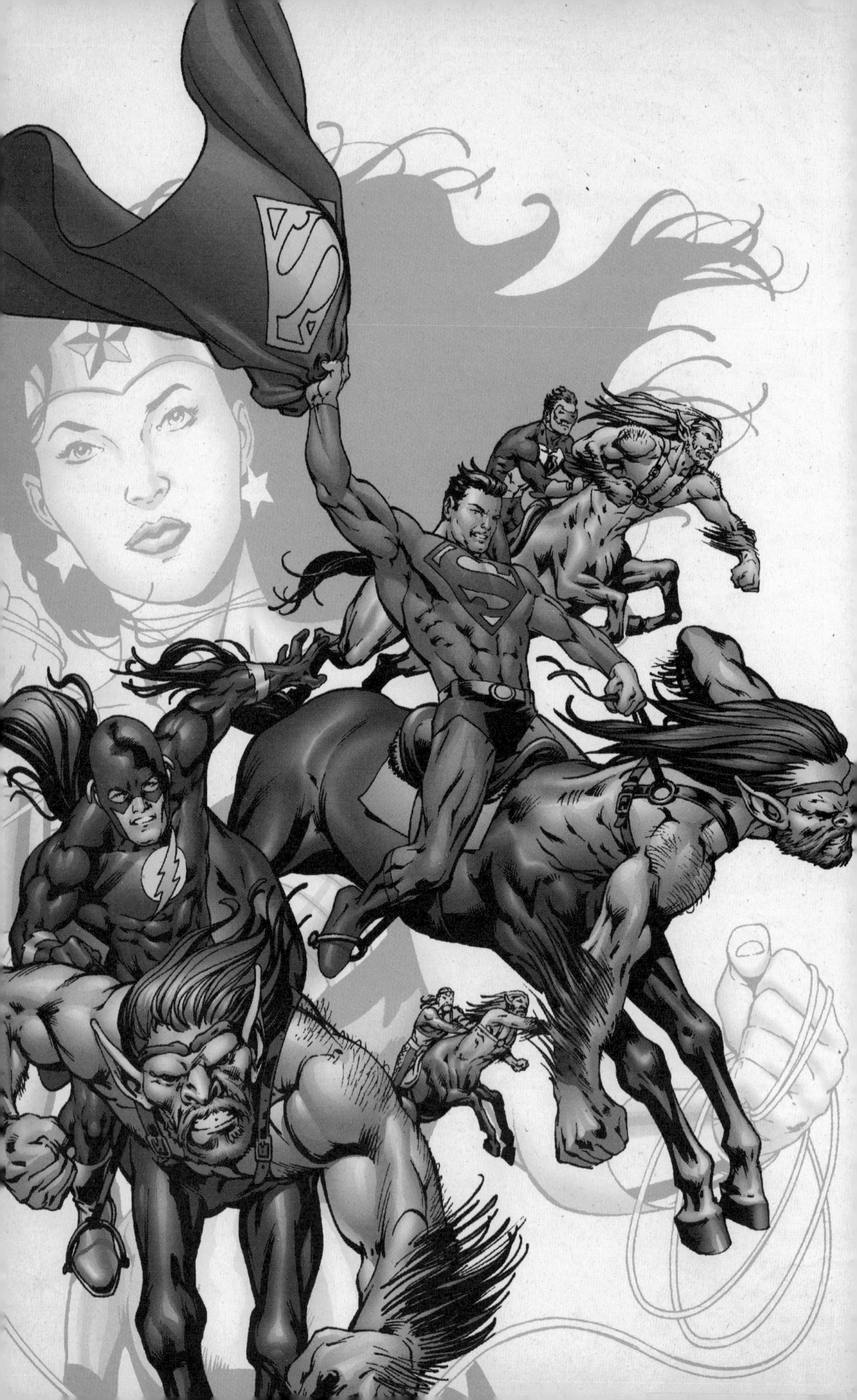

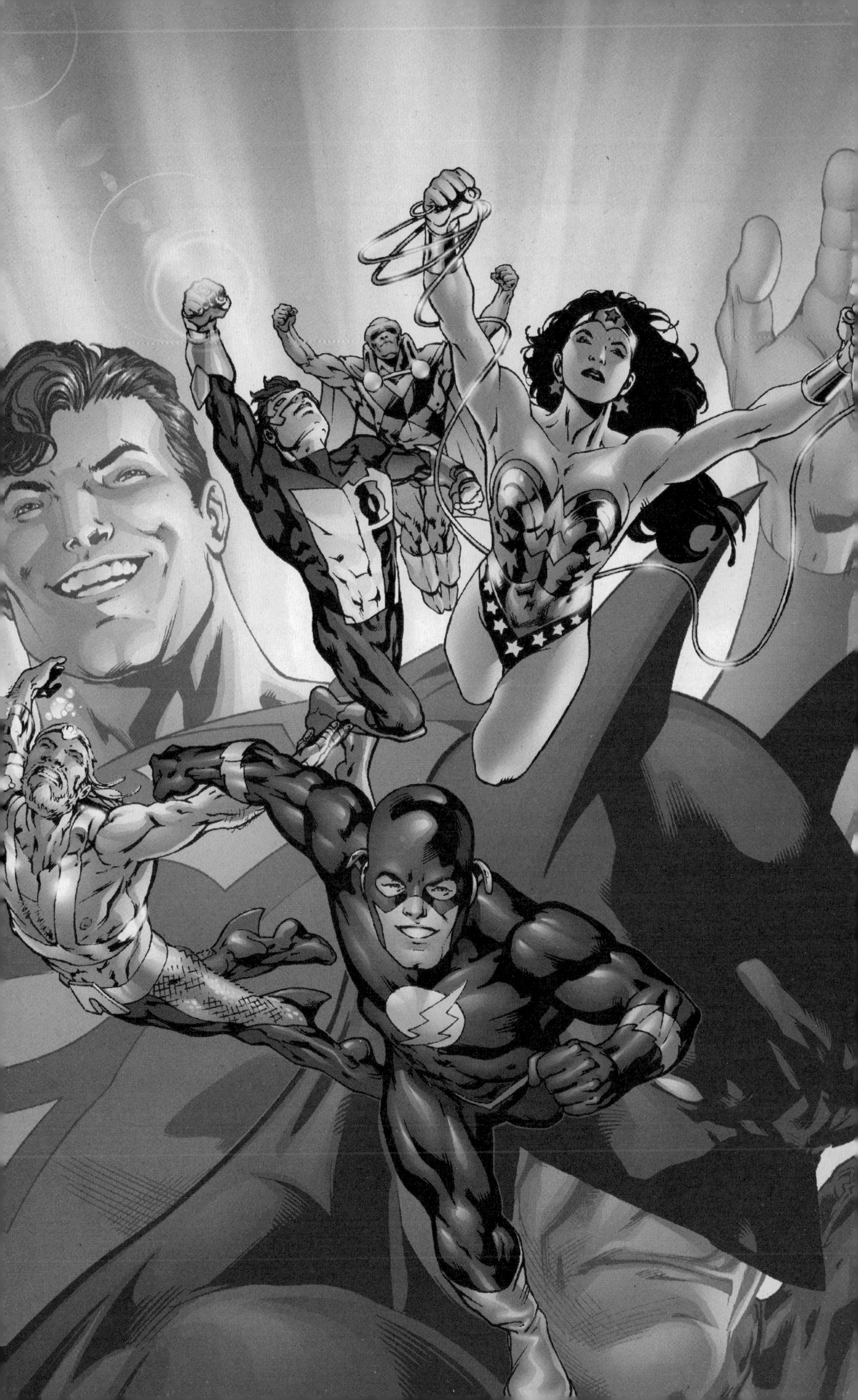

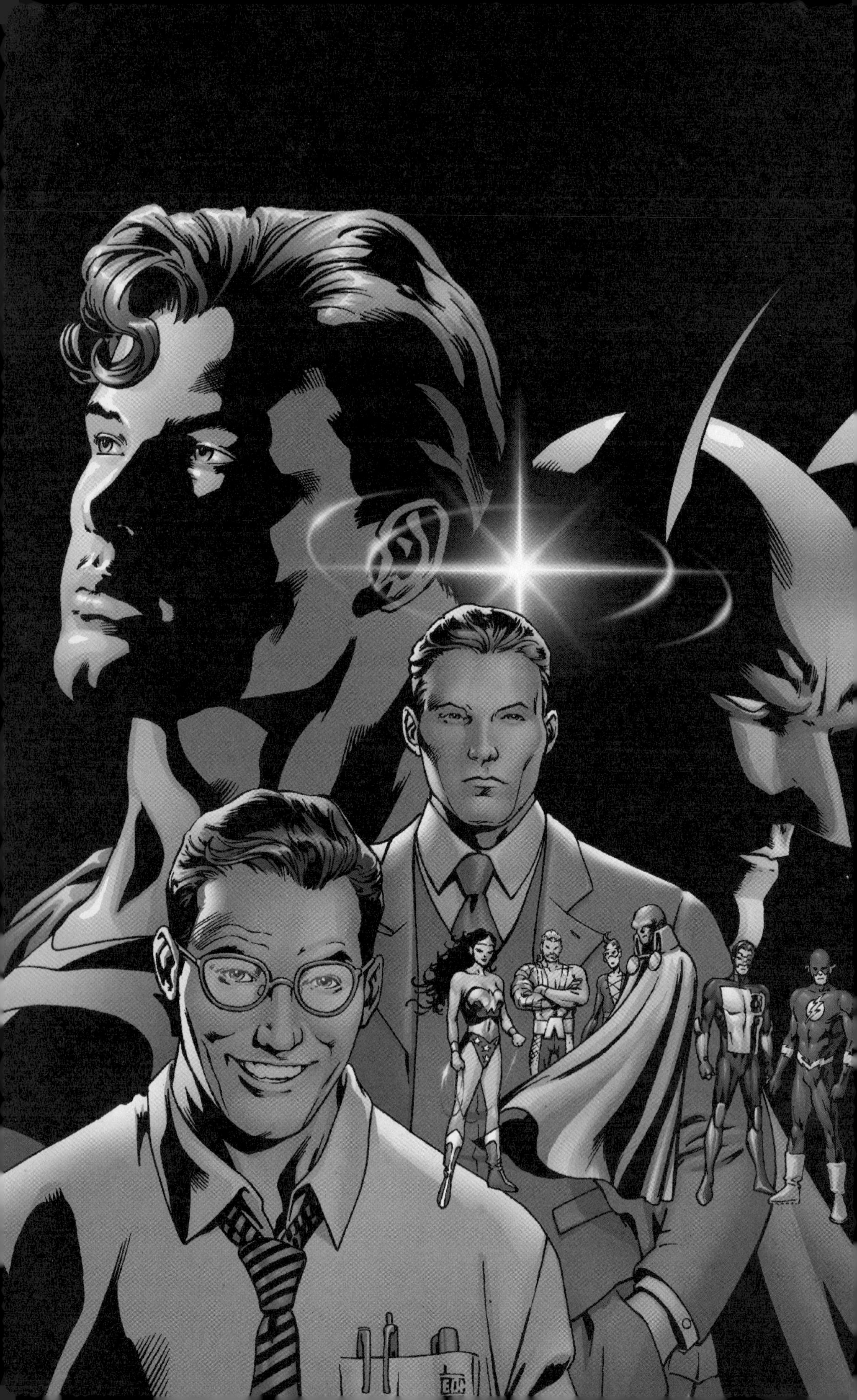

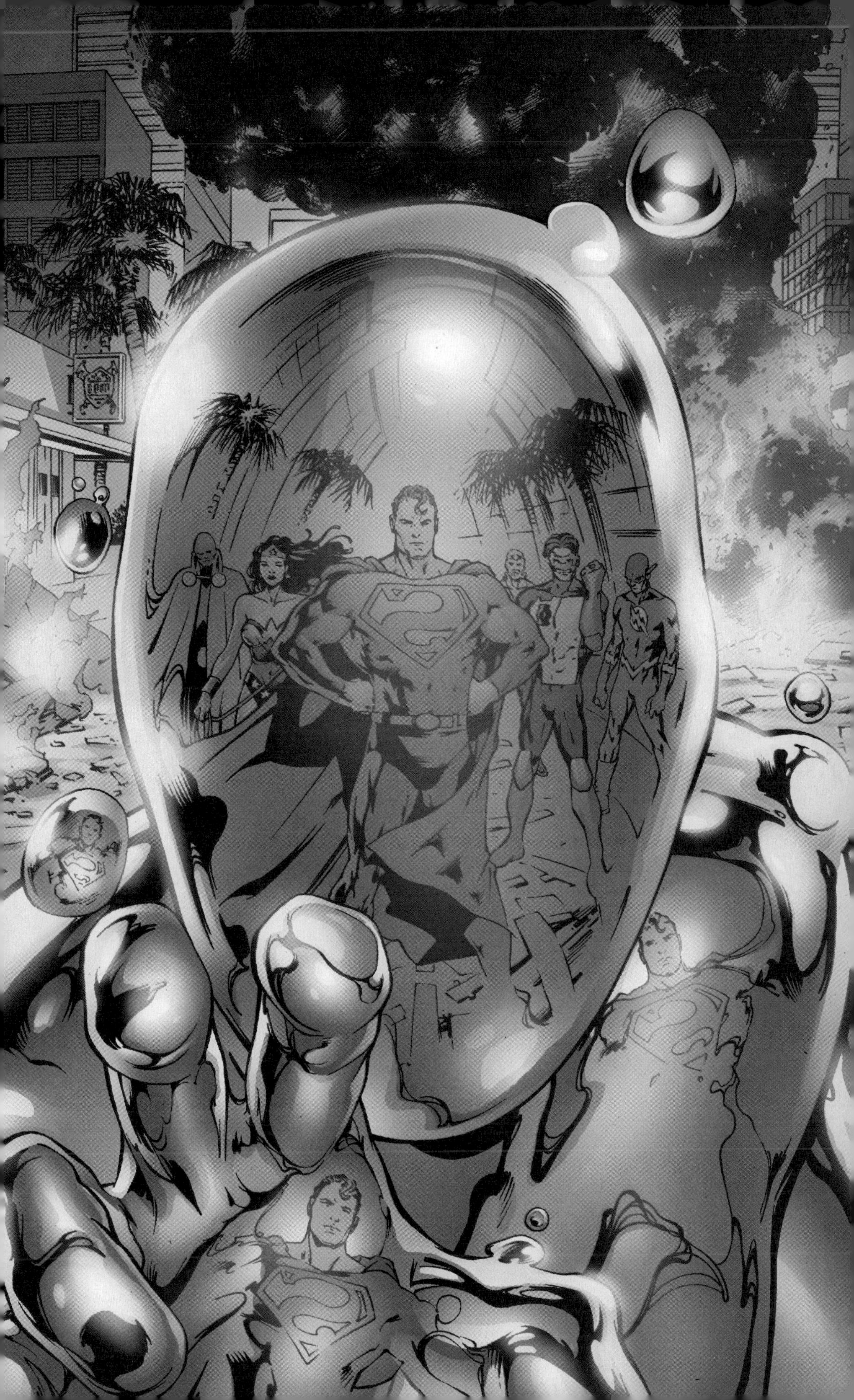

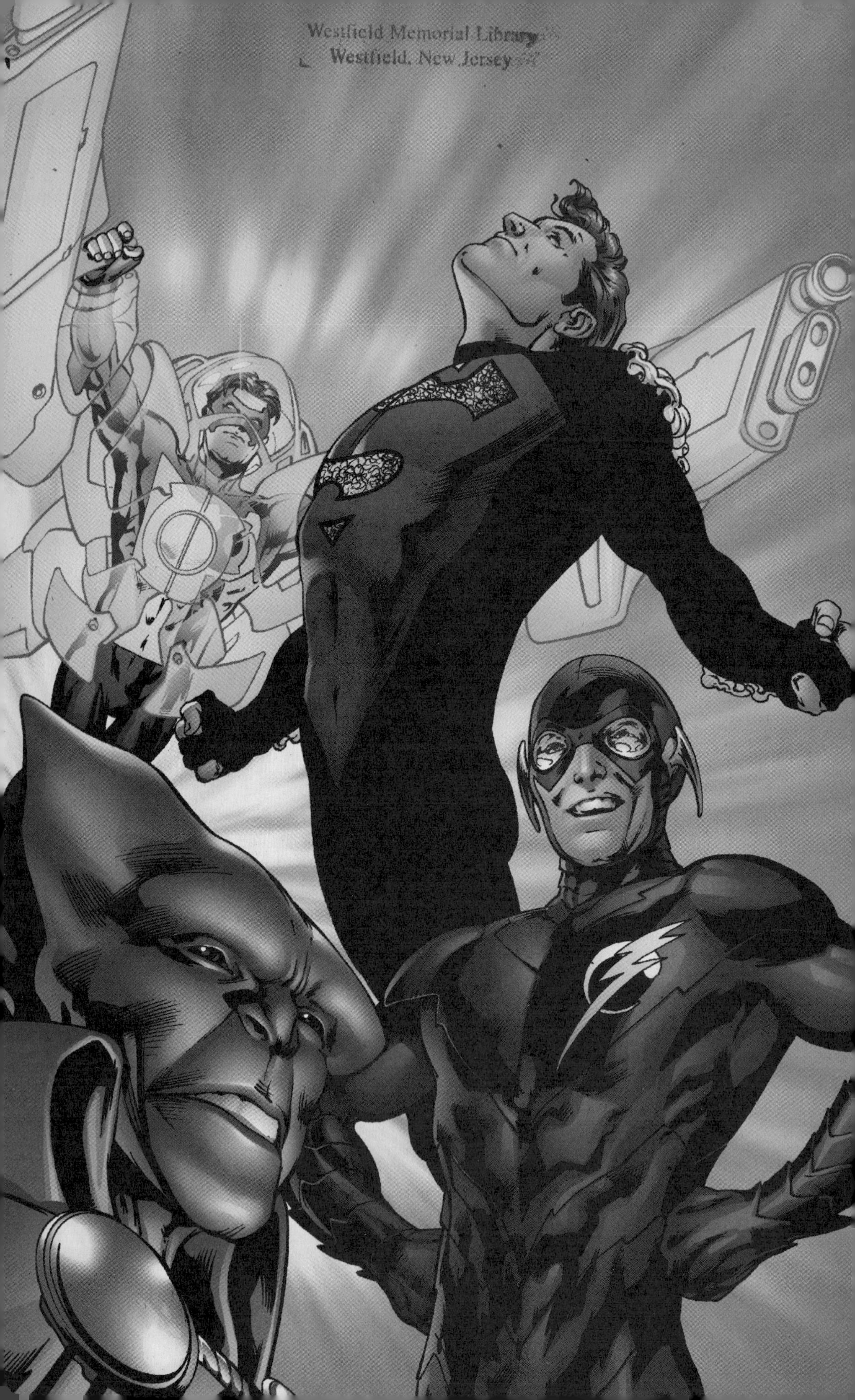

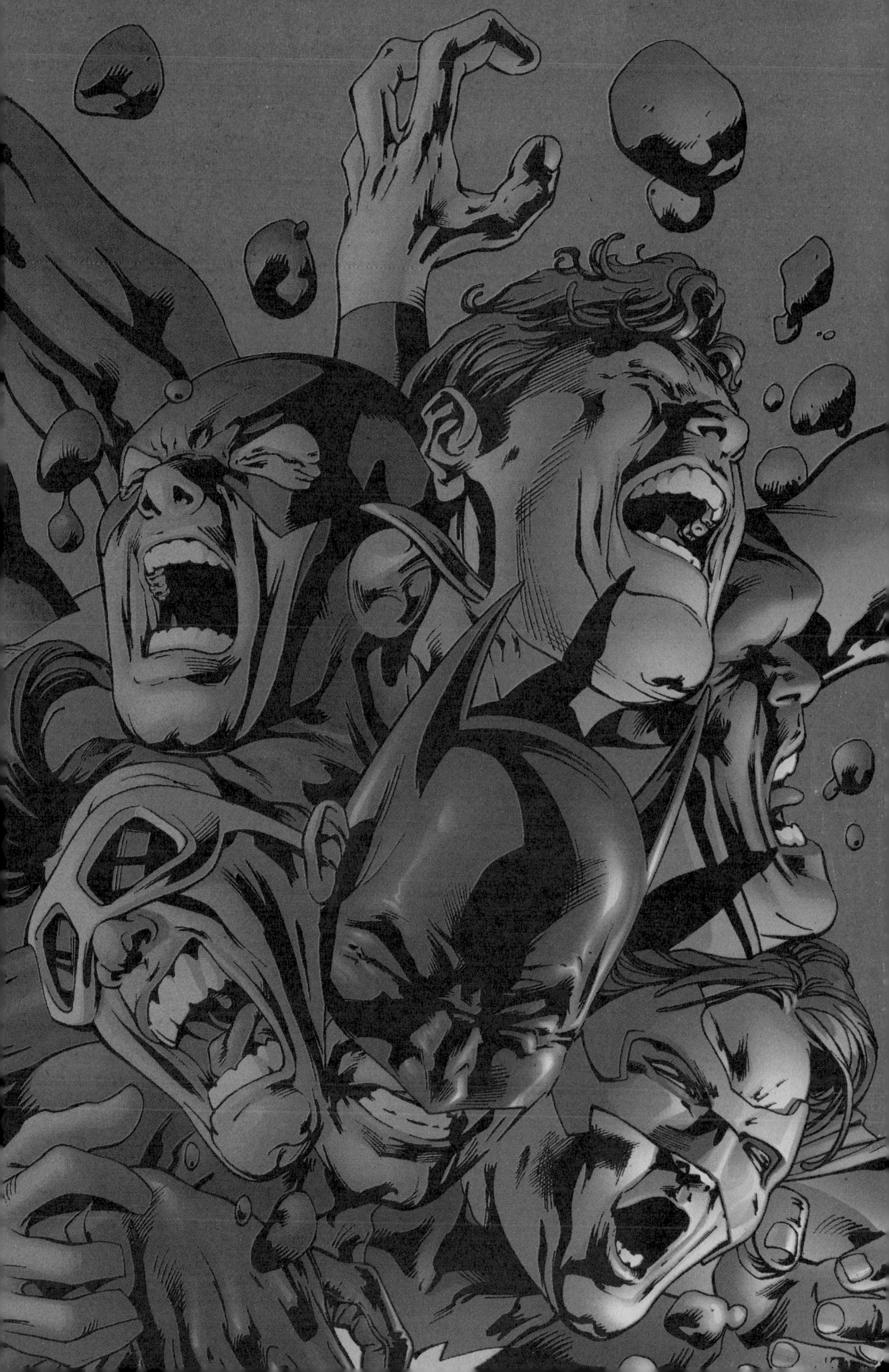

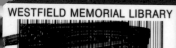

THE HEROES OF THE JUSTICE LEAGUE CAN ALSO BE FOUND IN THESE BOOKS FROM DC:

GRAPHIC NOVELS

JLA: EARTH 2
Grant Morrison/Frank Quitely

THE FLASH: LIFE STORY OF THE FLASH
M. Waid/B. Augustyn/
G. Kane/J. Staton/T. Palmer

GREEN LANTERN: FEAR ITSELF
Ron Marz/Brad Parker

WONDER WOMAN: AMAZONIA
William Messner-Loebs/
Phil Winslade

COLLECTIONS

JUSTICE LEAGUE: A NEW BEGINNING
K. Giffen/J. M. DeMatteis/
K. Maguire/various

JUSTICE LEAGUE: A MIDSUMMER'S NIGHTMARE
M. Waid/F. Nicieza/J. Johnson/
D. Robertson/various

JUSTICE LEAGUE OF AMERICA: THE NAIL
Alan Davis/Mark Farmer

JLA: AMERICAN DREAMS
G. Morrison/H. Porter/J. Dell/
various

JLA: NEW WORLD ORDER
Grant Morrison/
Howard Porter/John Dell

JLA: ROCK OF AGES
G. Morrison/H. Porter/
J. Dell/various

JLA: STRENGTH IN NUMBERS
G. Morrison/M. Waid/
H. Porter/various

JLA: WORLD WITHOUT GROWN-UPS
T. Dezago/T. Nauck/H. Ramos/
M. McKone/various

JLA: JUSTICE FOR ALL
G. Morrison/M. Waid/
H. Porter/J. Dell/various

JLA: YEAR ONE
M. Waid/B. Augustyn/B. Kitson/
various

JLA/TITANS: THE TECHNIS IMPERATIVE
D. Grayson/P. Jimenez/
P. Pelletier/various

THE KNIGHTFALL Trilogy
BATMAN: KNIGHTFALL Part 1: Broken Bat
BATMAN: KNIGHTFALL Part 2: Who Rules the Night
BATMAN: KNIGHTFALL Part 3: KnightsEnd
Various writers and artists

THE DEATH OF SUPERMAN Trilogy
THE DEATH OF SUPERMAN
WORLD WITHOUT A SUPERMAN
THE RETURN OF SUPERMAN
Various writers and artists

AQUAMAN: TIME & TIDE
Peter David/Kirk Jarvinen/
Brad Vancata

THE FLASH: BORN TO RUN
M. Waid/T. Peyer/G. LaRocque/
H. Ramos/various

GREEN LANTERN: A NEW DAWN
R. Marz/D. Banks/R. Tanghal/
various

GREEN LANTERN: BAPTISM OF FIRE
Ron Marz/Darryl Banks/
various

GREEN LANTERN: EMERALD KNIGHTS
Ron Marz/Darryl Banks/
various

JACK KIRBY'S NEW GODS
Jack Kirby/various

JACK KIRBY'S MISTER MIRACLE
Jack Kirby/various

JACK KIRBY'S FOREVER PEOPLE
Jack Kirby/various

STEEL: THE FORGING OF A HERO
Various writers and artists

WONDER WOMAN: THE CONTEST
William Messner-Loebs/
Mike Deodato, Jr.

WONDER WOMAN: SECOND GENESIS
John Byrne

WONDER WOMAN: LIFELINES
John Byrne

DC/MARVEL: CROSSOVER CLASSICS II
Various writers and artists

DC VERSUS MARVEL/ MARVEL VERSUS DC
R. Marz/P. David/D. Jurgens/
C. Castellini/various

THE AMALGAM AGE OF COMICS: THE DC COMICS COLLECTION
Various writers and artists

RETURN TO THE AMALGAM AGE OF COMICS: THE DC COMICS COLLECTION
Various writers and artists

THE FINAL NIGHT
K. Kesel/Marz/S. Immonen/
Marzan, Jr./various

KINGDOM COME
Mark Waid/Alex Ross

LEGENDS: THE COLLECTED EDITION
J. Ostrander/L. Wein/
J. Byrne/K. Kesel

UNDERWORLD UNLEASHED
M. Waid/H. Porter/P. Jimenez/
various

ARCHIVE EDITIONS

ALL STAR COMICS ARCHIVES Volume 1
(ALL STAR COMICS 3-6)
ALL STAR COMICS ARCHIVES Volume 2
(ALL STAR COMICS 7-10)
ALL STAR COMICS ARCHIVES Volume 3
(ALL STAR COMICS 11-14)
ALL STAR COMICS ARCHIVES Volume 4
(ALL STAR COMICS 15-19)
ALL STAR COMICS ARCHIVES Volume 5
(ALL STAR COMICS 20-23)
All by Gardner Fox/various

THE FLASH ARCHIVES Volume 1
(FLASH COMICS 104, SHOWCASE 4, 8, 13, 14, THE FLASH 105-108)
J. Broome/C. Infantino/
J. Giella/various

GREEN LANTERN ARCHIVES Volume 1
(SHOWCASE 22-23, GREEN LANTERN 1-5)
GREEN LANTERN ARCHIVES Volume 2
(GREEN LANTERN 6-13)
All by J. Broome/G. Kane/
J. Giella/various

JUSTICE LEAGUE OF AMERICA ARCHIVES Volume 1
(THE BRAVE AND THE BOLD 28-30, JUSTICE LEAGUE OF AMERICA 1-6)
JUSTICE LEAGUE OF AMERICA ARCHIVES Volume 2
(JUSTICE LEAGUE OF AMERICA 7-14)
JUSTICE LEAGUE OF AMERICA ARCHIVES Volume 3
(JUSTICE LEAGUE OF AMERICA 15-22)
JUSTICE LEAGUE OF AMERICA ARCHIVES Volume 4
(JUSTICE LEAGUE OF AMERICA 23-30)
JUSTICE LEAGUE OF AMERICA ARCHIVES Volume 5
(JUSTICE LEAGUE OF AMERICA 31-40)
All by Gardner Fox/
Mike Sekowsky/various

PLASTIC MAN ARCHIVES Volume 1
(POLICE COMICS 1-20)
Jack Cole

WONDER WOMAN ARCHIVES Volume 1
(ALL STAR COMICS 8, SENSATION COMICS 1-12, WONDER WOMAN 1)
WONDER WOMAN ARCHIVES Volume 2
(SENSATION COMICS 13-17, WONDER WOMAN 2- 4)
All by William Moulton Marston/
Harry G. Peter

TO FIND MORE COLLECTED EDITIONS AND MONTHLY COMIC BOOKS FROM DC COMICS, CALL 1-888-COMIC BOOK FOR THE NEAREST COMICS SHOP OR GO TO YOUR LOCAL BOOK STORE.

Visit us at www.dccomics.com

JLA0011